REGULATING COMPETITION IN THE DIGITAL NETWORK INDUSTRY

This book proposes a wholly new view on digital competition. It proposes that – rather than just competing within or for a market – digital firms compete to capture their own part of the digital network industry, constituting their digital ecosystem. Once they control the network's access points for competition, they become the de facto regulators of their ecosystems, allowing them to leverage their ecosystem power to capture new markets and expand their reach further across the digital network. Regulation that focuses on markets cannot capture these dimensions of power and competition. The system of progressive ecosystem regulation proposed in this book explains how ecosystem competition can be stimulated to create meaningful competitive pressures, open up the network to disruptive entry, and introduce real choice for users.

Jasper van den Boom is an assistant professor of EU competition law within the Europa Institute at Leiden University and an external researcher in the Shaping Competition in the Digital Age (SCiDA) project at the Heinrich Heine University Düsseldorf. He is an expert in the area of digital competition and its regulation. His work focuses on competition in and between digital ecosystems, the Digital Markets Act and its enforcement, and comparative legal research for competition and antitrust matters. This book is based on his PhD thesis written for Tilburg University, under the supervision of Prof. Giorgio Monti and Dr. Inge Graef.

GLOBAL COMPETITION LAW AND ECONOMICS POLICY

This series publishes monographs highlighting the interdisciplinary and multijurisdictional nature of competition law, economics, and policy. Global in coverage, the series should appeal to competition and antitrust specialists working as scholars, practitioners, and judges.

Regulating Competition in the Digital Network Industry

JASPER VAN DEN BOOM
Leiden University

CAMBRIDGE
UNIVERSITY PRESS

CAMBRIDGE
UNIVERSITY PRESS

Shaftesbury Road, Cambridge CB2 8EA, United Kingdom

One Liberty Plaza, 20th Floor, New York, NY 10006, USA

477 Williamstown Road, Port Melbourne, VIC 3207, Australia

314–321, 3rd Floor, Plot 3, Splendor Forum, Jasola District Centre, New Delhi – 110025, India

103 Penang Road, #05–06/07, Visioncrest Commercial, Singapore 238467

Cambridge University Press is part of Cambridge University Press & Assessment, a department of the University of Cambridge.

We share the University's mission to contribute to society through the pursuit of education, learning and research at the highest international levels of excellence.

www.cambridge.org
Information on this title: www.cambridge.org/9781009671699

DOI: 10.1017/9781009671712

When citing this work, please include a reference to the DOI 10.1017/9781009671712

First published 2026

Cover image: Vietnamese woman in the Mekong River picking water lilies in a circle formation photographed from a drone point of view, Mekong Delta, Vietnam - Getty Images

A catalogue record for this publication is available from the British Library

A Cataloging-in-Publication data record for this book is available from the Library of Congress

ISBN 978-1-009-67169-9 Hardback

I dedicate this work to my partner Chiara Colizzi.

Contents

List of Figures — *page* ix
List of Tables — xi
Preface — xiii
Acknowledgements — xv
Case Law and Decisions — xvii
List of Abbreviations — xxi

1 **Introduction** — 1

PART I THE COMPETITORS IN THE DIGITAL NETWORK INDUSTRY — 13

2 **Digital Goods, Platforms, and Ecosystems** — 15

3 **Digital and Non-digital Network Industries** — 52

4 **Digital Platforms: A New Natural Monopoly?** — 85

PART II THE DYNAMICS OF COMPETITION BETWEEN DIGITAL ECOSYSTEMS — 113

5 **Modalities of Ecosystem Competition** — 115

6 **Stages of Ecosystem Competition** — 135

7 **Theories of Harm for Ecosystem Competition** — 166

PART III A REGULATORY FRAMEWORK TO GOVERN ECOSYSTEM COMPETITION — 183

8 **Existing Regulatory Paradigms: EU, UK, and Germany** — 185

9 A New Regulatory Paradigm: Regulating Ecosystems 214

10 Conclusions 259

Bibliography 269

Index 283

Figures

2.1 A visualization of interdependent cluster markets *page* 45
3.1 An illustration of the digital supply chain 54
3.2 A simplified visualization of the digital network industry – own illustration 82
4.1 The feedback loop leading to self-reinforcing dominance in digital platforms 97
4.2 A simplified version of economies of scope in digital platform markets 102
4.3 The multiple outputs in ad-centric horizontal search 103
4.4 The economies of scope between different sides of the market and outputs on the consumer side 103
4.5 The extended cluster of search and advertisements offered on the Google Search platform 104
4.6 (a) Google Search query page as a gateway for its product ecosystem and (b) Google's inclusion of different loosely related outputs into its horizontal search results 105
4.7 The feedback loop associated with data-driven economies of scope 106
5.1 An illustration of the differentiated ecosystem strategies 123
6.1 The CMA analysis of Alphabet Group and Facebook filed 10-K reports 156
9.1 An exemplary overview of the regulatory pools and burdens in progressive ecosystem regulation 226

Tables

2.1 An overview of the differences between ad- and device-centric business models *page* 22
6.1 An overview of the different orientations of the MAGMA ecosystem 154
8.1 Gatekeepers, their core platform services, and relevant provisions 193
9.1 Obligations for the different regulatory layers under progressive ecosystem regulation 256

Preface

The digital economy is fundamental for the growth and functioning of our society, yet it is becoming increasingly concentrated under a small number of powerful undertakings. Digital undertakings often adopt platform-based business models, where they act as intermediaries between different sides of the market. The platform acts as an infrastructure where suppliers compete to offer their goods and services to end users. However, the role of digital giants generally goes far beyond acting as intermediary. Large digital firms operate vast conglomerates of connected digital products, collect immense amounts of data on consumers, transactions, and preferences, and set the terms for competition across a range of markets.

This book explains how competition in the digital economy works by adopting the view of digital markets as connected in a single digital network industry. All digital goods are, to a greater or lesser extent, connected to one another. Operators of vast digital conglomerates, here described as digital product ecosystems, use these connections between markets to leverage their position from one market to another. They are supported in doing so by the very nature of digital goods, the adoption of platform business models, and their ability to steer users to adopt their new services. As ecosystem operators expand their activity across a greater number of markets, they carve out an ever larger part of the network industry for themselves where they act as the de facto regulator. The ecosystem operator decides who gets to use their platforms to supply their services and compete, which products are interoperable with its proprietary products, platforms, and infrastructures, the terms and conditions for access, and sets standards. The ecosystem operator has the power to shape its part of the network industry as it sees fit.

Ecosystem operators are limited in their ability to exert this power if they face competitive pressures from other ecosystems. When there is competition, users can switch from one ecosystem to another if they do not like the terms set by one of the ecosystems. However, as the digital network industry becomes increasingly concentrated under a small number of large ecosystem operators, both business users and end users become increasingly locked in into the ecosystems of incumbents. There are less opportunities to switch to similar platforms to offer or consume services and even if there are substitutes, these are offered by an ecosystem operator with similar power to extract rents from its users and set unfavourable terms for competition. The weaker competition between ecosystem becomes, the more likely anti-competitive conduct and harms to consumers are to happen.

Concentration under a small number of large ecosystem operators does not just harm competition in markets and services that already exist. It also harms innovation and prevents the emergence of new technologies that may better serve users and be more efficient. As incumbents carve up the digital network industry in a small number of large subsegments, their ecosystems, they gain control over access points into competition. Entrants become dependent on the infrastructure offered by incumbent ecosystem operators, and the incumbents can use their access to data to identify potential competitive threats early. If a new entrant has a technology that may actually create a meaningful competitive threat, the incumbent can intervene to pre-empt disruption and competition. As all incumbents have the incentive to pre-empt disruption, they have incentives to prioritize the suppression of competitive threats over competition with one another.

This book provides an in-depth analysis of why digital markets are so prone to concentration, and why this results in the creation of vast multi-product ecosystems. It then explains how ecosystems compete with one another and what exactly constitutes ecosystem power. Ecosystem power, a non-structural form of power to leverage one's position across markets as to protect and expand the position of one's ecosystem, can be used to entrench monopolies and pre-empt disruption. The book provides clear theories of harm associated with this form of ecosystem power. That is not to say that ecosystems are inherently harmful to competition. In fact, ecosystem competition can produce great pro-competitive benefits that ensure that competitive pressures remain even when a market is monopolized. The book contributes by distinguishing between stages of ecosystem competition and describes when ecosystem competition goes from healthy to harmful. Finally, the book proposes a new type of regulation: progressive ecosystem regulation. This regulatory framework is based on theories of ecosystem competition and serves to create long-term sustainable competition between ecosystems that works for consumers. This wholly new view on digital regulation breaks with existing paradigms on regulation and envisions that healthy long-term competition is possible at the ecosystem level if properly regulated.

Acknowledgements

This book has been written during my time as a PhD student at Tilburg University. I am immensely grateful to my colleagues at the Tilburg Institute for Law Technology and Society (TILT) and the Tilburg Law & Economics Center (TILEC). I am particularly thankful towards my supervisors Giorgio Monti and Inge Graef. It has been a privilege to work with and receive guidance from my incredibly supportive mentors.

After my time at Tilburg, I have been able to further develop this book for publication while working with the amazing team at Heinrich Heine University Düsseldorf. Working in particular with Rupprecht Podszun, Sarah Hinck, and Birte Krüger in the project 'Shaping Competition for the Digital Age' has allowed me to grow as a researcher and deepen my understanding of digital markets and digital regulation.

I present this book with gratitude to my supervisors, colleagues, friends, family, and defence committee members Eric van Damme, Ariel Ezrachi, Damien Geradin, and Heike Schweitzer, as well as the academic community.

Case Law and Decisions

DECISIONS

Case B7-61/21, Alphabet, Bundeskartellamt Decision of 30 December 2021
Case B6-27/21, Meta, BKA Decision of 02 May 2022
Case B2-55/21, Amazon, BKA Decision of 05 July 2022
Case B 9-67/21, Apple, BKA Decision of 03 April 2023
Case B 6-26/23, Microsoft, BKA Decision of 27 September 2024
Case V-43/20, 'Google – Google News Showcase', Decision of 21 December 2022
Case B7-70/21, 'Google – Data processing', Decision of 6 October 2023
Bundeskartellamt, Google Automotive Services proceeding – Market test regarding commitments proposed by Google, Press Release of 20 December 2023
Bundeskartellamt, Extension of ongoing proceedings against Amazon to also include an examination pursuant to Section 19a of the German Competition Act (GWB), Press release of 14 November 2022
Bundeskartellamt, Bundeskartellamt reviews Apple's tracking rules for third-party apps, Press Release of 14 June 2022
Bundeskartellamt, First proceeding based on new rules for digital companies – Bundeskartellamt also assesses new Section 19a GWB in its Facebook/Oculus case, Press Release of 28 January 2021
British Telecommunications (Case IV.29.877), Commission Decision 82/861/EEC [1982], OJ L 360/36
Google/DoubleClick (Case M.4731), Commission Decision C(2008) 927 final [2008] OJ C 184/10
Microsoft – Tying (Case COMP/39.530), Commission Commitment Decision C2009 10033 [2009] OJ C 36/7
Microsoft/Yahoo (Case M.5727), Commission Decision C(2010) 1077 [2010], OJ C 95/1
Microsoft/Skype (Case M. 6281), Commission Decision C(2011) 7279 [2011], OJ C 268/12
Slovak Telekom (Case AT.39523), Commission Decision C(2014) 7465 [2014], OJ C 314/7

Facebook/WhatsApp (Case M.7217), Commission Decision C(2014) 7239 [2014] OJ C
Microsoft/LinkedIn (Case M.8124), Commission Decision C(2016) 8404 [2016], OJ C 388/4
Facebook/WhatsApp (Case No. M.8228), Commission Decision C(2017) 3192 final [2017] OJ C 134/22
Google Search (Shopping) (Case AT.39740), Commission decision C(2017) 4444 [2017] OJ C 9/11
Apple/Shazam (Case M.8788), Commission Decision C(2018) 5748 [2018] OJ C 106/16
Google Android (Case AT.40099), Commission Decision C(2018) 4761 [2018], OJ C 402/19
Google Search (AdSense) (Case AT.40411), Commission Decision C(2019) 2173 [2019], OJ C 369/6
Google/Fitbit (Case M.9660), Commission Decision C(2020) 9105 [2020] OJ C 210/32
European Commission, Commission opens non-compliance investigations against Alphabet, Apple and Meta under the Digital Markets Act, Press Release of 25 March 2024
DMA.100055, Meta – Article 5(2), Decision to open proceedings based on Art.20 and Art.29 of 25 March 2024
DMA.100193, Alphabet – Online Search Engine – Google Search – Art. 6(5), Decision to open proceedings based on Art.20 and Art.29 of 25 March 2024
DMA.1000185, Apple – Operating systems – iOS – Art. 6(3), Decision to open proceedings based on Art.20 and Art.29 of 25 March 2024
DMA.100109, Apple App Store, 5(4), Decision to open proceedings based on Art.20 and Art.29 of 25 March 2024
DMA.100203/4 – Art. 6(7) DMA, Apple Interoperability, Decision to open proceedings based on Art. 8 DMA of 19 September 2024
DMA.100206, Apple new business terms 5(4), 5(7), and 6(4), Decision to open proceedings based on Art. 20 and 29 of 24 June 2024
European Commission, Antitrust: Commission sends Statement of Objections to Amazon for the use of non-public independent seller data and opens second investigation into its e-commerce business practices, Press Release of IP/20/2077 10 November 2020 on sending a statement of objections in Case AT.40462 (Amazon Marketplace)
European Commission, Antitrust: Commission sends Statement of Objections to Apple on App Store rules for music streaming providers, Press Release IP/21/2061 of 30 April 2021 on sending a statement of objections Case AT.40437
European Commission, Antitrust: Commission seeks feedback on commitments offered by Amazon concerning marketplace seller data and access to Buy Box and Prime, Press Release IP/22/4522 on sending a statement of objections in Cases AT.40462 and AT.40703

European Commission, Antitrust: Commission opens investigation into possible anticompetitive conduct by Google in the online advertising technology sector, Press Release IP/21/3143 on sending a statement of objections in Case AT.40670

European Commission, Antitrust: Commission sends Statement of Objections to Apple over practices regarding Apple Pay, Press Release IP/22/2764 of 2 May 2022 on sending a statement of objections in case AT.40452 (Apple Pay)

European Commission, 'Pulling the plug on consumer frustration and e-waste: Commission proposes a common charger for electronic devices', Press Release IP/21/4613 of 23 September 2021: https://ec.europa.eu/commission/presscorner/detail/en/IP_21_4613

FCA Google AdTech Decision (Decision 21-D-11), Decision by the Autorite de la Concurrence of 7 June 2021 regarding practices implemented in the online advertising sector

Amazon FBA (Case No. 29925), Autorita Garante della Concorrenza e Del Mercato Decision, 30 November 2021

Apple Dating Apps (Case ACM/19/035630), Summary of the Decision by Autoriteit Consument & Markt of 24 August 2021

Facebook/Instagram (case ME/5525/12), Office of Fair Trading Decision of 14 August 2012

Facebook (Case B6-22/16), Bundeskartellamt Decision of 6 February 2019

CASE LAW

Case 41/83, Re British Telecommunications: Italy v Commission [1985] ECLI:EU:C:1985:120

Case C-202/88, French Republic v Commission of the European Communities [1991] ECLI:EU:C:1991:120

Case T-30/89, Hilti v Commission of the European Communities [1991] EU:T:1991:70

Case C-271/90, Kingdom of Spain, Kingdom of Belgium and Italian Republic v Commission of the European Communities [1992] ECLI:EU:C:1992:440

Case 53/92, Hilti AG v Commission of the European Communities [1994] ECLI:EU:C:1994:77

Case T-271/03, Deutsche Telekom v Commission of the European Communities [2008] ECLI:EU:T:2008:101

Case C-280/08, P Deutsche Telekom v European Commission [2010] ECLI:EU:C:2010:603

Case C-52/09, Konkurrensverket v TeliaSonera Sverige AB [2011] ECLI:EU:C:2011:83

Case T-336/07, Telefónica, SA and Telefónica de España, SA v European Commission [2012] ECLI:EU:T:2012:172

Case T-167/08, Microsoft Corp. v European Commission [2012] ECLI:EU:T:2012:323

Case C-295/12 P, Telefónica SA and Telefónica de España SAU v European Commission [2014] ECLI:EU:C:2014:2062

Case T-612/17, Google LLC v European Commission [2021] ECLI:EU:T:2021:763
C-165/19 P, Slovak Telekom v Commission [2021] ECLI:EU:C:2021:239
Case T-604/18, Google and Alphabet v Commission [2022] ECLI:EU:T:2022:541
Epic Games v Apple inc., 10 September 2021, Case 4:20-cv-05640-YGR, U.S. District Court, Northern District of California
United States v Microsoft Corporation, 253 F.3d 34 (D.C. Cir. 2001)
United States v Microsoft Corporation, Civil Action No. 98-1232 (TPJ), 14 September 1998, United States District Court
Unlockd Media Inc. v Google LLC, Case 3:21-cv-07250, 17 September 2021 United States District Court of Northern California
California Crane School Inc. v Google LLC, Alphabet Inc., case 4:21-cv-10001-HSG, 27 December 2021, United States District Court of Northern California
United States v Google LLC, Case 1:20-cv-03010, 20 October 2020, District Court of Columbia
German Federal Court, Order of 23 April 2024 – KVB 56/22 – Amazon
German Federal Court, Order of 23 April 2024 – KVB 56/22 – Amazon (2024)

Abbreviations

ACCC	Australian Competition and Consumer Commission
AFA	Anti-fragmentation agreement
AI	Artificial intelligence
API	Application Programming Interface
BKA	Bundeskartellamt
CJEU	Court of Justice of the European Union
CMA	Competition & Markets Authority
CPS	Core platform service
DMA	Digital Markets Act
DMCCA	Digital Markets, Competition, and Consumer Act
EEA	European Economic Area
EU	European Union
FRAND	Fair, reasonable and non-discriminatory
GAFAM	Google, Apple, Facebook, Amazon, Microsoft
GWB	Gesetz Gegen Wettbewerbsbeschränkungen
MADA	Mobile application distribution agreements
MNO	Mobile network operator
OECD	Organisation for Economic Co-operation and Development
OEM	Original equipment manufacturer
OHA	Open Handheld Alliance
OS	Operating System
PA	Placement Agreement
PCI	Pro-competition intervention
R&D	Research & Development
SDK	Software Development Kit
SMS	Strategic market status
UK	United Kingdom
US	United States
USD	United States Dollar

1

Introduction

The digital economy is fundamental for the growth and functioning of our society. Economic activities, commercial transactions, professional interactions, and even social relationships are increasingly enabled by – and facilitated through – digital technologies and infrastructures. The importance of digital undertakings is reflected in their value, both in terms of market capitalization and turnover; large user numbers; and how their activities span across markets and across the digital and physical realm.[1] Aside from economic indicators, digital undertakings are also increasingly active in the provision of (quasi-)public tasks, including activities related to public health, education, transport, communications, and access to information.[2]

Over the last decades, digital undertakings have become deeply engrained and embedded in nearly every aspect of our lives, exerting different types and dimensions of power.[3] Digital firms have created undeniable value and innovation and have acted as drivers of technological and societal progress. However, the growing societal dependence on a small number of large firms has increasingly led to concerns about the concentration of economic, social, and political power. Societal harms are reflected in concerns about the rising power of digital undertakings

1 Digital Competition Expert Panel, 'Unlocking Digital Competition' (2019); UNCTAD, 'Value Creation and Capture: Implications for Developing Countries' (United Nations Conference on Trade and Development 2019); Luigi Zingales and others, 'Stigler Committee on Digital Platforms – Final Report' (Stigler Center 2019); Commercial and Administrative Law of the Committee on the Judiciary Subcommittee on Antitrust, 'House Investigation of Competition in Digital Markets' (2020); Filippo Lancieri and Patricia Morita Sakowski, 'Competition in Digital Markets: A Review of Expert Reports' [2020] Working Papers 303, The University of Chicago Booth School of Business, George J. Stigler Center for the Study of the Economy and the State; Ariel Ezrachi and Maurice E Stucke, *How Big-Tech Barons Smash Innovation – and How to Strike Back* (HarperCollins 2022).

2 Christoph Busch, 'Regulation of Digital Platforms as Infrastructures for Services of General Interest' (2021) 09 WISO Diskurs.

3 Anna Gerbrandy and Pauline Phoa, 'The Power of Big Tech Corporations as Modern Bigness and a Vocabulary for Shaping Competition Law as Counter-Power' in Huub Brouwer, Michael Bennett and Rutger Claassen, *Wealth and Power* (1st edn, Routledge 2022) <www.taylorfrancis.com/books/9781003173632/chapters/10.4324/9781003173632-11> accessed 16 August 2024.

to control information flows, infringe on privacy and individual autonomy, or to undermine democratic discourse.[4]

The growing concerns surrounding the role of digital undertakings in our society, as well as the high levels of concentration in these markets, have sparked a global debate on how to reign in the powers held by private firms. This has resulted in the imposition of a large number of laws and regulations that oversee different aspects of digital activity. On the one hand, there is economic regulation, which aims to restore competition and fight concentration across markets. Competition law serves as a general framework to protect competition and promote the welfare of consumers. Now, competition law has been supplemented by novel types of economic regulation aimed specifically at digital firms and markets, including most prominently the Digital Markets Act (DMA) in the EU and the Digital Markets, Competition, and Consumers Act (DMCCA) in the UK.[5] Regulation similar to the DMA is also considered in various jurisdictions, while other jurisdictions are in the process of developing their own regulatory responses.[6] At the same time, there is a variety of social (i.e. non-economic) regulations aimed at the promotion of privacy, transparency, the safety of new technologies or the protection of labourers.[7] This book focuses on economic regulation and the role of competition law. Specifically, the work aims to enhance our understanding of competition in the connected network

4 See Digital Competition Expert Panel (n 1); Jacques Crémer, Yves-Alexandre De Montjoye and Heike Schweitzer, 'Competition Policy for the Digital Era' (2019); Australian Competition & Consumer Authority, 'Digital Platform Inquiry' (2019); Zingales and others (n 1); Subcommittee on Antitrust (n 1); Ezrachi and Stucke (n 1); Gerbrandy and Phoa (n 3).

5 Regulation (EU) 2022/1925 of the European Parliament and of the Council of 14 September 2022 on contestable and fair markets in the digital sector and amending Directives (EU) 2019/1937 and (EU) 2020/1828, OJ L 265/1 (Digital Markets Act); Digital Markets, Competition and Consumers Act 2024; Japan Fair Trade Commission, Cabinet Decision on the Bill for the Act on Promotion of Competition for Specified Smartphone Software (2024).

6 See, for instance, India's Digital Competition Bill 2024, Ministry of Corporate Affairs Government of India, Report of the Committee on Digital Competition Law (2024), Annex IV; Australian government, Digital platforms – a proposed new digital competition regime (2025).

7 See, for instance, Regulation (EU) 2019/1150 of the European Parliament and of the Council of 20 June 2019 on promoting fairness and transparency for business users of online intermediation service [2019], OJL 186/57 (P2B-Regulation) for transparency of digital platform operations; Proposal for a Regulation on a Single Market for Digital Services and amending Directive 2000/31/EC, COM/2020/825 final, proposal of 15 December 2020 (Proposal for the Digital Services Act) on content moderation and consumer protection; Regulation (EU) 2016/679 of the European Parliament and of the Council of 27 April 2016 on the protection of natural persons with regard to the processing of personal data and on the free movement of such data, and repealing Directive 95/46/EC OJ L 119/1 (General Data Protection Regulation) for privacy and data protection; Proposal for a Regulation of the European Parliament and the Council on European data governance, COM/2020/767 final, proposal of 25 November 2020 (Data Governance Act) for data flows; Directive (EU) 2019/790 of the European Parliament and of the Council of 17 April 2019 on copyright and related rights in the Digital Single Market and amending Directives 96/9/EC and 2001/29/EC for copyright protection and amending Directives 96/9/EC and 2001/29/EC OJ L 130/92; European Commission, Proposal for a Directive of the European Parliament and of the Council on improving working conditions in platform work, COM(2021) 762 final, proposal of 9 December 2021 for the rights of platform workers.

of digital markets by diving into competition between digital ecosystems, as to draw lessons for the regulation of digital markets and the objectives of regulating digital firms and activities.

Digital markets are the new frontier for competition law and regulation. The past two decades have allowed regulators and academics to observe and study digital business models and competition between digital firms, allowing for the development of methods for defining markets, new theories of harm, and new principles. This has allowed competition law to evolve, so that it can better capture and combat distortions of competition in digital markets, particularly digital platform markets. Digital platform markets are characterized by (among other things) their multisidedness, their global reach, technological adaptivity, the proliferation of free goods and services, the collection, processing and use of data as compensation for these free goods and services and the use of that data for advertising, personalization, and quality improvements.

Digital markets also exhibit a number of economic characteristics that are drivers of concentration. These are often linked to the exhibited novelties in digital business models. The platform business model, where the platform operator intermediates between different groups of users, creates network externalities (direct or indirect), which drives concentration on the demand side. The use of (personal) data leads to data-driven efficiencies and feedback loops, strengthening the position of larger undertakings with more capabilities to collect and process data, thus creating efficiencies on the supply side with higher levels of demand. There are also barriers to entry, as entrants have to overcome the so-called chicken-and-egg problem, which exists as newcomers have to attract multiple groups of users to their platform simultaneously. Consequently, entry requires the investment of sunk costs, but there is a high chance of failure. This chance of failure increases significantly for entrants when there are already established platform operators, as it is more difficult to attract and retain users when competing with a larger and more efficient digital firm. As a result of these economic characteristics, digital markets face structural competition problems. Platform markets tend to be highly concentrated and take shape as a monopoly or duopoly. Competition problems are further exacerbated as large digital undertakings often have opportunities to leverage their position from the platform market to adjacent markets, creating vast digital conglomerates that occupy a vast range of markets. These digital conglomerates are often described as ecosystems, where links across markets allow the digital undertaking to steer their users from one service to another. The development of these ecosystems of products is facilitated by cross-market efficiencies that are present in digital markets, such as the modularity of digital goods, economies of scope, and complementarities.

These novelties of digital markets required competition law and authorities to catch up, evolve, and identify new priorities. The European Commission has been a frontrunner in this, with its early investigations into Google's business practices.

However, even here it proved a challenge to conclude the investigation in a timely manner, leading to questions about the suitability of competition law to govern fast-paced and dynamic markets. In light of the dynamism of digital markets and short innovation cycles, there is a real risk that business models have already changed and competition has already been irreparably harmed by the time the investigation is concluded. Let alone by the time the remedies are imposed, start to produce effects, and litigation is concluded.

The length of competition law investigations and the perceived lack of timely interventions has led to calls for regulation to deal with the structural competition problems in digital markets. In 2022, the European Union introduced the first regulatory framework to deal specifically with competition in digital markets: the DMA. This was already preceded by the German reform of competition law with the introduction of Section 19a GWB, which aims to promote competition in digital markets specifically. The DMA is a consolidation of the experiences from competition law and the lessons from the studies of digital platform competition. The DMA consists of a set of ex ante rules that apply only to designated gatekeepers that are active in so-called core platform services. The DMA is developed with an eye on speedy enforcement and timely interventions: the core platform services are laid down in an exhaustive list of platform activities, to identify a gatekeeper the Commission can rely on presumptions created through quantitative thresholds and there is no economic analysis or efficiency defence required for the substantive obligations to apply. The substantive obligations mimic proposed resolutions to theories of harm that have already been investigated by competition authorities or for which there are active or potential investigations, and may include obligations to prevent steering, to promote interoperability, to make data available, or to prohibit anti-competitive activities such as self-preferencing. The design of the DMA reflects the spirit of the times in which it was drafted: there was an urgent need for regulation to remedy the harms caused by anti-competitive behaviour by large digital firms, and the DMA complements competition law by addressing its perceived gaps, namely that its slow to act and requires overly complicated analyses of harms.

The DMA is an important first step in regulating digital markets. Not only for breaking through the competition law versus regulation debate, but also for its ability to stop or mitigate the most urgent anti-competitive activities that we are aware of. However, the DMA is viewed here as – indeed – only the first step. The United Kingdom has introduced the Digital Markets, Competition, and Consumers Act (DMCCA) as their own response to competition problems in digital markets, and new regulation – often different from the DMA and DMCCA – is being introduced around the globe.[8]

[8] See Jasper Van den Boom and others, 'Digital Regulation Synthesis: Comparative Analysis of the DMA, Sec. 19a and the DMCCA' (2024) (1) SCiDA Discussion Paper, SSRN for a comparison of the DMA, DMCCA, and Sec. 19a GWB and references to other proposed digital regulation.

This book aims to look beyond this initial regulatory framework and aims to develop the theories and conceptual framework for future-proof regulation in digital markets. The underlying hypothesis of this work is that ultimately, competition in digital markets is competition between and in digital ecosystems within a digital network industry. Competition in digital markets is not competition *in* a market as we know it, nor is it simply competition *for* a market. Competition in digital markets is competition with many moving parts. It is not simply competition between one firm and another, but rather between groups of firms that collectively co-generate value through competition and cooperation. These firms are also not competing for one market but are rather competing by leveraging the total value proposition of their cross-market activities into entry into new markets and technologies, with an eye of securing direct access to different user groups and the ability to steer users. This book provides a conceptual framework to understand the digital network industry and the relevance of monopoly markets within the ecosystem, a theory on the stages of ecosystem competition in the digital network, and a conceptual regulatory framework that is able to capture and regulate the complexities of ecosystem competition as to stimulate sustainable competition.

The novelty of the proposed regulatory framework lies in how it frames competition between digital firms. Rather than looking at independent markets or platform services, the proposed framework approaches the issue as competition throughout a network of connected markets. Ecosystems are viewed as subsegments of this network, where the digital firm acts as the de facto regulator, allowing them to wield their private power throughout their parts of the network. The proposed regulatory framework draws lessons from experiences with sector-specific regulation in non-digital network industries, the application of competition law in digital markets, and the novel regulatory frameworks for digital to stimulate sustainable competition. This book proposes that a layered, asymmetric regulatory framework with the objective of creating an environment that protects and stimulates disruptive competition is best suited to create real long-term competitive pressure on incumbent digital ecosystem operators.

1.1 RESEARCH PURPOSE

The purpose of this book is to develop a novel conceptual framework to study competition in digital markets and to develop principles for the regulation of digital markets based on insights derived from its analyses. These analyses are conducted on the basis of insights from economics, management studies, and legal literature.

The book aims to answer the following question: 'How can insights from the regulation of network industries help to shape regulation in digital markets?'

The phrasing of the question allows one to explore the networked nature of digital goods without inferring that those regulatory interventions that were suitable in traditional networks can be transposed or that this transposition should be tested. Rather, it allows one to juxtapose traditional networks against digital networks, which may lead to regulatory insights. This clearly delimits the topic, without inferring any conclusions.

There are three sub-questions that together answer the main research question:

(1) What are the similarities and differences between traditional network industries and digital networks?
(2) How does competition exhibit itself in digital markets and under which circumstances do harms to competition occur?
(3) What lessons can be derived from the regulation of network industries for the regulation of digital markets and how can these lessons be implemented into a regulatory framework?

These three questions are answered across the three parts of the book. Part I explains the novelty of digital markets. This is relevant, as in non-digital network industries, the existence of natural monopoly in certain markets was often used as a justification for ex ante economic regulation. It was considered that in these natural monopoly markets, it is more cost efficient to have all demand fulfilled by a single supplier than by multiple suppliers, as marginal costs are reduced with additional produced units. As a result, competition may be considered impossible, undesirable or short-lived and potentially wasteful or destructive.[9] Due to the interconnected nature of markets in a network industry, the effects of having natural monopoly in one market could permeate throughout the rest of the network. Thus, regulation was not only required to prevent exploitative behaviour of the monopolist within the market itself but also for the functioning of the network as a whole.[10] Here, the book identifies a gap in the literature on competition between digital undertakings and regulation in digital markets. The debate on regulation often focuses on the

[9] In this book, desirable outcomes generally relate to increasing different types of efficiency. On the used definition of efficiency, see Alessio M Pacces and Louis Visscher, 'Methodology of Law and Economics', in Bart van Klink and Sanne Taekema (eds), *Interdisciplinary Research into Law* (Mohr Siebeck 2011) 4. 'Efficiency means that "given the resources initially available and their allocation, the members of a society have achieved the highest possible level of utility".' These efficiencies can entail cost-efficiency in production (productive efficiency), which is leading in the analysis of the natural monopoly concept in Chapter 2. Where it concerns the impact of regulation on efficiency, matters of allocative efficiency are also considered (i.e. the impact of regulation on the allocation of surpluses), consumer welfare (allocating a greater share of the total welfare with consumers), and/or dynamic efficiencies (the rate of innovation and investments to improve production processes or for the development of new technologies). It should be noted that the natural monopoly theory, relates to cost-efficiency. See to this extent OECD, 'Glossary of Industrial Organisation Economics and Competition Law' 62: 'Because productive efficiency requires that only one firm exist, natural monopolies are typically subject to government regulation. Regulations may include price, quality, and/or entry conditions.'

[10] Richard A Posner, 'Natural Monopoly and Its Regulation' (1969) 21 Stanford Law Review 548; Sanford V Berg and John Tschirhart, *Natural Monopoly Regulation: Principles and Practice* (Cambridge University Press 1988); Paul Joskow, 'Regulation of Natural Monopoly' in A Mitchell Polinsky and Steven Shavell (eds), vol 2 (Elsevier 2007) <https://EconPapers.repec.org/RePEc:eee:lawchp:2-16>; Christopher Decker, *Modern Economic Regulation: An Introduction to Theory and Practice* (Cambridge University Press 2015).

gatekeeper power held by a digital undertaking in its platform market(s), as well as its ability to leverage market power into adjacent (or connected) markets. However, this debate rarely extends to discussing whether the market failure is sufficiently strong that the platform market constitutes a natural monopoly. Moreover, the debate is often limited to the resulting gatekeeper power for the monopolist without discussing the impact of monopoly on the functioning of the broader network. There have been earlier attempts to apply the theory of natural monopoly to digital markets, but these are generally based on empirical observations in a small number of markets.[11] This book contributes to this discussion by creating a comprehensive framework to assess the natural monopoly characteristics of digital platform markets, which also includes theorization on the digital platform as exhibiting natural monopoly from a multi-output perspective.

Part II analyses how natural monopoly in a digital platform market impacts competition in the broader network by studying how competition in the digital network occurs. In order to answer this question, the book sets out an in-depth analysis on multi-product ecosystems as subnetworks within the broader digital network industry. From here, the book develops a theory of ecosystem power as to explain why conglomeration in digital markets is so prevalent. Here, the book argues that ecosystem power is related to the ability of the digital undertaking to leverage its power throughout the network as to carve out a larger subnetwork for itself by leveraging its users and resources into new markets. This is used to develop novel theories of harm which explain anti-competitive effects by looking at the effects of ecosystem power and gatekeeper power jointly. This helps to explain when abuses of gatekeeper power have anti-competitive effects and how they permeate throughout the ecosystem. Here, the book builds on the works of authors such as Gawer, Lianos, Jacobides, and Mandrescu as to create new insights into competitive strategies used by platform and ecosystem operators and clarify when these strategies produce pro- or anti-competitive effects.[12]

Part III develops a proposal for a regulatory framework which aims to stimulate competition at the ecosystem level to minimize harms associated with the abuse of gatekeeper power. The book proposes that the purpose of regulation of the digital network industry should be to empower entrants to enter into competition and facilitate disruptive innovation. By introducing uncertainty into competition, and raising

[11] See Francesco Ducci, *Natural Monopolies in Digital Platform Markets* (Cambridge University Press 2020); Herbert Hovenkamp, 'Antitrust and Platform Monopoly' (2021) 130 Yale Law Journal 1952.

[12] See Annabelle Gawer and Michael Cusumano, 'Industry Platforms and Ecosystem Innovation' (2014) 31 Journal of Product Innovation Management 418; Annabelle Gawer, 'Digital Platforms' Boundaries: The Interplay of Firm Scope, Platform Sides, and Digital Interfaces' (2021) 54 Long Range Planning 1; Michael G Jacobides, Carmelo Cennamo and Annabelle Gawer, 'Towards a Theory of Ecosystems' (2018) 39 Strategic Management Journal 2255; Michael G Jacobides and Ioannis Lianos, 'Ecosystems and Competition Law in Theory and Practice' (2021) 30 Industrial and Corporate Change 1199 <https://doi.org/10.1093/icc/dtab061>; Daniel Mandrescu, 'Tying and Bundling by Online Platforms – Distinguishing between Lawful Expansion Strategies and Anti-Competitive Practices' (2021) 40 Computer Law and Security Review 1.

the risk of disruptive entry, regulation can induce long-term competition between digital ecosystems. This proposed regulatory framework demonstrates that the regulation of digital markets can be based on different principles than those underlying regulation in non-digital network industries and those underlying existing proposals for regulation in digital markets. Underlying the regulatory framework proposed in this book is the idea that regulation can be used to stimulate competition between ecosystem operators throughout the digital network industry by empowering entrants to capture their own platform markets and develop their own ecosystems. This steps away from both the idea that regulation should focus on the monopoly as used in the regulation of non-digital networks and the idea that regulation should focus on gatekeepers or the dependencies of third parties on platforms, which is central in existing proposals for the regulation of digital markets.

The contribution of the proposed regulatory framework lies not only with the concrete lessons it provides for regulators but also contributes to the broader debate on the suitability of regulation. First, it contributes to the discussion by including considerations on dynamic competition and a focus on business models that were considered missing in the DMA.[13] As a result of including these considerations, the proposed regulatory framework strikes a balance between interventionism and non-interventionism as it regulates the interactions between ecosystems with an imbalance in power, while leaving competition between ecosystems of equal sizes unfettered. On the one hand, the book supports interventions in the form of behavioural regulation and recognizes the need for ex ante rules.[14] On the other hand, the book limits regulatory interventions to where they are absolutely necessary and

[13] See Sidak and Teece, 'Dynamic Competition in Antitrust Law' (2009) 5 Journal of Competition Law & Economics 581; Petit and Teece, 'Taking Ecosystems Competition Seriously in the Digital Economy' (OECD 2020); Petit, Big Tech and the Digital Economy: The Moligopoly Scenario (1st edn, Oxford University Press 2020); Petit and Teece, 'Innovating Big Tech Firms and Competition Policy: Favoring Dynamic over Static Competition' 41 (2021); Portuese, 'The Digital Markets Act: A Triumph of Regulation over Innovation' (2022) Information Technology 24 discuss the importance of dynamic competition and debate how regulation may have the unintended side effect of limiting innovation. These authors also argue in favour of recognizing the direct and indirect competitive pressures resulting from competition between ecosystems in deciding (how) to regulate digital markets.

[14] See Digital Competition Expert Panel (n 1); Zingales and others (n 1); Scott Morton and others, 'Equitable Interoperability: The "Super Tool" of Digital Platform Governance' (2021) 4 Digital Regulation Project, Policy Discussion Paper 1; Jenny, 'Competition Law Enforcement and Regulation for Digital Ecosystems: Understanding the Issues, Facing the Challenges and Moving Forward' (2021) 3 Concurrences 38; Cabral and others, The EU Digital Markets Act: A Report from a Panel of Economic Experts. (Publications Office 2021) <https://data.europa.eu/doi/10.2760/139337> accessed 14 December 2022; Cappai and Colangelo, 'Taming Digital Gatekeepers: The "More Regulatory Approach" to Antitrust Law' (2021) 41 Computer Law and Security Review 1; Wagner and others, 'Taming the Giants: The DMA/DSA Package' (2021) 58 Common Market Law Review 987; OECD, 'Ex Ante Regulation and Competition in Digital Markets' (OECD 2021); Busch, 'Regulation of Digital Platforms as Infrastructures for Services of General Interest' (2021) 09 WISO Diskurs; these works generally favour ex ante regulation or the introductions of presumptions into competition law as to resolve market failures and to limit large digital platform operators in their ability to exploit their gatekeeper power.

recognizes that markets are best governed by the forces of free competition. The proposed regulatory framework in the book is intended to be temporary and exist to stimulate competition, limiting the scope and duration of reliance on behavioural remedies.[15] The book also argues that structural measures should only be considered as a measure of last resort, as it argues that this would be inefficient and could harm competition at the ecosystem level, especially if it leads to further concentration of the network between a small number of large players.[16]

Second, the book brings together several streams of literature which have not been sufficiently connected. While there are works that focus on the identification of product ecosystems[17] and works that explore the relationships and interactions between digital networks and non-digital networks,[18] this book looks at how digital product ecosystems shape the digital network industry and how they exert competitive pressures on one another to develop a new type of regulatory framework. These combined insights from streams of literature in economics, management theory and legal scholarship open a new stream of literature which may inspire regulation for digital markets based on ecosystem competition within the digital network.

1.2 METHODOLOGY

The research in this book predominantly relies on a law and economics methodology.[19] As such, the book relies on mainstream economic theories such as theories

15 See Posner, 'Natural Monopoly and Its Regulation' (1969) 21 Stanford Law Review 548; Martin Cave, 'Encouraging Infrastructure Competition via the Ladder of Investment' (2006) 30 Telecommunications Policy 223; JA den Hertog, 'Review of Economic Theories of Regulation' (Utrecht School of Economics 2010); Wim Marneffe and Lode Vereeck, 'The Meaning of Regulatory Costs' (2011) 32 European Journal of Law and Economics 341; Decker (n 10); Ibáñez Colomo, 'The Draft Digital Markets Act: A Legal and Institutional Analysis' (2021) 12 Journal of European Competition Law & Practice 561; these works recognize that regulation generally leads to second-best outcomes when compared to competition and that regulation should be phased out where possible.

16 See Martin K Perry, 'Vertical Integration: Determinants and Effects' (1989) 1 Handbook of Industrial Organisation 183; Lina M Khan, 'The Separation of Platforms and Commerce' (2019) 119 Columbia Law Review 126; A Claici and others, 'The Economic Rationale for Vertical Integration in the Tech Sector: Hardware Devices to Software to Services: Strategic Risk-Taking, Innovation and Investments in the Pursuit of Efficiency and Consumer Value' (Copenhagen Economics 2020); these works discuss the rationale and efficiencies associated with (vertically) integrated business models and discuss the desirability of unbundling ecosystems.

17 See Jacobides, Cennamo and Gawer (n 12); Jacobides and Lianos (n 12); Daniel A Crane, 'Ecosystem Competition and Antitrust Laws' (2019) 98 Nebraska Law Review 412; Petit and Teece, 'Taking Ecosystems Competition Seriously in the Digital Economy' (n 13).

18 See JJ Montero and others, 'Digital Platforms: The New Network Industries? How to Regulate Them?' (2019) 21 Network Industries Quarterly <http://mir.epfl.ch/>; Juan Montero and Matthias Finger, *The Rise of the New Network Industries* (Routledge 2021).

19 On the concept of law and economics methodology, see Pacces and Visscher (n 9) 85–107. Here, it is noted that in law and economics, the economic approach operates on two distinct levels: first, human choice is analysed from an economic point of view and the predominant approach is the rational choice theory. The second level of the economic approach is the goals which are attributed

on transaction costs, rational choice, information asymmetries, regulatory costs, and the regulators imperfect access to information to determine whether – and if so what type of – laws and regulation can achieve desirable outcomes. The book combines insights from economics literature and management theory with a legal study to develop suggestions for regulatory interventions to the workings of digital markets, so that the proposed regulatory framework reflects the realities of competition and competitive conditions in digital markets.

The design of this research consists of a literature study that combines legal doctrinal research, regulation theory, economics literature, and management theory. The literature review relies on both primary and secondary sources. The primary sources on which the book relies are predominantly EU law, EU case law, and regulation that is imposed in European utility markets. Where relevant, the book will address law, case law, or regulation from other jurisdictions.

The secondary sources the book relies on are economic, management studies, and legal scholarly works that analyse the workings of network industries, digital markets, data, sector-specific regulation, and competition law. Economic literature is predominantly analysed to establish the workings of network industries and to identify possible natural monopoly market – also known as core network activities – in the digital network industry. In order to establish the concept of natural monopoly, the study of economic literature focuses on the characteristics of network industries and the theory of natural monopoly, as to provide a justificatory framework for the conclusions surrounding the networked nature of digital markets and the natural monopoly status of certain digital markets. In order to substantiate findings from the literature study, the book relies on empirical insights on the workings of digital markets and the (de)regulation of traditional network industries.

The main contribution of this research will be to the legal science and our understanding of regulation theory in relation to digital markets. The purpose of this book is to develop a conceptual framework for regulation that searches for optimal outcomes as to stimulate durable competition in the digital network industry. Findings from the economics and management studies literature should therefore be placed in the context of developing regulatory solutions.

to the legal system. Here, market failures are considered as the *raison d'être* of law. Legal rules are analysed as instruments to correct market failure or at least reduce its adverse consequences. It also notes that most legal economists follow a pragmatic, eclectic approach and that it is hard to fit this scholarship in a particular school. A review of methodology of law and economics must concentrate on the ideas which are shared by a vast majority of legal economists. Moreover, law and economics combines normative law and positive economies: a positive analysis provides statements of what the law and its effects are, and it aims at explaining and predicting law and its consequences. The result of the positive analysis sets the stage for a normative analysis, where it is discussed what the law should be. The positive analysis may already include implicit normative statements. In this work, the law and economics methodology should be understood as to ensure that normative statements on what the law should be are grounded in these facets of economic thinking, while leaving space for normative nature of legal scholarship.

Methods of data collection. This study has relied on peer-reviewed legal journals and economics journals. These have predominantly been found in the WorldCat, Wiley Online Library, Springer, or HeinOnline databases. Alternatively, sources have been found through the snowballing method or through recommendations from the network of the author.

When reviewing scholarly studies, the following search criteria were applied: the study has used only peer-reviewed works; used articles had to be published in either a legal, economic, management theories, or computer sciences journal; the book has only used English and Dutch literature; the scope has been limited to law and case law from the European Union or its member states, the United Kingdom, and the United States; finally, secondary sources had to relate to our understanding of regulation and economics in liberal market economies.

Validity. The internal validity of this study is safeguarded through reliance on a law and economics methodology and insights from management theory to develop the regulatory framework.[20] This approach allows for a positive justification for the normative statements on regulation. Moreover, both the literature and case studies rely on a mix of primary and reliable secondary sources of legal scholarship. Studying traditional network industries provides testable insights into the efficiency of regulation in creating or simulating competitive pressure, whilst the secondary sources provide insights into how this can – or cannot – be transposed onto contemporary digital markets.

1.3 OUTLINE

This book is divided into three parts. Part I studies the economic characteristics of digital goods and services, platform business models, ecosystems and the digital network industry. It sets the stage for the analysis in the later parts of the work by explaining the novelties of digital business models and ecosystems.

Part II develops new theories and concepts to capture the dynamics of ecosystems competition. Here, the book distinguishes between multi-actor and multi-product ecosystems, develops a conceptual framework for the different stages of ecosystem competition, and uses this framework to develop novel theories of harm related to ecosystem competition.

Part III discusses lessons for regulation. First, it looks at existing regulatory proposals and reforms of competition in the EU, UK, and Germany to explain the benefits and shortcomings of the different approaches. Subsequently, it explains how the conceptual system of progressive ecosystem regulation would be able to encompass good practices from all three jurisdictions while mitigating the weaknesses presented by each of the regulatory approaches.

[20] Where general economic terms are used, one can refer to OECD, 'Glossary of Industrial Organisation Economics and Competition Law', online for definitions, unless more specific or elaborate definitions are provided in the text of the book.

PART I

The Competitors in the Digital Network Industry

This first part of the book contains an analysis of the economic characteristics of network industries and digital markets. It is discussed how interconnected digital markets create a digital network industry of their own and how the nature of digital goods incentivizes the use of digital platform strategies and the creation of multi-product ecosystems. It sets the stage for later analyses by framing digital competition as competition in a broad digital network.

This part has two main contributions. First, it develops a framework to assess whether digital platform markets exhibit natural monopoly as a result of its economic characteristics and the presence of self-reinforcing feedback loops. Second, it sets out a theory on how digital natural monopoly in platform markets and multi-product ecosystems shape competition in the digital network. With this, it provides the foundation for the analyses conducted in the later parts.

2

Digital Goods, Platforms, and Ecosystems

This chapter discusses the characteristics of digital goods and services, platforms, and ecosystems. Its purpose is to create a comprehensive overview of what digital goods are and how they differ from non-digital goods and services (Section 2.1). This helps to understand how the nature of digital goods inspires the adoption of competitive strategies, including the adoption of digital platform business models and the emergence of digital ecosystems. The functioning of digital platforms is discussed in Section 2.2. Section 2.3 elaborates on the emergence of digital ecosystems and how they relate to digital platforms.

2.1 THE CHARACTERISTICS OF DIGITAL GOODS AND SERVICES

Digital goods and services form their own distinct category of products or outputs. In many instances, the difference is obvious. On the one side, there is a tangible, physical product that can be touched and consumed, which must be produced and transported and which may be scarce or at risk of irreparably breaking. On the other, there is an intangible digital product that can only be viewed or listened to and accessed through devices, which – once developed in code – can be duplicated with zero or near-zero costs and transferred and downloaded almost instantaneously. As a result, digital goods are rarely scarce, or scarcity is artificially introduced. One can easily delete an app and retrieve it again later, often with the data of the person still available. Hardware bridges the gap between digital and non-digital: while tangible, it is only valuable for the intangible software that it allows access to. This is how we experience the difference between digital and physical, but how exactly do digital goods differ from non-digital goods from an economics perspective? This section sets out the economic characteristics of digital goods as to explain how their nature and characteristics inspire new business models and new economic opportunities.

2.1.1 *Digital Goods Are Information Goods*

Software goods are information goods. The latter were defined by Varian in 1998 as 'anything that can be digitized, including a book, a movie, a record, or a telephone conversation'.[21] A rather broad definition, but helpful in distilling the essence of what differentiates physical goods from software. Later, Michael Hutter has tried to define information goods by virtue of their characteristics, arguing that there are three features that distinguish the information economy from the non-information economy: abundance, access, and network and communities.[22]

The *abundance* of information goods is a result of their non-exhaustive and non-rivalrous nature. Information goods are in principle public goods: as soon as information becomes available, anyone can use it. The use of information by one party does not diminish its value (non-exhaustive) nor does it exclude consumption by other parties (non-rivalrous).[23] This distinguishes information goods from physical non-information goods, where there is scarcity. The consumption or use of a non-information good by one party will exclude consumption or use by another. A piece of fruit can only be eaten once, and a t-shirt only be worn by one person (rivalry).[24] Even when goods can be reused, they tend to damage or depreciate over time.

As information goods can be easily duplicated, shared, and used by a large number of users, and scarcity is absence, this also changes how we conduct transactions.[25] Transactions related to non-information goods often happens through transferral: someone buys the piece of fruit or t-shirt and brings it home. For information goods, transactions generally happen through *access*: one can watch a movie on their TV, listen to music on a streaming device, or download an app without owning the (rights to) that movie, music, or application. Instead, the owners of the copyright to information goods provide access to their goods and services, often for remuneration or other forms of compensation. Access to utilize the property – rather than the transfer of property – becomes the basic institutional condition for the information economy.[26]

While information goods are abundant once created, there are often significant costs to creating the information itself in the form of research, compilation, and curation. For information goods, the bulk of the production costs are sunk costs, meaning that the majority of the costs are incurred for the development of the first copy.[27] Afterwards, information goods can be duplicated and disseminated at near-zero cost, allowing the license holder to recoup its investment.[28] Once generated,

21 Hal R Varian, 'Markets for Information Goods' 19.

22 Michael Hutter, 'Information Goods', *A Handbook of Cultural Economics* (Edward Elgar Publishing 2003) 263–268.

23 ibid 264.

24 cf Hal Varian, *Microeconomic Analysis* (3rd edn, Norton 1992); Varian (n 21); Hutter (n 22).

25 Hutter (n 22) 265.

26 ibid 263.

27 Varian (n 21); Hutter (n 22) 263–264.

28 cf Chris Anderson, *The Long Tail – Why the Future of Business Is Selling Less of More* (Hyperion e-book 2016); Alexandre de Streel, Marc Bourreau and Lauriane Giet, 'Digital Conglomerates and EU Competition Policy' (CERRE 2019); Marc Bourreau, 'Some Economics of Digital Ecosystems' (OECD 2020). Note for the OECD DAF/COMP/WD(2020)89; Lancieri and Sakowski (n 1).

the producer of the information good will generally attempt to disseminate that information to as many people as possible. This requires a completely different business strategy compared to non-information goods.

For non-information goods, there are costs associated with the production of each unit. Therefore, overproduction is costly, so the producer of non-information goods will try to ensure that supply matches demand. For information goods, where there is abundance, firms will try to aggressively get their product out there. As a result, abundance strategies rely on things like free giveaways and demo versions: giving away free newspapers, the free nature of social media and search engines for end users and the prevalence of previews for movies and demo versions of video games are all part of the abundance strategy.[29]

In some markets, the primary product is given away for free so that the user will purchase products in its aftermarket while others are damaged versions (versions that have only a part of the functionalities when compared to the full version) of the product.[30] These free goods allow users to familiarize themselves with the product and allows the undertaking to create a community surrounding its information product. While giveaways can be used in non-information markets for a short period of time, the presence of copying and distribution costs makes it unfeasible in the long term. For information goods with zero marginal costs, however, providing the goods free of cost and monetizing it in other ways is a viable long-term strategy.[31] This can be seen nowhere better than in digital markets, where free (or Freemium) goods have become the norm in many markets.[32]

The use of giveaways and free goods produces another important effect, namely that it helps to stimulate the creation of networks and communities.[33] Giving away information goods can help the producer identify how to best monetize them. This strategy is common in digital markets, by giving away the product to household consumers (end users) the firm stimulates adoption and builds a network. It can then see how the product is best monetized.[34] This could entail the introduction of advertisements, sales to enterprise customers, the use of a Freemium model (where users pay for an upgraded version), or a combination thereof. Once the information good is popularized, this may lead to social contagion, driving the demand for the product.[35]

[29] Hutter (n 22) 263–264; Michal S Gal and Daniel L Rubinfeld, 'The Hidden Costs of Free Goods: Implications for Antitrust Enforcement' (2015) 80 Antitrust Law Journal 521, 524–525.

[30] Hutter (n 22); Gal and Rubinfeld (n 29); Friso Bostoen, 'Online Platforms and Pricing: Adapting Abuse of Dominance Assessments to the Economic Reality of Free Products' (2019) 35 Computer Law & Security Review 263.

[31] Hutter (n 22) 263.

[32] Gal and Rubinfeld (n 29) 523–525.

[33] Hutter (n 22) 266–267.

[34] Amrit Tiwana, *Platform Ecosystems: Aligning Architecture, Governance, and Strategy* (Morgan Kaufmann 2013) ch 3.

[35] This self-reinforcing effects on the demand side of the market are referred to as network externalities, the principles of which are discussed in Section 2.2.

Once a user network is developed, a community may also form around the information product, especially in modern online networks: users that join an online community tend to provide content to that community. This can be observed not only in open-source projects but also in user participation such as entering search queries, making posts, or posting reviews. In these markets, the final product that is consumed by the users is ultimately a collaboration between the producer and those prosumers (producing consumers) that have contributed to the latest version.[36]

2.1.2 *Digital Goods Are Modular Goods*

Digital goods are generally modular (information) goods. A modular good consists of distinct building blocks called modules, which can easily be integrated into or removed from the final product, without it having to be completely redesigned. Modules can be reused across a range of different products, can be used to make different versions of a similar product at lower or higher price points, or can be used to add new functionalities to an existing product.[37] A modular design is not unique to digital products, as it also used in industries such as construction, art, or car manufacturing.[38] The modularity of digital goods is however particularly important in shaping the business models and competitive strategies of digital firms.[39]

The modularity of digital goods allows for the adaptation and evolution of digital products through component sharing within the firm and provides opportunities to co-generate value through component sharing between firms.[40] Component sharing within the firm simply means that a producer of different products can use a module from the production of product A for product B as well. For instance, a video-game producer may be able to reuse certain models, backgrounds, or pieces of code for the development of multiple videogames. As a result, its costs for producing the second and each subsequent game become lower than the production of the initial game.[41] Modularity lowers the average costs with the production of more products, at least as long as component sharing is available.[42]

[36] Gina Dokko, Aimée A Kane and Marco Tortoriello, 'One of Us or One of My Friends: How Social Identity and Tie Strength Shape the Creative Generativity of Boundary-Spanning Ties' (2014) 35 Organisation Studies 703.

[37] See Marc Bourreau, Pinar Dogan and Matthieu Manant, 'Modularity and Product Innovation in Digital Markets' (2009) 6 Review of Network Economics; Andreas Hein and others, 'Digital Platform Ecosystems' (2020) 30 Electronic Markets 87; de Streel, Bourreau and Giet (n 28); Hovenkamp (n 11); Jacobides and Lianos (n 12).

[38] Bourreau, Dogan and Manant (n 37) 2.

[39] cf Bourreau, Dogan and Manant (n 37); Annabelle Gawer and MA Cusumano, 'How Companies Become Platform Leaders' (2008) 49 MIT Sloan Management Review 28; de Streel, Bourreau and Giet (n 28); Jacobides, Cennamo and Gawer (n 12).

[40] Bourreau, Dogan and Manant (n 37) 3.

[41] Claudia de O Melo and others, 'Interpretative Case Studies on Agile Team Productivity and Management' (2013) 55 Special Section: Component-Based Software Engineering (CBSE), 2011 412.

[42] Bourreau, Dogan and Manant (n 37) 4–5.

Component sharing *between* firms is also highly important in digital business models, as it helps with building a network or community. Digital services such as Operating Systems generally comprise a mix of goods and services produced by the undertaking itself (its proprietary apps), as well as applications provided by third-party complementors, in this case software developers.[43] In fact, most of the applications that we use and access on our smartphones or personal computers are non-proprietary, but rather the result of a co-generation of value between the supplier of the OS and independent developers.[44] This is a result of component sharing: the OS supplier provides the Operating System as a stable core in which modules can be integrated, and the third parties provide the modules. Users can now mix and match different modules, personalizing their experience with the Operating System. The supplier of the Operating System does not have to curate the experience for each of its users but simply has to manage which modules become available (or are excluded from) the stable core that they provide.[45]

In digital software markets, the interaction between the modules from the supplier and external complementors are generally facilitated through Application Programming Interface (APIs). An API is a piece of code that is standardized and designed to be used by the providers of specialized modules. APIs are considered to be secure, as the provider of the specialized module only gets access to the information required to supply the specialized module.[46] Common examples of APIs are universal logins, third-party payment processing software, real-time comparison websites, and tools that allow third-party plug-ins into a piece of software. APIs are highly important for collaboration, innovation, and data monetization, and it is up to the supplier of an information good to determine to what extent they allow access to third parties into its software.[47]

In short, modularity is key to the adoption of platform business models, especially platforms like Operating Systems. Component sharing between firms allows the platform operator to develop a network of complementors which generate value on and for the platform. Meanwhile, both component sharing within and between firms is commonplace in digital markets, creating productive efficiencies.

43 cf Gawer and Cusumano (n 39); Gawer and Cusumano (n 12); Jacobides, Cennamo and Gawer (n 12); Jacobides and Lianos (n 12).

44 Wen Wen and Feng Zhu, 'Threat of Platform-Owner Entry and Complementor Responses: Evidence from the Mobile App Market' (2019) 40 Strategic Management Journal 1336; Competition & Market Authority, 'Mobile Ecosystems Market Study – Interim Report' (2021) Market Study Interim Report; Friso Bostoen and Daniel Mandrescu, 'Assessing Abuse of Dominance in the Platform Economy: A Case Study of App Stores' (2020) 16 European Competition Journal 431.

45 Bourreau, Dogan and Manant (n 37); de Streel, Bourreau and Giet (n 28); Bourreau (n 28); Jacobides and Lianos (n 12).

46 IBM Cloud Education, 'Application Programming Interface (API)' (2020) <www.ibm.com/cloud/learn/api>.

47 cf Bostoen and Mandrescu (n 44); Joost Rietveld and Melissa A Schilling, 'Platform Competition: A Systematic and Interdisciplinary Review of the Literature' (2021) 47 Journal of Management 1528.

2.1.3 *Devices, Advertisements, and Business Model Orientation*

A discussion of the difference between digital and non-digital goods is not complete without looking at hardware. Hardware provides the physical devices required to enter software and without it, software would remain inaccessible. But what is hardware? On the one hand, they are not quite information goods. After all, hardware can only be replaced by cloud computing to a limited extent.[48] One will still need a screen, headphone, or neural implement to access the digitized content. On the other, hardware goods have little to no value without software: a smartphone without software is not much more than a rectangular piece of plastic. While inextricably linked with one another, their production and proliferation does not follow the same principles and processes.

The difference between hardware and software is that hardware is a tangible good. Producing devices has a (sometimes significant) per unit cost, changing the cost distribution.[49] They are made out of (sometimes rare) materials, making them scarce. Hardware is also rivalrous and exhaustive; smartphones, computers, and headphones are personal items, and the second life of these products is (for now) limited. This means that commercial strategies aimed at proliferating hardware is different from software and likely more akin to non-information goods: transactions happen through transferral, supply is dictated by demand, congestion issues may arise, and the use of giveaways is limited.[50]

While there are differences between software and hardware, there are also similarities. For vital hardware components, the cost distribution often also consists primarily of high upfront investments and lower costs per unit. While there are costs to producing microchips, the majority of the costs consist of research and development, developing or buying the required machinery, and setting up an (informational) infrastructure.[51] Moreover, hardware is generally modular. Producers of personal computers, smartphones, or video-game consoles can reuse chips and semiconductors to create a range of low- and high-end devices, where the latter includes more or newer technologies than its cheaper counterpart.[52] It is also possible to reuse components from (for example) the development of personal computers for video-game

48 G Wang and J Unger, 'A Strategy to Move Taiwan's IT Industry from Commodity Hardware Manufacturing to Competitive Cloud Solutions' (2013) 1 IEEE Access 159.

49 Varian (n 24).

50 See ibid; Varian (n 21); Hutter (n 22); Anderson (n 28).

51 John Teel, '9 Costs That Factor into Mass Manufacturing a Hardware Product' (2017) <https://makezine.com/article/digital-fabrication/3d-printing-workshop/cost-manufacture-new-electronic-hardware-product/>; Hitesh Gambhava, 'How Much Does Hardware Product Development Cost?' *eFour* (16 September 2022) <www.efour.co/blog/hardware-product-development-cost/>.

52 This can be seen in generations of video-game consoles, which sometimes include a 'normal' version, a 'light' version, and a 'pro' version, which include slight variations. For example, the Playstation 5 has a discless version, a version with disc slot, and now a 'pro' version with some hardware upgrades.

consoles. This may include not only physical chips and nodes but also expertise, information, or other (in)tangible assets.[53]

Digital undertakings often – but not always – offer a combination of software and hardware in their portfolio. Some undertakings are – or were – fully focussed on delivering software. Alphabet and Meta have long provided solely software services in the form of search or social media. They have later branched out, Alphabet now produces its own smartphones and personal computers and Meta its own virtual reality headsets, but this shift to hardware has only happened later in their lifetime. Apple has always focussed on a mix of hardware and software, offering its proprietary applications only on its proprietary hardware. Amazon originated as an online bookstore, where the digital service (its website) was merely a conduit for the sales of its physical goods. There are also digital undertakings that only supply hardware, such as AMD, NVIDA, and ASML. This shows that there is variety in the strategies of digital firms and the strategies that they (can) use.

Here, it is helpful to understand the strategies of digital undertakings as a spectrum: from opened to closed and from monetization (ad-centric) to marketization (device- or sales-centric).[54] The business models of Alphabet and Meta are predominantly ad-centric: they give away free services to end users and are compensated through revenues from advertising. They strengthen their position in their advertising activities by collecting personal data. Thus, to reach more users with their ads and collect more data, they must aggressively proliferate their products. Consequently, they maintain a strategy of openness: their business strategies are focussed on adoption and growth to monetize this use later.

On the other side of the spectrum, there are producers such as AMD, NVIDIA, and ASML. They produce their goods in-house; there is little participation by third parties, and they do not use giveaways. They market their products, selling their devices to enterprises and/or end users with a margin. In between, there are Microsoft and Apple. Microsoft is mostly software-based, yet product-centric. It sells its Operating System and productivity software to enterprises to recoup its costs and is less focussed on advertising. Windows maintains very open strategies in some cases (Windows OS) and closed strategies in others (Microsoft Office). Apple is also device-centric and aims to sell its devices by offering highly complementary hardware and software. It makes use of controlled openness, allowing participation by third parties under strict conditions. Digital undertakings rarely rely on a purely open or closed strategy, but rather a mix of both. This is also demonstrated by NVIDIA's recent move towards the development of artificial intelligence[55]: know-how and resources from hardware development can be leveraged into software, and vice versa.

53 Bourreau, Dogan and Manant (n 37); de Streel, Bourreau and Giet (n 28); Bourreau (n 28); Jacobides and Lianos (n 12).

54 See eg Bourreau (n 28) 5–8; Bostoen and Mandrescu (n 44) 3–4; Rietveld and Schilling (n 47).

55 See NVIDIA, AI Solutions, Official website <www.nvidia.com/en-us/solutions/ai/>.

TABLE 2.1 *An overview of the differences between ad- and device-centric business models*

Advertisement-centric business model	Device-centric business model
Free access for consumers	Paid access for consumers
Monetized on a secondary side of the market	Marketized on the same side of the market
Open business models to attract a large userbase on both sides of the market	Closed business model to ensure high quality
High data dependence	Low data dependence

In principle, ad-centric and device-centric strategies can be distinguished on the basis of the characteristics presented in Table 2.1.

The chosen business model impacts the way digital goods and services are offered. A device-centric business model that relies on marketization and sales is able to recoup its costs by maintaining a one-sided business model. The undertaking can simply sell its goods and services to recoup its costs and turn a profit. However, digital undertakings may also choose to supply their goods and services on the basis of a digital platform model, where it acts as an intermediary to connect buyers and sellers, viewers and advertisers, or service providers and users.[56]

2.2 DIGITAL PLATFORMS: A REVOLUTION OF INDUSTRIAL ORGANIZATION

Digital platforms have become the widely adopted business model for digital firms. The digital platform should be seen as a novel form of industrial organization that changes the way value is created throughout a network.[57] To explore the value proposition of digital platforms, it is important to first define what exactly constitutes a digital platform and how this differs from non-platform markets.

The concept of a platform is nothing new: a platform is the *technology*, generally employed *by an intermediary* to act as a *gateway* between different groups of users. Any platform connects multiple groups of users, thereby creating multi-sided markets. For instance, a market for buyers on the one side of the platform and a market for sellers on the other side of the platform. This is what distinguishes the platform from traditional one-sided markets, where the producer of a good sells it to

[56] Todd Davies and Zlatina Georgieva, 'Zero Price, Zero Competition: How Marketization Fixes Anticompetitive Tying in Monetized Markets' 2–6.

[57] Literature on the novelty of the platform is robust, cf Rietveld and Schilling (n 47); Hein and others (n 37); Tiwana (n 34); de Streel, Bourreau and Giet (n 28); Scott Morton and others (n 14); Geoffrey Parker, Marshall Van Alstyne and Xiaoyue Jiang, 'Platform Ecosystems: How Developers Invert the Firm' (2017) 41 MIS Quarterly 255; Montero and others (n 18); Gawer (n 12); Martin Kenney and John Zysman, 'The Rise of the Platform Economy' (2016) 32 Issues in Science and Technology 61; Busch (n 2).

consumers or downstream customers.[58] For example, a newspaper that is sold for a few euros to cover its costs maintains a one-sided business model: the news agency produces the product and sells a product. A newspaper that is offered for free, and remunerated by advertisements, is a multi-sided business model: it acts as a gateway for advertisers to reach readers, and the news agency intermediates.[59] This is known as a *matching* platform: the newspapers attract readers by offering engaging content and mixes this with advertisements.[60] The more eyeballs on the newspaper, the more valuable the service becomes for advertisers. Ad-centric matching platforms receive payment for the placement of the advertisement, not per sale on the basis of those advertisements.[61]

A payment service provider offers an example of a transaction platform. The platform facilitates payments by offering the payment infrastructure in the form of cards and devices, which allows buyers and sellers to conclude transactions. The payment providers acts as the intermediary, and charges a small fee for each card payment. As the operator gets paid per transaction, this is known as a *transaction* platform.

The success of a platform depends on the size of the network of users that operate on it on both sides of the market. After all, it is only possible to act as a gateway by connecting A to B. This means that the operator of any type of platform must overcome the chicken-and-egg problem: they must provide value for different sides of the market simultaneously in order to attract users on different sides of the market.[62] It must first attract enough readers to be attractive for advertisers. However, as it depends on advertisers for revenue, it must attract advertisers quickly to cover its costs before the quality of the newspaper starts to suffer, or before it goes bankrupt. Many digital services use this model: Facebook and Google Search have offered their product for free to monetize it later and have grown into digital giants this way. Today, many applications rely on this business model still: games, video- or music-streaming services often rely on free but advertisement-driven business models. Hybrids are possible, and common, many services allow users to purchase an

58 Andrei Hagiu and Julian Wright, 'Multi-sided Platforms' (2015) 43 International Journal of Industrial Organization 162.

59 Julian Wright, 'One-Sided Logic in Two-Sided Markets' (2004) 3 Review of Network Economics 42; Bruno Jullien, 'Competition in Multi-sided Markets: Divide and Conquer' (2011) 3 American Economic Journal: Microeconomics 186; Hagiu and Wright (n 58).

60 Lapo Filistrucchi, Damien Geradin and Eric EC van Damme, 'Identifying Two-Sided Markets' [2012] SSRN Electronic Journal <www.ssrn.com/abstract=2008661> accessed 14 September 2021; L Filistrucchi and others, 'Market Definition in Two-Sided Markets: Theory and Practice' (2014) 10 Journal of Competition Law and Economics 293; Andrei Hagiu and Julian Wright, 'Multi-sided Platforms' (2015) 43 International Journal of Industrial Organisation 162; Bourreau (n 28).

61 Filistrucchi and others (n 60) 298–300.

62 Bernard Caillaud and Bruno Jullien, 'Chicken & Egg: Competition among Intermediation Service Providers' (2003) 34 The RAND Journal of Economics 309; Tiwana (n 34) chs 2–3; Crémer, De Montjoye and Schweitzer (n 4) 32.

ad-free version (the so-called Freemium model), and commercials were already commonplace in television and radio.

The workings of multi-sided markets, intermediation, and different types of transactions are not new to digital platforms, yet digital platforms differentiate themselves strongly from traditional platforms in multiple ways. While traditional platforms offer a set of specific services, the platformization of markets should be seen as a new model of industrial organization that has revolutionized industry and dislodged the 'firm' model as the incumbent model of industrial organization, at least in digital markets.[63]

Digital platform operators differ from traditional non-platform firms as they do not add value by producing something but rather coordinate and intermediate the supply of externally produced goods and services. At the same time, digital platforms differ from other multi-sided markets as their ability to coordinate and govern the users on either side of the platform reaches far beyond what we see in traditional multi-sided markets.[64] They do not just intermediate between groups of users but internalize the products and services offered by these users as to form their own multi-actor ecosystem: a collective of third parties and a firm that operates one or more digital platforms, where these third parties offer complementary goods or services on one or more of the platforms offered by that firm or consume the goods or services offered by that firm.[65] The ecosystem of complementors co-creates value together with the platform operator and raises the value proposition of its platforms by competing, cooperating, or entering into coopetition on the platform or with the platform operator.[66]

Compared to newspapers, radio, and television, digital platform operators (are able to) exert far more oversight, control, and direction over their different groups of users.[67] Modern digital platforms often integrate a far greater number of different third-party modules than non-digital platform businesses such as newspapers or television. Digital platform operators perform a number of tasks to maintain or elevate the quality of their platform: they develop standards, for instance, in the form of software development kits or through APIs, they set minimum quality standards, and even set prices for participation.[68] Digital platforms also have far greater capabilities to target and personalize their services as a result of the collection and use of

[63] See n 37.

[64] Tiwana (n 34); Jacobides and Lianos (n 12).

[65] Jacobides and Lianos (n 12); Philipp Hornung, 'The Ecosystem Concept, the DMA, and Section 19a GWB' [2023] Journal of Antitrust Enforcement jnad049.

[66] Tiwana (n 34); Giuseppe Colangelo, 'Evaluating the Case for Regulation of Digital Platforms' (2020) 26 The Global Antitrust Institute Report on the Digital Economy; Lancieri and Sakowski (n 1); Bostoen and Mandrescu (n 44); Jacobides and Lianos (n 12); Hornung (n 65).

[67] Tiwana (n 34); Montero and others (n 18); Jacobides and Lianos (n 12); Montero and Finger (n 18); Hornung (n 65).

[68] Tiwana (n 34); Bostoen and Mandrescu (n 44); Bourreau (n 28).

personal data.[69] This further allows them to strengthen their control over third-party complementors. Platform operators can make strategic use of their APIs. They allow third parties to connect but also use these APIs to obtain valuable information on user preferences and activities in real time, which enhances their ability to target advertising.[70]

The digital platform operator may be considered a *super intermediary*: digital platforms automate the interactions, aggregate a substantial amount of supply and demand in a market, and often even create the markets around them. Business and consumers have more power over the intermediated parties, than traditional intermediaries.[71] Therefore, digital platforms may have to be understood as a more powerful facilitator than an intermediary. The platform is the coordinator in their markets, as well as the super intermediary, a de facto regulator of its ecosystem of actors.[72] This is what distinguishes the digital platform operator from a non-digital intermediary: the digital platform is the infrastructure underlying a digital multi-sided market, or markets, where it generates value by aggregating users on the different sides of the market(s), coordinating the value propositions offered by these different actors, intermediating the interactions between the different sides of the market and determining how the generated value is allocated amongst players including the platform operator itself.[73]

For conceptual clarity in the analyses throughout this book, a strict distinction is maintained between *the platform* (as the technology), the *platform operator* (the intermediary that has the ability to impose rules), and the *multi-actor ecosystem* (the users that are active on the platform, which may include vertically integrated activities of the platform operator). By maintaining this distinction, it is easier to separate between (i) the value co-generated by its complementors in the ecosystem on the basis of the platform; (ii) the intermediary role of the platform operator, and (iii) the functioning of the platform operator as the de facto regulator of the multi-actor ecosystem.[74] This helps to better analyse these different activities as to understand

69 Marc Bourreau, Alexandre de Streel and Inge Graef, 'Big Data and Competition Policy: Market Power, Personalised Pricing and Advertising' (2017) CERRE Project Report; Competition & Market Authority, 'Online Platforms and Digital Advertising' (2020) <www.gov.uk/cma-cases/online-platforms-and-digital-advertising-market-study>.

70 Bourreau, de Streel and Graef (n 69); Competition & Market Authority (n 69); Victoria Fast, Daniel Schnurr and Michael Wohlfarth, 'Regulation of Data-Driven Market Power in the Digital Economy: Business Value Creation and Competitive Advantages from Big Data' (2022) 0 Journal of Information Technology.

71 Montero and Finger (n 18) 225–231.

72 Montero and Finger (n 18); Wagner and others (n 14).

73 Gawer and Cusumano (n 12); Kenney and Zysman (n 57); José van Dijck, David Nieborg and Thomas Poell, 'Reframing Platform Power' (2019) 8 Internet Policy Review 1; Pieter Nooren and others, 'Should We Regulate Digital Platforms? A New Framework for Evaluating Policy Options: Evaluating Policy Options for Digital Platforms' (2018) 10 Policy & Internet 264; Montero and others (n 18); Montero and Finger (n 18); Rietveld and Schilling (n 47).

74 Jacobides, Cennamo and Gawer (n 12); Jacobides and Lianos (n 12); Hornung (n 65) 402–404.

where value is generated and by whom, how competition *on* and *between* platforms takes place, and why or how anti-competitive behaviour may arise.

Take the example of Operating Systems: Windows, iOS, and Linux are all technologies on which software developers can deliver their goods and services to end users. Thus, they all fulfil the technological role of a platform. Microsoft and Apple act as intermediaries for Windows and iOS, they operate the central platform and have the ability to make decisions about how users connect with one another, and have the opportunity to charge a commission for interactions. Meanwhile, Linux is open source, so there is a peer-to-peer marketplace. Linux is a non-intermediated platform technology, this type of platformization often falls outside of the scope of inquiries into platform-based competition. Finally, there is the question of how the platforms are regulated. Linux is wholly unregulated, and Windows is barely regulated. Users can generally interact in any way they want and download everything directly of the web with minimal limitations. In contrast, Apple has created a heavily regulated and moderated environment where users can only download permitted applications via permitted means. As a result of this difference, Apple users are more intermediated than Windows users. Moreover, the risk of anti-competitive behaviour as a result of intermediation is absent for Linux as there is no intermediary. This is to say that not all platforms are the same, nor are the competitive risks associated with the existence of platforms.

2.2.1 *New Possibilities for Aggregation and Scale*

The value of digital platforms is – at least in large part – determined by the number of users they can connect to one another. Due to the informational nature of digital goods, digital platforms are exceedingly proficient at creating scale and connecting extraordinary numbers of users on the same or different sides of the market.[75] This section discuses three keystones: geographical range, ability for proliferation, and possibilities for coordination.

Global Networks

Digital firms are often global, allowing them to attract a far greater number of users than those found in similar non-digital networks: WhatsApp has outnumbered traditional players in markets for interpersonal communications. With over 1.5 billion users, the network operated by WhatsApp is one and a half times bigger than the largest telecom in the world, China Mobile, and over three times bigger than the largest telecoms provider in Europe.[76] However, WhatsApp is not even close to being the largest digital network: Meta has aggregated over 3 billion users on its Facebook and Instagram networks, and Google has exceeded 3 billion users for its

[75] Crémer, De Montjoye and Schweitzer (n 4) 32–34, 56–60.
[76] Montero and others (n 18) 3.

Android OS.[77] These networks far exceed any scale that would have been possible without the level of internet access and computing power that we have today. As the marginal costs for new connections are low, infrastructure is virtual, and digital products are not subjected to transportation, storage costs, or loss over distance, networks can become more geographically and numerically vast than ever.[78]

Aggregation on the side of end users does however not start to paint the full picture. The true value proposition of most digital platforms is the large amount of business users that offer their services and compete using the platform as infrastructure. Amazon's Marketplace has around 2 million sellers, and there are an estimated 26 million software developers that develop apps for Android and iOS alone. The number of developers active in the Windows ecosystem of actors far exceeds those numbers. In terms of ad-centric ecosystems, Meta and Alphabet both serve around 7 million distinct advertisers, that range from very large and with a global reach to very small and very local.[79]

New Levels of Abundance

The second keystone to aggregation by digital firms is the ability to aggressively proliferate high quality goods at near-zero cost. Abundance strategies have reached new possibilities for scale that go far beyond offering a free newspaper at a train station or the giveaway of a CD with demo software. Digital goods can be given away, indefinitely and in unlimited quantities, globally and in real time, while incurring near-zero costs.[80] These giveaways may range from low quality teasers to high-quality complex products. In some instances, the digital undertaking uses cross-subsidization to pay business users for the distribution of their free goods. In the *Google Android* case, it is described how Google expanded its position in the OS market by giving away Android OS to OEMs for free, while simultaneously paying these OEMs for the exclusive pre-installation of Google Search through revenue sharing agreements.[81] Giving away high-quality products for free has become the norm in digital markets, be it in the form of communications services, online social networks, search services, or content streaming. As giveaways make it easy to aggregate massive numbers of end users on the service, devising ad-centric strategies comes naturally to digital platform business. The strategy of 'free' is valuable

77 Alex Cranz, 'There Are over 3 Billion Active Android Devices' *The Verge* (18 May 2021); Hannah Murphy, 'Facebook Confronts Growth Problems as Number of Young Users in US Declines' *Financial Times* (22 October 2021).

78 Anderson (n 28); Montero and others (n 18) 3–4.

79 The number of active advertisers on Facebook has been taken from the official Facebook website: www.facebook.com> Insights to Go (accessed 12 January 2022); Google's number of advertisers is taken from Kylie Moore, 'Google Advertising Statistics for 2021' *Digital Third Coast* (2022).

80 cf Varian (n 21); Tiwana (n 34); Gal and Rubinfeld (n 29); Anderson (n 28); Chris Freeman and Francisco Louçã, *As Time Goes By: From the Industrial Revolutions to the Information Revolution* (Oxford University Press 2001).

81 Google Android (Case AT.40099), Commission Decision C(2018) 4761 [2018], OJ C 402/19.

because it helps digital platforms to overcome the chicken-and-egg problem. The foregone profits from giving these products away for free are later recouped when the platform has gained a value- and efficiency advantage over its competitors by virtue of network externalities, data, and the scale of their operations.[82]

New Opportunities for Coordination of Decentralized Assets: A New Form of Industrial Organization?

The third keystone to platform's ability to aggregate larger numbers of users than ever before is their ability to coordinate a large number of decentralized assets. By relying on external parties to produce the majority of what is offered on a platform, the platform operator can externalize costs while internalizing the generated value. Meanwhile, algorithmic coordination that is made efficient through the use of data helps to effectively steer production by a large an unstructured influx of third parties, while limiting coordination costs. As a result, platforms can integrate a seemingly infinite number of different users that offer niche services without a loss of efficiency.[83]

Digital platforms can be viewed as a form of industrial revolution that unlocks new possibilities for scale, in particular because of its ability to coordinate decentralized assets.[84] Finding efficient scale of production has always been a driver for changing business models: the emergence of railways, motorized vehicles and aviation have allowed for centralized production at a massive scale and the creation of global distribution networks to get the produced goods to users' home. It was these technological developments that made centralized production in factories so attractive around the turn of the twentieth century.[85]

To provide some historical context. Before the industrial revolution, a large portion of production happened through a decentralized 'putting-out' system, also known as domestic systems. Here, merchant employers put out material to rural producers that worked in their homes or workshops. Finished products were collected and returned to the merchant, who then paid these independent producers for their labour.[86] Here, the merchant provided an intermediation service similar to the platform providers of today: it connected suppliers of materials to suppliers of labour, allowed them to co-generate value, and collected and sold the outputs. This system was inefficient, as the merchant and goods would have to travel large distances to supply each of the domestic producers with materials, again to collect the goods, and then again to reach a point of sale.

82 Gal and Rubinfeld (n 29) 523–527.

83 cf Tiwana (n 34); Anderson (n 28); Jacobides, Cennamo and Gawer (n 12); Montero and others (n 18); Jacobides and Lianos (n 12); Montero and Finger (n 18).

84 cf Freeman and Louçã (n 80); Anderson (n 28); Parker, Van Alstyne and Jiang (n 57); Crémer, De Montjoye and Schweitzer (n 4).

85 A Chandler, *The Visible Hand: The Managerial Revolution in American Business* (Belknap Press 1993).

86 Britannica, The Editors of Encyclopaedia, 'Domestic system', Encyclopedia *Britannica* (14 February 2020).

With the emergence of technologies that allowed for mass production and transportation, came the emergence of the factory. This way, the materials and labours were brought to a single point of production, from where the outputs could be transported for wholesale or retail directly. The factory reduces coordination costs and creates efficiencies associated with reducing travel and transport time, standardizing production processes and outputs, and reducing the unnecessary duplication of materials. Overall, factory-based production and mass transportation significantly increased productivity and were drivers of new levels of wealth.[87] This centralized form of industrial organization is often referred to as the firm: the industrial organization as a firm allows the undertaking to lower transaction costs by internalizing processes rather than contracting those sources externally.[88]

The emergence of digital platforms now allows for a new mode of organization, combining the perks of decentralized production and mass transportation. As digital platforms can easily coordinate a large number of decentralized assets, they reduce the transaction costs associated with external contracting. This allows for a new form of industrial organization: the algorithmically coordinated putting out system. Rather than producing the goods internally, the digital platform is able to coordinate external value creation and internalize a part of this value as a reward for its coordination and intermediation services. Those that produce no longer need to be within a single firm but can rely on a third-party intermediary to reach their customers, even if these customers are geographically distributed.[89] Reliance on algorithms and Big Data allows the undertaking to automatically coordinate these interactions, which allows for an immense scale of operations while lowering transaction costs to a point that they become lower than those incurred in the employer–employee relationship.[90]

The platform hangs in between the firm and the market: it provides the technology – or digital infrastructure – that shapes the conditions for economic exchange. The players that depend on it act as if they are competing in a market, while the platform dictates their behaviour as if they were part of its firm.[91] It is important to note that any production activities undertaken by the operator of the platform take place within the ecosystem operated by the platform operator and should not be viewed as platform activities in themselves. Instead, entry into downstream markets to produce should be viewed as vertical integration between the platform upstream and the production of content downstream.[92]

87 Chandler (n 85) 102–106.

88 RH Coase, 'The Nature of the Firm' (1937) 4 Economica 386.

89 Montero and Finger (n 18); Tiwana (n 34); Kenney and Zysman (n 57); Erkko Autio, 'Orchestrating Ecosystems: A Multi-Layered Framework' [2021] Innovation 1.

90 Montero and Finger (n 18).

91 cf Gawer and Cusumano (n 12); Julie E Cohen, 'Law for the Platform Economy' (2017) 51 Davis Law Review 72; Digital Competition Expert Panel (n 1); Crémer, De Montjoye and Schweitzer (n 4); van Dijck, Nieborg and Poell (n 73); Lancieri and Sakowski (n 1); Rietveld and Schilling (n 47).

92 Jacobides and Lianos (n 12), 8, 10, 17, refer to competition between the platform operator's downstream activities and the third parties in the multi-actor ecosystem as vertical intra-ecosystem competition,

Online platforms promote the use of user-generated content, sharing, and collaboration. Capital has quickly taken advantage of these new modes of exchange by inserting themselves between the supply and demand of these services provided by independent workings, thereby embedding extractive processes into social interactions.[93] This has lowered barriers to creating and providing content is observed in practice in many markets: user-generated media content competes with professionally produced content, platforms such as Upwork allow local small entrepreneurs to provide their services globally and platforms such as Uber and Airbnb allow car- and homeowners to enter the markets for transport and tourism.[94] Digital platforms have an innate ability to access modes of supply that are unavailable without this level of coordination: end users are no longer merely passive consumers of goods, but they are invited to actively participate in generating outputs and exchanges.

The ability to add additional offerings without increasing costs makes digital platforms highly suitable to serve the long tail of demand. While traditional firms focus on selling a lot of a small number of products, digital platforms generate significant revenue by selling a little bit of a large number of products.[95] In markets for search for example, Google is able to distinguish itself by its ability to answer rare or unique search queries. In markets for media, platforms such as YouTube have allowed content creators to follow a small but dedicated following which has propelled some independent content creators to stardom, while a large group of content creators continues to put out content without ever reaching a large following.[96] In digital platform markets, demand follows supply: for everything that one puts out there, someone is willing to buy it.[97]

These combined characteristics – or keystone factors – help to understand the unprecedented scale of digital platforms: the nature of information goods allows for the creation of global networks, where users are aggregated by giving away goods freely or cheaply to build extensive networks which – once established – seem to create self-perpetuating demand by allowing for unprecedented levels of participation due to the modularity of digital goods and the ability of platform operators to coordinate decentralized assets. This helps to understand why digital platform operators must be viewed as *super* intermediaries: it is insufficient to simply connect different groups of users, the value of a platform for its users is largely determined by its ability to coordinate assets efficiently and distribute the surplus of value generated in a way that benefits everyone. For this, a platform needs the proper architecture and orchestration.

as it entails vertical integration of offering intermediation on one level and the production of a downstream good or service that would normally be part of the intermediated markets themselves.

93 Laurent Baronian, 'Digital Platforms and the Nature of the Firm' (2020) 54 Journal of Economic Issues 214, 215.

94 Montero and Finger (n 18).

95 See Anderson (n 28) chs 3, 8.

96 See Montero and Finger (n 18) pt I; Anderson (n 28) chs 3, 8.

97 See Anderson (n 28).

2.2.2 *The Coordination of the Multi-actor Ecosystem: Architecture and Orchestration*

The coordination of a digital platform rests on two key pillars: its architecture and the way it is orchestrated. First, the architecture of the platform determines how easy or difficult it is for third parties to connect, to find what they are looking for, to offer their goods and services, and which types of participation are allowed. In short, the architecture is (relatively) fixed: how is the platform designed and what are its functions and limits. Second, orchestration is the act of coordination by setting rules and terms for the activities performed on the platform.[98] This may be the checks the platform operator performs for quality control, how it allocates the generated value, and other gatekeeping activities.[99] To exemplify, the architecture determines, for instance, that an online marketplace allows for the buying and selling of third-party applications and not the buying and selling of physical goods. Thus, software developers can connect while sellers of physical goods cannot. Orchestration, in turn, relates to the minimum quality of software offered by third-party developers, the blacklisting of malicious software providers, and setting the percentage of commissions fees charged by the platform for each transaction.

Platform Architecture

Proper architecture of the platform allows the platform operator to reduce complexity for its users and to lower transaction and coordination costs. The most important functions of the platform's architecture are the possibilities for partitioning and systems integration. Partitioning refers to the subdivision of the ecosystem into different platforms and their complementary apps, while system integration refers to the coordination of the development activities among the platform and third-party developers.[100]

The platform operator may use APIs or software development kits (SDK) to create a well-partitioned platform. APIs or SDKs allow for the creation of 'black boxes': the platform allows compatibility with third-party services, without disclosing how the proprietary software of the platform functions. At the same time, third-party developers are ensured of compatibility with the platform without having to disclose how its app functions exactly. This way, the platform can maximize user participation and

[98] Tiwana (n 34); Amrit Tiwana, 'Evolutionary Competition in Platform Ecosystems' (2015) 26 Information Systems Research 150424094525000; Jacobides, Cennamo and Gawer (n 12); Peter C Evans and Annabelle Gawer, 'The Rise of the Platform Enterprise – A Global Survey' (2019) <www.thecge.net/app/uploads/2016/01/PDF-WEB-Platform-Survey_01_12.pdf>; Jacobides and Lianos (n 12); Hornung (n 65).

[99] Tiwana (n 34); Alessio Cozzolino, Leonardo Corbo and Paolo Aversa, 'Digital Platform-Based Ecosystems: The Evolution of Collaboration and Competition between Incumbent Producers and Entrant Platforms' (2021) 126 Journal of Business Research 385.

[100] Tiwana (n 34); Autio (n 89).

the creation of value by third parties without facing disincentives: as the platform does not share any sensitive information, the risk of accidentally sharing knowledge that may lead to competition is minimized. In fact, the platform operator strengthens its position in its respective market by setting standards for connection (through APIs) and code (through SDKs).[101]

This strengthening effect happens through system integration. Rules on systems integration determine whether and how the apps that are developed for the platform can be integrated (i) into the platform itself or (ii) into other apps on the platform. Where partitioning allows third-party developers to pursue their own goals in a comprehensible way (i.e. the developer is free to develop any app without disclosing how it is made), systems integration facilitates the co-creation of value by the platform and third parties: the platform determines how *all* 'black boxes' in the ecosystem may interact with one another. Not only does the platform determine how apps are integrated on the platform, but they also set the standards on how apps may interact with one another when provided on the platform. This creates value-driven lock-in, as app developers are dependent on the platform to co-create value amongst themselves.[102]

The role of the ecosystem architect is to create a unique form of multi-sided markets: not only does the platform facilitate the connection between multiple sides of the market, but it also governs the way in which these parties connect with one another and to what extent they are able to provide interoperable services. The architecture of the ecosystem has the purpose of reducing structural problems; the subsequent governance exercises by the platform may help reduce behavioural problems in the ecosystem. The architecture of the platform and its consequences for governance are inextricably linked. Choices in governance may have different consequences depending on the architecture of the ecosystem.

Platform Orchestration

As platforms act as coordinators of external production, it is not possible to rely on a command-and-control structure as seen in traditional firms.[103] While the latter relies on a hierarchical structure of managers over employees, no agreements on the distribution of authority exist within the ecosystem. The role of the platform is to orchestrate its downstream activities by putting in place mechanisms to reward successful third-party developers and may choose to put in place mechanisms punishing unsuccessful ones (while the latter is not a requirement for successful orchestration).[104]

[101] Tiwana (n 34).
[102] ibid.
[103] It is possible for the operator of a platform to vertically integrate as to internalize certain production activities, but this should be seen as the integration of downstream or upstream activities rather than as part of the platform activities undertaken by the digital enterprise.
[104] Tiwana (n 34); Erkko Autio and Llewellyn Thomas, 'Innovation Ecosystems: Implications for Innovation Management' (2014); Ron Adner, 'Ecosystem as Structure: An Actionable Construct

The platform operator acts as the de facto regulator of its own platform and performs the activities associated with this role. This means that the platform sets rules for access, content, competition, and aftercare, which shape how services are provided and who can provide them.[105] Moreover, the platform determines the division of rights and rewards by dividing authority between itself and its complementors, the collection of mechanisms through which it can exert control and the mechanisms for distributing rewards.[106]

First, in terms of *access rules*, the platform operator performs an important gatekeeper function.[107] Gatekeeping is a strict form of control by which the platform decides who can offer something on the platform and what they can offer. This is close to a command-and-control right as it is similar to an employer–employee relationship.[108] The platform operator may choose to allow or disallow certain actors to perform certain activities or block them from the platform altogether.[109]

For those complementors that do have access to the platform, the operator determines how they can supply their goods and services and under which conditions. These are *content rules*, as they shape what type of content and goods can be found on the platform.[110] The platform operator can exert control over content directly (minimum standards for quality, prohibitions of hate speech or self-harm content) or indirectly (issuing software development kits, terms and conditions for the use of APIs).[111] Here, the division of authority between the platform and complementors is particularly important. The division of authority determines which parts of the platform allow for compatibility and which do not. The platform decides on who holds 'platform decision rights' and 'complement decision rights'. The first set of rights refer to the authority to decide on platform functionalities, while the latter refers to the right to decide on complement functionalities.[112]

The division of these rights determines to what extent value creation is centralized or decentralized: a fully open-source project – such as Linux – allows users to both determine the functionalities of the platform and the complements which

for Strategy' (2017) 43 Journal of Management 39; Brice Dattée, Oliver Alexy and Erkko Autio, 'Maneuvering in Poor Visibility: How Firms Play the Ecosystem Game When Uncertainty Is High' (2018) 61 Academy of Management Journal 466; Autio (n 89).

105 Heike Schweitzer, 'Digitale Plattformen als private Gesetzgeber: Ein Perspektivwechsel für die europäische 'Plattform-Regulierung' [2019] ZEuP; Heike Schweitzer, 'The Art to Make Gatekeeper Positions Contestable and the Challenge to Know What Is Fair: A Discussion of the Digital Markets Act Proposal' (2021) 3 ZEuP 35.

106 Tiwana (n 34).

107 See eg Schweitzer, 'Digitale Plattformen als private Gesetzgeber: Ein Perspektivwechsel für die europäische 'Plattform-Regulierung' (n 105).

108 Tiwana (n 34).

109 Schweitzer, 'Digitale Plattformen als private Gesetzgeber: Ein Perspektivwechsel für die europäische 'Plattform-Regulierung' (n 105).

110 ibid.

111 Tiwana (n 34) chs 4–5; Hein and others (n 37) 93–95.

112 ibid.

are available on it, Alphabet's Android platform gives complement developers significant complement decision rights while retaining platform decision rights, and Apple's iOS maintains full control over its platform rights while exerting a high level of control through its complement decision rights.[113] In order to publish an app on Apple's App Store, complementors must subject themselves to high levels of oversight on quality and design, adhere to pricing obligations and use Apple's payment system. There is little oversight on what can be published on Android, at least in terms of pricing and quality (and even less so on Windows).[114] For a platform that is fully open source, any complementor can offer its own version of the platform itself. While this allows for a lot of freedom for complementors, it may also lead to security risks or unreliable forms of the platform.[115]

Beyond content rules, there are *competition rules*. Once it is clear what type of content can be offered, the platform may steer or determine how competition between complementors happens. This may relate to ranking, auctions, the use of fees, recommended prices, the placement of buy boxes, or any other type of activity that determines which complementor gains precedence over another or that influence the complementors' competitiveness.[116] These types of interventions are particularly important in relation to digital platforms, as they aggregate such a vast number of competing business users and the level of dependence that these business users have on the platform. Especially small producers are likely dependent on large platforms for the majority of their revenue. Consequently, they will be willing to adjust their competitive strategies largely to the demands of the platform. Any measures by the platform operator that may reduce their competitiveness, such as de-ranking or loss of access to certain functionalities, may mean the end of their business.[117] Pricing policy is also an important aspect of competition rules. It determines the allocation of value between the platform and users on different sides of the market. These policies may reflect to which extent complementors are dependent on the platform and vice versa. A platform that is actively working to overcome the chicken-and-egg problem will have to allocate value in a way that attracts either end users or business users. If the platform has an oversupply of business users, they will lower rewards for business users and use this to cross-subsidize the service for end users. Conversely, if there is an oversupply of end users the platform will offer more awards to business users to attract this group. Generally, to grow, the platform

[113] ibid.

[114] ibid; Montero and Finger (n 4); see also Google's official Guidelines on quality control (<https://android-developers.googleblog.com/2019/06/improved-app-quality-and-discovery-on.html>); Apple's App Store Review Guidelines (online: https://developer.apple.com/app-store/review/guidelines/).

[115] See Chris Hughes, Top 10 Open Source Software Security Risks – and How to Mitigate Them (12 July 2024, CSO Online), <www.csoonline.com/article/574615/top-10-open-source-software-risks.html>.

[116] Schweitzer, 'Digitale Plattformen als private Gesetzgeber: Ein Perspektivwechsel für die europäische 'Plattform-Regulierung' (n 105).

[117] See *Google Android*; *Google Shopping*; Van den Boom J, Winners & Losers: Game, Set and Match in Google Shopping? (SCiDA Blog, 17 September 2024).

will have to reward its users.[118] However, once the platform has matured and has become less dependent on attracting new users (or even retaining the existing user base), it can allocate more the generated value to itself. Thus, the attractiveness of prices for users (and competitive terms for business users) may reflect the overall competitive health of competition on the platform.[119]

Finally, the platform operator sets rules for aftermarkets, for instance, in the markets for updates, repairs, or transactions. Most digital platform markets may use of products offered in aftermarkets: transaction platforms rely on in-app payment systems that will generally have to provide certain levels of safety in terms of cybersecurity and protection from fraud. These can be vertically integrated (such as Apple's in-app payment system in the App Store) or offered by third parties (such as PayPal, iDeal, or credit card providers). For advertising platforms, an aftermarket exists related to the auctioning of advertisements. There are many firms specialized in performing Search Ad Optimalisation and creating advertising campaigns for their clients that are heavily dependent on platforms offered by Meta and Alphabet. The platform operator can determine who is allowed to participate in aftermarkets and how aftermarkets take shape through the architecture and orchestration of their platform. The health and size of aftermarkets depend to a large extent on whether the platform follows an open or closed strategy in this regard: does it make the aftermarkets for repairs exclusive to its partners or vertically integrated service points (Apple, Tesla), or does it invite anyone to perform repairs (Samsung, Alphabet)?[120]

Aftermarkets, and their connection with the digital platform, are best understood by looking at how platforms are embedded in an ecosystem of connected products and services. Digital firms often operate a vast collection of products and services that are connected to – yet independent from – their digital platforms. These are not just aftermarkets but may also be other horizontally, vertically, or diagonally related activities. Even most digital platforms consist of not one, but a number of integrated products and services. In order to understand how digital firms function, and the extent of their private rule-setting power, one must look at how their products and platforms are embedded within their multi-product ecosystems.[121]

118 Michael A Cusumano, Annabelle Gawer and David B Yoffie, *The Business of Platforms: Strategy in the Age of Digital Competition, Innovation, and Power* (2019); Evans and Gawer (n 98); Carmen Leong and others, 'Platform Leadership: Managing Boundaries for the Network Growth of Digital Platforms' (2019) 20 Journal of the Association for Information Systems.

119 Tiwana (n 34); Cozzolino, Corbo and Aversa (n 99); Petit and Teece, 'Taking Ecosystems Competition Seriously in the Digital Economy' (n 13); Friso Bostoen and Nicolas Petit, 'Platforms' Treacherous Turn' [2023] SSRN Electronic Journal <www.ssrn.com/abstract=4664056> accessed 22 August 2024.

120 Jacobides, Cennamo and Gawer (n 12) 2256–22260; Jacobides and Lianos (n 12) 8–10, 17.

121 Hornung (n 65); Ioannis Lianos, Klaas Hendrik Eller and Tobias Kleinschmitt, 'Towards a Legal Theory of Digital Ecosystems' (2024) <www.ssrn.com/abstract=4849340> accessed 22 August 2024; Ioannis Lianos and Bruno Carballa-Smichowski, 'A Coat of Many Colours – New Concepts and Metrics of Economic Power in Competition Law and Economics' (2022) 18 Journal of Competition Law & Economics 795.

2.3 DIGITAL MULTI-PRODUCT ECOSYSTEMS: A NEW PERSPECTIVE ON CONNECTED DIGITAL MARKETS

The emergence of digital product ecosystems has attracted attention from both academics and policymakers.[122] There is an ongoing attempt to properly capture what constitutes a digital multi-product ecosystem, how they function, and to capture how their presence impacts competition. The term 'ecosystem' is more than a metaphor, as there are attempts in both literature and law to operationalize the concept and to give it meaning. However, there is not yet a settled definition of what exactly constitutes an ecosystem.[123] A clear definition for the distinct multi-actor and multi-product ecosystem helps to understand how they function, compete, and which incentives digital firms have to expand beyond their platform to create multi-product ecosystems.

2.3.1 *Defining Digital Multi-product Ecosystems*

There are multiple reasons as to why it is hard to define the product ecosystem: product ecosystems are non-structural, hard to delineate, and evolving. Alphabet's ecosystem of products and services looked significantly different ten years ago than it does today and will look completely different again in ten years. However, even outside of the complexities of the product ecosystem itself, associated with changing technologies, demographics, and business models, there are two pitfalls that one may run into when trying to define the product ecosystem conceptually.

First, the conflation of the multi-actor ecosystem and the digital product ecosystems.[124] As noted previously, the multi-actor ecosystem consists of a platform operator and the complementors, which rely on that platform to sell or buy goods and services. The multi-product ecosystem however consists of the cross-market activities of a single digital undertaking and encapsulates the 'brand': it refers to the cross-market activities or vertical integration of undertakings such as Apple, Google, Amazon, Facebook, or Microsoft. User lock-in may be the result of actions in the multi-actor ecosystem (demanding exclusivity from complementors to offer goods and services on a platform) or from the multi-product ecosystem (Apple's focus on

[122] See Section 2.4 in reference to Crémer, De Montjoye and Schweitzer (n 4); Digital Competition Expert Panel (n 1); Zingales and others (n 1); Competition & Markets Authority, 'Online Platforms and Digital Advertising Market' (2019) Online Platforms and Digital Advertising Market Study – GOV.UK.

[123] In Case T-1077/23, ByteDance v. Commission, ECLI:EU:T:2024:478, Judgement of 17 July 2024, paras 128–130, the court itself notes that they are using a working definition. cf Jasper Van den Boom and Philipp Hornung, 'Ecosystems in the DMA – Bridging the Gap between Legal Text and Economic Reality' [2025] Journal of European Competition Law & Practice; Jasper van den Boom, 'Incumbent or Challenger? – Assessing Ecosystem Competition in the DMA' (2024) 20 Journal of Competition Law & Economics 409.

[124] Jacobides, Cennamo and Gawer (n 12) 2261–2267; Jacobides and Lianos (n 12) 1205; Hornung (n 65) 299–300.

complementarity between its proprietary products to create value-driven lock-in).[125] However, the mechanisms underlying lock-in are completely different and should be treated as such by regulators or relevant authorities. The first is the result of (contractual) obligations related to the use of the platform. In other words, it is the platform operator using its private regulatory power to demand certain behaviour from users that depend on the platform. The latter is the result of the connections between different products and platforms, as well as a lack of interoperability with products and services provided by competing suppliers. This lock-in is not the result of activity of *one* platform, but rather of the way the network of goods and product interoperate with one another and not with others.[126] While mandating interoperability may be one part to solving this puzzle, there are many other ways in which the connection between different products and platforms can steer user behaviour and lock them in into the product ecosystem of a single supplier.

In some instances, an attempt is made to bridge the gap between effects that arise from activity in the multi-actor ecosystem and multi-product ecosystem by defining what is referred to here as a 'platform ecosystem'. These may take shape as the ad-tech ecosystem, mobile ecosystem, or data ecosystem.[127] While looking at these conceptual platform, ecosystems may be helpful to understand the different sources of competition and competitive harms. These platform ecosystems are not distinct ecosystems of their own. Instead, a platform ecosystem is the practical manifestation of the confluence of activities in – parts of – two separate ecosystems: the multi-actor and multi-product ecosystem. Thus, to look at the so-called mobile ecosystem, is simply to look at how the multi-actor ecosystem and multi-product ecosystem function and interact in relation to a selected number of activities as chosen by the regulator.[128]

Second, there may be a failure to properly define the relationship between the broader product ecosystem and the core platform(s) of an ecosystem operator. For instance, the Australian Competition and Consumer Commission (ACCC) notes in its platform inquiry that Google is insulated in its search activities through economies of scale, and that Apple has insulated its position in mobile Operating Systems by limited switching of users and limited entry in the market for mobile Operating Systems.[129] This assessment skips past the insulating effects of the multi-product ecosystem in maintaining one's position. Google is entrenched in search not only due to the network externalities and economies of scale exhibited in this market but also through its position in mobile Operating Systems with Google Android, its web browsers, and activities in navigation, mapping, and reviews. There are also loosely

[125] See the discussions in Sections 3.2 and 4.1.

[126] Hornung (n 65).

[127] The term platform ecosystem is chosen as this was recently used to describe a confluence between the ecosystem of actors and products in *ByteDance* paras 128–129.

[128] See eg Competition & Market Authority (n 69) 9–19.

[129] Australian Competition & Consumer Authority (n 4) 8.

connected activities such the operation of Gmail, Google Maps, and voice assistants. Each of these activities generates data on users, which allows Google to refine its search and advertising services. Each activity in the multi-product ecosystem has multidirectional strengthening effects on activities in other markets.[130] For Apple, its position in mobile OS can be viewed as one of its core markets. However, the strategy of Apple revolves around creating a collection of products with high levels of complementarity. The strategies employed by both multi-product ecosystems differ significantly: Google relies on its multi-product ecosystem to increase traffic towards horizontal search as to generate revenue in that market, while Apple steers users of its iOS to adopt complementary Apple products. The differences in business models inspire the competitive strategies maintained by operators of multi-product ecosystems. Consequently, each multi-product ecosystem may exhibit shared characteristics but understanding the functioning of one ecosystem does not mean that those lessons are automatically transferrable to understand the functioning of another.[131] In order to generalize knowledge on the functioning of ecosystems, it is important to properly distinguish between activities in the multi-actor ecosystems related to different platforms and their functioning in that specific ecosystem, and to understand how this relates to ecosystem orientations (open, closed, marketization, and monetization).

Many attempts have been made to capture the functioning of product ecosystems by identifying their characteristics or by using existing labels to explain their functioning. For instance by looking at the products and services offered in a multi-product ecosystem as multi-product bundles that comprise the services offered both through the multi-actor and multi-product ecosystem.[132] These bundles consist of groups of complementary goods that are consumed by the final consumer and which can collectively create consumer lock-in to the benefit of the orchestrator.[133] However, not all connected services are bundled or consumed together. In many instances, connections between products exist indirectly in the form or shared data or shared inputs, bring their own efficiencies to the ecosystem orchestrator. Such a concept does not fully recognize the flexibility with which the consumer can use products in the ecosystem in various combinations, extracting different levels of benefits from complementarities or (data-driven) efficiencies. Perhaps, the multi-product bundle best describes a 'platform ecosystem' as referred to earlier, helping to delineate which products and services from the multi-actor and product ecosystem are likely to be consumed jointly.

Others have tried to distil the essence of a product ecosystem to its central characteristics, identifying five: (i) the platform and its members are not members of a

[130] This is elaborated on in Sections 5.2 and 5.3.

[131] Shili Shao, 'Antitrust in the Consumer Platform Economy: How Apple Has Abused Its Mobile Platform Dominance' (2021) 36 Berkeley Technology Law Journal 355; Bostoen and Mandrescu (n 44); Competition & Markets Authority (n 122); Davies and Georgieva (n 56); Crane (n 17).

[132] Jacobides and Lianos (n 12) 1200–1205.

[133] ibid.

single industry but participate in broad-spectrum competition across a variety of industry; (ii) ecosystems are marked by co-evolution which is driven by reciprocal interaction between heterogeneous ecosystem members, this reciprocal cycle leads to generativity in the form of new output, structure, or behaviour; (iii) the ecosystem consists of the platform and its complementors; (iv) ecosystems are marked by coopetition, a combination of competition and cooperation, towards the creation of new products, services, and innovation; and (v) they have a conscious direction, as there is self-organized leadership from the ecosystem orchestrator.[134] On the basis of these characteristics, the authors argue that one can best understand the nature of a multi-product ecosystem by looking at competition between multi-product ecosystems. Ecosystems are networks of business entities that work together to create and capture value, they are dynamic organizations whose strategies are fluid, and often reliant on the technical leadership of one or more firms that provide the core platforms around which other system members align their investments and strategies.[135] A valuable definition and delineation, at least in terms of how the multi-actor and multi-product ecosystem function jointly. However, a sharper definition of the multi-product ecosystem itself is still possible.

Here, I propose that a multi-product ecosystem should be defined as 'a collection of goods and services built around a digital platform or a group of digital platforms for which one undertaking is able to exercise control on terms for activities such as determining compatibility, coordination and the setting of standards. This collection of goods and services create synergies between one another and the digital platform(s) offered by the undertaking.'

These synergies can either be achieved by integrating these products and services into the offering of a platform operated by the undertaking or by looser links such as the internal sharing of data, reliance on complementary technologies, or the possibility to leverage the installed base. The latter form of connections between the products in the ecosystems that do not form a bundle or are not integrated into a platform can be understood as ecosystem linkages, which are 'intangible links between products that create economies of scope or user synergies without having to be part of the same bundle'.

The multi-actor ecosystem – which is discussed as a distinct phenomenon here but is generally deeply integrated with the multi-product ecosystem – consisting of 'the collective of third parties and a firm that operates one or more digital platforms, where these third parties offer complementary goods or services on one or more of the platforms offered by that firm or consume the goods or services offered by that firm. The ecosystem of complementors co-creates value together with the platform operator and raise the value proposition of its platforms by competing, cooperating or entering into coopetition on the platform or with the platform operator'.

[134] Petit and Teece, 'Taking Ecosystems Competition Seriously in the Digital Economy' (n 13) 6–9.
[135] ibid.

Together, they form platform ecosystems, in which multi-product bundles are offered and which exhibit the central characteristics described earlier.

2.3.2 *On-Platform and Cross-platform Expansion*

Digital platform operators are likely to have incentives to expand their collection of products both on the platform itself and beyond the platform. This expansion can take many shapes: the digital platform may vertically integrate to internalize upstream or downstream production activities; it may enter into markets that provide complementary services to those offered on the platform; it may enter into adjacent markets that have a shared user base, or it may expand by developing new platforms to which it can attract users. These different types of expansion may happen for different reasons, which are explored here.[136] Expansion into conglomerates comes naturally for digital firms. As digital goods are generally modular goods, the platform operator will develop new modules related to its existing portfolio of modules (products) and stable cores (platforms).[137] Some of these modules will be suitable for integration into the platform itself, expanding the functionality of the platform itself. This is called on-platform expansion. In other instances, the platform operator may find that its new module – while valuable – does not integrate well into its existing platform(s). The platform operator may then choose to offer this module as a stand-alone product or to develop it into a new platform service.[138]

On platform expansion allows the platform operator to increase its value proposition for its existing network of users.[139] Alphabet has integrated so-called Shorts on its YouTube platform. These are short videos similar to those one can find on TikTok. By integrating similar short videos on YouTube, Alphabet provides YouTube users with a new functionality, thereby providing more incentives for YouTube users to stay in the Alphabet ecosystem instead of visiting TikTok. Meanwhile, this expansion has positive effects for different groups of users of the YouTube platform: users gain access to a new functionality on the platform that they frequent, and advertisers can now offer similar advertisements on YouTube as they can on TikTok. In other

[136] cf Annabelle Gawer and Rebecca Henderson, 'Platform Owner Entry and Innovation in Complementary Markets: Evidence from Intel' (2007) 16 Journal of Economics & Management Strategy 1; Feng Zhu and Qihong Liu, 'Competing with Complementors: An Empirical Look at Amazon.Com' (2018) 39 Strategic Management Journal 2618; Wen and Zhu (n 44); Joost Rietveld, Melissa A Schilling and Cristiano Bellavitis, 'Platform Strategy: Managing Ecosystem Value through Selective Promotion of Complements' (2019) 30 Organisation Science 1232; Daniel Mandrescu, 'Tying and Bundling by Online Platforms – Distinguishing between Lawful Expansion Strategies and Anti-Competitive Practices' (2021) 40 Computer Law and Security Review 1; de Streel, Bourreau and Giet (n 14); Tristan Lécuyer, 'Digital Conglomerates and Killer Acquisitions – A Discussion of the Competitive Effects of Start-up Acquisitions by Digital Platforms' [2020] Concurrences.

[137] Hein and others (n 37) 88–89; Bourreau, Dogan and Manant (n 37) 3–5; Mandrescu (n 12) 8–10.

[138] Mandrescu (n 12) 2–10.

[139] ibid.

instances, on-platform expansion may only serve one group of users of the platform. For instance, YouTube has expanded its advertising offering by adding Surveys and unskippable advertisements. These new advertising functions add value for advertisers, but users may experience them as intrusive or annoying. In these cases, the platform operator must be careful to include on-platform expansion only to the point that it does not degrade the value of the platform for one category of users too much.[140]

Where the platform operator wonders about the suitability of integrating the new module on the platform, or where integration is simply not possible, it can choose to develop a wholly new platform to offer these services. This is cross-platform expansion.[141] After the acquisition of Twitter by Elon Musk, Meta announced that it would launch Twitter rival Threads. This is a wholly new platform to complement its Facebook and Instagram platforms. Meta, likely due to the different use case, presentation, and functioning of a Twitter-like platform, offers a new and separate platform while maintaining links between its services to embed it within its ecosystem.

Once users have been entered into the product ecosystem of a digital firm, the firm can try to steer users from one service to another. Steering can take place in many ways: recommendations, the creation of shared logins for all platforms, previews of content on one platform, rewards on the other platform, or simply through brand familiarity.[142] Consequently, the userbase captured on a new platform market may be steered towards the existing portfolio of products and services offered by the ecosystem operators, entrenching its position in its core platform markets. Conversely, the ecosystem operator may also steer its user base from its existing platforms and products towards its new services, facilitating entry into new markets.[143] Threads, for instance, has a shared login with Instagram, and Meta may use data collected from one service to the benefit of its other services. Cross-platform expansion allows the ecosystem operator to attract new users to its ecosystem: users that left – or were to leave – Twitter could now find an alternative in Threads. These users may not have been inclined to spend their time on Instagram but can now be entered into the Meta ecosystem nonetheless.[144] In the case of Twitter/X, it has ultimately turned out that the challenge came not from an established incumbent but rather the disruptive challenger Bluesky. This shows that while incumbents have

[140] ibid.

[141] ibid.

[142] cf Digital Competition Expert Panel (n 1); Crémer, De Montjoye and Schweitzer (n 4); Philip Marsden and Rupprecht Podszun, 'Restoring Balance to Digital Competition – Sensible' (Konrad Adenaufer Stiftung 2020); Schweitzer, 'The Art to Make Gatekeeper Positions Contestable and the Challenge to Know What Is Fair: A Discussion of the Digital Markets Act Proposal' (n 105); Lancieri and Sakowski (n 1); Mandrescu (n 12).

[143] Mandrescu (n 12) 2–10.

[144] Imran Rahman-Jones and Tom Gerken, 'Threads: Meta's Rival to Elon Musk's X Launches in EU' [2023] *BBC*.

an established position, times of transition still create opportunities for competitive entry and risks for incumbents if they fail to capture the shifts in demand.[145]

When integrating new services onto existing platforms, the ecosystem operator can extract more value from its multi-actor ecosystem related to that platform.[146] For instance, by adding more advertisements, YouTube can extract more revenue from the same hours of watched videos. However, when the ecosystem operator enters a new platform market, they cannot easily extract revenue from its new user base. As the platform is new, the ecosystem operator will have to again overcome the chicken-and-egg problem. This is easier for operators of large digital ecosystems, as they can steer their end users towards the new platform by creating complementarities, by (for instance) allowing users to export their content to the new platform, by offering rewards for going to the new platform, or simply by promoting it. Instead of more placing more third-party advertisements on YouTube, Alphabet may use some of its advertising time to promote its own new service for instance. On the advertiser side, the ecosystem operator likely already has (parts of) the advertising auctioning and serving infrastructure in place and has already built up trust and recognition with advertisers.[147] Moreover, if the digital firm has deep pockets, they can simply cross-subsidize the new service and wait with monetizing the new platform until the it has a sufficiently established base of end users.[148]

While cross-platform expansion requires more investments and efforts from the platform operator than on-platform expansion, it is a rewarding activity. Entry into a new platform market allows the platform operator to expand with new functionalities without risking a loss of users in its core platforms, it allows the platform operator to attract new users that had no interest in its other platforms due to heterogeneous demand and it opens up new sources of differentiated datasets. As such, cross-platform expansion is riskier, but equally if not more beneficial to the platform operator as on-platform expansion because it can help to entrench core markets or expand into new multi-actor ecosystems.[149]

2.3.3 *Understanding Digital Markets: On-Platform Clusters and Cross-market Linkages*

Digital platforms generally consist of a number of different modules integrated into a stable core. These modules are often viewed as functionalities of the platform.

[145] van den Boom (n 123); Gael Cooper, 'Bluesky Boasts More than 30 Million Users, Thanks to 'Twitter Quitters' *CNET* (31 January 2025).

[146] ibid.

[147] cf Gawer and Henderson (n 136); Wen and Zhu (n 44); Lancieri and Sakowski (n 1); Subcommittee on Antitrust (n 1); Mandrescu (n 12).

[148] Jasper Van den Boom and Peerawat Samranchit, 'Digital Ecosystem Mergers in Big Tech – A Theory of Long-Run Harm with Applications' [2021] Journal of European Competition Law & Practice 1.

[149] Mandrescu (n 12) 2–10.

However, in many instances, integrations of a service into the platform that seem natural can also be removed. How should we then view platform markets? On the one hand, the integration of different functionalities is what we have come to expect as users. It would not be desirable to have a distinct communications platform for text, voice calls, and video calls if there is an integrated alternative. On the other hand, opening up certain functionalities of the platform to competition or third-party participation may bring forward more user choice and efficiencies associated with competition. Hereunder, it is discussed how viewing digital platform markets as on-platform cluster markets may help to explain why we view digital platforms as distinct product markets while also recognizing that they can comprise a variety of functionalities and services.

On-Platform Cluster Markets

To explore the idea of an on-platform cluster markets, it is important to first look at the multi-sidedness of digital platforms and then at the multi-functionality of each side of the platform.

The first step in defining markets when digital platforms are involved is to assess whether the intermediation happens between multiple sides of a single market or between multiple interconnected markets. This assessment is important, as it allows competition authorities to assess the cross-market effects that arise between the different groups of users that are intermediated by the platform.[150] This cross-market effect may inspire strategies employed by the platform: does the platform intermediate by providing an audience or by facilitating transactions?[151] Does it choose to subsidize one group of users to attract the other, whether by zero-pricing on the consumer facing side or free development tools on the professional side?[152] Is lock-in on one side of the market sufficiently strong that users on the other side of the market are dependent on the platform to offer their service?[153] These questions may help one determine how the market for the offered intermediation should be defined, as well as with the identification of market power.

It has been argued that transaction platforms should be viewed as connecting two sides of the same market, while matching platforms should be viewed as connecting two distinct but interconnected markets. The rationale behind this is that transaction markets are characterized by the presence and observability of a transaction between two groups of platform users and – as a result – the platform can charge both a price for using the platform and for each additional use. As facilitating the

[150] Jens-Uwe Franck and Martin Peitz, 'Market Definition and Market Power in the Platform Economy' (2019) CERRE Tech, Media, Telecom Report 20–28.

[151] Filistrucchi and others (n 60) 9–19.

[152] Wright (n 59); Tiwana (n 34); Hein and others (n 37).

[153] de Streel, Bourreau and Giet (n 28); Andrea Prat and Tommaso Valletti, 'Attention Oligopoly' (2022) 14 (3) *American Economic Journal: Microeconomics* 530–557.

transaction is a single service, it should be viewed as taking place within a single market. In matching platforms on the other hand, distinct services are offered to distinct groups of users. This would warrant their treatment as distinct yet connected markets. There is no observable transaction, and there is not a single basic service. In advertising markets, there is a clear interrelationship between the different sides of the platform, as the market for advertisements cannot exist without a market to attract users. However, neither side of the market is interested in the services offered to the other side: advertisers do not care to create or consume content, and end users do not wish to make use of the tools necessary to auction and place advertisements[154].

In digital markets, the lines between a transaction platform and non-transaction platform may blur. First, transactions may not always be observable.[155] The provider of an Operating System does not necessarily know how many apps are downloaded on it, yet it can choose to monitor this (and even impose the use of its payment system). Conversely, while advertising is generally seen as a matching service, the pay-per-click model shows characteristics of a transaction platform.[156] Second, transaction and non-transaction services may be substitutes for one another. A complement developer may have the choice to supply a platform that uses either a subscription model or payments per usage with similar effects. Applying a multi-market approach makes it easier to understand the choices that are made on either side of the market: the end user has incentives to join a platform which differ greatly from the incentives by a complement developer. Letting go of the single-market paradigm allows one to assess a wider range of considerations on either side, as it does not presume that the users are related by a single basic service but rather choose their platform on widely diverging considerations.[157]

This study takes a multi-market approach to examine competition within platforms and ecosystems across all market types. This makes it easier to distinguish between the different activities performed on different sides and by different group when compared to a single-market narrative. It also explains how new sides or functionalities can be integrated or removed. For instance, online social networks used to be characterized by (passive) consumers, content creators (professional or prosumers), and advertisers. The emergence of the influencer blurred the line between content creator and advertiser and has introduced new means of monetization.[158] By exploring the 'influencer' market as its own distinct market that relies on functionalities (or modules) for advertising and content creation, one does not have to make an attempt to fit the influencer into the existing single multi-sided market

[154] Filistrucchi, Geradin and van Damme (n 60) 3–8.
[155] Franck and Peitz (n 150) 24.
[156] Filistrucchi and others (n 60) 3–9.
[157] Franck and Peitz (n 150) 9.
[158] Francisco J Martínez-López and others, 'Behind Influencer Marketing: Key Marketing Decisions and Their Effects on Followers' Responses' (2020) 36 Journal of Marketing Management 579.

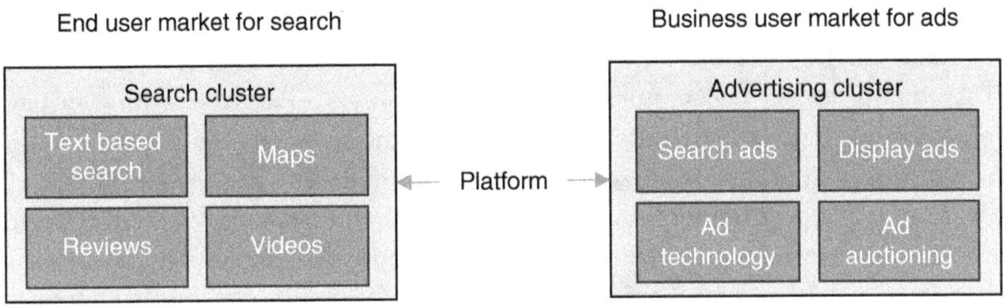

FIGURE 2.1 A visualization of interdependent cluster markets

paradigm. In a way, embedded advertising (i.e. promoting goods or services within the content) is simply a new module added to the platform.[159]

The second step in defining the relevant platform markets is to determine which cluster of modules is offered on each different side of the platform. The clusters are the so-called platform ecosystems and comprise offerings by both vertically integrated platform operators themselves and third parties. An example can be found in the market for horizontal search. Horizontal search, at its core, is simply a web crawling service that provides the user with a number of links to potentially relevant results. Google Search offers a cluster of search services, including but not limited to text-based search, reviews, location-based search (Maps) and video- or image results. This is the cluster for end users. End users do not need to consume each type of search result with each search but are free to do so without ever leaving the platform, or even the search results page. Meanwhile, the search results incorporate sponsored links (search advertisements), boxes with descriptions (display advertising) by use of its embedded ad auctioning and serving mechanisms (Figure 2.1). This is the cluster for advertisers. Advertisers may use a single type of ad services (e.g. only sponsored links) or pay for a range of services to promote their content, by mixing and matching between single services and bundles offered related to Google Search.

Not any group of products sold together constitutes a cluster market. A cluster market is defined by the presence of certain economies of joint provision, which can take the shape of cost savings or transactional advantages which are difficult to duplicate.[160] As a result, the firm is able to profit by raising its prices higher than its costs. The concept of the cluster markets recognizes that combining complements can lead to market power.[161] A cluster market is distinguished by the following characteristics: (i) most customers would be willing to pay monopoly prices for the convenience of receiving the defendant's grouping of products, or (ii) economies of joint provision make distribution of the cluster cheaper per good than distribution of

[159] ibid.
[160] Crane (n 17); Hovenkamp (n 11) 256–262.
[161] Hovenkamp (n 11) 256–262.

each separately, and (iii) the firms supplying one of the products in the cluster could not easily add the others as well.[162]

According to the first requirement, most customers should be willing to pay monopoly prices for the convenience of receiving the grouped products. While the markets in question are often zero price markets, one can view the steady rise of the number of advertisements on these platforms, the increase in the price of these advertisements on the other side of the market, and the inelasticity in demand in markets such as search and social media on both sides as an indicator that the platforms can extract monopoly rents from the consumer for their products.[163] Second, offering each of these services together through a single platform is efficient. As discussed earlier, it is efficient to integrate modules into a stable core, rather than offering them through separate channels. Moreover, complementarities of offering different functions jointly on a platform raise the value for users.[164] Finally, not every supplier of one of the cluster services can easily offer another. While the integration of Google Maps and location-based search in a search engine is value-enhancing, it is not a simple feat to start offering location-based search. Competitors like Ecosia or DuckDuckGo do not have the data or infrastructure required to offer their own mapping, navigation, and location-based search services. In other instances, the ability to provide equivalent clusters to a competitor depend on the size and formation of the multi-actor ecosystem: the provider of a new Operating System cannot simply expect that software developers will make the applications they have developed for Android or iOS interoperable.[165]

The idea of a cluster market is also distinct from the idea of a multi-product bundle. A multi-product bundle implies that the products are generally consumed together, but in the case of digital platforms there is often mixing and matching going on. There is no user that consumes everything that is available on Amazon Marketplace or the Apple App Store. However, these products are all offered together, and there is an expectation for users that these goods are *offered* jointly. After all, it is the value proposition of the platform and its multi-actor ecosystem in its totality that attracts users to the platform, rather than a single market or feature that the platform offers.[166] The value of the platform is determined by its vibrant downstream offering of goods and services, be they proprietary or offered by third parties.[167] The clusters offered on platform markets are dynamic, so they are susceptible to change and often expansion. At the same time, they are heavily connected

[162] Phillip Areeda and Herbert Hovenkamp, *Antitrust Law : An Analysis of Antitrust Principles and Their Application* (Aspen 1978); Hovenkamp (n 11) 256–262.

[163] See eg also the analysis of advertisement-based platforms by the Competition & Markets Authority (n 69).

[164] Economies of scope are discussed in more depth in Chapter 3.

[165] Areeda and Hovenkamp (n 162); Hovenkamp (n 11) 256–262.

[166] BRICS Competition Law and Policy Center, 'Digital Era Competition: A BRICS View' (BRICS 2021) 30.

[167] Tiwana (n 34) ch 4.

and jointly shape the expectations of users and their appreciation of the platform. By offering on-platform clusters, ecosystem operators can sell holistic outcomes such as access to safe mobility or a one-stop-shop for advertising.[168]

Beyond the Platform: the Efficiencies of Ecosystem Linkages

The modules integrated into a platform constitute its cluster, but how to best understand the cross-market conglomerate of platforms and products? If goods and services are not consumed together, or even offered through the same platform, how does presence in one market strengthen the position of the ecosystem operator in another? Here, it is important to understand the concept of ecosystem linkages.[169]

Ecosystem linkages are intangible connections between different markets that create some interdependencies, complementarity, or shared efficiencies. The value of the ecosystem as a whole, and the position of the ecosystem operator vis-à-vis its competitors, improves with the introduction of a new product even if that product is seemingly not connected to its other services. For instance, Google's development of healthcare technology such as algorithms for the detection of certain diseases is a single-sided and stand-alone activity.[170] However, Google's know-how in the development of algorithms and the data that is collected from this activity may still provide it with cost saving economies of scope, insights from data or other benefits that permeate throughout its ecosystem. In most instances, ecosystem linkages exist due to the collection and combination of data, the reuse or development of shareable expertise and technologies, or leveraging opportunities that allow for the steering of users or cross-subsidization opportunities.[171]

The development of on-platform clusters and expansive multi-product ecosystems are intrinsically linked with one another. Digital firms have many opportunities to develop new products and services, which can be intended as modules for integration with the platform, the integration of vertically related services, or specifically aimed at cross-platform expansion to capture new users. While designing modules, the ecosystem operator may find that rather than being integrated into the platform, they work best as a stand-alone product. This invites a process of experimentation and innovation: what is a commercially attractive module? How is it best offered to consumers (on or cross-platform expansion)? How can it best be monetized, or what function can it perform in the ecosystem?[172]

Expansion strategies can be the result of conscious attempts, where the ecosystem operator tries to gain a first mover's advantage by entering into a new market, possibly

[168] Lianos, Eller and Kleinschmitt (n 121) 32.

[169] Van den Boom and Samranchit (n 148); Lianos, Eller and Kleinschmitt (n 121) 14–16.

[170] Melanie Evans, 'Google Strikes Deal with Hospital Chain to Develop Healthcare Algorithms' *The Wall Street Journal* (26 May 2021).

[171] Gawer and Henderson (n 136); Gawer and Cusumano (n 12); Rietveld, Schilling and Bellavitis (n 136); de Streel, Bourreau and Giet (n 28); Bourreau (n 28); Hornung (n 65).

[172] ibid.

leveraging its position from its existing markets. However, expansion can also be the result of unintended innovation. Meta for instance, found that separating its Facebook Messenger service from the social media platform, and offering it as a stand-alone app, was more desirable than offering communications only through the platform. Entry is facilitated by the efficiencies derived from its multi-product ecosystem (whether due to its access to resources or valuable insights created from data), which allows the undertaking to capture market share in a new market relatively easily. Once the new product has been developed the digital undertaking determines whether it should integrate it into existing platforms, develop it as a new platform, offer it as a stand-alone product or abandon it. It is likely more attractive for a digital undertaking to pursue products which have stronger ecosystem linkages to its existing collection of products, as this enhances the value of the entirety of the ecosystem in a more significant way.

Competition between ecosystems works similarly as competition to systems, on which a large body of literature already exists.[173] Systems are generally viewed as collection of two or more components together with an interface that allows the components to work together. These goods often have little to no value in themselves but generate value jointly as a system. Non-digital examples include nuts and bolts to provide a fastening service or banking machines and debit cards. In the digital market, hardware and compatible Operating Systems provide a similar example. In competition between systems – as opposed to competition between individual products – there are three important considerations that must be managed: expectations, coordination, and compatibility.[174] Expectations on the user side are important as a consumer who purchases a component of a system must be able to form expectations about availability, price, quality, and compatibility with other system goods in the future. On the side of producers, coordination is necessary to ensure that the components within the system work well together. Finally, compatibility determines whether different systems are substitutes or complements to one another. Incompatibility can result from a coordination failure or as a deliberate choice to compete rather than to cooperate.[175]

[173] cf Michael L Katz and Carl Shapiro, 'Systems Competition and Network Effects' (1994) 8 Journal of Economic Perspectives 93; Hans-Werner Sinn, 'The Subsidiarity Principle and Market Failures in Systems Competition' (1996) 5411 NBER Working Paper Series; Hans-Werner Sinn, 'The Selection Principle and Market Failure in Systems Competition' (1997) 66 Journal of Public Economics 247; Carl Shapiro and David J Teece, 'Systems Competition and Aftermarkets: An Economic Analysis of Kodak' (1994) 39 The Antitrust Bulletin 135; Jeffrey Church and Neil Gandal, 'Systems Competition, Vertical Merger, and Foreclosure' (2000) 9 Journal of Economics & Management Strategy 25; Gregory Gundlach and Diana L Moss, 'Systems Competition and Challenges to Antitrust Thinking: An Introduction' (2011) 56 The Antitrust Bulletin 1; Norman W Hawker, 'Automotive Aftermarkets: A Case Study in Systems Competition' (2011) 56 The Antitrust Bulletin 57; Johannes M Bauer, 'Platforms, Systems Competition, and Innovation: Reassessing the Foundations of Communications Policy' (2014) 38 Special issue on Moving Forward with Future Technologies: Opening a Platform for All 662.

[174] Katz and Shapiro (n 173) 93–94.

[175] ibid 105–109; Nicholas Economides, 'Public Policy in Network Industries' (2006) 06–17 Working Paper Series New York University 469.

In systems competition, it is possible for the firm with a small, initial advantage to parlay its advantage into a larger, lasting one. Competition between systems within networks – or between incompatible networks – is intense, at least until a winner emerges. As such, these markets are often referred to as winner-take-all markets, and the process of falling in the favour of a single system is referred to as tipping.[176] In order to ensure that the market tips in its favour, the system's operator has incentives to make early and visible sunk expenditures into (new) products, as to gain the initial advantage and to signal to consumers that it is committed to developing the system. A hardware supplier may vertically integrate the supply of its associated software – or enter into long-term contracts – to ensure a steady supply of software down the line. This helps consumers to set their expectations, while resolving potential coordination and compatibility problems.[177] At the same time, the system operator has incentives to build customers' beliefs surrounding its own system while breaking down customer beliefs on competing systems[178]: Apple has incentives to convince users that the quality of its system is the highest, while arguing that the Microsoft ecosystem is difficult to use or unsafe. This makes new users more likely to adopt its system and makes it less likely for existing users to switch. Firms with established reputations, well-known brand names and ready visible access to capital have competitive advantages, much like well-established digital ecosystems.[179]

Many of the ideas surrounding systems competition apply directly in ecosystem competition, where similar considerations are made by product-ecosystem operators. Competition in these markets is based on a series of decisions with complex trade-offs: a system that does not facilitate enough collaboration may not be able to generate the value that is required to remain in the market, while opening up the system too much may lead to the emergence of a new system or technology that threatens its incumbency. This provides the operators of digital ecosystems with incentives to engage in the acquisition of potentially threatening start-ups, to copy and integrate services that are offered by its complementors or to refuse (to continue) compatibility with certain components or complementors.[180]

It also helps one to understand the strategic motives behind the continuous expansion of digital platform undertakings into new markets. Entry into new markets which include products that can be used as a component in the system – one way or another – allows the undertaking to set the standards in these markets and leverage their user base from one market to another. This allows the platform to attract new customers, lock-in existing customers and increase the stickiness of its system by preventing coordination or compatibility problems down the line. In

176 Katz and Shapiro (n 173) 102–107; Crémer, De Montjoye and Schweitzer (n 4) 30.

177 Katz and Shapiro (n 173) 93–95.

178 ibid.

179 ibid.

180 ibid; James Moore, 'Predators and Prey: A New Ecology of Competition' (1999) 71 Harvard Business Review 75; Jacobides and Lianos (n 12) 1200–1205.

order to expand its offering and the value of its ecosystem, the ecosystem operator may subsidize complementors on the condition of exclusivity or subsidize its own divisions which produce and sell complements (perhaps at a loss).[181] Each entry into a new market raises the value of the ecosystem and allow opportunities to place hurdles in the paths of rivals (for instance, by choosing incompatibility or preventing access to sources of complementary goods).[182]

Due to the existence of ecosystem linkages, the complementary goods offered by the digital product ecosystem do not have to be offered as a bundle to co-generate value[183]: the consumer can slowly buy products over time and having more products of the ecosystem generates increased value. As the value of the products offered by that brand increase for the user – as well as the costs incurred to buy the collection – the users' lock-in into the ecosystem grows. Ultimately, competition between digital firms goes far beyond competition for a single platform market. Instead, this competition must be treated as a type of competition between systems.[184] The novelty of digital ecosystems again relates to their potential for scale, geographic range, scope (across markets), the levels of data collection, oversight, control, and adaptivity of these systems.

2.4 CONCLUSION

This chapter has developed definitions and concepts to explain the nature of digital goods, the prevalence of digital platforms, and the emergence of vast digital ecosystems.

Digital goods are distinct from non-digital goods due to their informational and modular nature. Software is non-rivalrous and non-exhaustive, with high upfront and low marginal costs. As a result, purely digital goods can be proliferated rapidly and across a vast number of users, often at near-zero costs. Digital goods are also modular, leading to the reuse of inputs for the creation of a number of outputs. Both software and hardware modules can be integrated into – or removed from – a stable core easily. This invites component sharing within the firm and between firms, which has led to business models based on co-generating value between the digital firm and its complementors.

The co-generation of value often happens by adopting a platform business model. Digital platform operators connect different groups of users. The platform itself then

[181] cf Catherine Tucker, 'Network Effects and Market Power: What Have We Learned in the Last Decade?' [2018] Antitrust 72; Jacobides and Lianos (n 12); Mariana Mazzucato, Josh Entsminger and Rainer Kattel, 'Reshaping Platform-Driven Digital Markets', *Regulating Big Tech* (Oxford University Press 2021); Martin Moore and Damian Tambini (eds), *Regulating Big Tech: Policy Responses to Digital Dominance* (Oxford University Press 2021).

[182] Jacobides and Lianos (n 12) 1204.

[183] de Streel, Bourreau and Giet (n 28) 3; Hovenkamp (n 11); Lianos, Eller and Kleinschmitt (n 121) 12–14 note that ecosystem linkages raise complementarities and may create an effect similar to a bundle without bundling the goods.

[184] See discussion in Section 3.3.

serves as the technology or infrastructure for the supply and consumption of services and competition. Digital platform operators are able to achieve unprecedented levels of scale, participation, and coordination. As a result, the function of digital platform operators far exceeds the role of intermediary. Instead, the platform operator acts as the de facto regulator in its own multi-actor ecosystem that is built on the platform. The platform and its ecosystem of actors jointly generate value, but the platform operator sets terms and conditions for access, content, competition, and aftermarkets. Moreover, the platform operator determines how value is allocated between different parties. As a result, digital platform-based multi-actor ecosystems are characterized by the technological leadership of a single firm, which creates a single direction for a group of users and firms that depend on the platform.

The offering of the platform often comprises both third-party goods and services and proprietary services. The proprietary products and services may be viewed as part of the platform itself, or as a result of vertical integration. However, a platform rarely consists of just a singular service on either side of the market. The chapter has dedicated attention on how to understand the connection between different sides of a platform markets and the connection between the cluster of functionalities offered on it. Defining the platform service is not always easy, as the offering is dynamic, so it evolves and changes over time.

It is however natural for platform operators to evolve their offering of products and services, both on and outside the platform. Platform operators will develop new modules and products that can be integrated into the platform as to enhance the value proposition of the platform itself or leverage their innovative efforts or know-how into new markets. This expansion is beneficial for the digital firm as it allows them to capture new users, retain existing users, entrench their existing platforms and products, and to occupy new markets. Ultimately, digital competition is best understood as competition between systems: digital firms do not compete for a single platform or product market, but rather the enhance the value of their system as a whole in competition with other systems. Chapter 3 explains how these systems are all embedded into a singular digital network industry, and how this influences competition.

3

Digital and Non-digital Network Industries

Digital goods and services are distinct from their physical counterparts, as are digital strategies. However, the economic characteristics exhibited by digital markets demonstrate a large number of parallels to those exhibited in non-digital network industries. Examples of non-digital network industries are railways or energy networks. These are *physical networks*, consisting of physical lines (wires; rails) and nodes (transformers; stations). Digital goods and services together form a *virtual network*. Rather than being connected through physical lines and nodes, connections consist in complementarities, dependencies, and interoperability.[185] Meanwhile, the telecommunications network provides the physical network infrastructure required for the functioning of the digital network, bridging the digital and 'traditional' (i.e. physical) network sectors.[186] Digital goods, platforms, and ecosystems all function as part of this network. Despite the existence of vast product ecosystems, competing ecosystems do not function wholly independently from others: they use the same internet, tend to rely on the same hardware, and often interconnect with one another. Some ecosystem operators act as *carriers* for other ecosystems: Meta and Amazon's ecosystems heavily depend on the Operating Systems offered by Alphabet, Apple, and Windows to connect with users. Facebook, in turn, acts as an *amplifier* for the value of the ecosystems operated by Alphabet and Apple: by having access to Meta's services, their ecosystems become much more attractive for users. Despite their competition with one another, all ecosystems depend on a general underlying network, and often one another, to generate value.

Despite the differences between different types of digital and non-digital networks, they all demonstrate a number of shared economic characteristics. Namely, they are all characterized by the presence of network externalities, economies of scale and scope, complementarities, dependencies and requirements for compatibility and

[185] Claude Crampes, 'Network Industries and Network Goods' 39; Oz Shy, *The Economics of Network Industries* (Cambridge University Press 2004) ch 1; Economides (n 175) 8; Montero and Finger (n 18).
[186] ibid.

standards, as well as switching costs and lock-in effects.[187] As the output of one part of the network serves as an input for the other, services cannot be provided without the required infrastructure, but the infrastructure is only as valuable as the services provided through it. Energy infrastructure is only as the quantity of kilowatts that it transports from producer to user, much like a computer is only as valuable as the software that it runs.[188] This chapter sets out the economic characteristics of network industries for both physical and digital, to explain how a look at digital markets as network industries may help us to understand digital business models and competition.

The digital network industry is hard to delineate and should be understood as capturing *all software, all related hardware, and all tangible and intangible infrastructures required for the proliferation of that soft- and hardware*. This, much like information goods, may seem like too broad of a definition as first. It certainly means that the digital network industry is far vaster, geographically, in terms of user numbers, and in terms of captured products and services, than any non-digital network industry. Later, it will be discussed how this network is segmented into ecosystems, which shows both the possibility to delineate the vast digital network into smaller parts and the inherent interconnectedness between digital products and services.

The analyses in this work focus predominantly on the connection between software, hardware, and digital infrastructure. Definitions for digital goods, platforms, and ecosystems have been provided earlier. As a matter of clarification, the term digital infrastructure is used when referring to any type of software-based infrastructure that facilitate the undertaking in the process of supplying services or goods to end users. Digital infrastructures include those required for computation (such as algorithms), storage (such as cloud), data processing (data infrastructures), while physical infrastructure is used when referring to cables and wires. The discussion of physical infrastructure is limited as internet wires and nodes are understood as part of the telecommunications sector and already regulated in that light. Moreover, the physical network is subject to its own cost distribution and operational peculiarities. The digital supply chain is shown hereunder in Figure 3.1.

While this visualization of the network looks straightforward, the digital network is highly complex in practice. First, it consists of a vast and ever-changing number of technologies, products, and services. It is extremely difficult to meaningfully delineate digital networks. Physical networks such as railway networks are easy to delineate: they consist of railways and everything related to them. Digital networks however can exist independently, overlap with other physical networks, or even substitute traditional networks.[189]

Second, digital networks are characterized by varying vertical, horizontal, and diagonal relationships. Depending on how these products and services are connected

[187] Shy (n 185) ch 1; Decker (n 10) ch 5.
[188] Crampes (n 185); Shy (n 185) chs 1–3.
[189] Montero and Finger (n 18) pt I.

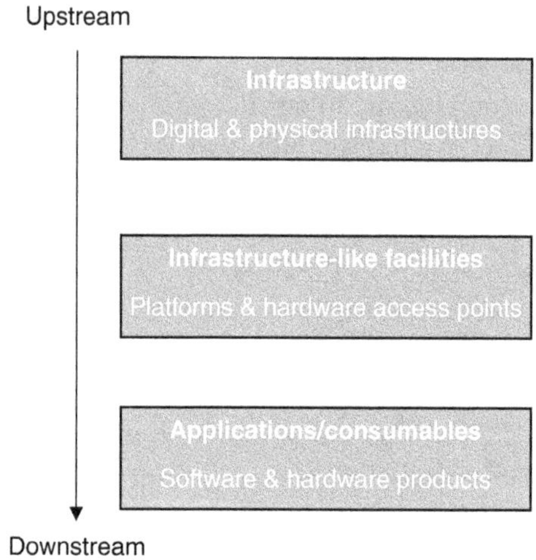

FIGURE 3.1 An illustration of the digital supply chain

they may form part of a single digital ecosystem or a group of ecosystems. A social media application likely has its own ecosystem of actors but also be dependent on the devices or Operating Systems offered by various other firms. Relationships and connections in the digital network industry are highly dynamic and multifaceted.[190]

Finally, digital networks are global networks, but not every service is globally available or aimed at a global audience.[191] This can make it hard to surmise the competitive relationship between different firms and services as this is highly context dependent. These peculiarities of the digital network are explored throughout this book. This chapter aims to first highlight the shared economic characteristics between digital and non-digital networks, to make the debate on its novelties more easily digestible.

3.1 THE ECONOMIC CHARACTERISTICS OF NETWORK INDUSTRIES: DIGITAL AND NON-DIGITAL

This section discusses the relevance of network effects, economies of scale and scope, complementarity and standards, and switching costs in network industries, and why they make these industries prone to concentration.

3.1.1 *Network Effects*

Network industries are named as such because they consist of a network of connected lines and nodes. This network encompasses the different levels of the value

[190] Petit (n 13).
[191] Montero and others (n 18) 6.

chain, all of which are required for the provision of the final service.[192] An electricity network consists of energy producers, which are connected to transmissions operators. Transmissions operators transport energy through wires with a high voltage capacity to distributors. These distributors use transformers to make electricity available for use on low-voltage networks for retailers, or directly for businesses, or consumers. Each of these actors depend on one another: produced electricity is worthless without the capacity to transport it, and transported electricity is useless if end users cannot consume it. This interdependency is at the core of every network industry and means that the development of the network must be carefully planned and curated. For a network to emerge, one needs producers, intermediaries (or infrastructure providers), and users.[193]

Networks are therefore subjected to so-called network externalities, also referred to as network effects. Network externalities refer to the phenomenon where the utility that a user derives from the consumption of the good is determined by the number of other agents consuming the good. In other words, the value of a network may increase (in case of positive network effects) or decrease (in case of negative network effects) with additional participants in the network.[194] In other words, where there are network externalities, demand begets demand. Consequently, networks are likely to expand where demand exists. High-density areas such as cities will have the largest demand for electricity and are historically most likely to be connected first. In rural areas, where demand is lower and more geographically distributed, it would generally take longer to be fully connected.[195]

There also needs to be a baseline of demand before connection to the network becomes attractive. One can think of railways. Here, demand is again high in high-density areas, leading to calls for a railway station. Once it is clear where the railway station will be placed, railway infrastructure can be built to connect the city to the broader network. It is likely inefficient – especially for smaller emerging railway networks – to connect each little village through its own train station. Consequently, a number of small villages may have to cooperate and coordinate their demand to build a station at a central location as to be connected to the network. Once the station is built, demand for railway services will grow, and more connections may be made in the area.[196]

192 Shy (n 185); Decker (n 10); Montero and Finger (n 18).

193 Decker (n 10).

194 Michael L Katz and Carl Shapiro, 'Network Externalities, Competition, and Compatibility' (1985) 75 The American Economic Review 424; Jean-Charles Rochet and Jean Tirole, 'Two-Sided Markets: A Progress Report' (2006) 37 The RAND Journal of Economics 645; Jean-Charles Rochet and Jean Tirole, 'Platform Competition in Two-Sided Markets' (2003) 1 Journal of the European Economic Association 990.

195 Milton Mueller, *Universal Service: Competition, Interconnection and Monopoly in the Making of the American Telephone System* (Syracuse University Books 2013); Decker (n 10).

196 Decker (n 10); Joskow (n 10).

Network externalities are more evident in the case of telecommunications networks. These networks are governed by very clear *direct* network externalities. A telephone network is only attractive for users if they can use it to reach other users, it again becomes more valuable if these are also users that they wish to reach and communicate with and again more valuable when the number of relevant users becomes greater. Here, the demand for the service is directly determined with the existing demand.[197]

Coordinating direct network effects is an important activity as it determines the value of the network: creating overcapacity may be wasteful and needlessly increase costs while creating too little capacity may lead to congestion. Both instances harm demand. If demand drops too much, this may lead to negative network externalities: as the popularity of the service shrinks it becomes harder to maintain the network and the losses may become self-sustaining: if a large group of users starts boycotting a social media or a communications platform, the remaining users are likely to leave eventually due to a lack of utility.

Balancing a network is difficult, peak loads on the network may demand extra capacity at some points in time and less capacity at others, making (some level of) real-time management an important part of the network operator's duties. The importance of proper coordination is particularly important in markets where poor coordination can be disastrous, such as markets that are sensitive to congestion, or where disequilibrium leads to a breakdown of supply. The latter is the case in electricity networks, where a blackout will occur if demand and supply are not balanced.[198] If networks do not scale properly, the costliness of the service may price out certain users and thereby reduce demand, leading to the decline of the network. Building too many railways for too few users, maintaining a telecommunications network for a too small number of users, may lead to an exodus from the network due to the unnecessarily high costs.[199]

Aside from direct network effects, there has been an increase in attention for indirect network externalities over the past two decades. In the early 2000s, Jean Tirole and Jean-Charles Rochet have formulated a theory of indirect network externalities in multi-sided markets.[200] Rochet and Tirole have studied how indirect network externalities occur in multi-sided markets, including media and payment card markets. These markets are called multi-sided as the supplier of a newspaper or payment

[197] Katz and Shapiro (n 157); Nicholas Economides, 'The Economics of Networks' (1996) 14 International Journal of Industrial Organisation 673; Mark Armstrong, 'Network Interconnection in Telecommunications' (1998) 108 Economic Journal 545; Albert-Laszlo Barabasi and Reka Albert, 'Emergence of Scaling in Random Networks' (1999) 286 4.

[198] Decker (n 10).

[199] cf Katz and Shapiro (n 194); Yannick A Mies, Heinz-Theo Wagner and Markus Vodosek, 'Understanding the Antecedents of Lock-In, Switching Costs and Network Externalities in the Context of Digital Innovation' in Tomás Bayón and others (eds), *Dynamic Capabilities and Relationships: Discourses, Concepts, and Reflections* (Springer International Publishing 2021).

[200] See eg Rochet and Tirole, 'Platform Competition in Two-Sided Markets' (n 194).

service connect two or more 'sides' of a market to one another: the newspaper connects readers on one side and advertisers on the other, a payment service provides an opportunity for users to pay merchants for their goods. In multi-sided markets, the provider of the intermediary service is often referred to as a platform. A platform can be understood as the technology through which others are able to connect and conduct their business.[201]

Indirect network effects are the externalities that arise not due to an increase or decrease of participants on the same side of the market but due to an increase or decrease in participation on the other side of the market. The value of the service on the side of the market A is determined by the size of the network in market B, and vice versa. Indirect network externalities can also be positive or negative, and this can differ per side of the market.[202] Just as it is important to properly coordinate direct network externalities, it is at least as important – if not more – to properly coordinate indirect network externalities. These types of externalities can be even more difficult to coordinate as there are multiple sides with diverging (and sometimes conflicting) interest.[203] As exemplified with the surplus of advertisers before, the platform operator must strike a fine balance between the interests of readers and advertisers.

Both direct and indirect network externalities are common characteristics in digital markets.[204] Direct network externalities are present in social media or communications services, and indirect network effects are relevant in all platform services where the digital firm acts as an intermediary.[205] As the platform offers an intermediation service, the attractiveness of the platform directly relies directly on its ability to match a group on one side of the market with the group on the other side of the market. The platform with the most expansive network on either side – and with the best matching technologies – will have a competitive advantage over others.[206]

[201] ibid 175–177; Rochet and Tirole, 'Two-Sided Markets' (n 194); Filistrucchi and others (n 60) 2; Jacobides and Lianos (n 12) 8–10, 17.

[202] Katz and Shapiro (n 194); Rochet and Tirole, 'Platform Competition in Two-Sided Markets' (n 194); Filistrucchi and others (n 60).

[203] Filistrucchi and others (n 60) 13, 14; Joseph Farrell and Paul Klemperer, 'Coordination and Lock-In: Competition with Switching Costs and Network Effects' (2007) 3 Handbook of Industrial Organization 1967; Mark Armstrong, 'Competition in Two-Sided Markets' (2006) 37 The RAND Journal of Economics 668; Rochet and Tirole, 'Platform Competition in Two-Sided Markets' (n 194) 991, 1018.

[204] See Nico Van Eijk and others, 'Digital Platforms: An Analytical Framework for Identifying and Evaluating Policy Options' (TNO 2015) <www.tno.nl>; OECD, 'Big Data: Bringing Competition Policy to the Digital Era' (OECD 2016) Background note by the Secretariat; Digital Competition Expert Panel (n 1); Crémer, De Montjoye and Schweitzer (n 4); Zingales and others (n 1); Lancieri and Sakowski (n 1); Hein and others (n 37).

[205] Rochet and Tirole, 'Platform Competition in Two-Sided Markets' (n 194); Wright (n 59); Rochet and Tirole, 'Two-Sided Markets' (n 194); Armstrong (n 203); Filistrucchi and others (n 60); Rietveld and Schilling (n 47).

[206] Wright (n 59); Tiwana (n 34); Anderson (n 28); Erik Brynjolfsson, Yu (Jeffrey) Hu and Michael D Smith, 'From Niches to Riches: The Anatomy of the Long Tail' [2006] MIT Sloan Management Review 13.

The platform operator also has to strike a balance between the interest of different user groups: too much advertising may drive away end users, while too little may reduce opportunities to invest in the quality of the service. For ride hailing services, rewarding drivers too much may make the service too costly for users (especially when there is competition), while rewarding drivers too little may lead them to leave the network, creating undercapacity and reducing the value of the service for end users. Digital businesses have to develop and scale their network, just like non-digital network services. Through careful balancing of interests, new platform operators can overcome the chicken-and-egg problem and attract users on all sides of the platform simultaneously.

As digital markets form a network, there are also cross-market network externalities. These cross-network externalities facilitate an undertaking in one digital market to leverage its network from that market into the other, simply by connecting the networks created in both markets. Network externalities are then enhanced as two networks merge into one.[207] The creation of a successful Operating System allows the supplier of that OS to steer users towards its proprietary services, and the integration of two social media networks (or creating strong links between them) can fuse two social networks into one. A digital undertaking may choose to enter into a new market to develop its network there or acquire another firm to capture a network of users and integrate them with its own.[208]

Digital undertakings also exhibit a novel form of network externalities, namely data-driven network externalities. These set themselves apart as their effects are not limited to the demand-side but actually produce supply-side efficiencies. Due to their complexity, these types of externalities are discussed in Section 3.2, where data as an input is discussed in depth.

3.1.2 *Economies of Scale and Scope*

Economies of scale and scope are supply-side efficiencies that make production processes more efficient as they increase their output in units (scale) or by producing joint outputs (scope). Production processes that are subject to economies of scale are characterized by the degree with which average costs are impacted with an increase in outputs. Economies of scale can be classified into three broad categories: constant returns to scale, increasing returns to scale, and decreasing returns to scale.[209] In the case of constant returns to scale, an increase in inputs causes the same proportional increase in output. When there are increasing returns to scale, the outputs of an undertaking increase disproportionally with an increase in inputs. With

[207] David P McIntyre and Arati Srinivasan, 'Networks, Platforms, and Strategy: Emerging Views and Next Steps' (2017) 38 Strategic Management Journal 141.

[208] Digital Competition Expert Panel (n 1); Mandrescu (n 12); Van den Boom and Samranchit (n 148).

[209] Richard A Posner, 'Natural Monopoly and Its Regulation' (1969) 21 Stanford Law Review 548; Joskow (n 10); Decker (n 10); Ducci (n 11).

decreasing returns to scale, each output increase in input leads to a proportionally smaller increase in output. This is not to be confused with diseconomies of scale, where an increase in input actually leads to a decrease in outputs. It is important to distinguish between constant returns of scale and increasing returns to scale when discussing economies of scale as a concept.[210]

Economies of scale are often discussed in relation to recouping the costs of infrastructure. Developing an infrastructure is often associated with high upfront costs (sunk costs and fixed costs) and relatively low costs per produced unit or connection (marginal costs). This creates returns to scale: the production of each unit allows the firm to spread out the cost for developing and operating the infrastructure, which makes the relative cost for producing each new unit lower. One may think of an electricity network, the infrastructure operator first has to lay all the wire needed for transport and connect homes and buildings to the network, which require significant investments. However, once the firm starts transporting electricity, the costs of transmitting 1,000 or 2,000 kilowatts is the same (depending on the capacity of the network). If the firm charges a set price for transport per kilowatt, it can recoup more of its costs by transporting 2,000 than it could by transporting 1,000, assuming its price reflects the recoupment of their investment. Once the main network is in place, there may still be new investments required to expand the network.[211]

There can also be increasing returns to scale where the sunk costs actually start decreasing while returns increase or stay the same. The first miles of wires that are installed to connect the producer to a transmissions operator are costly, as are the wires from the transmissions operator to distributor.[212] However, if the network reaches a high density urban area, it can make many new connections with short ranges of wire. The cost per new connection diminishes depending on the number of connections, and it transports more kilowatts on the basis of these cheaper connections. Thus, even if the value of each connection does not grow with every meter of wire, every meter of wire does become cheaper on average with each connection, creating larger returns per meter of wire in high-density areas.[213]

Information goods often exhibit strong increasing returns of scale: producing a high-budget action movie requires a significant investment, but once the movie is made available there are near-zero costs for each screening of said movie. The more the movie is watched in theatres or streamed on video-on-demand services, the more profitable the product becomes. Most software and hardware are characterized by the same cost distribution: developing a search engine, a social media, or a dating app are all characterized by high upfront costs for development, and these costs can

210 Joskow (n 10) 3–24; Decker (n 10) 11–68.
211 Decker (n 10) 267–316.
212 ibid.
213 ibid.

be recouped by growing the network of members.[214] Once the website is online, there are near-zero costs in connecting new members. Returns to scale are increasing as the value of the networks actually increases as they grow: a larger social media with a more extensive reach can charge a higher price to advertisers and a dating site with many (desirable) members can extract a greater premium from those searching for a date. Most digital services, even those aimed at selling products per unit (even physical products) exhibit economies of scale when serving the long tail of demand. In other words, their ability to match any niche request with a supplier. The more expansive the userbase of buyers, the more opportunities there will be for sellers in niche markets to sell. Conversely, the more sellers there are, the more likely that the niche demand will be satisfied. Serving one niche market as a specialty is likely not (very) profitable but serving a whole range of niche markets may generate more revenue than simply selling 'hit products'.[215] More users on either side of the market therefore create increasing returns to scale: the larger the userbases, the more likely that having additional users leads to more matches per user.

Economies of scope refer to a situation where producing multiple outputs together leads to cost-saving efficiencies. They cost-saving efficiencies may be due to complementarity in production processes, the existence of co-products, or the presence of shared inputs.[216]

Complementarity in production processes exists, for example, when the machinery to produce output A can also produce output B.[217] It is cheaper to produce blue, red, and yellow cups in a single factory than having a separate factory dedicated to the production of each, as all that is required is to change the dye in the machines. However, even if separate machines are necessary for each, it can still be cheaper to concentrate production within a single factory as the factory already has the know-how or transport network in place. Co-products exist when the production of output A leads to the production of output B as a by-product: a sheep herder produces both wool and meat, and can capitalize on both. The production of these products goes together naturally, no farmer would choose to produce the one and waste the other, assuming there is demand.[218] Finally, a shared input exists when an input can be used for the production of multiple goods: a producer of plastic cups can use the same plastic for different coloured cups but may also expand production to use the same plastic for the production of plastic plates and cutlery. In order to speak of

[214] cf Varian (n 21); Van Eijk and others (n 204); Crémer, De Montjoye and Schweitzer (n 4); Lancieri and Sakowski (n 1); Subcommittee on Antitrust (n 1).

[215] Erik Brynjolfsson, Yu (Jeffrey) Hu and Michael D Smith, 'Long Tails vs. Superstars: The Effect of Information Technology on Product Variety and Sales Concentration Patterns' (2010) 21 Information Systems Research 736; Brynjolfsson, Hu and Smith (n 206); Anderson (n 28).

[216] William W Sharkey, *The Theory of Natural Monopoly* (Cambridge University Press 1982); Joskow (n 10); Michael G Pollitt and Steven J Steer, 'Economies of Scale and Scope in Network Industries: Lessons for the UK Water and Sewerage Sectors' (2012) 21 Utilities Policy 17; Decker (n 10).

[217] ibid.

[218] ibid.

economies of scope, the marginal cost of producing output A should decrease when there is an increase in the production of B. This is called cost complementarity. That is to say, the cost of producing the goods jointly should create on average lower costs than producing each good separately.[219]

Economies of scope are often present in network industries, as infrastructures can be used for multiple purposes. Railways can be used for the transport of people and goods, or short-term and long-term transport, and telecommunications networks can supply both voice and video communications. By using the infrastructure for both purposes, the cost of offering these services jointly through that network is cheaper than to provide them separately. The infrastructure is the shared input for the provision of the different services offered on it. There may also be efficiencies related to vertical integration.[220] For instance, there may be a reduction in coordination costs or other inefficiencies by ensuring that one firm operates on multiple levels of the value chain. Any decision to unbundle undertakings, ensuring that activities across different levels of the value chain are supplied by different firms, should look at whether the efficiencies of introducing competition outweigh the efficiencies of integration.[221] Considerations on the benefits of vertical integration versus those of competition are particularly relevant in the discussion on digital markets: is it better to introduce behavioural remedies to curtail the anti-competitive behaviour of digital giants, or should digital giants be split up altogether? The benefits derived from economies of scope and vertical integration should be a prominent part of such debates.

Economies of scope are widely prevalent in digital markets. Due to the modularity of digital goods, almost every digital 'service' consists of a cluster of products and services. When we use our smartphone, we first see the user interface of our operating system, which creates a stable core for a cluster of software services and integrated platforms. App marketplaces – integrated into the OS – constitute their own platform market, yet also do not consist of a singular service, but rather of a cluster of APIs, drivers, and other connection interfaces offered by the ecosystem operator, as well as a large collection of third-party and proprietary apps that are offered through the platform, and integrated aftermarkets such as in-app payment systems. It may be hard to distinguish which offers are integrally connected to one another and which are vertically integrated but distinct markets. The app marketplace could not function without its infrastructure for connectivity and downloads, yet the choice to integrate an (exclusive) proprietary payment system is a design choice.[222]

219 ibid.

220 Martin K Perry, 'Vertical Integration: Determinants and Effects' (1989) 1 Handbook of Industrial Organisation 183; A Claici and others, 'The Economic Rationale for Vertical Integration in the Tech Sector: Hardware Devices to Software to Services: Strategic Risk-Taking, Innovation and Investments in the Pursuit of Efficiency and Consumer Value' (Copenhagen Economics 2020).

221 ibid.

222 Recently, the implementation of the Digital Markets Act has drawn attention to the importance of competition in the space for in-app payment systems, forcing Apple to change their business model

3.1.3 *Complementarity, Compatibility, and Standards*

Networks generally consist of interconnected products and services with interdependencies: services are offered on an infrastructure, and the infrastructure's value is derived from the services rendered on it. Without the one, the other can't exist or holds no value. The components that comprise a network are generally complementary to one another: the network encompasses generation, the wholesale and retail networks, offering these goods jointly in a single network makes the network attractive for more users, and more types of users. The larger the network becomes, and the more functionalities it has, the greater the value of the network.[223] This is particularly true for the digital network industry, which is hard to delineate and ever-evolving. The fundamental nodes for the digital network industry started with a number of computers that were not connected to one another. These were later connected to the internet. The internet started out small as well, connecting only a handful of academics, military officials, and other geeks. Over time, greater and greater numbers of users were introduced, more internet-based enterprises started to emerge, as did new products and services previously unimaginable.[224] For this growth and evolution to take place, the digital network industry needed standardization, interoperability, compatibility, and complementarity. Now, we see vast digital enterprises, which have been built on the standards that ensure connectivity; personal computers and smartphones can be found in the majority of households; and traditional networks are being complemented or even substituted by their digital counterparts. This is, however, not to say that parts of the digital network do not remain incompatible with one another: the digital network industry may be all encompassing, but it is not one singular and fully interoperable network in every aspect. Some parts are open, whilst others have taken shape as closed ecosystems.

To create a single network, compatibility is a requirement. Incompatibility between certain components, when these are incompatible two networks emerge. Examples can be found in the British railroads in the 1800s, where there were competing railway standards with a different width of tracks, meaning that trains had to

to allow third party payment systems. This emphasizes that while payment systems and app stores are highly complementary – and the inclusion of payment systems is necessary to make app purchases – they are still distinct markets that can be opened up for competition. In other parts of the cluster, this may be less evident but still valid, and the exercise of identifying which markets are distinct is important in opening up competition, as discussed in Chapters 8 and 9.

223 See Economides (n 197); Shy (n 185); Economides (n 175); Nicholas Economides and Lawrence J White, 'Networks and Compatibility: Implications for Antitrust' (1994) 38 European Economic Review 651; Farrell and Klemperer (n 203); Decker (n 10).

224 Kevin Featherly, ARPANET, Britannica, updated 15 July 2024 <www.britannica.com/topic/ARPANET>; Bethany Nowviskie, 'Eternal September of the Digital Humanities' in Matthew K Gold (ed), *Debates in the Digital Humanities* (University of Minnesota Press 2012) <https://doi.org/10.5749/minnesota/9780816677948.003.0025> accessed 22 August 2024.

be developed to ride on either the one or the other. These were incompatible, and required the production of different undercarriages for trains. Here, compatibility was ensured by introducing standards through law, requiring all railways to follow the legal standards.[225] Another example can be found in 1900s telephone networks in the United States, where AT&T's network competed with local independent telephone providers. As a result, customers would need two telephone sets to reach those connected to one network or the other. Ultimately, AT&T convinced legislature that a single telephone network would be best and absorbed the independent networks. This led to a single universal network, which would generally be considered efficient, yet AT&T was ultimately broken up into several regional networks to end their monopoly and its associated harms to the economy and consumers.[226] This shows that while it may be desirable to have a single network, this does not mean it is desirable to have that network operated by single firm or entity. Interoperability allows different firms to collaborate within a single network.

It is not always the case that a single network is better for users than having competing networks, although there are efficiencies associated with large networks, these must outweigh the benefits of competition. Competition between networks may be beneficial, depending on the circumstances.[227] The operators of a network can choose to compete through an open network strategy or a closed network strategy. With an open network strategy, the operator of the network tries to become the relevant standard and offers interoperability to providers of other networks. This strategy allows the network operators to share network externalities and compete on dimensions of price and quality. A network operator may also choose to a closed strategy and remain incompatible with other network providers. This means that its network is smaller, and they derive less value from network externalities, yet they can compete on the quality of the network itself. These strategies are relevant in digital markets, which are characterized by open (monetization) strategies on one side, and closed (marketization) strategies on the other. Competition between such networks is not new, yet it has taken new forms with the emergence of digital ecosystems.

The choice of a firm to engage in an open or closed network strategy depends on several of factors. First, the adoption of a single standard may be mandated by law, which takes away the choice an undertaking has in deciding its strategy. Second, the firm will consider its expertise on a certain standard and the cost of adopting that standard. Third, the choice on compatibility will depend on the relative benefit of keeping all the network externalities to itself by choosing incompatibility versus receiving half of the larger network benefits by sharing the network. Fourth, the choice on compatibility depends on the ability of a firm to sustain its dominant

[225] Montero and Finger (n 18).
[226] Mueller (n 195).
[227] Economides and White (n 223); Economides (n 197).

market position in an ensuing standard war if incompatibility is chosen.[228] Finally, the compatibility choice depends on the ability of firms to leverage any monopoly power that they manage to attain in new markets as a consequence of its incompatibility with the rest of the market.[229]

Similar considerations drive the decision to be interoperable or not for competitors in digital markets. Competition between Alphabet and Apple in the market for smartphone Operating Systems is a clear example. Until now, Apple has chosen a (mostly) closed strategy where it sells its hardware and software together and consciously remains incompatible with Alphabet's (and Microsoft's) Operating Systems. Apple has the required expertise to be a market leader in quality for its complementary and synergetic network of goods and services, and it is able to extract the benefits of maintaining its incompatible network by selling its devices for a high price, which users are willing to pay to get access to Apple's proprietary software and ecosystem. Moreover, Apple is able to leverage the synergies of its ecosystem to steer users from one product to another, stimulating users to not just buy the iPhone but also its laptops, tablets, wearables, and headphones. Apple clearly has an economic rationale to remain incompatible with Alphabet's open network, which allows virtually any third party to offer their complements. Instead, its value is generated by offering a highly curated collection of products and services. Now, with the DMA, there is the question whether Apple can maintain its incompatibility with other networks. Following the obligations in Art. 6 DMA, Apple will have to allow the installation of third-party software and app stores and to open up its ecosystem to new in-app payment systems and side-loading. This significantly impacts Apple's ability to differentiate itself from the other ecosystems and upsets the balance and stability of competition between the ecosystems. The question is then: will having multiple firms active in a single network yield better competitive results than having competing networks? This remains an open question, as the DMA is still at the precipice of its enforcement.

In short, high levels of complementarity between digital goods and services create value for users. Offering a collection of outputs on a single platform makes the

[228] As we will see later in this chapter, undertakings in digital markets may be inclined to refuse compatibility to protect their existing market position in certain markets that are within their digital ecosystems, regardless of whether they are dominant or hold a minority market share.

[229] Economides (n 175) 479–481 Based on the works of Economides (n 25); Shy (n 25), it is put forward here that the last three considerations are highly important in competition in digital markets. In these markets, choosing incompatibility in competition in certain networks may be the only way an undertaking can sufficiently differentiate its offering as to remain within competition. Some considerations by the undertaking may be altered due to the existence of ecosystems. Rather than safeguarding a dominant position in a certain market for instance, an ecosystem operator may choose incompatibility to carve out a part of the market and insulate this from competition. Part II will discuss these considerations in the choice to maintain an open or closed strategy in the context of competition in digital markets. Here, the reasoning builds on the idea set out in the work of Economides that the more intense the network externalities are, the stronger the incentive for a firm to break away and be incompatible from substitutes

platform more attractive to users. However, complementarity between goods and services may also lead to increased switching costs and lock-in: when a network of linked products and services is incompatible with devices offered by other suppliers, users may feel increasingly locked in into a network such as the one operated by Apple. Once a user has an iPhone, MacBook and Apple Watch, they may feel locked in as switching one device would require switching the others. Forcing interoperability helps to reduce this lock-in, but may also reduce the ability of the ecosystem operator to differentiate its offering of products and services and forego the efficiencies associated with the presence of competing networks.[230] The digital network industry is however peculiar in this regard, when compared to non-digital networks. Namely, this mandated interoperability does not relate to the network as a whole, but rather to segments of the networks, the digital ecosystems.[231] In the case of incompatible railway standards, interoperability requirements changed two competing railway networks into one. For digital markets however, there are not two networks but a single digital network with incompatible parts (at least not in the West, China's digital network may actually be considered as a separate network due to how it is governed).[232] Interoperability requirements for core platform services such as mobile operating systems therefore shift and upset the balance between ecosystems, threatening the segment of the network that they have carefully carved out for themselves and where they can exert their private power over third parties. Disturbing this equilibrium is the intention of the DMA, and not a side effect, as it pushes Apple and Alphabet to compete with one another in the market for open smartphone Operating Systems.[233] This is a situation where two incompatible networks are forced to become compatible by law, making all other (strategic) considerations moot.

[230] Mies, Wagner and Vodosek (n 199); Fiona M Scott Morton and others, 'Equitable Interoperability: The "Super Tool" of Digital Platform Governance' (2021) 4 Digital Regulation Project, Policy Discussion Paper 1.

[231] Ian Brown, 'Interoperability as a Tool for Competition Regulation' (LawArXiv 2020) preprint <https://osf.io/fbvxd> accessed 7 February 2022; Marc Bourreau, Jan Krämer and Miriam Buiten, 'Interoperability In Digital Markets' (CERRE 2022) Final Report.

[232] The distinct market for China in digital services is observed in the Google Shopping investigation, where the Commission considers the market for search global with the exception of China, which has barred Alphabet from providing its search services.

[233] Wagner and others (n 14); Schweitzer, 'The Art to Make Gatekeeper Positions Contestable and the Challenge to Know What Is Fair: A Discussion of the Digital Markets Act Proposal' (n 105); Marsden and Podszun (n 142); Rupprecht Podszun, Philipp Bongartz and Sarah Langenstein, 'Proposals on How to Improve the Digital Markets Act' [2021] Social Science Research Network; Giorgio Monti, 'The Digital Markets Act' (2021) 5 European Competition and Regulatory Law Review 90; O Andriychuk, 'Shaping the New Modality of the Digital Markets: The Impact of the DSA/DMA Proposals on Inter-Platform Competition' 44 World Competition 261; Damien Geradin and Dimitrios Katsifis, 'Strengthening Effective Antitrust Enforcement in Digital Platform Markets' [2021] European Competition Journal 1; Nicolas Petit, 'The Proposed Digital Markets Act (DMA): A Legal and Policy Review' (2021) 12 Journal of European Competition Law & Practice 529; Rupprecht Podszun, *Digital Markets Act – Article-by-Article Commentary* (Hart-Beck-Nomos 2024).

3.1.4 *Switching and Lock-In Costs*

Switching costs are costs that must be incurred by users for changing their current supplier of a good or service. These costs can take many forms: the purchase of a new device or machine, learning or training costs, a loss of expertise, emotional costs, or having to rebuild trust between parties. In the use of some products or service switching costs come naturally, for instance, in the use of machinery that requires a lot of training. A pilot will be able to fly a plane after many hours of practice and study, yet switching to flying a helicopter, would again require significant efforts. In other instances, switching costs can be increased by strategies of the supplier, for instance, by using its position in aftermarkets or connected products to keep users complacent. Here, the example of the Apple ecosystem is particularly salient: if switching smartphones mean that you can no longer use your wearables and headphones, you likely experience high switching costs when considering a smartphone from another provider.[234] In other instances, switching costs are the result of factors external to the firm, such as network externalities. Twitter users may feel that their preferred social media platform has degraded after its conversion to X, yet many stay on the platform as long the users they are interested in remaining on the platform.

In many instances, switching costs can be overcome. Users of a Windows-based personal computer may buy a MacBook next and incur the costs paired with learning how to use the new device and OS. Twitter users may try out other social networks such as Mastodon, with varying degrees of success. However, when switching costs become too high, users become locked in. Lock-in occurs when users cannot, or feel like they cannot switch from one supplier to another. So-called vendor lock-in is a recurring issue with large enterprises: once they have settled on a certain software solution, the costs of switching to a newer (and perhaps better) software seems to be taxing, causing them to remain with the old supplier. From the perspective of the undertaking, user lock-in is desirable as it may lead to higher willingness to pay for users for the product offered by the supplier.[235] From the perspective of the user – and competition policy – however, lock-in is likely considered negative as it provides the incumbent firm with power to engage in exploitative behaviour and reduce competition by leveraging its network across markets.[236]

In network industries, switching costs are high because of (i) the aforementioned network effects and (ii) because of the required coordination in a network.[237] As the

[234] The European Commission is currently in the process of coming to an implementing decision under Art. 8 DMA, where it makes it mandatory for Apple to become interoperable in terms of both software and hardware (DMA.100203 and DMA.100204, Apple Interoperability 6(7), Decision to open a proceeding of 19 September 2024).

[235] Mies, Wagner and Vodosek (n 199).

[236] Crémer, De Montjoye and Schweitzer (n 4) 8, 34, 58; Lancieri and Sakowski (n 1) 45–47.

[237] Farrell and Klemperer (n 203) 44.

value of a network is determined by the number of complementary lines and nodes that work together in cohesion, unbundling such an extensive network is likely to lead to a loss of efficiencies and raise concerns in coordination. Once a network of English academic literature is established, there are significant (learning) costs when the international community decides to switch to French. Similarly, coordination is required for an energy supplier that must maintain an equilibrium in the transmission of energy to incorporate new energy sources into its network without disturbing the equilibrium. These types of coordination costs may collectively lock users in into a suboptimal standard. However, once the standard has been chosen and widely adopted, it may be too costly (as a society) to promote the adoption of a better standard.[238]

These problems are of course more pronounced in network industries than in non-network industries due to the presence of strong network externalities, the need for complementarity and compatibility, and the presence of economies of scale and scope. Problems revolving around consumer lock-in are mitigated when there is an opportunity for users to multi-home, which refers to using several services at the same time. Users that are able to multi-home can use a new service without leaving the old service or learn to use the new service while relying on the old service at the same time.[239] The user of the Facebook Blue social media platform can use Instagram or Twitter at the same time. As all of these networks are freely provided to end users, there are little barriers for users to participate in more than one network. This allows users to switch. However, as the networks are unique and incompatible, it may still not be attractive for the user to fully leave any of the networks when adopting a new one.

3.2 THE DIGITAL REVOLUTION: DATA-DRIVEN EFFICIENCIES IN THE DIGITAL NETWORK

There are several economic characteristics exhibited by digital markets that are drivers of concentration: the presence of network externalities, economies of scale, and economies of scope. Section 3.1 has explained how the nature of digital products mean that these characteristics are present. However, digital markets are not just characterized by the presence of digital goods but also by the emergence of data as an important input for production. Digital technology has created a wealth of data, which in itself has become recognized as a resource that creates business value for firms. Access to data is often seen as the secret to success in digital markets, and privileged access to data is seen as a driving factor behind the competitive advantage and strong dominant positions held by today's digital superstar firms.[240] A look

[238] Farrell and Klemperer (n 203) 58–59.
[239] ibid 70; Rochet and Tirole, 'Platform Competition in Two-Sided Markets' (n 194) 992–993.
[240] See eg Fast, Schnurr and Wohlfarth (n 70).

at the economic characteristics of data as an input explains why they are a driver of concentration: data as an input itself creates novel data-driven network effects, economies of scale, and economies of scope.[241]

Data is simply information. Access to information – and reliance thereon for competition – is nothing new, much like multi-sidedness is not a new phenomenon. However, data has become more important for competition in digital business models as the collection, processing, use, and effects of data have reached unprecedented scales. This relatively new access to vast amounts of data and processing capabilities has resulted in so-called Big Data. Big Data consists of large, heterogeneous, unstructured or semi-structured, and generic purpose datasets.[242] In order to make use of Big Data, large-scale computers and non-structured software methods (i.e. algorithms) are a necessity to extract value from the data in a timely manner.[243] Traditional non-digital businesses made use of small and structured datasets: outcomes of focus groups and questionnaires, data on the success of competitors, literature on competitive strategies, and so on. Digital businesses are able to collect vast amounts of personal and non-personal data directly as a by-product of interactions with their products and services. This gives deep insights into user behaviour, possible improvements, and the human psyche. The collected data is unstructured, uncurated, and updated live. Without sufficient computing capacity, it would be impossible to process all this data to create meaningful insights. Attempts at human processing of such quantities of data would likely result in diminishing returns, or diseconomies of scale, as drawing insights from such a deluge of data is simply too complex. With the use of algorithms, however, incoming data can be processed in real time and used for experimentation, personalization, customization, and targeting.[244]

To understand the dimensions of Big Data, Laney's three V's are a helpful analytical tool. Big Data is characterized by its volume, variety, and velocity.[245] Under the condition that there is sufficient capacity to process the data, it becomes more valuable with increased volume (economies of scale), variety (economies of scope), and velocity (speed of processing).[246] As data is generated through interactions with

[241] ibid 202–229; European Commission (2016) Online Platforms and the Digital Single Market Opportunities and Challenges for Europe. Available at: https://eur-lex.europa.eu/legal-content/EN/TXT/?uri=CELEX:52016DC0288

[242] Ioanna D Constantiou and Jannis Kallinikos, 'New Games, New Rules: Big Data and the Changing Context of Strategy' (2015) 30 Journal of Information Technology 44, 2–10; Fast, Schnurr and Wohlfarth (n 70) 202–229.

[243] OECD, 'Big Data: Bringing Competition Policy to the Digital Era' (n 204) 5–15.

[244] See Doug Laney, '3D Data Management: Controlling Data Volume, Velocity and Variety' [2001] Meta Group Research note; OECD, 'Big Data: Bringing Competition Policy to the Digital Era' (n 204); Enric Junqué de Fortuny, David Martens and Foster Provost, 'Predictive Modeling with Big Data: Is Bigger Really Better?' (2013) 1 Big Data 215; Fast, Schnurr and Wohlfarth (n 70).

[245] Laney (n 244).

[246] ibid.

users, data gives rise to data-driven network externalities. A greater userbase, and a greater number of interactions with a digital service, create more data. This data helps the undertaking to improve its services.[247] The improved service attracts more demand, growing the userbase and the number of interactions. The novelty of data-driven network externalities – when compared to traditional network effects – is that increases in adoption not only lead to increases in demand (i.e. produce effects on the demand-side) but actually leads to cost-saving efficiencies (i.e. effects on the supply-side). In other words, where traditional network effects only cause the perception that the value of the service increases, data-driven network externalities actually cause the service to become better as the network grows.[248]

The emergence of Big Data, and the associated data economy, data-driven business models, and data-driven efficiencies, is truly a revolution in terms of resources for productivity. The cost of producing personal and non-personal data is immensely low as machine-generated data is produced as an inseparable by-product of the use of digital services.[249] Modern businesses have found ways to collect, process, and capitalize on this data for a number of purposes. This section explains how data helps digital undertakings to coordinate decentralized assets, to create economies of scale and economies of scope, and how data-driven network externalities change the value of networks.

3.2.1 *Data to Train Algorithms: Coordination and Predictive Modelling*

The *Oxford Dictionary* defines data as (emphasis added) 'facts or information, especially when examined and used to find out things or *make decisions*'. As such, there is a natural interest to use the increasingly widespread collection and processing of data to improve decision making. In the case of digital firms, such decision-making often happens by developing and training algorithms.[250]

The emergence of Big Data infrastructures has created the opportunity to engage in predictive modelling based on massive, real-time datasets.[251] This increased

[247] See ibid; OECD, 'Big Data: Bringing Competition Policy to the Digital Era' (n 204); Junqué de Fortuny, Martens and Provost (n 244); Fast, Schnurr and Wohlfarth (n 70).

[248] Fast, Schnurr and Wohlfarth (n 70) 202–229.

[249] Jens Prüfer and Christoph Schottmüller, 'Competing with Big Data' (Tilburg University, Tilburg Law and Economic Center 2017) 1.

[250] Junqué de Fortuny, Martens and Provost (n 244); University of Antwerp and others, 'Mining Massive Fine-Grained Behavior Data to Improve Predictive Analytics' (2016) 40 MIS Quarterly 869; Nestor Duch-Brown, Bertin Martens and Frank Mueller-Langer, 'The Economics of Ownership, Access and Trade in Digital Data' (2017) 1 JRC Digital Economy Working Paper.

[251] In light of the definitions set out in Section 3.1, data infrastructures should be understood as the computational power required to store, use and analyse data including server space, algorithms and other facilities required to use data to create value. The undertaking will also have to develop infrastructure-type facilities, where they can establish a connection between the user of the product and the data-infrastructure as to collect data from its users.

access to data is joined by increases in computing power and memory, as well as improved algorithms and algorithmic understanding. This has allowed models to be built from very large datasets.[252]

Predictive modelling and algorithmic decision-making have been applied in industries on the basis of smaller datasets, for instance, in the market for credit scoring. The algorithms used for this kind of predictive analysis based its decision on rather rich descriptive data such as demographic features, past purchasing and payment behaviour as well as debts. For these decisions predictive analysis is rather simple: predictive analysis is used to predict a target variable, and the algorithm is developed using small sets of training data for which the value of the target is known. These targets are often set based on a vector of features.[253] One could imagine that for credit scoring, a person with large outstanding debts and a high level of purchases is less likely to receive a good credit score than a person with a high level of purchases but no outstanding debt. The algorithm can also consider the profession of the person, monthly income, and perhaps how many years from retirement the person is to fine tune credit scores.

Big Data is currently opening the doors to use predictive modelling in markets where the features that decide the value of the target are not so clear. Digital undertakings – in particular big digital platforms – are increasingly relying on large quantities of sparse, fine-grained feature data, such as that derived from the observation of the behaviour of individuals. The rich descriptive data discussed earlier consisted of summaries of individual behaviour (total purchases, total debt, etc.).[254] This novel behavioural data on the other hand relates to the fine-grained behaviours themselves: data on an individuals' visits to a massive number of websites can be used for targeting online display advertising and data on an individual's geographic location can be used to target mobile advertisements for local businesses (even in real time).[255] Aside from being highly specific (fine-grained), the data is sparse as most of the user behaviour gives little or no indication about the target of prediction or wider trends.[256] These extensive datasets on individuals and their behaviour as to make a predictive analysis about their potential future choices are referred to as *high-dimensional datasets*.[257]

Aside from high-dimensional dataset, digital platforms also increasingly have access to *large population datasets*. Rather than focusing on fine-grained and sparse data on one specific individual, these types of datasets consist of data of a massive number of individuals.[258] This type of data allows algorithms to detect

[252] Junqué de Fortuny, Martens and Provost (n 244).
[253] ibid; René Arnold and others, 'Is Data the New Oil? Diminishing Returns to Scale' [2018] 29th European Regional ITS Conference, Trento 2018 17.
[254] Junqué de Fortuny, Martens and Provost (n 244) 216.
[255] ibid 217.
[256] ibid 215–218.
[257] Lancieri and Sakowski (n 1) 84; Junqué de Fortuny, Martens and Provost (n 244) 217.
[258] Lancieri and Sakowski (n 1) 87; Zingales and others (n 1).

hidden patterns in user behaviour across a large group of users or to determine societal trends. Where the high-dimensional dataset is particularly useful for quality improvements such as personalization of services, personalized recommendations, or targeted advertising, the latter type of data is particularly useful for the identification of new markets, the development of new (versions of) products or new functionalities, as well as the coordination of assets or inventory.[259]

Modern algorithms are able to discover patterns in swaths of data that could not be analysed by humans.[260] With automated processing, predictive models can be built on sparse and fine-grained data, algorithms continue to demonstrate marginal improvements in their predictive performance continue to persist even to massive scale.[261] In fact, certain telling behaviours cannot even be observed without access to massive sets of data. Particularly, in markets where rare-but-important behaviours make up a substantial portion of the data, massive data may improve predictive modelling. These insights indicate that firms which have access to massive datasets to train their algorithms may indeed have a considerable advantage over firms with smaller datasets and that this advantage may be more pronounced in markets where the fulfilment of demand in the long tail is important (such as search).[262] Moreover, it challenges the notion that data collection exhibits decreasing returns to scale at some point. In predictive modelling that was based on more rich descriptive data, it was generally understood that collecting too much data on too many features led to less accurate predictions. Looking at the data-collecting behaviour of large digital firms, this is likely not the case for predictive modelling as done by modern digital platforms.[263] There may be diminishing returns, but this just means that the marginal increases in quality become less great with more collected data, there are still benefits to collecting more data. If diseconomies of scale do set in at some point, we have clearly not reached that state yet.[264] Even if collecting more data is not particularly useful for the improvement of the service in question, data may still be used to strengthen one's position or create quality improvements in connected services.[265]

So, what do data-driven efficiencies in coordination look like in practice? We see it in the business models of ride-hailing apps such as Uber or e-commerce marketplaces such as Amazon. Uber has real-time access to the location of its drivers and passengers. Consequently, the algorithm tries to match supply and demand in different geographic locations at any given time: if there are many potential passengers and few riders in the city centre of Brussels, prices and compensation for riders goes

[259] Brynjolfsson, Hu and Smith (n 215) 1580–1596.

[260] Duch-Brown, Martens and Mueller-Langer (n 250) 6–8.

[261] University of Antwerp and others (n 250) 870.

[262] Anderson (n 28); Cedric Argenton and Jens Prufer, 'Search Engine Competition with Network Externalities' (2012) 8 Journal of Competition Law and Economics 73.

[263] University of Antwerp and others (n 250).

[264] Shoshana Zubanoff, *Surveillance Capitalism* (Profile Books 2019).

[265] This is discussed later in this chapter, when data-driven economies of scope are discussed.

up so that supply increases. If there are many riders and few passengers, prices and compensation for riders go down so that more people may consider taking an Uber. What sets Uber's data-based strategies apart from taxi companies is its ability to match demand and supply at a highly fine-grained level, rather than estimating. Algorithms are also able to process historical data to predict future demand: access to information on concert dates by a popular artist inform the algorithm that – historically – there was high demand for Uber drivers at the end of these concerts. The algorithm can raise prices in anticipation to attract drivers to start up its app, drive down to the location, and wait for the end of the concert, so-called surge pricing. The more data becomes available to the algorithm, the better Uber's ability to anticipate surges and lulls in demand and coordinate its independent drivers to minimize frictions and waiting times. Meanwhile, e-commerce platforms such as Amazon use data to minimize storage and sorting costs for themselves and their complementors. Amazon has deep insights into consumer purchasing behaviour and the available stock of its third parties: by matching demand and supply through predictive modelling, Amazon generally knows how much sales of a certain product will be made, and which seller it should recommend to match consumption with available stock. This also allows Amazon to verify where there is more demand than supply, driving vertical integration into downstream markets and the development of Amazon in-house products.

3.2.2 *Data-Driven Economies of Scale*

Data is information, thus exhibiting the cost structure associated with information goods. Data is non-exhaustive and non-rivalrous and can be used and reused by various users simultaneously without any loss of quality. To make use of data, one must put in place an infrastructure for its collection and processing. Once this infrastructure is in place, the generation of data and adding data points for processing have near-zero marginal costs. This cost distribution gives rise to increasing returns to scale: the more data that is processed on the infrastructure, the lower the average cost per data point. Moreover, increases in collected data lead to (at least over a large range) disproportionally great increases in efficiency or outputs.[266]

There are generally three types of fixed or sunk costs that must be incurred: first, a digital product must be developed and adopted by a large number of users. As data as an input is created by user interactions, one cannot generate user data without offering a product that users wish to interact with. Second, investments must be made in the hardware (servers, computing power) that are required to

[266] Jens Prüfer and Christoph Schottmüller, 'Competing with Big Data' (2021) 69 The Journal of Industrial Economics 967; University of Antwerp and others (n 250); Duch-Brown, Martens and Mueller-Langer (n 250); Junqué de Fortuny, Martens and Provost (n 244); Inge Graef and Jens Prüfer, 'Mandated Data Sharing Is a Necessity in Specific Sectors' 103 Economisch Statistische Berichten 298; Constantiou and Kallinikos (n 242).

store and process the data. Third, costs must be made to acquire the human capital (software engineers) to develop the algorithms that are required to harness data-driven efficiencies.[267] Once the product is developed and the infrastructure is put in place, both the creation and collection of data, as well as its use in training algorithms is negligible. Data are created as a costless inseparable by-product with each user interaction.[268] The marginal costs of storing additional data is near zero.[269] Finally, the cost of having the algorithm process additional data is near zero.[270] As a consequence, data analysis in itself exhibits economies of scale, separately from the increasing returns to scale that are created through data analysis in the provision of digital services.[271] Firms may lower the required investment of sunk and fixed costs by acquiring data from data-brokers, or through data-sharing, this is discussed later in the context of regulatory interventions. Generally, however, the initial creation of data entails the creation of the infrastructure and follows this cost distribution.

The generated data can be used for a number of quality improvements or cost-saving efficiencies. The main examples include quality improvements and service personalization, personalized recommendations, and targeted advertising.

Quality Improvements and Service Personalization

The collection of user data allows digital undertakings to improve the quality of their offerings. The analysis of clickstream data, which can be enriched by additional data from other sources, allows the undertakings to derive general insights about users' browsing behaviour and provides the undertaking with the opportunity to adapt the design and interfaces according to its primary business goals. Undertakings with advertisement-centric business models would like to ensure that they attract as many users as possible and retain their attention for the longest possible times, as to maximize the users' exposure to advertisements. Device-centric businesses on the other hand will try to convert visits into sales.[272]

In addition, the digital undertaking can exploit data as to improve the presentation of its content and improve navigation elements by running usability studies and field experiments while tracking changes in consumer behaviour.[273] High-dimensional

267 Fast, Schnurr and Wohlfarth (n 70); Bourreau, de Streel and Graef (n 69); see also the discussion in Section 3.1 on choice to forego short-term profits or incur losses for the sake of long-term network building and to this extent, Lina M Khan, 'Amazon's Antitrust Paradox' (2017) 126 The Yale Law Journal 710.

268 Prüfer and Schottmüller (n 249) 968.

269 ibid.

270 de Streel, Bourreau and Giet (n 28) 9.

271 Bourreau (n 101), 2–4.

272 Bourreau (n 28) paras 19–20.

273 Fast, Schnurr and Wohlfarth (n 70) 5; Michael Trusov, Liye Ma and Zainab Jamal, 'Crumbs of the Cookie: User Profiling in Customer-Base Analysis and Behavioral Targeting' (2016) 35 Marketing Science 405.

datasets allow for quality improvements such as personal recommendations or better targeted advertisements, while broad dimensional datasets allow the platform to discover macrotrends. It may help undertakings find which functionalities are most used, which need to be changed, what users are interested in as new products or new functionalities, and how to coordinate existing assets better. Quality improvements may occur both gradually or in real time.[274] For instance, Uber may be able to gradually determine optimal prices to maximize indirect network effects by attracting the optimal number of drivers and passengers. For Uber, real-time improvements are just as important: it allows Uber to decide if they need to make it attractive for additional riders to offer their service at a given time, for instance, when there is a football match or big concert in town. It can do so by making drivers aware that there are opportunities for profitable rides or by promising better premiums to its drivers through surge pricing.[275]

Personalized Recommendations

User profiling and the analysis of browsing and transaction history allow for personal recommendations, which are at the core of the value proposition by certain categories of digital undertakings. Providing users with personalized recommendations simplifies users' purchasing decisions or consumption choices by highlighting offers that match their interests and by reducing their search cost.[276] It also makes it easier for users to discover niche products which allows the digital undertaking to serve the long tail of demand, which allows the digital undertaking to attract a larger and more diversified base of customers. As a consequence, the ability to personalize recommendations has a significant impact on the ability of the firm to generate revenues as well as the consumption behaviour by its customers.[277] Besides the ability to attract more niche demand, product recommendations also allow the undertaking to push successful 'superstar' products on consumers, incentivize consumers to make unplanned purchases, or to make follow-up purchases of complementary goods in the aftermarket that raise the value of the main product.[278]

[274] Prüfer and Schottmüller (n 249); Fast, Schnurr and Wohlfarth (n 70); Jan Krämer and D Schnurr, 'Big Data and Digital Markets Contestability: Theory of Harm and Data Access Remedies' [2021] SSRN Electronic Journal <www.degruyter.com/document/doi/10.1515/9781400879762-024/html> accessed 26 October 2021.

[275] Uber, How Surge Pricing Works, Official website: <www.uber.com/us/en/drive/driver-app/how-surge-works/>.

[276] Bourreau, de Streel and Graef (n 69); University of Antwerp and others (n 250).

[277] Fast, Schnurr and Wohlfarth (n 70); Brynjolfsson, Hu and Smith (n 206); Brynjolfsson, Hu and Smith (n 215); Anderson (n 28).

[278] See Fast, Schnurr and Wohlfarth (n 70); Brynjolfsson, Hu and Smith (n 215); Gal Oestreicher-Singer and Arun Sundararajan, 'The Visible Hand? Demand Effects of Recommendation Networks in Electronic Markets' (2012) 58 Management Science 1963; Shuk Ying Ho and Kai H Lim, 'Nudging Moods to Induce Unplanned Purchases in Imperfect Mobile Personalization Contexts' (2018) 42 MIS Quarterly: Management Information Systems 757.

Personalized recommendations allow the firm to attract more users on both sides of the market and to generate better margins from the users it has attracted. The success of personal recommendations relies on the data to which the platform has access. As a consequence, privileged access to high-quality data provides an incumbent platform with a competitive advantage over competing platforms.[279] Aside from this, platforms may also use personal recommendations to gain a competitive advantage when competing directly with their downstream clients, for instance, by favouring their own products or certain preferred third-party complementors.[280]

Targeted Advertising

Digital advertisement platforms set themselves apart by their ability to target specific groups of users and personalize their advertisements. Non-digital advertising lacks the ability to engage in the same in-depth targeting as digital media. While advertising in newspapers and on television can be aimed at target audiences to some extent, the ability of these media to target individuals or specific groups of users pales in comparison to digital platforms.[281] Digital undertakings that rely on an advertising business model will generally offer their services to end users at zero price, which allows them to collect data on users as to improve their ability for targeted advertising.[282] The UKs Competition and Market Authority (CMA) has conducted an in-depth inquiry into digital advertisement markets and its two dominant players: Google and Facebook. The study by the CMA looks into the immense value generated in digital advertising markets, as well as the high levels of concentration in these markets. In the UK, the revenue generated in digital advertising markets has exceeded that of non-digital advertising markets, and 90 per cent of the total revenue goes to just Google and Facebook.[283] The CMA differentiates between keyword (search) advertising, open display advertising and owned and operated display advertising. In search advertising, sponsored results are shown as the result of users search queries. In display advertising, users are shown picture or video ads alongside the product or content they are interested in. The open display market consists of the owned and operated display market by Google and Facebook and the open display market where publishers such as online newspapers compete in real time to sell advertising inventory to publishers.[284] According to the CMA, the first

[279] See Fast, Schnurr and Wohlfarth (n 70); Gediminas Adomavicius and others, 'Do Recommender Systems Manipulate Consumer Preferences? A Study of Anchoring Effects' (2013) 24 Information Systems Research 956.

[280] Zhu and Liu (n 136). See Google Search (Shopping) (Case AT.39740) Commission decision C(2017) 4444 [2017] OJ C 9–11.

[281] Competition & Market Authority (n 69) 196–217; Fast, Schnurr and Wohlfarth (n 70) 202–229.

[282] Fast, Schnurr and Wohlfarth (n 70) 202–229.

[283] Competition & Market Authority (n 69) 10.

[284] ibid 262–290.

type is particularly useful to promote clicks to conversions, while the latter allows the user to familiarize themselves with certain products.[285]

Data are important to facilitate three types of targeting: (i) context-based targeting, (ii) segment-based targeting, and (iii) behaviour-based targeting. The first refers to targeting based on the content of a website. The second splits consumers into homogeneous groups in order to customize advertisements based on the associated group characteristics and the third type of targeting is based on past online behaviour by the individual consumer such as search queries, transaction history, and visited websites.[286] Behavioural targeting in particular relies on comprehensive user profiles that are based on the analysis of the collected user data.[287] While the effectiveness of digital advertising has been disputed, recent empirical studies provide evidence for a positive relationship between targeted advertising and advertising effectiveness, which includes findings on a positive correlation between targeted advertising in online sales, purchasing intention of consumers, website visits, clickthrough rates, and view-through rates. The timing and placement of the targeted advertisements seems to be of particular importance for its success.[288] Targeted advertising – and the immense value created in these markets – thus seems prone to concentration under the largest providers of online advertisements. This again highlights the competitive advantage of undertakings with privileged access to Big Data.[289]

3.2.3 *Data-Driven Economies of Scope*

Data also generates economies of scope: there are economies of scope associated with the processing of data, and data-driven economies of scope in the provision of service.

Economies of Scope in the Processing of Data

Economies of scope in the processing of data exist because of complementary production processes and the nature of different types of data as co-products with cost complementarity. First, data is a co-product of user interactions with the developed digital product. As such, economies of scope exist in the operation of a digital service and engaging in data analysis. As data processing leads to cost savings in the operation of digital services and the development of new digital products, data are to be considered a complementary co-product to the provision of digital services.[290]

[285] ibid 218.
[286] Fast, Schnurr and Wohlfarth (n 70) 204–215.
[287] ibid 204–205.
[288] ibid 206–208.
[289] Competition & Market Authority (n 69); Fast, Schnurr and Wohlfarth (n 70).
[290] Prüfer and Schottmüller (n 249) 968–969.

Second, there are economies of scope in collecting data from multiple sources, which shows effects akin to having complementary production processes. Once the algorithm is in place to process data for a specific purpose in market A, it can also utilize data collected in market B. After incurring the sunk costs to collect data in market B, it can be copied, stored, and reused in market B at near-zero marginal costs.[291] After all, data are – unless made exclusive (for instance, for strategic reasons) – a non-rivalrous and non-exhaustive good that can be accessed, used, and reused by multiple (potentially infinite) parties. Absent technical restrictions, data collected in one market can be used across an indefinite range of algorithms for an indefinite amount of uses.[292]

Conversely, data collected in one market may also help the undertaking model new algorithms or improve existing algorithms in other markets. The value of accessing additional datasets in market B to improve the algorithm in market A has been demonstrated in practice: Google developed Gmail and offered it freely to consumers as to scan the content of their emails, improving its targeted advertising algorithms.[293] Rubinfeld and Gal explain why processing more data from more sources within a single firm leads to cost savings. They argue that this advantage exists because incumbents with more portholes from which to gather data, who have a substantial database to which they can compare new data or process unique data synthesis and analysis tools, may enjoy a competitive comparative advantage.[294] This highlights the nature of data as a shared input.

In short, there are data-driven economies of scope in the operation of multiple digital products: all services create data which can be used as a shared input, there are cost savings in increasing the quality of all services with data created in all other services and the marginal costs of reusing data is near zero. This gives rise to cost complementarity: the creation of multiple outputs (cost-saving efficiencies) jointly lowers (or does not increase) the creation of all other outputs.

Not only does the processing of data in itself become more cost efficient when reused across multiple algorithms, it also leads to better results in predictive modelling. Data processing leads to better results when it is based on multiple datasets, rather than one.[295]

This increase in efficiency for modelling can be exemplified by looking at the market for targeted advertising: Google's presence in the market for search, mobile

[291] de Streel, Bourreau and Giet (n 28) 8.

[292] cf Inge Graef, 'Data as Essential Facility Competition and Innovation on Online Platforms' (Katholieke Universiteit Leuven 2016) <http://lib.ugent.be/catalog/rug01:002276080>; Arnold and others (n 253); Fast, Schnurr and Wohlfarth (n 70).

[293] Montero and Finger (n 18) pt I.

[294] Daniel Rubinfeld and Michal Gal, 'Access Barriers to Big Data' (2016) 59 Arizona Law Review 339, 342–343.

[295] Duch-Brown, Martens and Mueller-Langer (n 250) 38; see also University of Antwerp and others (n 250); Fast, Schnurr and Wohlfarth (n 70).

OS, Maps, web browsers, email, comparison shopping, and reviews (etc.) provides it with unique and somewhat related datasets, which can be used to build a comprehensive user profile. This allows Google to target users based on both high-dimensional datasets, consisting of their current location, past preferences, searches, and perhaps personal communications and large population datasets such as reviews and business of restaurants. Analysing only one dataset, for instance, past purchasing behaviour, would not allow for the same quality of personalized recommendations

Data-Driven Economies of Scope Related to Cross-market Expansion

Aside from the cost-saving efficiencies of the joint processing of datasets, there is also a widely held belief that diversified undertakings enjoy cost-saving economies of scope in entering new markets.[296] In fact, data can be referred to as a general-purpose shared input: it can be used to identify in which untapped markets user demand exists, how to best access this demand, it provides insights into the desired quality, may help train algorithms to improve the quality, and help to develop the product once the market has been entered.[297] The possibilities for cross-market expansion are supported by the modular design of digital products in general, but data are considered to be a key driver for the tendency of digital markets to expand across different markets.[298] In its investigation into competition in digital markets, the US House subcommittee noted that undertakings with sufficient technical expertise and/or access to consumer data can apply this resource in a new market at low costs, reduce costs of entry, and extend its reach across adjacent markets with relative ease.[299]

It is possible to differentiate between economies of scope used in horizontal, diagonal, or vertical expansion. Horizontal expansion is the expansion into products that compete with one another. For instance, Instagram and Facebook are both social media which would directly compete with one another. Diagonal expansion can be found in entering the market for desktop-based, mobile-based, and voice-based search. While these goods are not as close competitors as two similar social media, operating one of these services allows the undertaking to use search queries from one service to create results in other services. Having access to all three types of search data may allow the undertaking to further enrich its results by enriching the data with location data (mobile) or by voice recognition (which allows for more certain verification of the user that conducts the search at any given time). Diagonal

[296] Fast, Schnurr and Wohlfarth (n 70); Crémer, De Montjoye and Schweitzer (n 4); Subcommittee on Antitrust (n 1).

[297] Nestor Duch-Brown, 'The Competitive Landscape of Online Platforms' (2017) 4 JRC Digital Economy Working Paper 1; de Streel, Bourreau and Giet (n 28); Subcommittee on Antitrust (n 1); Crémer, De Montjoye and Schweitzer (n 4).

[298] Bourreau, Dogan and Manant (n 37); de Streel, Bourreau and Giet (n 28); Hein and others (n 37).

[299] Subcommittee on Antitrust (n 1) 45.

expansion allows the undertaking to enter into complementary markets that are neither directly horizontal or vertically related to its occupied markets, providing them access to complementary technologies and datasets, which create economies of scope. Diagonal expansion can happen into closely related markets (such as different markets for search) or loosely related markets. For instance, Google's access to extensive location and navigation data as well as information on infrastructure may help its expansion into autonomous technologies such as self-driving cars. Amazon's expansion into the provision of server space with AWS has also provided it with useful insights and the server space to expand into a range of complementary or loosely connected markets, which are potentially connected through its Prime Membership.

As increased access to data allows the undertaking to enter markets more easily and more cost efficiently, and the processing of data from more datasets leads to cost-saving efficiencies and an increase in quality in existing products, a feedback loop comes to exist. The more markets a digital conglomerate spans, the more data it can collect from various sources. This makes the digital conglomerate more efficient in providing its existing services and entering new markets. This creates strong incentives for digital undertakings to expand across a large number of markets.[300]

3.2.4 *Data-Driven Network Externalities*

Data-driven network externalities set themselves apart from direct or indirect network externalities as they create actual cost-saving efficiencies in the supply of the product or service. Generally, the value-increasing effects of direct and indirect network externalities are limited to the demand side: having additional participants in the network raises the perceived value of the network for users and make them more inclined to join (creating an upward sloping curve of demand).[301] However, the perceived increased value exists only in the eye of the user, as users can now make additional connections. There is no cost-saving efficiency that leads to lower average costs of production.[302] In telecoms, having more users connected to the communications network raises the value but does not make delivering the service more efficient or a higher quality. Would the users leave the network, the telecoms operator would not be better at delivering the service than it was before the participants had joined.

Data-driven network externalities are also not the same as dynamic economies of scale, which are completely supply-driven. Dynamic economies of scale exist when the production of a specialized good has high learning costs. As such, becoming

[300] Fast, Schnurr and Wohlfarth (n 70); Competition & Market Authority (n 69).

[301] Katz and Shapiro (n 194); Rochet and Tirole, 'Platform Competition in Two-Sided Markets' (n 194); Rochet and Tirole, 'Two-Sided Markets' (n 194); Filistrucchi and others (n 60).

[302] Prüfer and Schottmüller (n 249) 996–998.

more experienced in the production of a complex good such as an aircraft allows the producer to become more efficient when producing more of the same good. This type of economies of scale lacks the network externality aspect that characterizes data-driven network externalities.[303]

Data-driven network externalities are unique as they require participation on the demand side of the network to increase efficiency on the supply side of the network. They are not cannot be easily copied by competitors or destroyed with the arrival of a new technology, as their existence is dependent on the presence of an installed base of users.[304] The supplier of a search engine relies on the data generated by its users to develop its network and create important insights into sorting and ranking results. This efficiency in sorting the search results cannot be duplicated without extensive access to user data.[305]

These network externalities lead to a unique feedback loop where producing more outputs (interactions) leads to the creation of more inputs (data), which can be used to produce higher quality outputs more efficiently, which in turn attract more interactions. The efficiencies associated with this data have been outlined earlier: they are not just limited to improving the same service (data-driven returns to scale) but also in developing new functionalities or improving products in other markets (data-driven economies of scope).[306] Due to the importance of data in training algorithms – which are key drivers behind quality improvements in the personalization or customization of service or targeted advertising or in the coordination of fragmented assets – data-driven network effects may also be referred to as algorithmic network effects.[307]

The self-reinforcing feedback loop exhibited as a result of data-driven efficiencies helps to explain why concentration is so prevalent in digital platform markets. Markets with strong traditional network effects are also prone to concentration. However, here there is an expectation that the monopoly can be contested: Myspace was early in the market for social media. However, as demographics changed so did preferences. Facebook displaced Myspace after the latter had a three-year reign as the dominant social media. Meta, in turn, seems stickier and better able to anticipate shifts in demand. This is at least in part due to its access to data and ability to predict shifts and developments in digital. The ability to process data at a large scale means that larger platforms are in fact more efficient as a result of scale economies, while they are able to better insulate themselves from competition through cross-market expansions that is also facilitated by data.

The relevance of data is not limited to novel digital platforms. Even traditional networks are increasingly complemented with a 'data layer' that helps with the

303 ibid.

304 ibid; Fast, Schnurr and Wohlfarth (n 70) 204–214.

305 Argenton and Prufer (n 262) 73–105.

306 Fast, Schnurr and Wohlfarth (n 70) 204–215.

307 Montero and Finger (n 18).

coordination of supply and demand: energy networks increasingly use artificial intelligence to efficiently use produced renewable energy, coordination in railways happens through automated means and predictive modelling, and large parts of the telecommunications sector have been fully substituted by digital data-driven services. The role and relevance of data are thus not wholly limited to competition between digital platforms and ecosystems but should be viewed as a general revolution in productivity. The emergence of Big Data has made personal and non-personal data valuable inputs, with new uses and promises. The ability to process vast quantities of data creates data-driven incumbency advantages for the largest digital firms, which causes structural concentration in digital markets. The interplay between digital ecosystems and data-driven business models is particularly strong. This raises the question, how similar or different is competition in digital and non-digital networks?

3.3 COMPETITION BETWEEN NETWORKS IN DIGITAL AND NON-DIGITAL SECTORS, IS IT DIFFERENT?

Competition between digital firms and ecosystems is best understood by looking at their position in the digital network industry. Competition scholars have coined different terms to best describe digital competition: nascent competition, indirect competition, dynamic competition, and so on. However, these terms and their underlying theories rarely help to understand why it is exactly in digital markets that this novel form of competition has become the norm.

There are past examples of competing networks and competing systems. Competing networks can be geographically delineated or on the basis of demand. The extent of a single network is often determined by the cost distribution of the underlying infrastructure, and the question when having one supplier is more cost-efficient than having multiple. Competition between systems takes place as competition between standards: one type of video format or another, wooden pegs or nuts and bolts? Competition between systems often – but not always – ends in the adoption of a single standard. So why is competition between systems, or ecosystems, so persistent in digital markets?

Digital competition is not quite competition between networks, and not quite competition between systems. Instead, the product ecosystems offered by digital undertakings and their associated multi-actor ecosystems seem to be a delineable segmented network within the digital network industry. It is not like competition between systems, where good A is *only* valuable if good B also exists. However, the presence of platform A does mandate the proliferation of service B. While the existence of platform C may further enhance the value of platform A and products B, D, and E. The digital firm first emerges within the network industry to build its own networks and develop its system and standards. Once it is able to capture its first markets, it can expand further in the network, capturing new nodes in the process. By strategically opening the ecosystem to participation in some areas, while closing participation in others, it is able to carve out a piece of the digital network industry where it exerts control.

This helps to understand why competition between ecosystems is so persistent in the digital network industry. Undertakings are not simply competing at the market level but are rather competing to control larger parts of the network. There is friction at the borders of their ecosystems, where they enter into new markets and emerging technologies, but the core of the network is relatively stable. The larger their ecosystem becomes, the more its platforms become entrenched: more business users and end users depend on the platform for their commercial activity, use the standards and software development kits provided by the ecosystem operator, have developed their expertise and know-how specifically for participation in that ecosystem, have made investments and have become used to dealing with the ecosystem operator. It is not just a conglomerate, it is a vibrant and thriving hub where value is co-generated, not unlike Silicon Valley itself.

Figure 3.2 serves to provide a visual for competition in the digital network industry, albeit highly simplified. To understand competition between digital undertakings and ecosystems as part of a network, it helps to identify the goals of competition. Ultimately, these undertakings compete for resources and users: resources exist in end users, business users, data, and the ability to set standards, and other intangible privileges such as access to financing and (political) influence.[308] The most successful undertakings are closest to the different categories of users, allowing them to steer users and collect the vastest amounts of data. As they control the access points

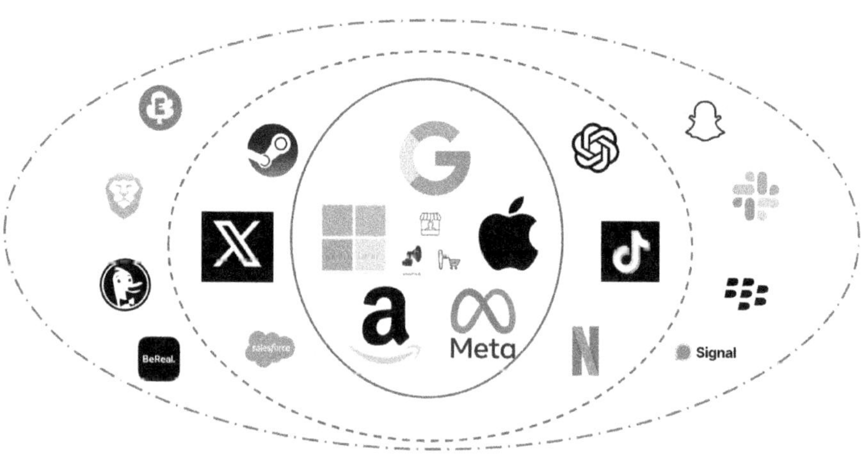

FIGURE 3.2 A simplified visualization of the digital network industry – own illustration

[308] See eg M Bennett, H Brouwer and R Claassen (eds), *Wealth and Power: Philosophical Perspectives* (1st edn, Routledge 2022) <https://doi.org/10.4324/9781003173632>, which explores various forms of power held by digital firms throughout its chapters. See also Ezrachi and Stucke (n 1).

to users, other digital undertakings are increasingly dependent on the most prominent ecosystem operators for access to the user. Access points should be broadly understood and may include platforms, infrastructures, facilities, or resources (data) that entrants need to be able to use in order to reach end users and business users, or to supply their goods and services. The central ecosystems can use this dependency to collect more data and further expand their competitive advantage, for instance, by making access to APIs dependent on the collection of generated data. In the visualization, the big digital ecosystems in the inner circle control the largest number of platforms and services, have the greatest numbers of users, collect the most data, and have the best access to finances.[309] Parties in the second circle have developed their own user networks, and in some instances started to expand into new product markets to develop a product ecosystem but will generally still rely heavily on the ecosystems of those in the inner circle. Platform operators in the outer circle are trying to capture their platform market but are either still entrants or have stagnated in growth. These platforms operate within their niche, on the outskirts of the digital network. Their position is precarious, as they may be forced to leave the market if they fail to achieve scale.

What is then the role of digital platform markets in this form of competition in this perspective? Digital platforms are generally where digital product ecosystems start, and they tend to be anchors around which the ecosystem is built. Those at the outskirts of the network try to capture platform markets, seemingly a first step in entering long-term competition. The platforms seem to form the stable core of the digital ecosystem, from where expansion throughout the network can happen. Looking at competition in the digital network through this lens also helps us to understand why it is not easy to introduce competition by means of competition law proceedings, and provides lessons for regulation. Can we really expect that competition between ecosystems intensifies by intervening at the level of markets, or platforms?

In non-digital network industries, regulatory intervention generally aimed to open up competition at the level of the infrastructure. In many instances, this started with introducing competition at the level of services, as trying to create competition for the infrastructure itself seemed to great of a step. As a result, parts of network industries were opened up to competition, while others ended with regulated monopolies. This type of regulation is referred to as natural monopoly regulation. The question now is how competition can be introduced in digital markets: what parts of the ecosystem can – and should – we open up to competition, and do core platform services fulfil a similar function in ecosystems as natural monopoly markets did in traditional network industries? Section 3.4 dives deeper into these questions.

[309] cf Bennet and others (n 308); Lianos, Eller and Kleinschmitt (n 121); Sai Krishna Kamepalli, Raghuram Rajan and Luigi Zingales, 'Kill Zone' (2020) No. 27146 National Bureau of Economic Research Working Paper Series <www.nber.org/papers/w27146>; Lianos and Carballa-Smichowski (n 121); Ezrachi and Stucke (n 1).

3.4 CONCLUSION

This chapter has discussed the similarities and differences between digital and non-digital networks, as to explain how competition in digital markets can be framed as competition within a network, but that it is still governed by different principles than competition in non-digital markets.

There are several shared economic characteristics between digital and non-digital network industries: network effects, economies of scale and scope, complementarity, compatibility, and standard-setting, as well as switching and lock-in costs. This leads to connections and interdependencies: one output is an input for another and one digital firm relies on the services of another to supply its products and services. There is also the risk of high levels of concentration and the emergence of bottleneck markets.

At the same time, cost distributions, competitive strategies, and limitations are still different in digital markets. Indirect network externalities are more important, increasing returns to scale are greater, and the network is more vast and more complex, consisting of many loosely connected but distinct markets that serve a wide variety of purposes. The presence of data-driven efficiencies further exacerbates concentration effects, and the nature of digital goods leads to cross-market expansion into vast ecosystems.

The chapter concludes by explaining how framing digital markets as a network industry helps to understand competition between and within ecosystems and the role of platforms in competition within the network. Looking at digital product ecosystems as segments of a singular network industry, helps to identify where they clash with one another and where friction exists. It also provides a novel perspective on the dependency of smaller ecosystem operators on larger ecosystem operators: they often operate key platforms and infrastructures necessary to reach end users. This goes beyond the role of a platform as an important gateway, it is rather the collection of platforms, products, and infrastructures operated by the incumbent ecosystem operator that can steer users towards or away from emerging platform operators. Platforms are important in themselves as gateways, but perhaps even more so in how they form stable cores from which the multi-actor and multi-product ecosystems of expand. Incumbents can use platforms to entrench their central position in the network, while entrants may try to leverage their position in a platform market to develop their own ecosystem and infrastructures.

4

Digital Platforms

A New Natural Monopoly?

This chapter discusses the theory of natural monopoly, how it applies in non-digital network industries, and whether it could apply to certain digital markets. The theory of natural monopoly dictates that in some markets it is more cost efficient to have a single supplier than multiple suppliers, which makes the market prone to concentration under a single firm. It has often been used to justify economic regulation such as regulated prices or access to ensure that the market functions properly while a fair share of the generated value is allocated with consumers. Section 4.1 discusses the theory of natural monopoly and sets out the characteristics of natural monopoly markets. Section 4.2 studies whether, and if so under which conditions, digital platform markets could be considered natural monopoly. Finally, Section 4.3 looks at the relationship between platform monopoly and ecosystem competition to explain why competitive pressures governing digital markets differ from those governing non-digital markets.

4.1 THE THEORY OF NATURAL MONOPOLY AND ITS APPLICATION IN NON-DIGITAL NETWORK INDUSTRIES

The theory of natural monopoly was often central in debates on the regulation of traditional network industries. In the past, networks such as those for railways, telecommunications, or energy were often considered natural monopoly. This led regulators to believe that the market would be best suited by vertically integrated, state-owned monopolies, which was long the standard mode of supply in – at least European – networks.[310]

[310] cf Posner (n 209); Sharkey (n 216); Berg and Tschirhart (n 10); Charles E Mueller, 'Computer Software Is a Natural Monopoly – Predatory Pricing and Efficient Scale' (1998) 29 Antitrust Law & Economics Review 99; Peter Z Grossman and Daniel H Cole, *The End of a Natural Monopoly: Deregulation and Competition in the Electric Power Industry* (Elsevier 2003); Joskow (n 10); Eric K Clemons and Nehal Madhani, 'Regulation of Digital Businesses with Natural Monopolies or Third-Party Payment Business Models: Antitrust Lessons from the Analysis of Google' (2010) 27 Journal of

Later, the theory of natural monopoly became more refined. Economists developed theories related to the efficiencies of monopoly versus efficiencies associated with competition and defined technological definitions to identify the shared economic characteristics of natural monopoly markets. This led to a distinction between parts of the network, where competition was considered possible and cost-efficient (competitive network activities) and parts of the network where competition was not possible, or where monopoly was more cost-efficient, which are core network activities. The core network activity is the segment of the market that is naturally monopolistic and often operates as a bottleneck between the upstream and downstream segments of the markets.[311]

Common contemporary examples of core network activities are infrastructures for the transmission of high-voltage energy and the distribution of low-voltage energy, the local loop in telecommunications, and railroad networks. Natural monopoly can be a temporary phenomenon. The generation of energy was viewed as a natural monopoly for a long time, but with the arrival of new technologies and an increase in demand of the market, competition in these markets is now considered efficient.[312] Natural monopoly should then not be viewed as something static and permanent but should rather be viewed as a classification that can be applied in a certain segment of a market over a period of time. Natural monopoly may also exist in a certain geographical area or over a certain size of demand. It is possible that when transport costs become lower, or demand for a certain service increases significantly, a market segment is no longer a natural monopoly.[313] The idea that a certain market is natural monopoly should not be viewed as a permanent representation of the economic realities. Instead, the status of natural monopoly for specific markets or infrastructures may change with developments, or simply reflect a regulatory choice.

There are however technical definitions of natural monopoly, which explain what type of cost distribution a natural monopoly tends to have. Economists have developed a single-product and multi-product perspective on natural monopoly to explain when sunk and fixed costs, economies of scale, economies of scope, and network externalities may create a natural monopoly market.

4.1.1 *The Single-Output Perspective on Natural Monopoly*

The single-product natural monopoly is technically defined by the existence of specific cost distributions between fixed costs and marginal costs, which lead to

Management Information Systems 43; Neil W Hamilton and Anne M Caulfield, 'The Defense of Natural Monopoly in Sherman Act Monopolization Cases' 33 31; Ducci (n 11).

311 Decker (n 10) ch 3.

312 See eg Monica Greer, *Electricity Cost Modeling Calculations* (Academic Press/Elsevier 2011).

313 Decker (n 10); Joskow (n 10).

economies of scale that cause subadditivity of the single firm. Subadditivity refers to a situation where it is more cost efficient to have one operator fulfil the entirety of demand than it is to have multiple suppliers. Subadditivity happens when fixed costs are sufficiently high and marginal costs are sufficiently low. The low marginal costs lower the relative cost per produced unit, helping the supplier to recoup their investments into developing and maintaining the infrastructure (sunk and fixed costs).[314] It can be the case that the sunk and fixed costs are sufficiently high that they can only be properly recouped if the operator of the infrastructure fulfils all demand. Alternatively, natural monopoly can exist because economies of scale continue to make the cost of production lower with each produced output, thereby making the price for consumers the lowest when they are all purchasing their goods from the same producer. Natural monopoly is a market with subadditivity of the single firm.[315] It may be the case that at some point diseconomies of scale set in, which means that after a certain point of production it becomes more expensive to produce additional outputs. This is the case if the production of new outputs requires investing in new facilities or capacity. Natural monopoly may persist if subadditivity remains even in light of diseconomies of scale, but if diseconomies of scale are persistent this will create opportunities for entry at some level of demand. Thus, it can be the case that natural monopoly only exists over a specific range of demand.[316]

Natural monopoly may also be limited to a certain geographical range. For instance, electricity gets lost when its transmission or distribution exceeds a certain range. This makes it cost inefficient to have a single point of production, and multiple competing networks may develop from different points of generation. As a result, natural monopoly may occur locally or regionally. In these cases, (extremely) high sunk and fixed costs may cause natural monopoly even in the absence of strong economies of scale.[317] This explains why many countries have regional distribution systems operators and transmissions systems operators that act as the monopolist in a geographic area defined by regulators.

Alternatively, a local or regional natural monopoly can be associated with economies of density. The local loop in fixed telephony or in internet infrastructure – also known as the last mile – is generally considered to exhibit natural monopoly. It is expensive to lay the wires in each neighbourhood that serve as the infrastructure for telecommunications but adding additional users to the network had low marginal costs. This leads to economies of scale that are even more pronounced in densely populated areas.[318] This means that it may only be efficient for the provider of wireless and broadband networks to supply all of the market if they have sole

[314] Posner (n 209); Joskow (n 10); Decker (n 10); Grossman and Cole (n 310).
[315] Posner (n 209); Joskow (n 10); Decker (n 10); Grossman and Cole (n 310).
[316] Decker (n 10) 17.
[317] Joskow (n 10); Decker (n 10).
[318] Decker (n 10).

operating rights in the urban local loop. This may warrant, for instance, the introduction of universal access obligations or the right to be connected: the monopolist will have sole rights to serve the highly profitable parts of the market, but only if it also supplies loss-leading connections. This is a barter between the regulator and the regulated: the regulated entity is protected from cream-skimming in profitable areas, and the regulator can ensure internet access in rural areas or for economically disadvantaged groups.

In traditional networks, the natural monopoly status of a market is generally due to the sunk costs largely required to create the infrastructure and the fixed costs associated with maintaining it. However, in markets with strong increasing returns to scale, natural monopoly may exist also in the absence of high fixed costs. These markets – unlike those previously discussed – can exhibit natural monopoly over *any* range of output and will become only more cost-efficient with any increase in scale. For particular products that have zero transportation costs, low to zero marginal costs, and which exhibit increasing returns to scale (in the limited sense of each additional input creating a disproportional increase in outputs) may qualify as naturally monopolistic in the single-product context.[319]

The discussion in this section is based on a single-output perspective. Single output means, in this case, that it is assumed that the monopolist only supplies one type of product or output. This is an assumption which allows economists to develop models where natural monopoly can be attributed solely to a combination of costs and economies of scale. Section 4.1.2 discusses how in a situation where the monopolist produces multiple output, economies of scope become relevant in determining whether natural monopoly exists. It is not the purpose of this book to develop new economic models or theories related to natural monopoly, but rather to create an intuition based on existing theories and models developed in economics. Consequently, only three scenarios for natural monopoly from a single-output perspective are considered here:

1. *High fixed and sunk costs combined with economies of scale create a natural monopoly without diseconomies of scope after a certain level of outputs.* The combination of high fixed and sunk costs may create a situation where the operation of the infrastructure is only viable after a minimum level of demand is supplied. When the largest share of demand must be supplied by the undertaking for its operation to be economically viable, this constitutes a natural monopoly, as developing a competing infrastructure would not be economically viable.[320]
2. *High fixed costs combined with economies of scale create a natural monopoly over a certain range of demand, with diseconomies of scope after a certain level*

[319] Joskow (n 10); Decker (n 10).
[320] ibid.

of outputs. The combination of high fixed and sunk costs creates a situation where the operation is only viable after a minimum level of demand is supplied. However, there may also be a maximum demand, which can be served before diseconomies of scale set in. The natural monopoly status of the undertaking then depends on the level of remaining demand. If remaining demand is too low for competition to be economically viable, the natural monopoly will remain but will not operate at maximum efficiency. In a scenario where there is a sufficient share of demand served under diseconomies of scope for competition to outweigh the efficiencies of a monopoly, the natural monopoly ceases to exist.[321]

3. *Increasing returns to scale, combined with any level of sunk and fixed costs create a natural monopoly*. With increasing returns to scale, the operation of the monopolist becomes more efficient with each output produced. As there is a disproportionate increasing in outputs for every new input, it is more efficient to aggregate all demand under a single supplier. This maximizes increasing returns to scale. Depending on the strength of increasing returns to scale, different levels of sunk or fixed costs may create a natural monopoly. Under extreme increasing returns to scale, there may be a natural monopoly even at low or zero fixed costs.[322]

4.1.2 *The Multi-output Perspective on Natural Monopoly*

In the multi-output context, subadditivity of the single firm can exist when there is a specific cost distribution of fixed costs combined with efficiencies of co-producing goods (economies of scope) which leads to a decrease in average costs of production (also referred to as multi-product economies of scale). This perspective looks at the efficiencies of supplying a variety or bundle of goods. It may be evident that there is a bundle of distinct goods, but it is also possible that what seems to be a single output actually constitutes multiple separate outputs. This is the difference between looking at railroads as if they only facilitate 'rail transport' or if it is possible to distinguish between multiple services within rail transport such as passenger transport, freight transport, long-distance transport, short-distance transport, and so on. When rail transport is defined as one service, one would focus on economies of scale. By identifying different co-products that are offered by relying on railroads, one can focus on economies of scope and cost complementarity.[323] Empirical research has demonstrated that most natural monopoly markets consist of a multiple-product output market.[324]

321 ibid.
322 ibid.
323 Sharkey (n 216).
324 See ibid; Joskow (n 10); Decker (n 10).

In the multi-output context, the presence of economies of scale in the supply of one of the products is considered necessary nor sufficient to establish natural monopoly.[325] Economies of scope can be highly relevant in understanding why certain markets exhibit natural monopoly, even when economies of scale could perhaps not justify why they are naturally monopolistic when they are viewed from a single-product context. A failure to see the multiple outputs produced by the single supplier may lead to false conclusions about whether natural monopoly exists.[326]

Natural monopoly based on economies of scope can exist in light of cost complementarity or due to trans ray convexity. Cost complementarity refers to a situation where the increase of the production of any (one) output, reduces the marginal cost of producing all other outputs. An example of a natural monopoly that persists on the basis of cost complementarity can be found in DSL internet and telephony markets. DSL internet connections are provided through the unused space of the normal phone line. This layer of digital packet transmission is paired with the voice transmission that happens through phone lines and these two transmissions do not disrupt one another. Increasing the amount of DSL connections on a fixed phone network creates cost-saving efficiencies and does not increase the marginal costs of providing voice telephony. There is cost complementarity in delivering the two services jointly, as any increase in DSL connections *or* voice telephony leads to declining average costs for the provision of the services together.[327] It is therefore cost efficient that the monopolist that operates the telephony network also supplies the DSL infrastructure, at least absent regulation that opens up this infrastructure for competition.

Natural monopoly may also exist as the result of trans ray convexity. This refers to a situation where the joint production allows for the compensation of diseconomies of scale that would otherwise be prohibitive. This can be clarified with a hypothetical example: imagine a scenario where a transport service provider faced with low demand decides to bundle freight and passengers on a single train. This may lead to diseconomies of scale due to the length or weight of the train, but it may be the only way to cost effectively transport both cargo and passengers if having two trains is too expensive.[328] In other words, it is possible that a market can only exist because of the existence of a joined market or a co-product. It is a logical consequence that the monopolist that supplies product A is also the only party that can supply product B, thereby establishing its monopoly for both outputs.

Finally, there is a situation where when the cost function exhibits both economies of scope and declining average incremental costs for all products. It is more

[325] See Sharkey (n 216); Joskow (n 10); Decker (n 10).
[326] Sharkey (n 216) 74–80.
[327] Nicole Schmoll, 'What Is the Difference between a Regular Phone Line & a DSL Line?' *It Still Works* (29 August 2017) <https://itstillworks.com/difference-between-regular-phone-line-dsl-line-17760.html>
[328] Joskow (n 10).

cost efficient to produce the different outputs within a single firm, and each of the products exhibit economies of scale independently. Economies of scope may exist, for instance, as a result of having single governance structures and managerial processes. There may be a natural monopoly with such a cost distribution, but this can also be attributed to the economies of scale of both goods independently.

These three scenarios for natural monopoly from a multi-output perspective are helpful to understand why concentration happens as a result of cross-market connections. Economies of scope, as well as complementarities, are important drivers of concentration in digital markets. Section 4.2 explains in more detail why platform monopolies generally cannot be viewed as the result of economies of scale alone: most platforms consist of an on-platform bundle, which is falsely viewed as a single service. The effects of economies of scope on cross-market concentration have been underassessed in decisional practices and literature on digital markets but have recently gained more attention with ecosystem theories of competition.[329]

4.2 APPLYING THE THEORY OF NATURAL MONOPOLY TO DIGITAL PLATFORM MARKETS

Digital markets and competition between digital firms show parallels with competition in network industries, and both types of industries also exhibit similar economic characteristics. Bottleneck markets in non-digital network industries are often regulated on the basis of the idea that these markets exhibit natural monopoly.[330] This section aims to answer the question if the same logic applies to the regulation of digital platform markets. Digital platforms fulfil a similar function as infrastructure does in non-digital markets: platforms allow for the provision of services by a vertically integrated undertaking as well as its competitors, they serve as an input for the production of outputs at the service level and often exhibit high levels of concentration.[331] The Digital Markets Act, which aims to promote contestability and competition *for* markets, rather than competition *in* the market, seems to be based implicitly on the idea that high levels of concentration (or even monopoly) are unavoidable outcomes of competition between digital platforms.

329 Van den Boom and Samranchit (n 148); Jasper van den Boom, 'Incumbent or Challenger? – Assessing Ecosystem Competition in the DMA' (2024) 20 Journal of Competition Law & Economics 409; Lianos, Eller and Kleinschmitt (n 122); Paul Heidhues, Mats Köster and Botond Kőszegi, 'A Theory of Digital Ecosystems' [2024] SSRN Electronic Journal <www.ssrn.com/abstract=4991830> accessed 13 December 2024; Hein and others (n 37): Van den Boom and Samranchit, for instance, found that the European Commission has hardly considered economies of scope and complementarities explicitly in merger decisions related to digital platforms up until 2021. The General Court first provided a clear definition for ecosystems in the Google Android judgement, Case T-604/18, Google v. Commission, [2022] ECLI:EU:T:2022:541, 104–105.

330 Posner (n 209); Joskow (n 10); Decker (n 10); den Hertog (n 15); Grossman and Cole (n 310).

331 Ducci (n 11).

This section applies the theory of natural monopoly to digital platforms, as to provide an in-depth analysis of the similarities and difference between core network activities in non-digital markets (i.e. bottleneck markets with natural monopoly) and core platform services in the digital network (i.e. highly concentrated digital platform markets that constitute an important gateway for business users to reach end users). The main findings of this section are that digital platform markets exhibit economic characteristics that lead to self-reinforcing dominance and structural competition problems. In some instances, it can be argued that natural monopoly may exist. However, digital markets are still very different from non-digital markets: the cost distribution, causes of concentration, and the overall effects on competition are different. It is not evident that similar regulation is suitable for both digital and non-digital monopolies.

4.2.1 *The Single-Output Perspective on Digital Platform Monopolies*

In 1998, Varian argued that software was a textbook example of a naturally monopolistic cost distribution: the largest share of the costs is incurred in the product development phase (fixed costs) and marginal costs of copying and transporting the goods are zero or near-zero (economies of scale). However, while there was concentration in the market for operating systems in the late 1990s and early 2000s with the emergence of Microsoft's Windows OS, there was no indication that the market for software was not competitive. In fact, Varian argued that there was aggressive competition to become the biggest software provider.[332]

At that time, IBM was just overtaken by Windows as the most popular provider of operating systems.[333] In the early 2000s, competition in digital markets was indeed intense: AltaVista lost its dominant position to Google, and the incumbent Myspace lost its dominant position to Facebook.[334] While the incumbency AltaVista and Myspace were short-lived, the dominant positions held by Google and Facebook have proven significantly more durable.

The analysis of natural monopoly in digital markets can begin by looking at the fixed costs associated with digital platforms. The development of digital products does require an undertaking to incur significant sunk costs. This may lead to high barriers to entry, as investments cannot be recouped and there may be risks involved in developing a new software product.[335] The costs of developing a digital platform

332 Varian (n 21).

333 Timothy Bresnahan, Shane Greenstein and Rebecca M Henderson, 'Schumpeterian Competition and Diseconomies of Scope: Illustrations from the Histories of Microsoft and IBM', *The Rate and Direction of Inventive Activity Revisited* (National Bureau of Economic Research, Inc 2011).

334 See Rebecca Greenfield, 'What the Web Looked Like before Google' *The Atlantic* (27 September 2013); Competition & Market Authority (n 69) 132–133.

335 Varian (n 21); John M Newman and others, 'Antitrust in Digital Markets' (2019) 72 Vanderbilt Law Review 1497.

that is required to supply digital intermediation services are also significant, barriers to entry in these markets are likely even higher than in single-sided software products, as the digital undertaking must invest in overcoming the chicken-and-egg problem and develop the most attractive offer to do so.[336]

A digital platform may be started with relatively low costs. For instance, Google's search platform was developed on the basis of four funding rounds totalling USD 26.1 million.[337] This allowed Google to become dominant in the market for horizontal search prior to its Initial Public Offering in 2004. The costs to build a search engine that would be able to compete efficiently with Google now would require a significantly higher upfront investment. This is exemplified by Microsoft's submission in the Microsoft/Yahoo merger[338]:

> Barriers to entry into this market appear to be high and include, among others, hardware, cost of indexing the web, human capital, cost of developing and updating the algorithm and IP patents. Microsoft estimates that the capital expenditure required to enter the market is approximately USD 1 000 million in hardware and USD 1 000 million in human capital. On top of that, Microsoft estimates that a new entrant would have to spend several billions of dollars to develop and update the algorithm. Finally, Microsoft explains that there are very significant costs that a new entrant would have to bear related to the necessity to have a large database.

Aside from upfront investments, fixed costs must be incurred periodically to grow the network and ensure it remains efficient. An example can be found in the datacentres established by Google. In its early years, Google's service provision relied on 112 servers that Google founders Brin and Page had built from cheap materials. By 2014, Google had spent an estimated $5 billion on the construction and operation of its data centres, out of which an estimated $2.82 billion are reoccurring fixed costs for the operation of the servers.[339] Google has continued to expand by building data centres in multiple US states and EU Member States, such as Canada, Japan, Singapore, Brazil, Australia, and Taiwan. The amounts that Google invests in the expansion of its datacentres remains substantial, with an exemplary $1.8 billion investment in its Oregon site, $773 million in a datacentre in Eemshaven the Netherlands, and a $2 billion investment in its Oklahoma site. The total capital expenditures in 2016 (during these datacentre expansions) were just under $10.2 billion, of which most can be accounted for by its datacentres and land acquisition.[340]

336 Caillaud and Jullien (n 62); Tiwana (n 34); Hein and others (n 37).

337 Google, *Google receives 25 million in equity funding*, Press release of 7 June 1999 <https://googlepress.blogspot.com/1999/06/google-receives-25-million-in-equity.html>; Crunchbase, 'List of Google's 4 Funding Rounds Totaling $26.1M' (online, 2000) <www.crunchbase.com/search/funding_rounds/field/organisations/funding_total/google> accessed 16 December 2022.

338 Microsoft/Yahoo (Case M.5727), Commission Decision C(2010) 1077 [2010], OJ C 95/1, para 111.

339 Yevgeniy Sverdlik, 'Google: From 112 Servers to a $5B-Plus Quarterly Data Center Bill' *Datacenter Knowledge* (23 July 2014).

340 Datacenter Knowledge, 'Google Data Center FAQ, Part 2' (26 August 2008).

This demonstrates that the fixed costs required to compete with a mature platform and ecosystem operator are significantly higher than competing in an emerging market. This gives insight into a one driver of self-reinforcing incumbency: as the more mature digital network grows in scale, higher upfront investments are required to compete with it. The risk that the novel platform fails is relatively high: digital platform markets are often characterized by competition for the market, rather than competition on the market. If the platform fails to become dominant, it will likely leave the market.[341] Thus, the larger the platform becomes, the higher the barriers to entry. At some point, entry into these markets may become blockaded.[342]

Sunk costs are however not the main driver of natural monopoly in digital markets.[343] While there is a cost distribution with high fixed costs and low marginal costs for digital platforms, early platforms were not naturally monopolistic and their dominance often was not durable. The fixed costs associated with the development of digital platforms are also not nearly as high as those required to develop traditional physical network infrastructures. Examples can be found in telecommunications: in the US, the creation of a telecoms network has been a long and arduous process in the United States, where it took AT&T and a number of independent telecommunications operators several decades to create the lines that spanned the entirety of the territory.[344] In the EU, the development of telecommunications infrastructures was a prerogative of the state and funded by public money. Even currently, the roll-out of a 5G network for telecommunications is marked by co-operation between public and private entities to ensure that such a network can be financed.[345]

Concentration is so prevalent in digital markets for a multitude of reasons: the stickiness of modern platforms' dominance is driven by a specific form of increasing returns to scale in the provision of data-driven digital services: increasing returns to adoption.[346] Due to the role of the platform as a coordinator of

341 Brynjolfsson, Hu and Smith (n 206); Hein and others (n 37); Digital Competition Expert Panel (n 1); Crémer, De Montjoye and Schweitzer (n 4); Zingales and others (n 1).

342 Ezrachi and Stucke (n 3) argue that the value of the entire ecosystem operated by digital undertakings is greater than the sum of its parts. This means that the larger and more established the ecosystem, the more sunk costs are required to provide something of equal or greater value. Even if a new undertaking could match the existing ecosystem product for product, the absence of an established multi-actor ecosystem and data flows would still not allow the entrant to match the value proposition of the incumbent ecosystem.

343 See the analyses by Ducci (n 11); Hovenkamp (n 26) on the existence of natural monopoly in digital markets.

344 See Tim Wu, *The Master Switch: The Rise and Fall of Information Empires* (Alfred A Knopf 2011); Mueller (n 195).

345 It is estimated that telecom providers in the US alone will have to invest $275 billion to develop a nationwide 5G network, see Accenture, 'Tackling the Costs of a 5G Build' (3 August 2018).

346 Nicolas Petit, *Big Tech and the Digital Economy: The Moligopoly Scenario* (1st edn, Oxford University Press 2020) also refers to increasing returns to adoption and describes it as a scenario where output can grow unconstrained and describes how output may be grown strategically to keep out competitors. This book adds a dimension to the increasing returns to adoption associated with digital platforms that leads to supply-side efficiencies related to growing output. See also Cozzolino, Corbo and Aversa

fragmented assets and geographically distributed demand, combined with direct, indirect, and data-driven network externalities, the platform becomes more cost efficient as it becomes adopted by more users. In other words, increased demand creates supply-side efficiencies. Monopolization is demand-induced, but the effects of increased demand are not limited to the demand-side. Instead, platforms with a large userbase will enjoy increases in supply-side efficiencies. Several feedback loops contribute to the prominence of demand-induced monopolization in digital platform markets.[347]

The first feedback loop exists due to the role of the platform as intermediary and the large reach of platforms give rise to strong direct and/or indirect network externalities. Adoption on one side of the market has positive effects on demand on the same and/or other side(s) of the market. Digital networks are often far vaster than non-digital networks, both in terms of geographic range and user numbers. The WhatsApp communications network is more expansive than the network of any traditional telecoms provider.[348] Other digital networks, including social media, operating systems and e-commerce, are most often (near-)global as well.[349] Digital platforms are also likely to intermediate between more groups of users than traditional network industries and are more dependent on user participation. Social media networks are driven by user-generated content. This content drives engagement by different user groups and is free for the platform operator. This gives rise to a new range of interactions that it can facilitate. As a consequence, the value of the platform – as perceived by a participant in its digital network – grows significantly with additional users. This feedback loop related to network externalities has often been associated with the tipping of digital platform markets in the favour of one incumbent.[350]

Due to the role of the digital platform as an intermediary and coordinator of fragmented assets, the increase of users on any side of the market also leads to supply-side efficiencies. This is the second feedback loop: demand-induced supply side efficiencies. As the platform matches externally produced goods and services, rather than producing them themselves, the only 'product' supplied by the platform is intermediation. An increase in participation in its downstream market raises the value and efficiency of its intermediation service.[351] One can observe this in ride-hailing platforms, for instance, having additional drivers leads to actual supply-side

(n 74); Andrew Shipilov and Annabelle Gawer, 'Integrating Research on Interorganisational Networks and Ecosystems' (2020) 14 Academy of Management Annals 92.

347 Damien Geradin, 'What Should EU Competition Policy Do to Address the Concerns Raised by the Digital Platforms' Market Power?' (2018) DP 2018-041 TILEC Discussion Paper.

348 Montero and others (n 18).

349 Kenney and Zysman (n 57); Evans and Gawer (n 98); Montero and others (n 18).

350 Crémer, De Montjoye and Schweitzer (n 4); Zingales and others (n 1); Digital Competition Expert Panel (n 1); Jenny (n 14); Subcommittee on Antitrust (n 1); Lancieri and Sakowski (n 1).

351 Anderson (n 28); Brynjolfsson, Hu and Smith (n 206); Brynjolfsson, Hu and Smith (n 215).

efficiencies: more consumer choice, decreased waiting times, and additional opportunities for the platform to spread out its fixed costs over more rides. For business users – the drivers – the platform becomes more efficient as they have access to more rides, perhaps in closer proximity. Ducci also observes these benefits of having a larger network but attributes the concentration mostly to increased network externalities. This work argues that while it is true that parties on both sides of the market experience this as a result of network externalities, the faster and better intermediation constitutes a supply-side efficiency from the perspective of the platform operator.[352] The participants on one side of the network are the inputs for intermediation, while the outputs are the results of the intermediation by the platform. In line with the definition of increasing returns to scale: any additional participation on one side of the network leads to a disproportional increase in outputs (intermediations or matches), creating increasing returns to scale.[353]

The third feedback loop exists due to data-driven economies of scale and data-driven network externalities, which again strengthens the increasing returns to adoption from the first and second feedback loops. The addition of each new user does not generate value just through the new potential connection it delivers but also due to the data it creates with each interaction.[354] As this data can be used for the improvement of the quality of the intermediation service provided by the digital undertaking, there are increased cost-saving efficiencies associated with having the largest network. This gives rise to a feedback loop that works in the opposite way as the one previously discussed: each output (intermediated interaction) provided by the undertaking generates user data which serves as an input for providing its intermediation service.[355]

These three concurrent feedback loops lead to a self-reinforcing dominance for the largest platform: the larger it becomes, the higher the fixed costs to duplicate it; the more users it gathers, the better it becomes at intermediating and the more intermediating it does, the more data it collects to improve its intermediary services (Figure 4.1). These efficiency gains raise the fixed costs of duplicating the network, continuing the cycle.

Drivers and Limitations of Monopolisation in Digital Platforms

While the operation of a digital platform exhibits a strong self-reinforcing feedback loop, it is not evident that this means that platforms should be considered as exhibiting natural monopoly. It is especially unlikely that *all* digital platforms exhibit

[352] Ducci (n 11).

[353] Joskow (n 10); Xing-Zhou Zhang, Jing-Jie Liu and Zhi-Wei Xu, 'Tencent and Facebook Data Validate Metcalfe's Law' (2015) 30 Journal of Computer Science and Technology 246.

[354] Prüfer and Schottmüller (n 249); Geradin, 'What Should EU Competition Policy Do to Address the Concerns Raised by the Digital Platforms' Market Power?' (n 347); Ducci (n 11); Fast, Schnurr and Wohlfarth (n 70); Montero and Finger (n 18).

[355] Prüfer and Schottmüller (n 249) 996–1002; Fast, Schnurr and Wohlfarth (n 70) 204–214.

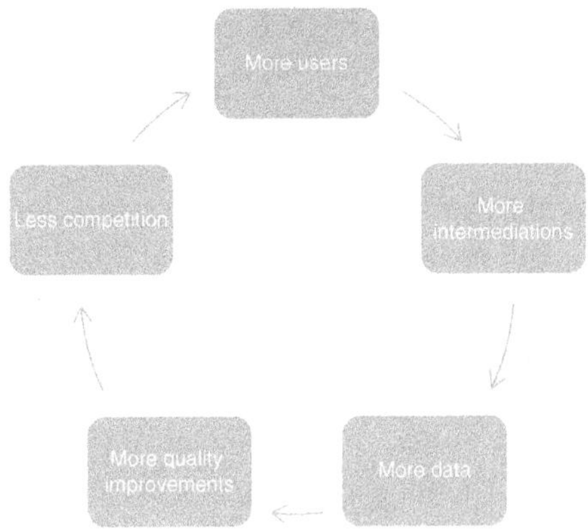

FIGURE 4.1 The feedback loop leading to self-reinforcing dominance in digital platforms

natural monopoly. Just like non-digital networks are different from one another, so are digital platforms. Some are highly data dependent, while others are not. Some are purely digital, while others mix digital and physical goods. On the demand side, some platform markets have homogeneous demand, while others are characterized by heterogeneous demand. Hereunder, the drivers and limitations of monopolization are briefly discussed.

DIGITAL VERSUS PHYSICAL First, there is a difference between purely digital platforms and digital platforms that facilitate the delivery of physical services. While a digital platform generally operates in a network that operates on virtual lines (digital connections), it may still depend on physical nodes to deliver the service (parcel delivery, drivers for ride-hailing apps). This means that unlike services that are delivered both by virtual lines and nodes (web-based intermediaries, apps), physical services have higher marginal costs and that these networks may face issues such as congestion problems.[356] There are variables and problems that may create opportunities for entry. It is not evident that it is more efficient to have one firm offer logistics and delivery in a vertically integrated way, competing delivery services can specialize in efficiently offering non-standard delivery services or luxury ride-hailing. Entry is likely to remain feasible.

As the marginal costs and coordination efforts related to providing a physical service are significantly higher, abundance strategies are less sustainable. An app developer incurs a one-time effort and will then be remunerated over time with each download. A driver for a ride-hailing app or a seller on Amazon however will want to be compensated every time they deliver the service. If the reward is

356 Mohammad Nabil Almunawara and Muhammad Ansharib, 'Multi-sided Networks of Digital Platform Ecosystem: The Case of Ride-Hailing in Indonesia' (2020) 30 Asia Pacific Journal of Information Systems.

insufficient, the complementor will likely leave the platform.[357] This again leads to opportunities for entry: a new platform may offer better rewards to riders for a certain period of time to capture a network, or focus on highly profitable segments of the ride-hailing market.

As a consequence of the existence of constraints in the form of higher marginal costs, increased coordination costs and geographical limitations, the supply of services through physical nodes is less likely to be naturally monopolistic on the basis of economies of scale. After all, the networks are likely less geographically vast than in pure software markets, which in turn weakens the feedback loop associated with increasing returns to adoption. Even if the company is (quasi-)global, such as Uber or Amazon, they will have to develop local or regional networks per area. This leaves more room for competition by a local ride-hailing service or e-commerce supplier, which may have better insights into local needs or delivery networks and thereby compete in a cost-efficient manner.

DATA-DEPENDENT VERSUS DATA-INDEPENDENT (OR DATA AGNOSTIC) The data dependency of digital markets differs strongly per platform service. The data dependency of search engines is well established: search engines require user queries and click-data to be finetuned and provide the best results.[358] In fact, any market that requires some form of sortation, recommendation, personalization, or targeting exhibits some level of data dependence.[359] Ad-centric platform businesses are generally particularly data-dependent, as the value proposition of online advertising is largely determined by whether it can target the intended audience.[360]

There are also digital ecosystems where access to data is less important. Undertakings such as Microsoft and Apple, which primarily sell their software and/or hardware directly, do generally not rely on highly personalized services. As these undertakings do not rely on advertising as a primary source of income, they do not need to establish comprehensive user profiles to create value. In these markets, the success of an undertaking is not dependent on its access to data, while it is still strengthened by having an installed base. This does not mean that these platform operators have no use for data at all: access to data may still produce insights into potential product quality improvements or the development of new products.[361] However, the less important access to data is in the continued commercial success of the undertaking, the less pronounced the efficiencies derived from data-driven economies of scale and data-driven network effects in that market. As these efficiency gains are less pronounced, it diminishes the effects of the self-reinforcing data-driven feedback loop.

357 Tiwana (n 34).

358 Argenton and Prufer (n 262); Competition & Market Authority (n 69); Ducci (n 11); Hovenkamp (n 11).

359 Competition & Market Authority (n 69) 255 et seq.

360 Casey Newton, 'How YouTube Perfected the Feed' *The Verge* (30 August 2017).

361 Apple/Shazam (Case M.8788) Commission Decision C(2018) 5748 [2018] OJ C 106/16, para 312 et seq.

AD-CENTRIC OR DEVICE-CENTRIC The size of a platform and the data dependence of the business model may also rely heavily on whether the platform is ad-centric or device-centric. Ad-centric ecosystems have as their objective to build as large networks as possible on the consumer facing side of the market, as to connect the user base on that side of the market with advertising on the other side of the market.[362] This business model means that the efficiencies derived from the self-reinforcing feedback loop may be more pronounced for several reasons.

First, the ad-centric ecosystem may be able to gather a larger user base by providing the service freely to end users. Unlike the device-centric ecosystem – where there is an incentive to convert attention into sales – the supplier of an ad-centric ecosystem will focus on attracting more users and incentivizing them to act more with the network.[363]

Second, as the ad-centric ecosystem is by definition multi-sided, there are often additional sides to these networks. This leads to stronger network externalities as each new user increases the number of possible connections that can be made. In device-centric ecosystems the digital platform likely intermediates between a producer and a buyer, leading to a two-sided market.[364] An ad-centric ecosystem on the other hand will likely connect end users, professional content creators (publishers), and advertisers, as well as potential amateur content creators or other parties.[365] The value of an ad-centric ecosystem is directly determined by its ability to intermediate.[366] While a product-based ecosystem may differentiate itself in terms of price and quality of the goods, the ad-centric ecosystem must supply the product with the highest quality as to retain users on its platform.[367] As such, the increasing returns associated with having more users are stronger in these ecosystems.

Thirdly, as data is a highly important input for ad-centric ecosystem, these markets are more likely to be highly data-dependent, strengthening the efficiency gains from the data-driven feedback loop. In short, ad-centric ecosystems enjoy stronger

362 Competition & Market Authority (n 69) 336.

363 Bourreau (n 28) 4–7.

364 Hein and others (n 100); Rahul Kapoor, 'Ecosystems: Broadening the Locus of Value Creation' (2018) 7 Journal of Organisation Design 12 note that product-based platforms are more likely to employ a business model that is akin to a single-sided strategy, albeit less internalized.

365 Competition & Market Authority (n 69) 117–130; Montero and Finger (n 18).

366 See eg Competition & Market Authority (n 141) for in-depth study of revenue generating activities of ad-centric platforms.

367 The high quality of the product is necessary to convince buyers to adopt the network in early stages of developing the network, but this does not mean the dominant platform has to continue to deliver the highest quality product indefinitely. In OECD, 'Quality Considerations in Digital Zero-Price Markets' (2018) DAF/COMP(2018)14 it is argued that quality can be degraded at a later time when users are locked in into the service; Gal and Rubinfeld (n 29) note that the supplier of a high-quality good can later bundle it with low-quality goods; according to Pinar Akman, 'A Web of Paradoxes: Empirical Evidence on Online Platform Users and Implications for Competition and Regulation in Digital Markets' (2022) 217 Virginia Law and Business Review 1. Consumers are also often incorrect in their assessment of the quality of a product.

increasing returns to adoption, both those that are derived from users as an input for the intermediary service and data-driven network externalities. While data dependency is not directly linked to an ad-centric nature of the ecosystem, it is likely higher in markets that rely on advertisements as these rely more on personalization, customization, and targeting.

USER-GENERATED V. PROFESSIONAL CONTENT The self-reinforcing feedback loop also depends on the level of interactivity required from users, and how user groups are remunerated. A succinct example can be found in the difference between video-sharing platforms or online social networks on one side, and video-on-demand streaming platforms on the other. The first type of platform is highly dependent on content provided by its end users, thus requiring a large network of end users. In order to ensure that amateur content is presented to interested audience, a high level of curation is likely necessary. The better the sharing platform is able to use data, the better its recommendations, and the more value it has for users.

For video-on-demand (VOD) services, curation is still important but less data dependent. A streaming platform will be interested in the consumption behaviour of end users, but its portfolio of available videos is smaller and more likely centred around a number of high quality productions. For these platforms it is likely not viable to host all available content, as it is either too pricey in terms of licensing intellectual property rights or because competing streaming services/video-game marketplaces demand exclusivity from their suppliers or even produce content in a vertically integrated way. The necessity of having a large network of end users exists because it allows the VOD-service to cover its costs but does not intrinsically determine its value.

HOMOGENEOUS V. HETEROGENEOUS DEMAND Markets with differentiated products are less likely to exhibit natural monopoly. The need for such differentiation is largely driven by heterogeneity in demand: users may want products with distinct prices and quality parameters.[368] One user may have high willingness to pay for a product with a more streamlined design and better privacy protection, while another user may prioritize buying the product for a lower price (or even zero price). This difference in user demands may exist between subsegments of end consumers but may also be because undertaking have to serve both residential and commercial customers. This can be exemplified through the considerations of the Commission and the effects of the *Microsoft/Skype*[369] and *Facebook/WhatsApp*[370] mergers. In the latter, it became clear that consumers are likely to choose the largest network that is available for free, in particular when the quality of the product is high. When looking

[368] Hovenkamp (n 11) 1996 et seq.
[369] See Microsoft/Skype (Case M. 6281) Commission Decision C(2011) 7279 [2011], OJ C 268/12.
[370] See Facebook/WhatsApp (Case M.7217), Commission Decision C(2014) 7239 [2014] OJ C.

at *Microsoft/Skype* however, the Commission rightfully notes that enterprises are not likely to adopt a 'first-best' attitude towards professional communication software.[371]

The existence of heterogeneous demand may allow entrant platforms to attract users as to overcome the chicken-and-egg problem even when there is already an established incumbent, as the entrant can try to appeal to niche demand that is not well served by existing incumbents. One can think of dating apps or social networks: gay dating apps, dating apps for people with children, or based on certain interests allow for experimentation and ultimately expansion. Different types of social networks can focus on different types of social interactions, be it based on a social graph or communities based on shared interests, or different forms of communication. Whatever the reason may be for heterogeneous demand, it may prevent the emergence of a natural monopoly in the single-product context.[372] For natural monopoly in digital networks – which relies on the aggregation of all demand on a single platform as to maximize efficiencies – the existence of concurrent standards may be sustainable.

A Single-Output Perspective on Monopolisation

Digital platforms are subject to self-reinforcing dominance, but to varying degrees. When looking at concentration on the basis of economies of scale, it is possible that some platforms exhibit natural monopoly. This argument has been made in the market for horizontal search, which is characterized by its nature as a purely digital, highly data-dependent, and generally ad-centric service. Moreover, demand for horizontal search is homogeneous: users want a broad range of potentially applicable outcomes. For more specialized search, there are separate platforms or functions that perform vertical search. Finally, horizontal search simply crawls the web for content supplied by others, without having to negotiate copyright or remuneration for linking to that service. It is due to these characteristics that concentration in horizontal search is particularly strong.

Looking at the self-reinforcing dominance of certain platforms in light of the identified drivers and limitations helps to determine how strong the self-reinforcing feedback loop is: video-sharing services such as YouTube demonstrate similar characteristics as horizontal search, albeit that the generated content must be specifically suitable for the platform. Social media platforms are purely digital and data-dependent but will see more heterogeneity in demand. Ride-hailing apps require the provision of physical services, limiting the size of the network. At the same time, these business models experience significant data-driven efficiencies. The likelihood and durability of monopolization depends on how these characteristics are mixed and matched: services like horizontal search that encompass only drivers of monopolization may naturally result in global monopolies, while services that also experience limitations are less likely to lead to durable monopolies. To assess whether natural monopoly exists, one should

371 See eg Van den Boom and Samranchit (n 148).

372 Hovenkamp (n 11) 1996–2024.

first look at the cost distribution (i.e. how high are the fixed costs and how strong are increasing returns to scale) and then see if there are limiting factors that allow for competition or create geographical or numerical limitations to monopolization.

4.2.2 *The Multi-output Perspective on Digital Platform Monopolies*

Adopting a multi-output perspective allows for a detailed look at the services offered through a singular platform and allows one to take into account the effects associated with economies of scope and complementarity. Complementarity is an important driver of demand and thereby plays an important role in the self-reinforcing feedback loop: more demand leads to more interaction, which leads to more data, which leads to better services.[373] These better services are – at least in part – the result of economies of scope: the reuse of shared inputs and complementary processes, the presence of co-products such as data, and the economies of scope associated with data-processing and multi-sidedness, lead to high levels of cost complementarity in jointly producing and offering digital goods through a single platform.[374]

The idea that a platform is the technology used to supply multiple outputs comes naturally. After all, the platform is – by its very nature – multi-sided. Due to this multi-sided nature, any platform offers distinct outputs to different sides of the same market. Hereunder, the market for horizontal search on the Google Search platform shows that it offers an interrelated search service on the consumer-facing side of the market and targeted advertisements on the advertiser-facing side of the market (Figure 4.2).

There are economies of scope when offering both search and advertising on the same platform. After all, the platform and the infrastructures for data collection and processing serve as a shared input for the provision of both the search service and the advertising service. The same data that can be used to improve and personalize search results and also to improve targeted advertising. Offering these services jointly on the same infrastructure leads to cost-saving efficiencies in the collection and processing of the data as well as in improving the quality of the delivered services.[375]

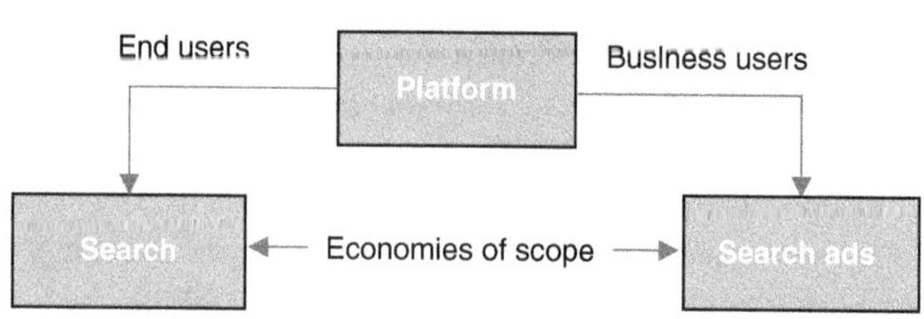

FIGURE 4.2 A simplified version of economies of scope in digital platform markets

[373] Prüfer and Schottmüller (n 266) 967 et seq.
[374] See eg Van den Boom and Samranchit (n 148).
[375] cf Junqué de Fortuny, Martens and Provost (n 244); Duch-Brown (n 297); Fast, Schnurr and Wohlfarth (n 70).

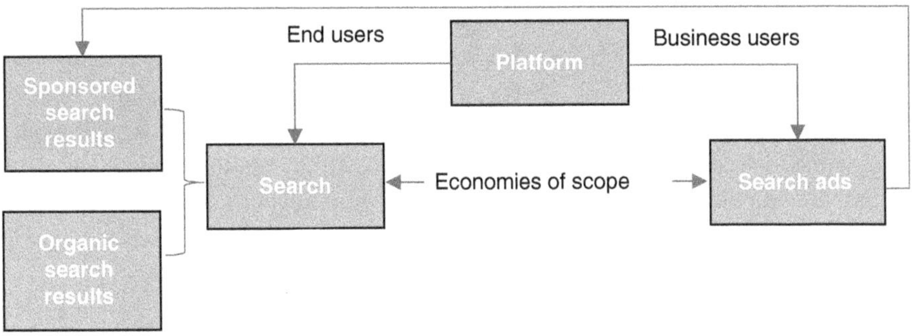

FIGURE 4.3 The multiple outputs in ad-centric horizontal search

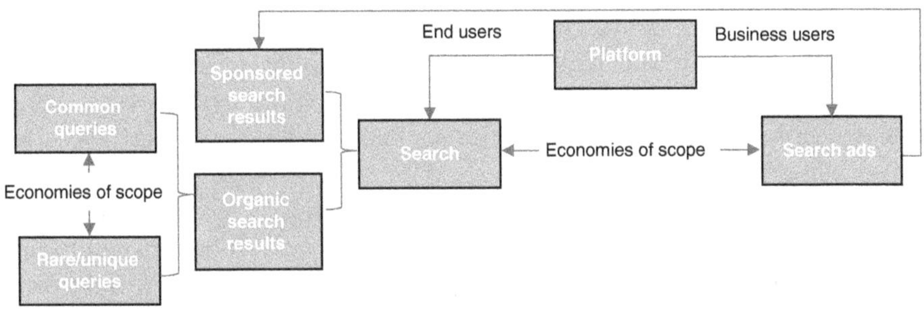

FIGURE 4.4 The economies of scope between different sides of the market and outputs on the consumer side

The joint provision of these services also leads to the supply of multiple outputs on the consumer facing side of the market. Search advertising happens by including sponsored results together with organic search results on the same page. Thus, in an ad-centric platform that provides search, the platform inherently produces two outputs: sponsored and organic search results (Figure 4.3).[376]

Further distinctions between outputs can be made still. The leading search engine can set itself apart by its better ability to answer rare or unique search queries.[377] It is expected that a horizontal search engine answers all common search queries. However, the quality of the search engine is ultimately determined by its ability to deliver answers to rare or unique search queries. Only by having access to enough search query data and click-data is the platform able to train its algorithm to infer what results are sought by users that enter unique searches (Figure 4.4).

The view on platform offerings can be expanded by looking at the clusters of products offered jointly on the platform. A more complex view of the multiple outputs

[376] Ducci (n 11). argues that there are three types of search results: organic, sponsored and self-preferential. For the sake of clarity this book will view self-preferential as sponsored, and sponsored can be understood as non-organic search results for the sake of this analysis.

[377] See Argenton and Prufer (n 262).

shows that Google Search is a platform that consists not only of horizontal search but also vertical search (Google Shopping) and review and recommendation services (i.e. Google Review and Google Maps) are bundled into horizontal search. This shows the economies of scope derived from the modularity of digital goods. Technologies used for horizontal search may be useful in creating efficient vertical search technologies as well, and reviews and recommendations services be efficient in determining what users are looking for with their horizontal and vertical search queries and determine levels of quality for the search results.

On the advertising side, having technologies and databases that make targeted advertising in search advertising markets more efficient may also help display advertising and vice versa. Having insight into user responses in both types of advertising creates a better understanding of the interests of users and how to convert advertisements into sales.

Moreover, there are economies of scope between the two sides of the market. One example is how technologies and know-how from display advertising may make the comparison-shopping service more attractive. These types of spill overs create economies of scope derived from the modular design of digital products, as well as data-driven economies of scope (Figure 4.5).[378]

This collection of outputs is associated with the supply of search in an ad-centric ecosystem. The economies of scope and complementarities exhibited in jointly supplying these different services as a 'one-stop-shop' model (on both sides of the market) make the offered cluster of goods more attractive to customers on either side of the market as those offered by competitors that offer only one of these services.

The number of outputs that can be supplied on a single platform's cluster can be expanded by introducing other outputs that are more loosely related to the primary functions of the platform. The platform may choose to include other services such as

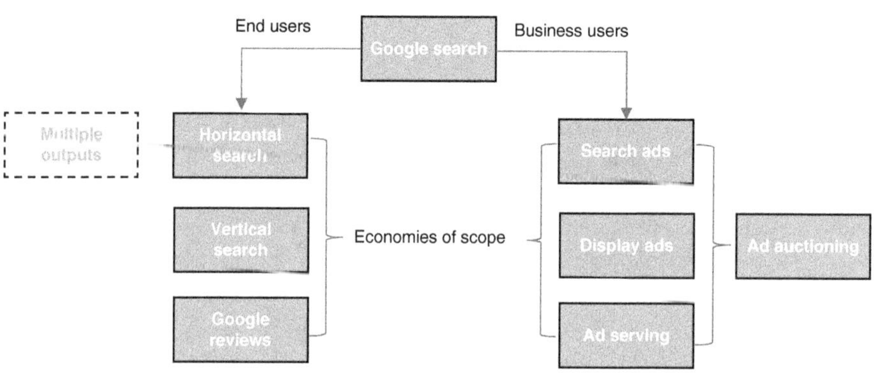

FIGURE 4.5 The extended cluster of search and advertisements offered on the Google Search platform

[378] See Areeda and Hovenkamp (n 162); Hovenkamp (n 11).

navigation- and location-based search (Google Maps), search for videos (YouTube), search for Apps (Play Store), and so forth.

Google's multi-product ecosystem expands far beyond these services and beyond search-based services and has the potential to span dozens or hundreds of markets. In fact, when a user accesses the Google search page now, the search page presents the user with a drop-down menu where a plethora of other Google services can be accessed using the horizontal search page as a gateway, these range from links to YouTube, the Play Store, Google News, shopping comparison services, your personal Google Drive for file storage, your photos, Google's text processing software, educational software, and so on.

Meanwhile, with each horizontal search result, Google includes a basic description of the service, comparisons, reviews, and sponsored links to other comparison services. This shows that – while a cluster can be delineated – the operator of a multi-product ecosystem can use its platform to either cluster a series of goods on platform or provide a gateway into its wider multi-product ecosystem. While these markets may not be part of the cluster and ecosystem linkages may be weaker, it is likely that many spill-overs and cost-saving economies of scope exist for which it is difficult to determine their exact effects. It is however clear that the development of a multi-product ecosystem strengthens the incumbent's position in the dominated markets and its multi-actor ecosystems (Figure 4.6).

The informational and modular nature of digital goods, and the role of the platform as a stable core from where on-platform or cross-platform expansion is a natural process, creates distinct self-reinforcing effects.

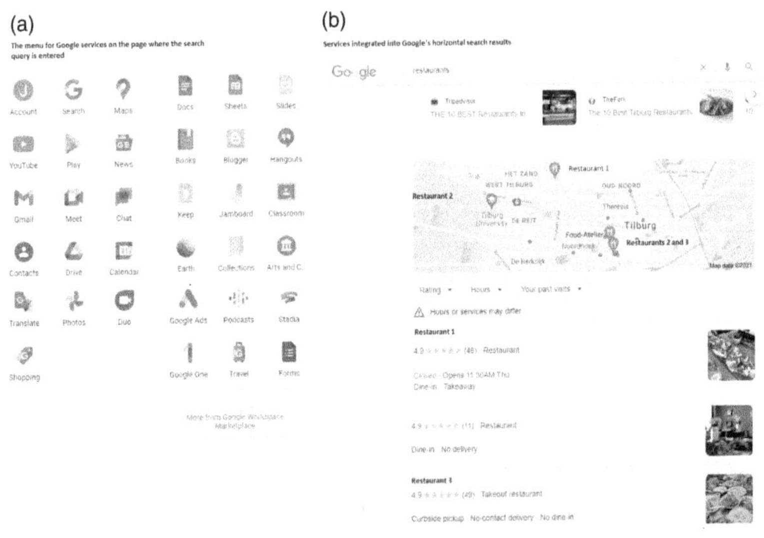

FIGURE 4.6 (a) Google Search query page as a gateway for its product ecosystem and (b) Google's inclusion of different loosely related outputs into its horizontal search results

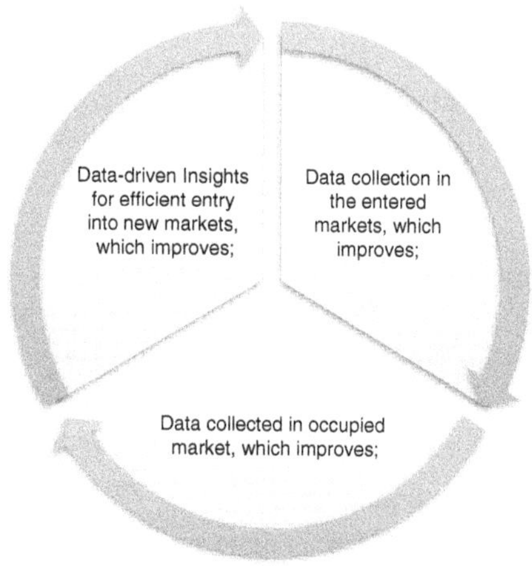

FIGURE 4.7 The feedback loop associated with data-driven economies of scope

First, the presence of economies of scope and complementarity between the multiple outputs offered through digital platforms strengthens the feedback loop described in Section 4.2.1, as they contribute to both increases in demand- and supply-side efficiencies.

Second, economies of scope, complementarity, and the process of expansion through new modules create natural incentives for cross-market expansion. Activity in one digital market creates three types of resources that can be reused and/or leveraged into entry into new markets: (i) modules, (ii) users, and (iii) data. The digital firm produces new products and services that may be used for on-platform expansion or cross-platform expansion. Cross-platform expansion is facilitated if the firm can steer its users from its existing platforms and products towards its new platforms and products. At the same time, launching new platforms and products allows the firm to attract new users that can be leveraged back to its existing services. Similarly, data obtained through existing platforms and modules may show opportunities for entry into new markets, and data collected from a variety of platforms and products may help to create quality improvement or cost-saving efficiencies in the existing offering of the firm.

The feedback loop is bidirectional: dominance in the platform market supports cross-market expansion and cross-market expansion strengthens dominance in the platform market (Figure 4.7). This second feedback loop feeds into the first, identified in Section 4.2.1.

4.3 PLATFORM MONOPOLY AND ITS ROLE IN ECOSYSTEMS: NATURAL OR ARTIFICIAL?

There is a case to be made for the classification of digital platforms as exhibiting natural monopoly, or at least similar characteristics as natural monopoly markets in non-digital network industries. A cost distribution with relatively high fixed costs and sunk costs and low marginal costs, increasing returns to scale and scope, and the existence of data-driven network externalities and efficiencies are structural causes of concentration. Moreover, concentration within a platform market – and even across markets – is associated with an actual increase in efficiencies in the form of cost savings or quality improvements.[379]

There are however limitations, not all platforms should be considered natural monopoly, and in many instances competition should be possible and efficient. Competition is also observed in practice: there are competing Operating Systems, social media networks, and online marketplaces. However, competition often happens by offering differentiated products, which are embedded in differentiated multi-product ecosystems. This makes it hard to discern whether they should be viewed as separate markets, both practically and for the sake of competition law. In *Google Android*, the Commission argues that there is a distinct market for licensable mobile OS (Android) and non-licensable mobile OS (iOS). This way, both undertakings have a monopoly in their own market, and the abuse of dominance provision can be applied. If looked at digital product markets like this – where each differentiated product constitutes its own market – one could classify a number of markets as natural monopoly.[380] In practice, competition in digital markets is more intense than one would suspect if there was a clear case of natural monopoly. This type of competition is however often described as indirect or nascent: competition is not between to substitutable services, but innovation in one service may lead to competition or contestation of the monopoly of its competitor.[381] This is likely a more realistic view of competitive pressures in digital markets: digital platform markets are governed by strong self-reinforcing feedback loops that cause monopoly or dominance, yet this monopoly is less stable than it was in non-digital core network activities.

There is a big difference between digital platforms and infrastructure as found in non-digital network industries. The latter is a natural monopoly because the costs of duplicating the service are prohibitively high, leading competing infrastructures to be cost inefficient. These technologies are – when compared to digital markets – relatively static: while an infrastructure that was once used for voice telephony may

379 See the analysis in Chapters 2 and 3.

380 Case AT.40099, Google Android, Commission Decision of 18 July 2018; see eg Scott Morton F and Van den Boom J, Are competition authorities equipped to combat entrenched digital monopolies? – Lessons from the US and EU antitrust cases against Google, SSRN Electronic Journal on why the distinction between licensable and non-licensable OS is not in tune with market realities. The US Department of Justice treated Apple and google as competitors to establish a monopoly in search; United States of America U.S. Department of Justice, State of Arkansas, State of Florida, State of Georgia, State of Indiana, Commonwealth of Kentucky, State of Louisiana, State of Mississippi, State of Missouri, State of Montana, State of south Carolina, and State of Texas, plaintiffs, v. Google LLC, Defendant, 2020 WL 6152114 ("USDOJ Search Complaint").

381 cf Petit (n 13); Hornung (n 65); Van den boom (n 329).

be updated and reused to supply internet, it is very costly and time consuming to *replace* the entire infrastructure. Consequently, introducing competition in non-digital network industries generally happened at the service level, while the monopoly on infrastructure was left intact. In digital platform markets, monopoly is the result of demand-driven self-reinforcing feedback loops, not because the cost of producing the infrastructure is prohibitively high. Entrants that rely on the infrastructure of incumbents to provide their services have opportunities to build their own infrastructure over time. In fact, some entrants may choose to fully rely on their own infrastructure to offer their services altogether. As digital markets are more dynamic and sunk costs are lower, competition at the infrastructure level *should* be easier to achieve. Barriers to entry at the service level are relatively low, especially if the entrant has access to the infrastructure of incumbents to provide those services. So then, what is the problem with competition in digital markets?

First, it should be acknowledged that opportunities for direct competition with an incumbent platform operator are likely very limited. Due to the existence of feedback loops, incumbent providers of search, e-commerce, social media, or other platforms are more efficient in providing intermediation, have access to more resources, and are able to use those resources more cost efficiently and effectively. An entrant that tries to compete with Google search by offering an exact equivalent is highly likely to fail, as they simply cannot duplicate the efficiencies of scale and scope or the network externalities enjoyed by Google. However, indirect competition remains a possibility. Existing competing suppliers of general search try to differentiate themselves through privacy (DuckDuckGo), sustainability (Ecosia), or marketization-based business models (Brave). Entry at the service level, that is, providing search services, can happen either by relying on the infrastructure provided by Alphabet, which licenses its web-search engine, or by the creation of one's own search engine (Mozilla). The question is then how indirect competition leads to contestability, and why this is so rare.

It is proposed here that persistent competitive problems are the result of vast digital product ecosystems. Here, core platform services act as bottleneck markets, but problems in digital markets are more complex than those observed in non-digital network industries. It is not that competition or contestability is impossible, but rather that entry and attempts at contestability are easily thwarted by the incumbent ecosystem operator. The ecosystem operator acts as the de facto regulator within its segment of the digital network industry. As incumbents hold a central position in the digital network, entrants must interact with one or some of the incumbents' services to gain access to users, entering them into the ecosystem of the incumbent as co-generators of value themselves. The ecosystem operator also has access to vast amounts of information and insights related to the competitive efforts of those that operate in its ecosystem: the ecosystem operator can track user behaviour to see which entrants are successful, which types of users go to these platforms, and how this impacts the incumbent's ecosystems. This allows the incumbent to identify potential threats early and eliminate them (foreclosure) or appropriate them (acquisitions). The ecosystem operator is also likely to have the ability to foreclose entrants through a two-pronged strategy: the first prong is to offer or modify its own services to compete more directly with those offered by the entrant. The incumbent is able to adapt or enter the new market quickly as a result of economies of scope, complementarity and data. The second prong is to use leveraging and steering strategies to steer users away from the platform of the entrant and into its own, draining the entrant of resources.[382]

This is – at its core – the same issue that arises when natural monopoly is present: if the monopolist is allowed to vertically integrate, it can abuse its power as the operator of the infrastructure to foreclose entry or give preference to its own downstream activities. The operation of ecosystems is however more multifaceted and complex than the operation of non-digital infrastructures and therefore harder to regulate. Moreover, there are still more opportunities for contestability in digital markets than there would be in light of a vertically integrated natural monopolist, as digital ecosystems thrive on the participation of third parties and innovation. In short, there are many parallels between non-digital and digital network industries, and the function of core network and core platform activities.

However, there are also important differences in how ecosystem operate and how competition occurs in the fluid and changing digital network. The importance of multi-product ecosystems to carve out a part of the network for oneself creates continued competitive pressure. Large ecosystems consist of a number of markets that encompass a number of platforms where they are often dominant or hold a monopoly. While competition for these markets may not happen directly, competition at the ecosystem level persists. If the lack of competitiveness can indeed be attributed to the power of incumbent ecosystem operators in their network, this would imply that more competition at the level of product ecosystems could limit their ability to abuse their power and create long term competition. After all, it is harder to wield one's power over players of an equivalent size and importance, which are less dependent on the network of the incumbent. Moreover, having competing ecosystems that offer similar (yet possibly differentiated) services provides more choices for end users and business users, mitigating switching costs and issues related to lock-in. Finally, contestation of a monopolized digital platform service may not be possible directly in light of structural causes of concentration, but allowing entrants to develop their platforms and modules over a longer period of time may help them to discover the mix of modules, products, and platforms to ultimately challenge the incumbent platform operator directly.

Competition happens by leveraging one's ecosystem into competition for a market. Leveraging can be used defensively or offensively in ecosystem competition. Incumbents are able to insulate their platforms from competition by leveraging

382 Theories of harm are developed in Chapter 7.

their resources to and from its platforms into its surrounding ecosystems. This further strengthens their platform monopoly and makes contestation harder. At the same time, entrants will try to capture a platform market that indirectly competes with the services offered by incumbent ecosystem operators. Once they have captured their platform market, they can try to expand their multi-product and multi-actor ecosystems to decrease their dependence and increase their resources and efficiency of operation. This offensive use of leveraging and ecosystem expansion may be key to sustainable competition in digital markets.

4.4 CONCLUSION

The emergence of the digital platform has led to traditional network industries to become platformed. This can happen either due to substitution of the traditional network suppliers or by operating on the traditional infrastructure while introducing a new data layer. These markets are characterized by direct and indirect network externalities, as well as economies of scale and scope, which may lead to natural monopoly in certain segments of the market.

The increasing returns to scale in the provision of digital goods through digital platforms are significant, both due to the nature of digital products and the presence of data-driven efficiencies. In some instances, these efficiencies may be strong enough to create subadditivity of a single platform from a single-product perspective. In these markets, fixed costs are lower than in traditional natural monopoly, but there are strong efficiencies associated with an increase in scale due to increasing returns to adoption and data-driven network externalities.

The presence of these phenomena lead to three concurrent feedback loops, which may cause natural monopoly: the more mature a platform is, the higher the required investments to compete, which leads users to aggregate on a smaller number of platforms; the more users are aggregated on the platform, the higher value and more efficient its intermediation service, which leads to more interactions; and the more interactions with the platform, the more data it can collect to make its services more efficient, which raises the required investments to compete with the platform.

When viewed from a single-product perspective, natural monopoly is likely to occur in markets which are highly data-dependent and where demand is homogeneous. The latter makes it easier and more efficient to aggregate all demand on the platform, while the first ensures that this aggregation leads to a greater cost advantage. Moreover, networks that are purely digital may lead to stronger network externalities and efficiencies as they can become global in scale and this leads to efficiencies directly. Digital platform networks that rely on physical nodes to deliver their services may experience hindrances such as transportation or other costs which fragments the network.

Adopting a multi-product perspective may further help one to understand natural monopoly in digital markets. The creation of a multi-output platform strengthens the feedback loops observed in a single-product context: adding more functionalities and products on the platform increases the required investments to compete with it, which attracts more users that interact with the platform for more varied services and in more ways, and this creates more voluminous and varied data, which leads to economies of scope associated with data. The different outputs offered on a single platform are likely cluster markets, as there are economies of joint provision of multiple digital goods and services to the modular design of digital products and the subsequent super modularity between digital goods and the platform. From a multi-product perspective, it is increasingly likely that there is subadditivity of a single platform that offers a range of outputs. These individual outputs may exhibit increasing returns to scale themselves but providing them jointly leads to further efficiencies.

The existence of natural monopolistic platforms does however not preclude the existence of competitive pressures due to the presence of multi-product ecosystems. As the multi-product ecosystems lead to economies of scope between a larger collection of more loosely related products, and ecosystem linkages lead to high complementarity between products even when they are offered and purchased separately, the multi-product ecosystem can be leveraged to compete in a market. This may be used offensively: where the digital platform can foreclose competition in otherwise competitive markets, or potentially try to compete with naturally monopolistic platforms. Alternatively, the multi-product ecosystem can be used defensively to retain market share in markets that could be considered natural monopoly markets: absent the leveraging of the ecosystem, the market would likely choose one winner as this system is the most efficient, but by creating strong ecosystem linkages, the ecosystem can protect its platform from envelopment. This chapter has made an argument that the existence of competitive harms may be related to the existence of a small group of incumbents, which dominates a large part of the digital network industry. Empowering entrants to develop their own multi-product ecosystem may allow competition at the ecosystem level to emerge, which may ultimately lead to competition for core markets or disruption of existing business models.

PART II

The Dynamics of Competition between Digital Ecosystems

This second part of the book looks at how competition in- and between digital ecosystems take place. The main contribution of this part is the development of a concept of ecosystem power, an analysis of competitive strategies, and the identification of four stages of ecosystem competition: (i) launch, (ii) expansion, (iii) maturity, and (iv) incumbency.

This part concludes with the idea that harms to competition arise when the network industry is characterized by stage 4 ecosystem competition. Here, a small group of large incumbent ecosystem operators covers a large part of the network industry. These incumbents have incentives to focus on pre-empting entry and suppressing or absorbing disruptive innovation, rather than competing intensely with one another. Their incumbency across different platform markets and related product markets also provides them with the ability to do so, as their position, power over processes, resources, and ability to monitor entry provide them with control over access points into the digital network and the ability to pre-empt competitive entry.

5

Modalities of Ecosystem Competition

Competition between ecosystems is a novel type of competition found in the digital network industry. There are elements of ecosystem competition that are akin to competition between systems, but ecosystem competition is more complex as it also entails competition within the ecosystem itself. Complementors compete with one another atop platforms, and platform operators can vertically integrate and compete in upstream or downstream markets. The nature of digital products, as well as the presence of data, leads to expansion of digital firms across markets that are horizontally, vertically, and diagonally related. The idea of ecosystems helps to capture the complex interactions between and dynamics of this new type of industrial organization.

This chapter explains how ecosystem competition happens between varying parties and at different levels and the role of the platform in shaping ecosystem competition (Section 5.1). Section 5.2 explores how operators of digital ecosystems use differentiation to escape intense competition and find an equilibrium, which helps them to solidify their position in the digital network. Finally, the notion of ecosystem power is explored and developed. This concept of power provides a counterpart for market power (as related to competition within the market) or gatekeeper power (as relevant for platforms) especially for the ecosystem level (Section 5.3).

5.1 INTER-ECOSYSTEM, INTRA-ECOSYSTEM, AND VERTICAL COMPETITION

There are three types of ecosystem competition: inter-ecosystem, intra-ecosystem, and vertical ecosystem competition. The first refers to competition between multi-product ecosystems, as ecosystem operators try to capture their part of the digital network industry. The second refers to competition within multi-actor ecosystems that compete on a platform and is largely important as a determinant of the value of a platform. Vertical ecosystem competition relates to competition between the ecosystem operator and its complementors in its multi-actor ecosystem, through vertical integration and entry into markets by the platform operator. These three types of competition are interconnected, yet the distinction is helpful to understand who the subjects of competition and competitive pressures are, and which type of potential anti-competitive behaviour may arise.

5.1.1 *Inter-ecosystem Competition*

Inter-ecosystem competition is akin to inter-brand competition: Google versus Apple, Apple versus Microsoft, and so on. Competition happens between the entirety of the Google and Apple ecosystem, including both its multi-actor and multi-product ecosystem, across a range of markets. What sets ecosystem competition apart is its complexity. In inter-brand competition, a consumer may choose between Coca Cola or Pepsi, or one of their many respective soft drinks, substituting one with the other depending on price, quality, or other considerations. In inter-ecosystem competition, consuming products has consequences that permeate across the multi-product and multi-actor ecosystems due to the existence of ecosystem linkages and externalities: interactions with Google Search create data that benefits Google's advertising capabilities, creating value for its advertisers. Data is then reused, and the revenue generated from these advertisements is cross-invested, with potential effects on the quality of Android OS or for the development of a new product such as Google's Artificial Intelligence. These new developments may benefit or harm the third-party complementors that depend on Google's services. Large numbers of interactions or transactions may shape competition in unexpected ways.

Ecosystem operators compete for the attention of end users, business users, and other resources simultaneously, establishing their position in the digital network. Inter-ecosystem interactions are also complicated, as they may compete and cooperate at the same time in different areas: Google and Apple supply competing mobile Operating Systems, yet Google also pays Apple to be the default search engine on Apple devices.[383] Meta is dependent on Google to supply Instagram, Facebook and WhatsApp to Android users, but competes with Google in the market for display advertising. Ecosystem interactions can roughly be divided into three categories: direct competition, indirect competition, or collaboration.

Direct competition happens horizontally and implies substitutability between the products. One Operating System versus another or one web browser versus another are some examples. This type of competition is closest to inter-brand competition as we see it in one-sided markets: end users or business users can substitute the product of one brand for the product of the other. Direct competition does happen, but mostly happens at the outer boundaries of the ecosystem, especially when it involves large ecosystem operators. When a new technology emerges, such as (at the time) smartphones, digital voice assistants, or artificial intelligence, large ecosystem operators tend to enter this market and compete intensely until a standard emerges. Afterwards, some will leave the market or significantly reduce their

[383] See USDOJ Search Complaint (n 381).

investments, while others differentiate their products and compete indirectly (or not intensely).[384] Microsoft has exited the market for smartphone and related Operating Systems, Alexa has emerged as the most popular voice assistant, and the outcome of the race for AI products is yet to be seen. Where two incumbents remain within a single market, they often differentiate their services and the orientation of their ecosystem: one offers high-end products and the other focuses on reducing costs, one is device-centric and the other ad-centric, and so forth. Smaller platform or ecosystem operators may try to compete directly as well: Ecosia, DuckDuckGo, and Brave have entered into competition with Alphabet in the market for horizontal search, and Snapchat and TikTok compete with Meta in the market for social media.

Secondly, competition may occur indirectly between digital cluster markets and in the markets that are adjacent to the cluster. By establishing strong ecosystem linkages between the on-platform cluster and other platforms or products offered by the platform, the ecosystem operator can raise its value proposition by creating new expectations for consumers and user synergies.[385] By adding value to its product ecosystem, the ecosystem operator is able to compete over the same userbase by offering products that are not direct substitutes for one another. For instance, one could say that the Apple Watch and an Android smartphone do not compete directly with one another as users will not deem them substitutable. However, a user that wants to use the Apple Watch will be incentivized to also choose the iPhone and iOS, as there are strong ecosystem linkages between Apple's handheld and wearables.

Indirect competition by establishing ecosystem linkages is important in digital ecosystem markets as it allows the ecosystem operator to leverage its user base from one product or platform to another, allowing it to compete with the ecosystem in its entirety rather than in single-product markets. Examples can be found in competition between Amazon and Netflix. Amazon has tied its Prime Video into the broader Prime subscription package, so that users that subscribe to Prime for other services also gain access to its video platform. This allows Amazon to enter into competition with Netflix without having to offer a platform of equal value, attracting users through the use of an abundance strategy and by giving away Prime Video for those who subscribe to its ecosystem through Prime.[386]

Finally, there are collaboration and coopetition.[387] The value of the platform and product ecosystem is largely dependent on products from its complementors, these

[384] Tiwana (n 34), ch 2, calls this competition for the dominant design.

[385] cf Tiwana (n 34); Jacobides and Lianos (n 12); Mandrescu (n 12); Van den Boom and Samranchit (n 148).

[386] See Amazon's official website: <Amazon.com> Digital Services & Content > Prime Video > Setting up > Is Prime Video Included with Amazon Prime? Here it is explained that all types of memberships provide access to Prime Video, see also Josh Wilson, 'How Amazon Video's ECommerce Approach Is Giving Them an Edge in the Streaming Industry' *Forbes* (29 August 2022).

[387] Barry Nalebuff and Adam Brandeburger, *Co-Opetition* (Profile Publishers 1997); Maxime C Cohen and Renyu Zhang, 'Competition and Coopetition for Two-Sided Platforms' (2022) 31 Production and Operations Management 1997.

complementors may also be competitors or competing ecosystems. There are small complementors, such as indie app developers or SMEs that sell on Amazon, and there are large complementors. Meta is a complementor to both Apple and Android, offering their social media on their Operating Systems. This makes Meta partially dependent on Apple or Android as providing the infrastructure for its ecosystem, as they act as Meta's *ecosystem carrier*. However, this dependence is still limited due to inter-ecosystem competition between Apple and Google: if Android does allow users to access Instagram and Facebook, and iOS refuses to have Meta apps on the iPhone, many users will likely switch to Android because they experience social media as a 'must have'. Meta works as an *ecosystem amplifier*: an OS that allows users to use Meta's social media services is simply more valuable to most users than an OS that does not. This does not mean that there is no competition in other markets, but the inherent cooperation between ecosystem operators does lead to a coopetition as the norm: compete in one market and cooperate in another. For smaller entrants that offer services that are not considered must-haves, the risks of exclusion are greater. Incumbent ecosystem operators provide them access to resources and markets, by offering access to their platform and associated modules, but can also change their terms, enter into competition, or revoke access to the detriment of its complementors. These issues are related to competition within the ecosystem.

5.1.2 *Intra-ecosystem Competition*

Intra-ecosystem competition specifically refers to competition between the complementors that are active on a platform, not between complementors and the operator of the platform.[388] By competing with one another, complementors generate value for themselves and the platform operator. The presence of intra-ecosystem competition is an important factor in value generation for the platform operator: having more complement developers often makes the platform more valuable for end users,[389] and a healthy degree of competition may lead to associated benefits as the complement developers compete by offering their services at lower prices or higher quality or by offering more innovative products. For instance, Uber drivers will ensure that they have a high level of customer satisfaction, as bad reviews may cause the algorithm to favour competing drivers. This results in a higher quality service for users.[390]

[388] Bourreau (n 28); Crane (n 17); Jacobides and Lianos (n 12) 1201–1208.

[389] Hein and others (n 37) 89 attribute this to super modularity. It must be noted that it is doubtful whether advertisers contribute to the value of the platform, outside of allowing the platform operator to offer the service at a price of zero to end users.

[390] Federal Trade Commission, 'The "Sharing" Economy – Issues Facing Platforms, Participants & Regulators' (2016) discusses the efficiencies of rating-systems in ensuring quality in ride-hailing services. Aside from promoting competition, the ratings system also allows users to set expectations for the service.

The terms of engagement for this type of competition are set by the platform, as it exercises a certain control over prices, quality, methods of supply, and the use of certain complementary systems (such as its payment system, App Store, dispatch service, etc). It is the platform which – in large part – decides how the generated value is allocated across the parties on its platform.[391] The terms offered by platform operator determine in part the attractiveness to enter into intra-ecosystem competition for complementors, while complementors in part determine the value of the platform itself, a complex relationship. For platform operators that are still in need of growth, terms offered to business users are often beneficial to create a vibrant downstream ecosystem. Mature platform operators however may be tempted to extract more value for themselves. New terms and conditions can be imposed under threat of retaliation, or entry into vertical ecosystem competition.[392]

5.1.3 *Vertical Ecosystem Competition*

Vertical ecosystem competition refers to competition between the platform operator and the complementors in its multi-actor ecosystem. Vertical ecosystem competition is the result of vertical integration. First, the platform operator depends on third parties to supply goods and services and acts as an intermediary. Later, the platform operator may decide that it is positioned well to offer certain goods and services themselves, entering into competition with those complementors: the development of a proprietary app or the sale of in-house goods are forms of vertical integration related to app and e-commerce marketplaces. There is an inherent conflict of interest in acting both as a private regulator (upstream) and competitor (downstream), skewing competition in the favour of the platform operator, often heavily.[393]

There is likely an asymmetric position of power between the platform and its operator, especially where it concerns smaller complementors that do not supply 'must haves'. Here, the platform can continue without the complementor without a significant loss of value, but the complementor needs the platform to provide its services. At the same time, the platform can gather data on the sales or activities of the complementors (and complementors that offer similar services) leading to information asymmetry. The platform owner can use the insights derived from this data to enter the market where the complementor operates in a highly efficient way.[394]

391 cf Tiwana (n 34); Julian Nowag, 'The UBER-Cartel? UBER between Labour and Competition Law' [2016] SSRN Electronic Journal 1; Mazzucato, Entsminger and Kattel (n 181); Cozzolino, Corbo and Aversa (n 99); Bostoen (n 30).

392 Bostoen and Mandrescu (n 44); Cozzolino, Corbo and Aversa (n 99); Rietveld and Schilling (n 47); Bostoen and Petit (n 119).

393 Zhu and Liu (n 136); Wen and Zhu (n 44). The Court of Judgement of the EU has recognized this inherent conflict of interest in Case C-333/21, European Superleague Company, ECLI:EU:C:2023:1011, Judgement of 21 December 2023.

394 See the study on competition between the platform and its complementors by Zhu and Liu (n 136).

Vertical competition between the platform and its complementors has given rise to this new range of competitive harms that are based on this power dynamic. While vertical competition between an upstream supplier and downstream customer are not new, the relationship between the platform and the complementor is more complex. The complementor is not simply the customer of the platform but is an entity which engages into competition with others exclusively on the infrastructure of the platform, while being bound by the rules it sets. This high level of dependence on the platform by the complementor makes the nature of the abuse of gatekeeper power somewhere in between exclusionary and exploitative. There are however strong links between inter-ecosystem competition and vertical ecosystem competition: abuses of gatekeeper power become less likely when there is strong inter-ecosystem competition, and strong ecosystem competition is more likely when there is healthier intra-ecosystem competition.

5.1.4 *The Interplay between Different Forms of Ecosystem Competition*

Inter-, intra-, and vertical ecosystem competition are intrinsically linked to one another. Platforms are the base technology on which the multi-actor ecosystem is developed and form the stable core for multi-product ecosystems. At its inception, the supplier of any platform will have to attract different groups of users to overcome the chicken-and-egg problem, this is a perquisite to expand beyond the platform into a multi-product ecosystem. A digital firm that simply offers a number of digital products is simply a digital conglomerate, missing a layer of complexity. Without a multi-product ecosystem, the platform operator is wholly – or definitely largely – dependent on third parties to generate any value, driving it to offer beneficial conditions for its complementors. Absent users, there is no intra-ecosystem competition, and thus no platform. Without platforms (and their surrounding ecosystems of users and products), there is no inter-ecosystem competition.

The position of the platform operator grows, at first, by developing and supporting its multi-actor ecosystem. The need to attract these users shape its strategies to engage in inter-ecosystem competition and vice versa. Let's say there are two new video-sharing services, trying to enter the market on the basis of venture capital. One platform offers users that upload their videos a small fee (a hypothetical €0,001) per view, while other does not remunerate users at all. Users would logically choose the platform where they get remunerated, over one where they do not. The second platform is incentivized to offer remuneration as well, which is equivalent to that offered by the first platform. This could be by including a similar payment system, or by adopting an ad-centric business model, allowing its users to place advertisements or engage in sponsorships. The existence of both platforms provides the complementors with bargaining power: if one platform offers poor terms, the user will exclusively upload its videos on the other platform. The larger and more influential the complementor, the greater its countervailing buyer power. However, if one of the platforms leaves the markets, and inter-ecosystem competition weakens, the user is dependent on a single platform, reducing its bargaining power. Dependence gives the platform operator power, even without entering into competition directly: the platform operator can give the bargaining complementor less favourable terms for the supply of its services, for instance, by limiting access to functionalities or demonetizing its content. At the same time, the platform operator can favour complacent complementors by giving them preferential rankings or offering other benefits. As inter-ecosystem competition weakens, dependency grows. As dependency grows, intra-ecosystem competition becomes more likely to favour the platform operator, even if it is to the detriment of complementors.

Over time, the platform operator may choose to engage in vertical competition. They start to produce in-house content, which is cheaper than paying the remuneration they initially offered third-party complementors. The position of complementors becomes even more precarious: if they try to exercise their countervailing buyer power, the platform can attempt to compete with them directly, substituting the independently created content with its own. When inter-ecosystem competition is strong, and alternatives exist, complementors may act collectively by boycotting the service after certain changes, or important complementors may take their business and leave for the competitor. Contrarily, when complementors are very dependent on the platform, there is little they can do but wait until they face vertical competition. The ecosystem operator can increasingly internalize production, excluding complementors. Over time, the ecosystem operator internalizes whole segments of the network that were previously co-generating value: Amazon becomes less of a Marketplace, and more of a store, Google becomes less of a search provider, and more of an information provider (a meta search service), or Uber starts using its proprietary self-driving cars. As vertical integration grows, intra-ecosystem disappears, and inter-ecosystem competition weakens over growing pats of the digital network. The more inter-ecosystem competition weakens, the worse the conditions for competitors in the multi-actor ecosystem, and the more opportunities to vertically integrate. This is yet another self-reinforcing feedback loop that governs digital competition.

5.2 ECOSYSTEM ORIENTATIONS: COMPETING THROUGH DIFFERENTIATION AT THE ECOSYSTEM LEVEL

Competition through differentiation is a key element of competition in digital markets. Digital goods can easily be differentiated as they are modular. It is relatively easy to create different versions of the same product (i.e. a free version and a paid version; a low-end or high-end product), and it is possible to offer similar yet differentiated services by integrating different modules: Twitch and YouTube both provide video-sharing services. Twitch however differentiated itself by offering opportunities for live chats and feedback when YouTube did not. Twitch also differentiated its platform by allowing content creators to monetize their services through voluntary tipping or subscriptions, rather than monetization through advertising. By differentiating its services to attract its target audience, Twitch was able to enter the market for video-sharing despite YouTube's dominance in this area.[395] As noted earlier, for competition between platforms, differentiation is key: they can choose to maintain an open or closed, ad-centric or device-centric business model.

Differentiation is also relevant at the level of product ecosystems. Here, differentiation is more diffuse and harder to quantify than in competition at the platform level. As such, it is described here as an 'ecosystem orientation'. Product ecosystems generally evolve from their core platforms, as the ecosystem operator starts its cycle of innovation and expansion from the captured platform market. Consequently, activities in new markets will often be somewhat related – especially in the initial development of the product ecosystem – so that power can be leveraged between the core platform service and the rest of the ecosystem.

Some ecosystems start out with a strategy of openness: the product ecosystems operated by Alphabet and Meta are based on revenues derived from advertising. As advertisements require eyeballs to be monetized, this has pushed their ecosystem in the direction of openness: offering new services beyond their initial platform are focussed on collecting more data and offering more venues for advertising: Android is licensed at zero cost, Gmail accounts are free, Google Maps is provided for free, all to sustain the advertisement-based business model. Apple's ecosystem is closed, and device-centric. Apple offers high-quality goods and focuses its branding and communications on safety and security. In principle, there is little that would prevent Apple from entering into advertising markets. If Apple would choose to do so, they could build an advertising ecosystem around Safari and its other proprietary services where it could develop its own advertising ecosystem. Instead, Apple actively pushes its ecosystem away from advertising towards more device-centric business models. The introduction of the Apple Tracking Transparency policy has reduced monetization through advertising for Apple app developers, instead pushing them towards direct sales for their apps.[396] For Apple, it is seemingly more attractive to differentiate iOS on the basis of quality and privacy than to enter into competition in advertising markets.

While hard to quantify, it can be observed that most large ecosystems find their orientation and specialize in a certain direction: Microsoft's product ecosystem has come to focus heavily on productivity and enterprise software; Meta is focussed on consumer communications; Alphabet is focussed on search and information; Apple focuses on high-quality consumer products and specific sectors; and Amazon focuses on retail and logistics.[397] They compete in some areas, such as Microsoft's

[395] See for an overview of differences, Kilham E, Twitch vs. YouTube Streaming: What's the Difference? (Lifewire, 8 February 2021).

[396] Reinhold Kesler, 'The Impact of Apple's App Tracking Transparency on App Monetization' [2022] SSRN Electronic Journal <www.ssrn.com/abstract=4090786> accessed 30 August 2024.

[397] Busch (n 2) 7–10.

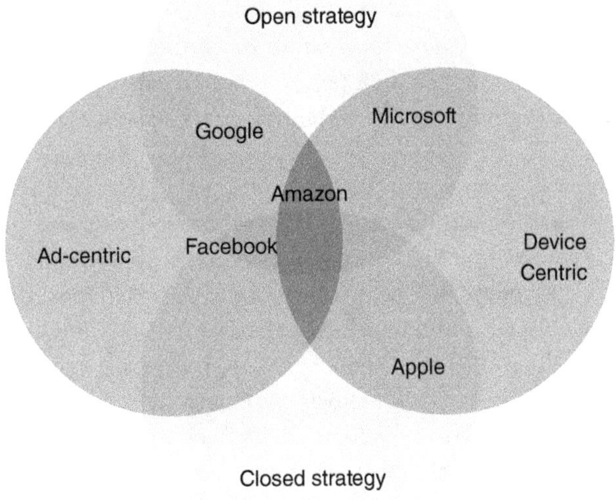

FIGURE 5.1 An illustration of the differentiated ecosystem strategies

cloud service Azure with Amazon's cloud service AWS. However, this competition does not touch the core of their ecosystems and the orientation of those ecosystems (Figure 5.1). It seems that the more elaborate large ecosystems become, the less intensely they compete with one another. Chapter 6 discusses why this may be a natural outcome of the growth and development of ecosystems, looking at different stages of ecosystem competition.

A big difference between ecosystem orientation and platform differentiation is that the product ecosystems does not face the same limitations as the digital platform, allowing the digital conglomerate to pursue a strategy of diversification, making its ecosystem more adaptive and resilient.[398] By entering into the provision of cloud services, Amazon has diversified its ecosystem away from being wholly dependent on e-commerce. Microsoft, supported by its revenues from Windows and enterprise software, has entered durably into markets for video-game consoles and has built an ecosystem of products surrounding Xbox, which is leveraged back into PC gaming on Windows.[399] Meta has expanded into Virtual Reality and the Metaverse, in an attempt to capture a new mode of communications and play. None of these

[398] Wu (n 344).

[399] One high-profile acquisition was that of Activision for €69 billion, see Case M.10646, Microsoft/Activision Blizzard, Commission Decision of 15 May 2023. Earlier, Microsoft had already acquired high-profile game studio Bethesda for €7.5 billion, see Tom Warren, Microsoft Completes Bethesda acquisition, promises some Xbox and PC exclusives (The Verge, 9 March 2021).

acquisitions seem to be the core business of the ecosystem operators, yet entry into these markets allows them to find new business opportunities. While entry often does not relate to the core operations of the ecosystem, they do access predominantly opportunities from where they can leverage their existing capabilities and resources, and which strengthen their position in their existing platforms. This type of diversification strengthens the survivability of firms, as well as their monopoly in their core markets.[400]

Understanding the relevance of the different orientations of digital product ecosystems helps to understand the source of their power. Ecosystem power is more complex than gatekeeper power as it expands beyond a single service and across an entire segment of the network. The presence of the ecosystem operator in multiple markets allows it to steer and control its user bases between markets and to steer their business activities.[401] As the product ecosystem becomes more entrenched in a certain area of activity: be it productivity for enterprises, consumer communications, e-commerce and logistics, high-end digital goods, or information, the more dependent users that are highly specialized in these areas becomes on one ecosystem operator. Furthermore, as specialization and differentiation of large ecosystem providers increases, the less competitive pressures there will be.

5.3 A THEORY OF ECOSYSTEM POWER

5.3.1 *Modalities of Economic Power and Their Relationship to Gatekeeper and Ecosystem Power*

Competition law has generally relied on the concept of market power to inform investigations and enforcement. Market power generally refers to a type of economic power that provides one firm or a collective of firms that operate in a certain product market to increase prices and allocate scarce resources in an inefficient manner.[402] Not all forms of market power are considered problematic. In fact, from the perspective of Schumpeterian competition the drive for market power – or the existence thereof – may even spur innovation.[403] In EU competition law, market power is only problematic where it leads to undue restrictions of competition, either through cartelization or because it has resulted in the dominance of one firm or a collective of firms.[404] Thus, one must distinguish the nature of certain types of economic power on the one hand from theories of harm related to that type of economic power on the other.

[400] Wu (n 344).
[401] See eg Heidhues, Köster and Kőszegi (n 329); Lianos and Carballa-Smichowski (n 121).
[402] Lianos and Carballa-Smichowski (n 121) 978 et seq.
[403] Cédric Argenton and others, 'Can Abuses of a Dominant Position Be Tackled More Effectively?' [2023] Report for the Dutch Ministry of Economic Affairs & Climate ch 2.
[404] Richard Whish and David Bailey, *Competition Law* (11th edn, Oxford University Press 2024).

While market power is an important concept in competition law, it is far from the only source of economic power. Economic power generally is the institutionalized control over resources. Economic power coordinates people's activities through cooperation: people exchange resources they own through mutually agreeable transactions that benefit everyone who engages in them. If this were not the case, they would not agree to the exchange.[405] Nobody forces complementors to be a part of the multi-actor ecosystem that operates on a platform, there is some benefit for third parties to do so. From the 'economic power perspective', the resources held by one party, and the need for access of others to those resources, shape power dynamics. Bargaining power exists due to scarcity: when labour is scarce, the worker can negotiate, but when jobs are scarce, the employer holds the cards.[406] Market power or monopoly power exists because one firm controls a significant share of the available resources or production capacity, therefore allowing them to limit output and increase prices without entry. Conversely, purchasing power exists when there is competition for the attention of a single buyer or a group of buyers, who can then set terms and conditions. Ecosystem operators have economic power: they control access to platforms, which constitute important gateways, providing them with intermediary – or gatekeeper – power. They decide which complementors gain access to end users, and vice versa, and under which conditions. When access to a platform is a 'must have' for different sides of the market, the platform operator has asymmetrical bargaining power, allowing them to set prices and conditions as they see fit.[407]

The power of operators of multi-actor and especially multi-product ecosystems goes far beyond a simple measure of market power. A look at the ontology of different types of power shows a complex interplay of multiple modalities of power. Ecosystems are shaped by power related to (i) resource dependence, (ii) power through processes, (iii) positional power, and (iv) power through coercion.[408]

First, the question as to who has power within the ecosystem starts with the question of resource dependence. Entrant platforms must overcome the chicken-and-egg problem: they must attract end users and business users by allocating value to both groups of users, possibly at the expense of its own resources. Entrant platforms are often loss leading, supported by venture capital, during this part of the process. Here, complementors often have significant bargaining power: end users receive high-quality and free or cheap services and business users are remunerated well.

[405] Randall G Holcombe, 'Economic Power' in Randall G Holcombe (ed), *Coordination, Cooperation, and Control: The Evolution of Economic and Political Power* (Springer International Publishing 2020) 50 <https://doi.org/10.1007/978-3-030-48667-9_3>.

[406] ibid.

[407] Damien Geradin, 'What Is a Digital Gatekeeper?' (*Platform Law Blog*, 24 February 2021) 5; Christian Rusche, 'On Gatekeepers and Structural Competition Problems' (2021) 56 Intereconomics 205; Cappai and Colangelo (n 14).

[408] See eg Lianos and Carballa-Smichowski (n 121); Heidhues, Köster and Kőszegi (n 329).

Think of Uber or Lyft in their early days: cheaper than taxi's, while offering attractive terms for drivers. A loss-leading business model sustained through venture capital.

As the platform continues to grow and evolve, the question of process-based power comes into play: which party can affect the others' conduct when there are conflicts in power?[409] When the resource dependence of a platform operator (i.e. its dependence on complementors) is high, it will not be able to impose terms and conditions on its users. When a video-sharing platform is one of many, it cannot unilaterally decide to introduce large amounts of advertisements without end users abandoning the platform. However, once access to the platform is a must have for certain types of content, users are more likely to accept the platform operators terms even if it harms their interests. With the process-based view of power, we can see when the balance of economic powers tips from favouring users to favouring the platform operator.[410]

The idea of a platform as being a 'must have' has to do with its positional power. When networks are heavily centralized, the central actor becomes able to extend its influence to tip towards sustainable dominance. Once the position of a platform operator in a certain segment of the network industry is established, it can use the network for its own purpose rather than the purpose for which the network was initially developed.[411] A platform operator with a high number of users and more connections between those users will find it easier to stay in power. This has been observed with changes to WhatsApp and X: despite resistance from their user bases to changes in privacy, moderation, or ownership, users tend to stick with the platforms that they know and where they have developed connections.[412]

Once the platform operator is sufficiently entrenched by virtue of its resources, position, and its ability to influence the behaviour of its users, it gains the ability to coerce those in its ecosystems and around them. Coercion allows the platform operator to steer its users towards certain choices without direct use of force or violence.[413] This goes what has been described related to process-based definitions of power. Here, the platform operator can make a choice despite a conflict of interest, such as introducing more advertisements to the displeasure of advertisers. With coercion, the platform operator gains the ability to steer users to make choices they otherwise would not make. These choices can be related to different activities. First, it may relate access to the platform in question, for instance, by signing up to ancillary services to make use of the platform or through exclusivity agreements. Second, it may relate to removal from the platform, for instance, by banning software developers from the platform if they do not adhere to requirements set by the platform operator. Third, they may have to do with access to other resources or platforms, for

[409] Lianos and Carballa-Smichowski (n 121) 802–803.
[410] Christian Rusche (n 407); Bostoen and Petit (n 119).
[411] Lianos and Carballa-Smichowski (n 121) 804–813.
[412] ibid 813.
[413] ibid 800–802.

instance, by making it mandatory to use the logistic services operated by the platform operator downstream to gain access to or preferential treatment on the platform itself. Coercion thus relates to involuntary choices, often as the result of an absence of alternative reasonable choices.[414]

Ecosystem power should thus be understood as a form of power that allows the ecosystem operator to manipulate the behaviour of its users across a variety of markets by virtue of its economic power. Ecosystem power grows not only in relation to the position of the firm within the platform market but also its surrounding markets. The connection between the primary market (the platform) and secondary markets (related product markets) allows the ecosystem operator to leverage power throughout the value chain as to shape the platform, the value chain, the relevant aftermarkets, and even loosely connected markets.[415]

5.3.2 *Ecosystem Power: The Power to Control and Shape the Network*

Section 5.3.1 has set out the fundamentals of ecosystem power. Now, the focus turns towards how to measure such power and to make the concept of ecosystem power operational. Market power is a helpful tool to determine the extent to which an undertaking or a group of undertakings can influence competition within a certain market. The concept of market power, as well as the process of defining markets, are considered to be imperfect and subject to limitations, but ultimately help competition authorities to assess behaviour within a specific conceptual framework.[416]

A similar concept is necessary for ecosystem power. The ecosystem concept has found its way into decisional practices, both in competition law and DMA enforcement. However, the concept remains ill-defined and susceptible to change. It seems that – at least the European Commission – continues to use the ecosystem concept as a metaphor instead of an operational term.[417] A study of the designation decisions under the DMA shows that the Commission uses the term ecosystem in nearly every designation decision to date, yet the Commission neither provides a clear definition of what it considers the ecosystem to be nor does it consistently assess the benefits for the ecosystem operator or the harms to competition.[418] In EU competition law, the Commission has used the ecosystem concept and given it consequence in the context of mergers, again without providing a clear definition.

In the assessment of *Google/Fitbit*, the Commission refers to the Google ecosystem, Apple ecosystem, wearable OS ecosystem, Android ecosystem, and AdTech

414 ibid.
415 ibid 810 et seq.
416 Pinar Akman, 'A Preliminary Assessment of the European Commission's Google Android Decision' [2018] Competition Policy International 8; Louis Kaplow, 'MARKET DEFINITION: IMPOSSIBLE AND COUNTERPRODUCTIVE' (2013) 79 Antitrust Law Journal 361.
417 Hornung (n 65) 435.
418 Van den Boom and Hornung (n 123).

ecosystem. It is unclear at any given time how exactly these ecosystems are delineated. In the more recent Booking/eTraveli decision, the Commission elaborates more on what it considers to be the effects of the presence of ecosystems. Here, it explains that 'Booking's growth projections for the flight "Online Travel Agency" (OTA) market in the EEA, ecosystem, increase of barriers to entry, and/or expansion on the hotel OTA market in the EEA, cross-sell, and harm to hotels and potentially to consumers.'[419] In more general terms, the Commission notes that "in cases where the acquirer operates an ecosystem that benefits from strong positive network effects, which act as a significant barrier to entry, the risk to competition resulting from an acquisition is not limited to the foreclosure of rivals' access to inputs, but extends to the strengthening of dominance as it fortifies the dominance of the ecosystem, in part because the new services add value to the consumers for which they are complements and in part because they help retain other users for which they are partial substitutes."[420] In both instances, the Commission explains the harms associated with the presence of expansive ecosystems, yet it does not explain what the ecosystem is, or what the nature of this type of power and its associated harms is perceived to be.

The General Court has given the Commission a definition for ecosystems, at least in essence, in two instances. First, in *Google Android*. Here, the Court explained that 'in a digital "ecosystem", which brings together several categories of supplier, customer and consumer and causes them to interact within a platform, the products or services which form part of the relevant markets that make up that ecosystem may overlap or be connected to each other on the basis of their horizontal or vertical complementarity.'[421] In ByteDance, the General Court repeated its definition from Google Android, and added a definition for the multi-product ecosystem explaining that 'a digital platform ecosystem may consist of one or more Core Platform Services and other services connected to them, for example by means of technological links or interoperability; this is liable to exacerbate entry barriers for competitors of those undertakings and increase the cost of switching providers for end users, making it more difficult for existing or new market operators to compete with those undertakings or contest their position.'[422]

With this, the Court has defined both the multi-actor and multi-product ecosystem. The first consists of the platform and the several categories of suppliers, which create horizontal or vertical complementarities, the latter is defined as a (in the case of the DMA core) platform service that is connected to other products and platforms by means of technological links or interoperability. The Court also sets out some of the associated harms: exacerbating entry barriers, increasing switching costs, or harms to competition.[423]

[419] Commission Decision M.10615, Booking/eTravel [2024], para 41.
[420] ibid, para 204.
[421] Case T-604/18 Google Android [2022] ECLI:EU:T:2022:541, para 116.
[422] ibid, para 128–129.
[423] Van den Boom and Hornung (n 123).

A clear concept of ecosystem power remains missing however. Heidhues and others juxtapose competition between ecosystems against competition between single firms. Their analysis explains how ecosystem operators tend to prioritize takeovers of new markets in early stages and try to obtain default access points in later stages. There are short-run efficiencies in this type of competition, but long-run effects are ambiguous. First, the ecosystem operator competes on the merits and enters into markets through acquisitions of by offering high-quality services. Once the ecosystem operator is well positioned; however, it can continue to occupy access points and leverage its power from one market to another to keep users with its proprietary platforms, even if better alternatives are available.[424] Similar observations have been made by Jacobides and Lianos, who explain that issues in assessing competition in ecosystems must be addressed by studying the nature of ecosystem dependencies head-on, studying the lock-in that the ecosystem orchestrators can impose on complementors and users by inducing non-generic co-specialization that restricts competition and entry. It is the very structure of the ecosystem and the ability of the dominant player to be at the core of the multi-product ecosystem, which leads to competition problems, rather than dominance in a particular market.[425] Jacobides and Lianos put forward that market power in digital markets should be measured by the ecosystem orchestrator's capacity to impose additional commitments on its customers or complementors by threatening to foreclose their access to other sides of the market or other benefits they could derive from the non-generic complementarities that are unique to the platform.[426]

This book adds to that by arguing that the ability of the ecosystem to abuse its gatekeeper, power is derived from the lack of competitive pressures in inter-ecosystem competition. If the users of an ecosystem cannot switch to a competing multi-product ecosystem or if the costs of switching are too high, the ecosystem operator can extract more rents from its users without losing them. At the same time, the ecosystem orchestrator can reduce inter-ecosystem competition by wielding its gatekeeper power in its multi-actor ecosystems. It can extract additional rents and resources, for instance, by collecting excessive data. This can be leveraged into inter-ecosystem competition. Moreover, the platform can prevent the emergence of competitors in inter-ecosystem competition by foreclosing them before they develop into meaningful competitors. As such, it is argued here that gatekeeper power (the ability to engage exercise control over complementors and users within the ecosystem) and ecosystem power (the ability to lock consumers in by escaping from inter-ecosystem competition) are two concurrent yet distinct powers.[427]

Ecosystem power should then be understood as 'the ability to leverage one's position in – and from – its occupied markets to capture new markets or entrench

[424] Heidhues, Köster and Kőszegi (n 329) 2–7.
[425] Jacobides and Lianos (n 12) 1205 et seq.
[426] ibid.
[427] See Chapter 7 on the relationship between these types of power.

its position in its occupied markets through strategic behaviour in one's multi-actor and/or multi-product ecosystem.' An ecosystem operator can leverage its ecosystem power through behaviour such as tying and bundling, fusing networks of users or leveraging its userbase across markets, creating or strengthening ecosystem linkages to create value-driven lock-in, or by denying compatibility with actual and potential rivals. This allows the ecosystem operator to leverage its existing collection of products and services to enter into new markets (leveraging offensively) or to insulate its core markets from competition (leveraging defensively). The presence of ecosystem power should not be viewed as inherently problematic. Similarly to the concept of market power, ecosystem power tends to lead to competitive harms when one undertaking has too much of it. When a firm has too much ecosystem power, it gains control over access points for competition in the digital network industry. When the digital network industry is occupied by a small number of large incumbent ecosystem operators, they gain increased opportunities to raise entry barriers and foreclose potentially disruptive entrants. This specific problem associated with ecosystem power is developed further in Part II, where a theory on the different stages of ecosystem competition and theories of harm are developed.

Broadly, ecosystem power should be viewed as non-structural (cross-)market power. The power to behave unilaterally from consumers and competitors is not derived from having a large market share in a single market, but rather from the ability to leverage market power between markets, lock-in consumers, the subsidization of complementors and cross-subsidization between profitable and loss-leading products, and foreclosure of access to essential inputs or refusing to deal with competing ecosystems.[428] The consumer that enters into the network of the ecosystem is nudged by the ecosystem to purchase the relevant complements, which further increases its sunk costs, switching costs, and subsequent lock-in.[429]

This non-structural market power significantly impacts the justificatory power of market shares in the relevant market as an indicator of market power. Using the relevant market focuses on a single component within a system. This system consists of intrinsically linked complementary goods, the value of which must be determined by looking at those goods jointly. As such, competition authorities and regulators should no longer look at markets independently but must assess the power of an ecosystem as a whole. The value and power of ecosystems together is greater than the sum of its parts, and that assessing market-specific behaviour does not capture this power.[430] Measuring deviations on the average within this single market fails to

[428] See Jacobides and Lianos (n 12) 1221.

[429] ibid.

[430] See eg Mark Lemley and Matthew Wansley, 'Coopting Disruption' [2024] Cardozo Legal Studies Research Paper No. 2024-24 1; Ezrachi and Stucke (n 1) on how ecosystem operators pre-empt disruption.

appreciate the dynamics of inter-ecosystem competition between different multi-product ecosystems.[431]

The assessment of cross-market power and indirect competitive pressures exerted through inter-ecosystem competition add a layer of complexity to the assessment of harms associated with ecosystem power when compared to assessing issues related to market power. Not only is ecosystem power non-structural, the significance of ecosystem power is also determined by the competitive position of competing ecosystem operators and its ability to exert direct and indirect competitive pressures, as well as the ability of users of the ecosystem to multi-home or leave the ecosystem.

In short, ecosystem power is a form of non-structural economic power that is related to the ability of a firm to use its position in a number of markets to steer users and complementors as to lock them into the proprietary ecosystem of the firm. When inter-ecosystem competition is strong, ecosystem operators will compete intensely to take over markets through acquisitions and the proliferation of high-quality goods, which creates short-term efficiencies. When inter-ecosystem competition weakens, the ecosystem operator gains ecosystem power, which allows it to use its power in terms of resources (and access to resources), control over processes, and positional power to steer and coerce customers and complementors to leverage its position across markets or to sustain its monopoly in its captured market. Ecosystem power can lead to competitive harms if it is significant enough that it allows the ecosystem operator to win competition for markets, even if it degrades the quality of its services, increases prices, or lacks innovation. It can do so because it can prevent competitors from entering the market or growing by steering users away from the potentially disruptive service, by denying it access to resources or infrastructures, or by acquiring the service in its infancy.

5.3.3 *Ecosystem Power and Market Power: Alternatives or Complementary?*

In determining the ability of an ecosystem operator to leverage its ecosystem power, or exploit its gatekeeper power, the importance of market power in a single-product market is diminished, but not irrelevant. Studying market power in specific types of markets may help to identify from which markets the ecosystem operator leverages its market power, or which core markets it is trying to protect through leveraging. Such an analysis is particularly relevant where it concerns platform markets that are extremely prone to concentration, or even exhibit (digital) natural monopoly. These markets often form core markets underlying the competitive strategies of multi-product ecosystems and monopolizing such a market may facilitate leveraging. The presence of natural monopoly allows the monopolist to charge additional rents with a limited risk of entry, which can be used to subsidize entry into new markets. Alternatively, the monopolist can forego extracting additional rents to lock-in

[431] Jacobides and Lianos (n 12).

users into its platform. The operator of one or more platform markets which exhibit digital natural monopoly may have enhanced abilities to leverage and strengthen its position in inter-ecosystem competition.

Firstly, the presence of monopoly power within a market enhances gatekeeper power, as it diminishes the possibilities for users to multi-home or switch: advertisers that wish to engage in search advertising are largely dependent on Google search, as Google holds a monopoly in search. Secondly, the presence of monopoly power enhances the possibilities to leverage this strong intra-ecosystem position into inter-ecosystem competition. In *Google AdSense*, for instance, Google allegedly demanded exclusivity from advertisers to exclude the emergence of competition in horizontal search through other ecosystems.[432] It is emboldened in this behaviour because of its monopoly in search advertising. Thirdly, the presence of digital natural monopoly markets allows the platform to develop its ecosystem around these core markets as to differentiate itself from others. This happens both by redirecting users back to its core markets where revenue is created or data is collected, as well as by insulating its core markets from competition (either by collaborating with other ecosystems or by occupying adjacent markets).[433]

This book thus views ecosystem-, gatekeeper-, and market power as distinct but related powers. The ability of an ecosystem operator to exploit its gatekeeper and ecosystem power depends on three conditions: (i) the presence of competing ecosystems of a similar size, which engage in direct competition with the incumbent in some markets; (ii) the possibilities for users to multi-home between ecosystems; and/or (iii) the possibilities for users to switch between ecosystems.[434] These conditions are shaped partly – but not exclusively – by the monopolization of one or more platform markets by the ecosystem operator.

These three criteria can be exemplified by looking at competition between large ecosystems. Apple and Google provide an example where large ecosystem operators compete directly in the market for operating systems and app stores. Therefore, complementors have the ability to multi-home, and users have the ability to switch between handhelds. When the user switches handhelds, they also enter into the rival ecosystem.[435] The ability for users to switch can be reduced by switching costs, either derived from the value of the platform or due to the loss of user synergies derived from ecosystem linkages. The presence of inter-ecosystem competition does however diminish gatekeeper power as users and complementors have alternatives. This in turn also limits ecosystem power as the ecosystem orchestrator is limited in wielding its gatekeeper power to leverage its userbases from one product

[432] Google Search (AdSense) (Case AT.40411) Commission Decision C(2019) 2173 [2019], OJ C 369/6.

[433] cf Mandrescu (n 12); Hovenkamp (n 11); Lianos and Carballa-Smichowski (n 121); Heidhues, Köster and Kőszegi (n 329).

[434] See Chapter 8 for theories of harm.

[435] Competition & Market Authority (n 44) 29.

to another. While these are limiting factors, complementors to the respective app stores may still be dependent on access to the platform for a significant share of their revenues.[436] Moreover, end users can switch handhelds, but most users do not multi-home between both mobile ecosystems concurrently.[437] Gatekeeper power thus still persists. This is further amplified as the question on access to the app store is not limited only to that market, but rather to the ecosystems as a whole.

Competition between Apple and Facebook provides an example of ecosystems, which do not compete directly with one another in either of their core markets. Apple operates a closed-product ecosystem focussed on selling a bundle of products, while the latter has developed an ad-centric ecosystem focussed on consumer communications and social media. For these ecosystems, collaboration is more attractive than competition in most instances and the competitive pressures they exert on one another are therefore generally weak. This also means that there is no real effect on the incentives or possibilities for users to switch out of one ecosystem and into the other. Apple has recently demonstrated that it can still leverage the position of its ecosystem into competition with Facebook. Apple's renewed ambitions to move into advertising and the choice to block Facebook and other third parties from gathering certain data on Apple devices.[438] This demonstrates that dependence of a rival on an incumbent ecosystem – even if the rival is an incumbent as well – brings inherent competitive risks for the dependent party. Facebook has estimated its losses in revenue following the Apple decision at USD 10 billion.[439] This shows that even if parties are not fully dependent on a platform, decisions by the platform operator to disallow certain activities can lead to substantial losses for the complementor. Substantial losses of revenue following strategic decisions by a platform operator are even more critical for smaller platform operators that are still trying to capture their market than they are for a rival incumbent.

5.4 CONCLUSION

This chapter has discussed the fundamental concepts to understand the competitive dynamics of ecosystems. Ecosystem competition takes place in and between two types of ecosystems: the multi-actor ecosystem and multi-product ecosystem. The first consists of the platform operator and the complementors that use their platform

[436] Bostoen and Mandrescu (n 44) 7–13.

[437] Competition & Market Authority (n 44) 39–40.

[438] See Kif Leswig, 'Apple's Ad Privacy Change Impact Shows the Power It Wields over Other Industries' *CNBC* (13 November 2021); this article discusses how Apple has benefitted from its prohibition of third-party tracking in developing its own advertising capabilities, Facebook COO Sheryl Sandberg notes that Apple has now secured a source of direct data for themselves, while Facebook is excluded from gathering that direct data on Apple devices. This may ultimately hurt Facebook's ability to target Apple users with advertising while Apple can use privileged access to data to do so.

[439] Ben Gilbert, 'Facebook Blames Apple after a Historically Bad Quarter, Saying iPhone Privacy Changes Will Cost It $10 Billion' *Business Insider* (3 February 2022).

to offer their services and compete, while the latter consists of the different platforms and products operated by a single ecosystem operator. Competition happens within these ecosystems: different complementors compete with one another on the platform (intra-ecosystem competition), and the platform operator itself can compete with its complementors as a result of vertical integration into downstream activities (vertical ecosystem competition). Competition also happens between multi-product ecosystems: Apple and Google compete with one another, both via their products and by making their multi-actor ecosystems compete with one another (inter-ecosystem competition).

Competition within the ecosystem and between ecosystems are related to one another. The value of a platform is determined largely by the vibrance of its multi-actor ecosystem. Complementors co-generate value with the platform operator. Consequently, a platform with a bigger and more productive multi-actor ecosystem is more valuable than a platform with a small and unproductive multi-actor ecosystem. The operator of the multi-actor ecosystem thus has to attract users to its platform to gain a stronger position in inter-ecosystem competition. However, the relationship between the ecosystem operator and its multi-actor ecosystem is determined by inter-ecosystem competition. If inter-ecosystem competition is strong, the platform operator may risk losing complementors if it enters into vertical competition or takes a larger share of the generated value for itself. If inter-ecosystem competition is weak, or absent, complementors do not have alternatives to offer their goods and services. This means that the ecosystem operator can exert more control over their complementors and extract greater rents. Control over one's multi-actor ecosystem is often understood as gatekeeper power.

The power of a firm in inter-ecosystem competition is a counterpart of gatekeeper power, namely ecosystem power. This chapter describes ecosystem power as a form of non-structural market power that is related to the ability of a firm to use its position in a number of markets to steer users and complementors as to lock them into the proprietary ecosystem of the firm. Ecosystem power governs the dynamic of inter-ecosystem competition: if firms cannot gain access to competitive resources needed in digital markets (users, data, and finances), they cannot enter into competition with the incumbent ecosystem operator. The ecosystem operator can leverage its resources to enter into new markets as to attract new users or to steer users or resources away from competitors. When there is an emerging market, the incumbent ecosystem operator can invest heavily to occupy this market as a means to keep its existing users in its ecosystem, to attract new users into its ecosystem, to steer users away from potential competitors, and to prevent investments into competitors. The larger the ecosystem becomes and the more markets it occupies, the greater its positional power and its power over processes and resources becomes. As the ecosystem grows, the firm is able to expand their power over larger segments of the digital network industry, where it can act as the de facto regulator (gatekeeper), determine who gets to enter into competition, and steer innovation and the use of resources.

6

Stages of Ecosystem Competition

Competition between ecosystems evolves and changes depending on where ecosystem operators find themselves in terms of the maturity of their ecosystem, the intensity of inter-ecosystem competition, and technological developments. This chapter develops a conceptual framework for stages of ecosystem competition, which may help to explain under which conditions competition is intense or weak, innovation is higher or lower, and different groups of users are better or worse off.

The theory on stages of ecosystem competition builds on works by Gawer, who has theorized that platforms can find themselves in a launch stage or maturity stage, marking a shift in their competitive strategies.[440] This conceptual framework goes a step further, both in terms of scope and classifications. It asks the question in which stage of competition product ecosystems are in relation to the digital network industry and identifies four stages related to inter-ecosystem competition: inception, growth, maturity, and incumbency.

There is a gradient transition between stages of ecosystem competition in which an ecosystem operator finds itself. There is no clear line or moment where ecosystem competition moves from one stage to the next. The categorization should be treated conceptually, as to help understand changes in the business model of ecosystem operators or changing competitive dynamics across digital markets and to determine the status of the digital network overall. If the digital network is occupied by stage 1 and 2 ecosystem operators, competition is likely healthy and intense, and innovation is high. Small and medium-sized ecosystem operators compete intensely to become the dominant standard, actively finding their place in the network. This should result in the emergence of stage 3 ecosystem operators. Entrant platform operators and small ecosystem operators are often loss-leading, as they try to capture their platform markets, expand, innovate, and pivot. Once they have managed to secure their position, they aim to turn profitable. These are mature ecosystems that can determine their own strategy and direction. Mature ecosystem operators may however grow into incumbents, who govern vast parts of the digital network industry

[440] Gawer (n 12) 1–4.

and operate across a large number of platform and product markets. These incumbents have the incentives and ability to suppress stage 1 and 2 ecosystem operators, ultimately weakening inter-ecosystem competition within the entire network, to the detriment of complementors, entry, and innovation.

6.1 STAGE 1: INCEPTION – THE EMERGENCE OF A NEW PLATFORM

The first stage of ecosystem competition is the emergence of a new platform. The platform may offer a wholly new service, be the result of platformization of existing services (such as ride-hailing vis-à-vis taxi services), or it can be that a new platform operator is challenging the existing platform operator to become the dominant design (for instance, the contestation of Facebook vis-à-vis Myspace as the dominant social media). This stage of ecosystem competition is characterized by intense competition and often associated with experimentation. The new platform operator must try to tip the market in its favour by attracting end users and complementors. To do so, it will often rely on abundance strategies, a strategy of openness, and by giving rewards to participants on either side of the market. This often results in short-term efficiencies yet also causes platforms to be loss-leading in their growth stages.

Competition to become the dominant design happens in almost all markets. After initial stages of experimentation in terms of design, features, and capabilities, markets will gravitate towards certain design principles and standards on the basis of consumer preferences.[441] As the dominant design is chosen, a mass exit of competitors follows. The dominant design determines the expected norms that must be met in order to attract the interest of users. This does not mean that every potential competitor has to adopt the same technology but simply that the quality and perceived value of the platform must be high enough to become a credible competitor.[442]

In many markets, the dominant design is not just offered by a single firm. For instance, there are a large number of espresso machines available, offered by different firms. While these espresso machines often have a similar design and method of use, there is no lack of competition. In digital platforms, competition to become the dominant design is intense and often short-lived, resulting in a monopoly or duopoly, as it relies on the creation of vast multi-actor ecosystems. For emerging platform operators, their main objective is to overcome the chicken-and-egg problem as to escape the 'launching stage'. Platforms will continue to rely on give-aways and growth strategies until they are able to push others out of the market and consolidate their user networks.[443]

441 Tiwana (n 34) ch 2.

442 Tiwana (n 34).

443 Mandrescu (n 169) 3–11; see also Gawer and Cusumano (n 39); Gawer and Henderson (n 136); Evans and Gawer (n 98); Gawer (n 12) on the launch and maturity phases of digital platforms and ecosystems.

While the initial fixed and sunk costs of creating a platform are relatively low compared to traditional infrastructure markets, self-reinforcing effects take over to entrench the incumbent platform operator. Network externalities, economies of scale and scope, and data-driven advantages will increase the gap between the incumbent platform operators and entrants, making their position harder to contest. Once the platform operator escapes the launching stage and enters a period of relative quietness, it can focus on harnessing the benefits of economies of scope and complementarities to develop new services and expand across markets, allowing it to leverage its established position within the platform market to diversify and enter into the second stage of competition.[444]

6.1.1 *Empirical Observations on Competition in the Emerging Platform Stage*

Today's largest platforms have all started out in their inception stage and have escaped their launch stage by employing the strategies as described earlier. Of course, the conditions governing the digital network industry at the time were different than they are now as there were less opportunities for the collection and processing of data, and existing incumbent digital firms were not as large as they are now. However, today's GAFAM platforms have all started out by either offering a wholly new platform service, substituting an existing service, or by winning contestation against the dominant incumbent. This analysis will highlight how the GAFAM companies were able to rise to prominence and which disruptive innovations they used to capture and sustain their position, as well as the competition between some of these ecosystems. Each discussion will end at the end of stage 1, when the GAFAM platform operators captured their first platform market.

First, the success of Google and Facebook as the contemporary ad-based ecosystems is based on their use of innovative strategies such as data analytics, the use of algorithms, a first mover's advantage into targeted advertising and internalizing external ideas. It is often argued that Google and Facebook do not necessarily have a first mover advantage in search, as other horizontal search and social media platforms came before them. However, both Google and Facebook relied on a combination of sustained and disruptive innovations to conquer their markets. Their disruptive innovations were related in particular to the analysis of data and reliance on complementors. Google and Facebook – both highly data-dependent ad-centric ecosystems – were able to create sustainable dominance and profitability rather quickly.[445]

Second, early competition between Microsoft and Apple was intense. Apple held the first mover advantage into personal computers, while Microsoft held a strong

[444] Brynjolfsson, Hu and Smith (n 215); Montero and others (n 18); Crémer, De Montjoye and Schweitzer (n 4); Digital Competition Expert Panel (n 1); Petit (n 13); Hovenkamp (n 11).

[445] A Hartung, 'How Facebook Beat MySpace' *Forbes* (14 February 2011); S Fraz, 'A Journey through Time: The Progression of Search Engines from Altavista to Google' *Medium* (9 August 2023).

position in software markets.[446] yet its market position was heavily threatened by Microsoft's reliance on an open business model that allowed third parties to offer their Windows operating system. Microsoft could offer personal computers at a lower price point allowed them to outcompete Apple, nearly pushing the latter off the market.[447] In many ways, Apple lost the competition for the operating system market and was only able to secure a position in this market in second-stage competition. Windows' monopoly position in operating systems allowed it to rapidly become profitable, while its smaller competitor Apple was unable to remain profitable in light of intense competition and failure to retain scale.

Third, the emergence of Amazon demonstrates the importance of aggregating demand on a platform and ultimately expanding into a cluster market. Amazon was able to develop a large customer base on its bookselling platform by virtue of private financial backing, its novel e-commerce strategies, and discounts. However, even when becoming the third largest bookseller in the United States, Amazon remained to be a consistent loss-leader, losing millions per year to provide its service. It is only after Amazon had expanded into offering a cluster of goods on its e-commerce platform and its expansion into other ventures such as music and video sales that it was able to secure a small quarterly profit. Amazon's strategy has shown the importance of aggregating demand on a platform at any cost, only to leverage one's user base into more and more connected markets.[448]

For Amazon, it is argued throughout the chapter that its profitability continues to increase by an offering that consists of an increasing amount of vertically, horizontally and diagonally integrated goods. As discussed in Chapter 4, the competition in markets that involve physical goods and services may operate under different principles than those for software goods. In these markets, economies of scale paired with vertical integration and economies of scope are more important to become profitable than it would be in pure software markets.

Google and Facebook: The Emergence of the Data-Driven Business Model

Google's origins famously lie with its horizontal search engine. Before Google, AltaVista was the most popular search engine, together with smaller search providers such as Yahoo and AskJeeves. AltaVista, founded in 1995, stood out as it was the first full web text search,[449] and its technology allowed for much faster results that brought back a large number of web pages. The search service offered by AltaVista

[446] Wu (n 344). Kapko M, History of Apple and Microsoft: 4 Decades of Peaks and Valleys (CIO, 7 October 2015).

[447] ibid.

[448] Khan (n 267). See also AD Pizio, 'People Think Amazon Is an E-Commerce Company, but 74% of Its Profit Comes from This Instead' [2024] *Motley Fool*, even at the time of writing Amazon's cloud services are only ca. 16 per cent of its total revenue but 74 per cent of its profits.

[449] Often referred to as WebCrawlers, an automated software program that tries to collect all relevant websites on the internet.

became popular instantaneously, with 300,000 search queries entered on the first day and 19 million searches per day by the end of its first year. It enjoyed its leadership position, but in 1998 Sergey Brin and Larry Page launched the Google search engine.[450] Google set itself apart by its PageRank algorithm, which automatically sorted the search results by relevance. After a mere two years, Google had overtaken the incumbent AltaVista – which still manually curated its search results – as the most popular search engine, which it remains until this day.

Both AltaVista and Google innovated search in their own ways, as the first introduced web crawling software, and the latter introduced algorithmic sorting. There are however two differences between Google and AltaVista that may explain the difference in their sustained market power: first, Google was able to continuously innovate by internalizing the network externalities in the market; it used user queries to update its search algorithm and increase its efficiency.[451] This type of innovation sustained existing technologies. Second, Google was able to engage in disruptive innovation by being the first to choose a business model based on targeted advertising.[452] By harnessing economies of scale related to user generated data both in the provision of the consumer facing service and the advertiser facing service, Google was able to become and remain the most effective horizontal search engine.

AltaVista tried to compete with Google by complementing their services with more powerful search technologies and gradually turning into a portal which combined multiple services such as its translation software Babel Fish. AltaVista was unable to catch up with Google in terms of efficiency, which continued to pre-empt any attempts by AltaVista to regain its position in horizontal search. The market had already tipped in its favour by 2002, and Google was able to maintain its dominant position in search. By 2004, when Google entered the second stage of digital competition and started forming its multi-product ecosystem, it had already won the battle for horizontal search.[453] AltaVista was acquired by Yahoo in 2004, which used its technologies to try (and fail) entering into competition in the market for horizontal search itself.

Google's rise to dominance within the horizontal search market was rather swift, and it did not take Google long to become profitable through its targeted advertisements. Google became profitable in 2001, three years after its inception.[454] Since then, it has steadily increased its profits together with its expansion both in the market for horizontal search and across markets.[455] Google's rapid expansion into a

450 Miguel Portela Pereira and others, 'Standards Wars: Google vs. Altavista' (Aalborg University – Course: Standardization 2015) <www.researchgate.net/publication/277311538>.

451 ibid; Sergey Brin and Larry Page, 'The Anatomy of a Large-Scale Hypertextual Web Search Engine' (1998) 30 Computer Networks and ISDN Systems 107.

452 Pereira and others (n 450) 10 et seq.

453 ibid.

454 Simon Bowers, 'Google Hits on Profit Formula' *The Guardian* (8 August 2001).

455 In 2001, Google had a USD 35 million on its balance sheet and a profit of around USD 7 million. In 2020, Google generated USD 183 billion in revenue, USD 147 billion of which came from online

multi-product ecosystem can be explained by its ad-centric nature – which creates incentives to collect more data from more sources – as well as the nature of horizontal search as a digital natural monopoly market. Google was able to reach profitability quickly compared to Amazon at the turn of the millennium or contemporary start-ups such as Uber. This may support that becoming profitable happens more quickly in a digital natural monopoly market than in a platform market that does not exhibit digital natural monopoly.

Facebook relied on a similar targeted advertising business model as Facebook to create its first revenues, yet its road to dominance differed from Google significantly. Facebook started as FaceMash, developed by Mark Zuckerberg in his second year at Harvard University. FaceMash offered a 'hot or not' comparison service where the photos of two female students attending Harvard University were presented next to one another and users could vote which of the women was more attractive.[456] Facebook, inspired by FaceMash, was intended to be a directory featuring photos and basic information of students attending Harvard University, which later expanded by including more universities, high schools, employees of certain companies, and ultimately the global population.[457]

Facebook did not enjoy a first mover's advantage. In fact, the incumbent at the time of Facebook's inception was Myspace, which had a robust user base, supplied a plethora of functionalities and was – at the time of Facebook's inception only recently – acquired by New Media Corporation, providing it with funding and professional management. The question is then how Facebook managed to overtake the incumbent which seemingly held all the cards. One strategy Facebook used to overtake Myspace was to rely fully on its community and the market to determine how the Facebook platform was going to take shape and evolve. Myspace tried to use professional management to determine the future of the undertaking and create a curated selection of functionalities. Facebook on the other hand relied on 'White Space management': no rules, no plans, no forecasted markets or demographic, and no foretelling uses. Facebook allowed third parties to supply their games on Facebook and allowed users to log into these games with their Facebook profile.[458]

Popular games such as Farmville attracted large numbers of users and ensured they spent time on Facebook. Facebook listened to suggestions by users on new ways to connect, new functions or applications to be introduced, to find the next promotion, and so forth. In short, Facebook relied on the external ideas generated

advertising; Megan Graham and Jennifer Elias, 'How Google's $150 Billion Advertising Business Works' *CNBC* (13 October 2021). Google made a USD 18.5 billion profit with an increase of 62 per cent in revenue when compared to the same quarter of the previous year; see also David Streitfeld, 'Google's Profits Soar as Revenue Rises 62 Percent' *New York Times* (29 July 2021).

456 Katharine A Kaplan, 'Facemash Creator Survives Ad Board' *The Harvard Crimson* (19 November 2003).

457 Ellen McGirt, 'Facebook's Mark Zuckerberg: Hacker. Dropout. CEO' *Fast Company* (1 May 2007).

458 Ross Pruden, 'How Facebook Used White Space to Crush Myspace' *TechDirt* (19 January 2011); Adam Hartung, 'How Facebook Beat MySpace' *Forbes* (14 January 2011).

by its user base to innovate. Facebook's reliance on third-party complementors to create value allowed it to innovate faster than an undertaking, which tries to create all ideas internally. By early 2010, Myspace abandoned its ambitions as a social media and tried to redefine itself as an 'entertainment destination', ultimately disappearing into the fringes.[459]

Facebook managed to cement its position as the dominant social media by internalizing the network externalities in the market and the ideas of its users. In its early stages, Facebook advertising was less successful than Google's. Facebook's display advertising interrupted the content experience and were deemed to be essentially ineffective. However, by 2011 Facebook was able to incrementally improve the targeting of its ads by gathering more user data, developing the algorithms and gaining access to data such as GPS localization data which greatly increased the efficiency of its targeted ads.[460] Unlike Google in horizontal search, Facebook was unable to pre-empt the emergence of potential competitors in social media such as Twitter and Instagram. The demand for diversified social networks threatened Facebook's position in social media and created the risk that Facebook itself could disappear into oblivion just like Myspace had, unless it cemented its position by creating a multi-product ecosystem.

Microsoft versus Apple: From Competition in the Market, to Frenemies, to Inter-ecosystem Competition

Apple was famously founded in a garage in suburban America by Steve Wozniak and Steve Jobs. Steve Wozniak developed the Apple I computer in 1976 and Apple II computer in 1977. In the mid 1980s, Apple revolutionized personal computers with the introduction of the Macintosh, entering into disruptive innovation by introducing a graphical user interface (GUI), rather than relying on simple code, as well as the introduction of the floppy disk and the mouse.[461] Apple's products were richly engineered but expensive, and by the 1990s, they faced declining sales and revenues as they were outcompeted Microsoft, which started proliferating personal computers at a lower price point with its Windows Operating System.

Microsoft became successful with the development of the Disk Operating System (DOS). Microsoft, founded in 1975 by Bill Gates and Paul Allen, found its success after striking a deal with IBM to provide its DOS on IBM hardware. This meant that for each IBM computer sold, royalties were paid to Microsoft. In 1985, Microsoft released Windows as the GUI extension for its DOS. Over the 1990s, Microsoft's success increasingly stemmed by selling its easy-to-use Windows operating systems

459 Hartung (n 458).

460 Kevin Curran, Sarah Graham and Christopher Temple, 'Advertising on Facebook' (2011) 1 International Journal of E-Business Development 26.

461 Wu (n 82) describes the collaboration between Wozniak and Jobs in developing the first Mac computers.

on personal computers used for personal use by consumers. By the end of the decade, Microsoft was the first software company to achieve over USD 1 billion in revenues and captured 90 per cent of the market share for personal computer operating systems.[462]

Apple – which was unable to find any sustained or disruptive innovations in the 1980s and 1990s after Wozniak and Jobs had departed from the company – was only weeks away from bankruptcy in 1997. The company was ultimately saved by a share purchasing deal by Microsoft, which involved both a financial injection and a commitment by Gates that Microsoft Office software could be made available on Apple software.[463] This allowed Apple to remain in the market, which ultimately led to Apple's resurgence as an important player in the digital market with its invention of the iPod and the development of its multi-product ecosystem. The discussion on the upcoming stages of competition focuses on how Apple built a multi-product ecosystem that functioned as a 'walled garden' to lock its users in and allowed the Apple ecosystem to isolate itself from competition.

Microsoft was able to retain its dominance in personal computer operating systems over the decades. It has successfully pre-empted challenges to its dominance both by its scale and the network externalities in the market, as well as its use of strategic behaviour to pre-empt the emergence of potential competitors. Most famously, Microsoft bundled Internet Explorer free of charge with its operating system to foreclose its potential competitor Netscape, leading to the famous *Microsoft* antitrust case in 2000 in the US as well as the EC commitment in 2009.[464]

The challenge to Microsoft's success came not through the emergence of a new computer operating system or the development of middleware that functioned without an Operating system, but by the emergence of innovative handheld technologies: the iPod and the iPhone. Apple's smartphone allowed users to access similar – albeit more limited – functionalities as it could on the personal computer, this could pose a serious threat to Microsoft's position and profitability down the line and created the risk of indirect competition. Microsoft responded by focusing more on the development of its multi-product ecosystem.[465]

While Microsoft failed to expand into mobile markets, it instead focussed on the development of a multi-product ecosystem based on professional productivity

[462] John Cowling, 'A Brief History of Microsoft – The Worlds Biggest Software Company' (*DSP Explorer*, 8 February 2016) <https://content.dsp.co.uk/a-brief-history-of-microsoft-the-worlds-biggest-software-company>.

[463] Stephen Silver, 'August 6, 1997 – The Day Apple and Microsoft Made Peace' (*Apple Insider*, 6 August 2018); Ben Thompson, 'Apple's Middle Age' (*Stratechery*, 5 February 2018) <https://stratechery.com/2018/apples-middle-age/>.

[464] United States v. Microsoft Corporation, 253 F.3d 34 (D.C. Cir. 2001); Microsoft – Tying (Case COMP/39.530) Commission Commitment Decision C2009 10033 [2009] OJ C 36/7.

[465] Charles Arthur, 'Microsoft Threatened as Smartphones and Tablets Rise, Gartner Warns' *The Guardian* (4 April 2013).

software. Despite enjoying its strong position in personal computer operating systems – which can arguably be classified as naturally monopolistic within its market – Microsoft ultimately had to enter into the development of a multi-product ecosystem to prevent potential envelopment attacks by another multi-product ecosystem down the line. Meanwhile, Apple recaptured its position in the digital network industry through its innovative iPod and later iPhone, from which they developed an expansive, but closed, multi-product ecosystem.

Amazon: An Aggressive Growth Strategy – Forfeiting Profit to Aggregate Demand

Amazon famously started out as an online bookseller. In 1994, Jeff Bezos founded Amazon as a way to capitalize on the potential growth market of web commerce. Bezos chose to sell books through his online platform due to the large potential market, the low price that could be offered for books and the tremendous selection of titles. Before settling on books, Bezos had also considered compact discs (CDs), computer hardware, or videos. It is presumable that the articles were selected for the potential to serve a wide range of demand and to achieve economies of scale. Amazon tried to achieve this scale by enticing users to rely on its platform to purchase their books by offering discounts of 10 to 30 per cent, providing recommendations based on reading habits or preferences and e-mail alerts to notify customers of new books in the areas of their interests.[466] Amazon used these strategies to develop a large customer base to which it would sell a wide array of e-commerce goods later. However, throughout its IPO in 1997 and its acquisition of two bookselling platforms in the UK and Germany, Amazon remained to be a consistent loss-leader.[467] In 1999, Amazon started to welcome third-party sellers on its platform, which was key to its success.[468] In 2001, Amazon had incurred a total of USD 3 billion in losses, before turning its first quarterly profit in the fourth quarter of that year. This profit came after Amazon started to allow third-party sellers and to expand into new product lines with its e-commerce products and new markets such as those for music and video products.[469]

Amazon also did not have a full 'first mover's' advantage. At the time of Amazon's transition into becoming a broader e-commerce platform, eBay was still the market leader in the industry. According to statements by Bezos in front of the judiciary committee, Amazon was able to overtake eBay as the most popular platform by focussing on supporting its third-party sellers. These sellers made up around 5% of sales on the Amazon platform in 1999 but make up over 60% of sales on the

466 Funding Universe, 'Amazon.Com, Inc. History' (*Funding Universe*) <www.fundinguniverse.com/company-histories/amazon-com-inc-history/>.

467 ibid; Khan (n 267).

468 Jeff Bezos' 'Testimony before the Subcommittee on Antitrust, Commercial, and Administrative Law'.

469 Funding Universe (n 466).

Amazon platform today. The secret to Amazon's success, according to Bezos himself, is the following[470]:

> It was only by focusing on supporting sellers and giving them the best tools, we could invent that we were able to succeed and eventually surpass eBay. One such tool is Fulfilment by Amazon, which enables our third-party sellers to stow their inventory in our fulfilment centres, and we take on all logistics, customer service, and product returns. By dramatically simplifying all of those challenging aspects of the selling experience in a cost-effective way, we have helped many thousands of sellers grow their businesses on Amazon.

Amazon's origins show that it had to rely on the ideas, products, and services by third-party complementors to outcompete eBay and the online solutions offered by physical stores such as Barnes and Nobles first, and later Walmart and Target. To create this vibrant downstream community, Amazon first attracted users on the consumer-facing side by offering sharp discounts and incurring losses, to then attract third-party sellers that could sell to that user base. The final quote by Bezos shows that – to retain its position in e-commerce and retail – Amazon had to expand into a multi-product ecosystem to achieve the economies of scale and scope that made it cost-efficient for third-party sellers to offer their products on the Amazon platform.

6.2 STAGE 2: GROWTH – EXPANSION INTO A MULTI-PRODUCT ECOSYSTEM

Stage 2 ecosystem competition is characterized by on-platform and cross-platform expansion. The operator of an incumbent (stand-alone) platform is granted some reprieve from the intense competition it faces in stage 1, yet it is nothing like the 'quiet life' lived by monopolists in traditional markets. The monopoly (or entrenched position) in the platform market allows the platform operator to identify growth opportunities. The platform operator can again start experimenting, yet this time it is not to establish its position vis-à-vis competitors in the same market but to see how it can expand its offering of products and services. The platform operator will start to see how it can leverage its position to and from its occupied markets as to anchor its core platform service and insulate it from competition by surrounding it with linked platforms and products, whilst also attracting new users by proliferation across markets.

The platform operator has to make a number of strategic considerations. First, it must choose whether to prioritize short-term gains or long-term competitive dominance. Its monopoly in a certain market allows it to stop relying on give-aways, instead raising prices. For instance, a ride-hailing company that has successfully captured a certain city could choose to raise prices for ride-hailers or raise its commission fees for drivers. In practice however, many of the larger incumbent ecosystems of today have

470 ibid.

chosen not to raise their prices for short term gains. Instead, these platforms tend to continue operating while facing significant losses while they are sustained through venture capital. Today's large ecosystem operators have generally maintained a strategy of long-term competitive dominance, focussing on horizontal, vertical, and diagonal expansion and strengthening user lock-in. This is especially true for the newer GAFAM companies: Google, Facebook, and Amazon, which had to enter the market later than Microsoft and Apple, and have therefore directly adopted these modern growth strategies.[471] Hence, the second stage of competition is referred to as the growth stage: now that the first platform has been captured, the ecosystem operator attempts to grow into an elaborate and interlinked digital multi-product ecosystem.

The second strategic consideration relates to the role of complementors. As the incumbent enters into new markets, it must make sure that it remains attractive to the complementors that helped it to capture its position. This is especially important where it relates to vertical integration. As the risk of vertical ecosystem competition grows, complementors may start to look for alternatives if they fear expulsion from the platform. Platform operators will continue to share rewards with their complementors as they grow, even if it creates losses. Google's revenue sharing agreements with OEMs are a good example of this: the platform operator enters into new markets and attempts to attract complementors there by giving them more give-aways as well. This is to signal to complementors in the new market and existing multi-actor ecosystems that the expansion of the platform operator into new markets benefits everyone.[472] In the case of Google, they first offered a beneficial deal to OEMs: a free high-quality Operating System, a free bundle of applications, and sharing in search revenue. It was not until much later that Google actually started to impose restrictive terms on OEMs and developed its own Pixel smartphone series. This strategy has been described as 'open early, closed late'. In the second stage of ecosystem competition, ecosystem operators generally prefer the 'open early' strategy, as to close off parts of the ecosystem during the third stage.

The third strategic consideration is when and where to start closing off parts of the ecosystem for complementors. Participation by complementors brings significant experimentation while externalizing these costs for the firms. Complementors will develop new applications, features, functionalities, or forks as to co-generate value with the ecosystem operator. Thus, it is attractive for the ecosystem operator to invite participation in many areas of activity. At some point however, the ecosystem operator will want to centralize more of the granted platform and decision rights as to give clear direction to the development of the ecosystem and to develop user expectations for the brand. Referring again to Google Android, the Operating System is in principle Open Source, thus allowing OEMs and developers to create forks of Google Android that could diverge heavily from what Google considers to be

471 Khan (n 267); Ezrachi and Stucke (n 1).
472 cf Rietveld and Schilling (n 47); Evans and Gawer (n 98); Cusumano, Gawer and Yoffie (n 118).

desirable. Google started offering Android OS with free licenses in 2005, and some Android forks arose. By 2012, Google made it mandatory for OEMs to enter into anti-fragmentation agreements. As competition waned with the decline of Blackberry, Google gained more opportunity to close off parts of its ecosystem to prepare itself for the maturity stage.[473]

The fourth and final strategic consideration is then how to evolve in terms of technology and business models. As discussed earlier, competition between digital ecosystems happens across a range of markets and can be more or less intense depending on the level of differentiation. Once the ecosystem operator has firmly established the reigns over its multi-actor ecosystems and is able to determine the direction of the development of its ecosystem better, it will look into how it can achieve a period of relatively relaxed competition at the ecosystem level. The empirical observations below show how growing ecosystem operators will evolve through acquisitions, the development of services, and the improvement of its platforms to differentiate itself from existing incumbents in terms of the nature of its services, its openness, its data dependency, and its target audience. By strongly differentiating one's ecosystem from the incumbent ecosystem operators, the growing ecosystem operator can signal that it is looking to establish an equilibrium at the ecosystem level rather than competing with the incumbent ecosystem operator head-on. The discussion of stage 3 and 4 ecosystem operators argues that this benefits all large ecosystem operators, while creating negative effects for entrants in stage 1 ecosystem competition and ultimately end users in the long term.

6.2.1 *Empirical Observations on Competition in the Growth Stage*

Apple provides a clear starting point for the discussion on stage 2 competition. At the end of the first stage of competition in the market for desktop operating systems, Apple was at the end of its rope and facing bankruptcy, saved only by the graces – and investment – of its competitor Microsoft.[474] However, 1997 marked the starting point of its return to relevance with the return of Steve Jobs and the development of a new and revolutionary vertically integrated strategy that involves three Apple products: the iMac, the iPod, and iTunes.

The first product to launch was the iMac, a novel Apple computer that managed to attract clients with its modern design and ease of use. Apple created a portfolio of digital products that would only be available to Apple computers. These included video-editing software, the QuickTime video player, but most importantly iTunes.[475] iTunes was revolutionary in its own right. It started as a music player that

[473] Alissa Cooper, Jasper Van den Boom and Zander Arnao, 'Considerations for Effective Search Competition Remedies' (2024) Knight Georgetown Institute Report.

[474] Silver (n 463).

[475] Brandon Griggs and Todd Leopold, 'How iTunes Changed Music, and the World' *CNN* (26 April 2013).

allowed Mac users to listen to digitally stored music in 2001 but quickly evolved into a digital marketplace for music with DRM copyright protection. Rather than buying physical CDs, users could buy and download a single for 99 cents. This created a legal way to acquire diversified music affordably, in a time where operations such as Napster and Kazaa allowed users to pirate music creating a decline in sales in the music industry.[476]

The final ingredient behind Apple's return to relevance was its revolutionary mp3 player: the iPod. The iPod – with its smooth design and large storage space – rapidly became the most popular mp3 player in the market. However, besides creating revenue through direct sales, the iPod was the perfect leveraging vehicle for iTunes. Music on the iPod required installation through iTunes, while iTunes was available only on Mac. This allowed Apple to leverage its market power in the mp3 market to its music marketplace and vice versa by tying the use of one to the other.[477] Ultimately, these types of ties would lead back to the iMac. Jobs had envisioned Apple's 'Digital Hub' strategy, where the Mac became the central hub of everyone's digital lives.[478] In 2003, when the iTunes music player evolved into the iTunes Music Store, Apple allowed the installation of iTunes on Windows. This allowed Apple to significantly expand its reach by strategically entering into the Microsoft ecosystem.[479] This was however not the end of Apple's Digital Hub strategy, which is still central to Apple's competitive strategy today. However, instead of leading back to the iMac, the Digital Hub has moved to the Cloud and takes shape in the form of continuous synchronization between Apple products. As the old iPod was replaced with the iPod Touch and the iPhone, a computer was no longer a necessity to access apps such as iTunes and the internet.

Apple's development of the iPhone is a clear example of how indirect competition may threaten another ecosystem's core markets. Windows was the comfortable monopolist in desktop Operating Systems, and competing directly, by entering into the market with a new desktop OS, would have been extremely difficult. However, by transforming the mobile phone into a pocket computer, it became possible to challenge Windows monopoly in Operating Systems by developing a mobile OS that could compete for its user base.[480] Apple was also able to displace incumbents in the market for mobile phones such as Blackberry by adopting a platform or multiactor ecosystem strategy. In 2007, Blackberry was in a similar position to previously discussed incumbents such as Myspace or eBay; it commanded over 50 per cent of

476 Nicola Sharpe and Arewa Olufunmilayo, 'Is Apple Playing Fair? Navigating the iPod FairPlay DRM Controversy' (2007) 5 Northwestern Journal of Technology and Intellectual Property 302; Griggs and Leopold (n 475); Charles Arthur, 'iTunes Is 10 Years Old Today, Was It the Best Idea That Apple Has Ever Had' *The Guardian* (24 May 2017).

477 Sharpe and Olufunmilayo (n 476).

478 Jan Porter, 'The Rise and Fall of iTunes: Apple's Most Hated App' [2019] The Verge.

479 ibid.

480 See eg Gawer and Cusumano (n 12).

the market share in mobile markets and had a loyal customer base and access to vast financial resources. By 2012, Blackberry had trouble retaining 1 per cent of the market share in mobile telephony, while Apple and Google took over its market. Blackberry failed to adapt to the ecosystem strategy.[481] Apple was able to disrupt the market for mobile phones by opening itself up to third-party complementors, allowing it to beat Blackberry in competition in the same way it was beaten by Microsoft, and the same way Facebook beat Instagram. However, Apple soon returned to its ideology of central planning and redirecting users to its other products, leaving it vulnerable to envelopment attacks by Google.

Google acquired Android in 2005 as to enter into the market for mobile Operating Systems. However, unlike Apple which focussed on a vertically integrated iPhone – iOS structure, Google created the Open Handheld Alliance (OHA) in 2007. Original equipment manufacturers (OEMs), mobile network operators (MNOs), and third-party app developers could freely use the Android Operating System if they became participants in the OHA.[482] This allowed Google to quickly proliferate its Operating System through a large variety of devices. Google harnessed the innovative power of multiple OEMS such as Samsung, HTC, and later Huawei, Xiaomi, and Oppo. This strategy allowed Google to offer a series of differentiated phones with different hardware specifications and different prices, which was an effective way of aggregating user demand and creating a user base. Google also exercised less oversight over its third-party app developers than Apple, which allowed the Play Store to quickly build up a greater offering of more varied apps than the Apple ecosystem. By 2010, Google's Android overtook Apple as the most popular Operating System. Thus, after trumping Blackberry by relying on a multi-actor ecosystem strategy, Apple was quickly overtaken by Google which opened up its ecosystem even more to third-party participation. At the moment of writing, Google is considered to have between 75 per cent of the total operating system market share and close to 100 per cent of the licensable operating system market share.[483]

This is dynamic competition in action[484]: at the same time Apple engaged in indirect competition with Microsoft's monopoly in desktop Operating Systems, Google entered into competition with Apple in the market for smartphone Operating Systems.

481 Tiwana (2014), 3.

482 See *Google Android* (Case AT.40099), Commission Decision C(2018) 4761 [2018], OJ C 402/19 paras 120–131; 148–154.

483 *Google Android* (Case AT.40099), Commission Decision C(2018) 4761 [2018], OJ C 402/19 paras 442–460, the Commission differentiates between licensable OS and non-licensable another. For total OS users it shows that in July 2016, 2156, million users had installed Android OS while 518 million users had installed iOS, amounting to about 75 to 80 per cent of the market for Google Android. In 2021, Statcounter notes that Android has around 72% of the market, iOS around 26%, and that the rest is divided among smaller OS providers such as Samsung and KaiOS. See data on Statcounter, *Mobile Operating System Market Share Worldwide, August 2020 to August 2021* (Statcounter, August 2021) <https://gs.statcounter.com/os-market-share/mobile/worldwide>.

484 Petit (n 13).

However, Google arguably entered this market as the development of mobile search threatened its monopoly position in the horizontal search market, which was based on desktop web-browsing. This idea is corroborated by the Commission's findings in Google Android, which describe how Google has leveraged its search engine into Mobile Operating Systems through anti-fragmentation agreements, mandatory app installations, and revenue sharing agreements if Google search was the exclusive default search machine on Android devices.[485] Meanwhile, Microsoft's attempted entry into the mobile OS market as a response to Apple and Google's entry into the mobile OS market failed and Microsoft left the mobile market.[486]

The competitive pressures these undertakings experienced from one another shaped the strategies of these undertakings: Apple focussed on its vertically integrated walled garden and it uses network effects and complementarities to lock-in its existing user base and maximizing profit by having users purchase multiple Apple products. Google continues to focus on growth and expansion as to gather and collect more data and create more sources of revenue through an ever-expanding multi-product ecosystem. Google will continuously invest in R&D and market entry in order to achieve and sustain more growth into more markets. Meanwhile, Microsoft has maintained its open business model on desktop – freely allowing any third-party software – while focussing its own product offering on productivity software.

While Microsoft, Apple and Google were entangled in an intense competitive process with one another, Facebook and Amazon had their own reasons for expansion into a multi-product ecosystem. For Facebook, its monopoly position in the social media market was arguably less stable on a stand-alone basis than Google's monopoly in search or Microsoft's monopoly in desktop Operating Systems. Facebook rather experienced competitive pressure from other social media which could be 'the next best thing'. Especially faced with heterogeneous user demands and – even in its early stages of development – backlash from data gathering practices, Facebook's monopoly seemed barely anchored and easily contestable.

At the same time, users' move to mobile forced Facebook to adapt its strategy as well, as the mobile phone would be a likely new access point for all consumer communications including social media. As a response to this, Facebook acquired Instagram in 2012 to prevent direct competition, and WhatsApp in 2014 to cement its position in person-to-person consumer communications services. Twitter, which is not focussed on building closed social networks but rather serves as a user commentary newsfeed of sorts did not directly threaten Facebook's position as the primary social network.

With the acquisition of Instagram in 2012 and WhatsApp in 2014, Facebook has secured sufficient routes to user data and cross-market network externalities to

485 Google Android (Case AT.40099), Commission Decision C(2018) 4761 [2018], OJ C 402/19, para 155 et seq.

486 Todd Haselton, 'Departing Windows Chief Terry Myerson Explains Why Microsoft Failed in Smartphones' *CNBC* (29 March 2018).

strengthen its dominance in the user-facing side of the market and to secure its position in display advertising from potential entrants.[487] Facebook's ecosystem is possibly the least expansive of the big five, as it is very focussed. It has however developed a very strong position in its segment of the network. Facebook is building an ecosystem which allows it to become the primary supplier of consumer communications services. Even Facebook's purchase of virtual reality technology supplier Oculus happened with the idea in mind that virtual reality could become a new communications platform.[488]

Any other services offered by Facebook are services that allow users to connect in new ways, that provide bartering and selling opportunities or content consumption which can be paired with display advertising. Thus, the mission of Facebook seems clear, monetizing communications between consumers. In doing so, Facebook cooperates closely with other firms: its platform can be accessed through Microsoft's, Apple's, and Google's ecosystems.

Amazon's expansion into a multi-product ecosystem was driven by a mixture of pursuing long-term competitive superiority and short-term profitability. As described by Khan, Amazon was willing to forego profitability in order to expand its position in e-commerce. The continued existence of Amazon was determined largely by the unrelenting willingness of investors to support Amazon. Khan noted that Amazon expanded into a large range of markets adjacent to e-commerce in order to insulate its position in this market from competition and grow its market share as an online retailer.[489] At the same time however, Amazon expanded its multi-product ecosystem into new directions which were seemingly unrelated to e-commerce and not necessarily aimed at building a long-term competitive advantage in the market for e-commerce. Most notably was its entry into the market for server space with AWS. This part of the strategy employed by Bezos is viewed here as a way to secure short-term profitability elsewhere, while Amazon focussed on aggregating demand on its activities related to e-commerce. This idea is supported by a statement made by Bezos in front of the US House subcommittee investigating digital markets:

> A lot of observers characterized Amazon Web Services as a risky distraction when we started. 'What does selling compute and storage have to do with selling books?' they wondered. No one asked for AWS. It turned out the world was ready and hungry for

[487] On the use of acquisitions to strengthen one's position through economies of scope and complementarities, see eg Van den Boom and Samranchit (n 148).

[488] Drake Baer, 'The Real Reason Facebook Bought Oculus: "Virtual Reality Will Be the On-Ramp to Optical Computing"' *Business Insider* (21 November 2014) in reference to Zuckerberg's Facebook post of the 25th of March where he announced that the purchase of Oculus was a 'a new communication platform. By feeling truly present, you can share unbounded spaces and experiences with the people in your life. Imagine sharing not just moments with your friends online, but entire experiences and adventures.' This post can be found at <www.facebook.com/zuck/posts/im-excited-to-announce-that-weve-agreed-to-acquire-oculus-vr-the-leader-in-virtu/10101319050523971/>.

[489] See eg Khan (n 267).

> cloud computing but didn't know it yet. We were right about AWS, but the truth is we've also taken plenty of risks that didn't pan out. In fact, Amazon has made billions of dollars of failures. Failure inevitably comes along with invention and risk-taking, which is why we try to make Amazon the best place in the world to fail.
>
> —Jeff Bezos (2021)[490]

Ultimately, both the server space and profits of AWS became the backbone of the expansive Amazon ecosystem. Amazon has developed a highly diversified offering of goods and services while maintaining at its core a vertically integrated and developed e-commerce infrastructure. It not only offers a marketplace, but it also produces its own goods, has its own auction house, and has developed a shipping and logistics network that rivals USPS. Outside of this vertical integration, Amazon's conglomerate has expanded horizontally and diagonally to an extent that it is sometimes argued that they are working towards becoming 'the monopolist of everything'.[491]

In short, digital undertakings have expanded from their platform into elaborate multi-product ecosystems, often for different reasons. It may help them safeguard their incumbency in core revenue generating platform markets, add value to their services through ecosystem linkages, harness efficiencies, or allow them to differentiate themselves from others. The development of the multi-product ecosystem may also be used to solidify their position in offering important societal services such as communications or help them build a long-term competitive advantage and short-term profits. Once the multi-product ecosystem is sufficiently developed, competition between the ecosystem operators reaches maturity, and an equilibrium can be found as to enter into stage 3 ecosystem competition.

6.3 STAGE 3: MATURITY – FINDING EQUILIBRIUM AND THE PATH TO PROFITABILITY

The third stage of ecosystem competition is maturity, which happens when the incumbent ecosystems are sufficiently established and diversified that they have softened inter-ecosystem competition. The ecosystem operator is then able to exert its power within the ecosystem, as to move away from growth strategies into strategies to become (more) profitable. In other words, this is the shift towards the 'closed late' strategy.

The ability of ecosystem operators to withdraw the rewards for its complementors and to extract the rents for themselves is demonstrated in later stages of ecosystem competition. Prices increase, commission fees become higher, terms for business users become worse, and the risk of anti-competitive behaviour through abuses of gatekeeper power grows.[492]

490 Jeff Bezos, 'Testimony before the Subcommittee on Antitrust, Commercial, and Administrative Law' (n 468).

491 Khan (n 267).

492 See eg Friso Bostoen and Nicolas Petit, 'Platforms' Treacherous Turn' [2023] Network Law Review.

While there are negative effects for business users and end users, it is argued here that these changes are not necessarily anti-competitive. Platform operators create unsustainable expectations for business and end users during their growth stages. Users become accustomed to free high-quality services, and business users are overrewarded for their participation in order to outcompete other ecosystems. However, no business can continue to be loss-leading indefinitely. Over time, platform operators *must* increase prices or introduce additional advertising (e.g. decrease quality for end users) to become and remain profitable and to create stability. This also makes sense from the perspective of the venture capital investors that have helped the platforms to grow: they have supported the platform while it was loss-leading and are now expecting returns. Without the maturity stage, investments in emerging platforms would likely significantly decline.[493] The attempt to escape intense competition and prioritize profits should thus be seen as natural, the question is then to which extent these profits can be justified through economic rationale. This is what sets apart stage 3 competition from stage 4 competition. In the latter, the ecosystem operators are behaving akin to monopolists or duopolists and extract excessive rents from users.

Maturity requires differentiation, at least to a certain extent, to escape intense competition. Microsoft and Apple both operate primarily device-centric ecosystems.[494] However, while Microsoft employs an open strategy which welcomes collaboration with third parties, Apple has developed a closed integrated ecosystem. Amazon has an ecosystem that is highly device-centric but also functions in similar ways to an ad-centric ecosystem as it relies on data to personalize and recommend certain offerings, whether it be through advertising or in its sorting of relevant e-commerce results. Finally, Google and Facebook offer ad-centric ecosystems. The Google ecosystem is open on the consumer-facing side; it invites the participation of OEMs and complement developers in Android and the Play Store and focuses on indexing the websites provided by third parties. It uses the data generated in these activities to generate data for its advertising services. Facebook on the other hand is more closed: it gathers data from its proprietary social media and communications services to gather data and target advertising. Differentiation between the largest ecosystem operators allows them to concurrently extract high revenue and profits, without taking away another ecosystem's piece of the pie.[495] As each ecosystem

493 Sai Krishna Kamepalli, Raghuram Rajan and Luigi Zingales, 'Kill Zone' (2020) No. 27146 National Bureau of Economic Research Working Paper Series <www.nber.org/papers/w27146> describes how Big Tech allegedly creates Kill Zones on the basis of the same underlying principles: venture capitalists will not invest in firms that are unlikely to achieve maturity.

494 Bourreau (n 28) 2–10.

495 Shao (n 131) describes differentiation between Google and Apple in relation to their smartphone OS business strategies: 'In the ostensible American mobile platform duopoly between Apple's iOS and Google's Android, significant differentiation has already reduced head-to-head competition, with Apple emphasizing privacy, security, and user experience while Google offers lower price points at the expense of monetizing user attention.' This book argues that these types of decisions are made systematically across markets enveloped within a product ecosystem as to differentiate the ecosystem

creates revenue from different sources, and the profits are high enough to remain on top of their respective collection of markets, competition between the largest digital ecosystems weakens and they gain the opportunity to focus more on extracting revenue from their existing userbase.[496]

The strategies employed by ecosystems are one way to differentiate themselves from others. However, each ecosystem has also developed itself around a core idea or core functionality. Google has positioned itself as an ecosystem for information, focussing primarily on revenue generated from gathering and indexing information. Its ventures into navigation, self-driving vehicles and other productivity software are also based (at least partly) on Google's capacity to collect and process information. Even Google's specialty in advertising – search advertising – is based on the use of information to create comprehensive user profiles and match them with the product they are looking for.[497]

The Facebook ecosystem – which is closest to Google in terms of strategy – is a communications ecosystem. Facebook does not gather and index information but rather lets users share information between them. Facebook's ecosystem consists of number-dependent and -independent messaging and social media apps through which a large share of consumer to consumer and business to consumer communications occurs.[498] Facebook's online display advertising is more communications focussed as Google's keyword advertising, as display advertising is generally aimed more at making users aware of the product, where keyword advertising is focussed more on conversions.[499]

Amazon's ecosystem can best be understood as a commerce ecosystem. Amazon's e-commerce platform is a product search engine, which helps users to navigate an almost unmanageable range of goods offered on its platform. Amazon also provides fulfilment services, which emboldens its position as the leading commerce ecosystem with its expansive logistics and shipping services.[500]

Microsoft is increasingly shaping itself into a productivity ecosystem or enterprise ecosystem. While Microsoft is still the leading provider in household desktops, it seems that this is no longer the core activity on which Microsoft focuses. Instead, Microsoft has been steadily expanding its productivity software from its proprietary Office products into Microsoft Dynamics 365. This cloud-based productivity hub bundles Microsoft's Office products, its Customer Relationship Management

experience as a whole. Gawer and Cusumano (n 39); Gawer (n 12) describe the importance of expanding into a multi-product platform and making scope decisions in order to retain one's position of leadership in the platform market and beyond.

496 Competition & Market Authority (n 155), paras 15–25 notes that while the Google and Apple ecosystems have a 'vice-like grip' on important core platforms for mobile devices, their source of revenue differs substantially: Apple makes over 80% of its revenue from device sales, while Google generates over 80% of its revenue from different types of advertising. The report also notes that both firms are highly profitable.

497 ibid, Competition & Market Authority (n 176).

498 Busch (n 2).

499 Competition & Market Authority (n 69).

500 Busch (n 2).

Software and its Sales Intelligence Solutions together with its Azure cloud computing services. Microsoft's expansion into LinkedIn, its acquisition of Skype and the development of Teams all point towards an attempt of Microsoft to develop a software service for universal productivity and communications in enterprises.[501]

Finally, Apple has differentiated itself by establishing the products in its ecosystem as luxury goods. Apple has captured a segment of the market with high willingness to pay and has been able to compete with the ad-centric ecosystem which offer goods at a low price point by focussing on quality and design and establishing strong ecosystem linkages. This is exemplified not only by the price point of Apple products but also the spending behaviour of Apple customers in App Stores for example. Bostoen and Mandrescu note that Apple App Store users spend on average ten time as much on apps than Google Android users.[502] According to data compiled by the American Customer Satisfaction Index, Apple was also the brand that users feel most connected to, as well as the most popular brand name, reaffirming the enjoyment users derive from Apple's integrated bundle of high-end products.[503] Apple's ecosystem could be considered a 'luxury' ecosystem, or at least a closed and vertically integrated ecosystem that serves to escape competition.

By differentiating both the ecosystem's focus and the strategies which are employed, the ecosystems have found an equilibrium in which they can compete in some product markets, while insulating their core markets.[504] This may also mean that a duopoly comes to exist in some markets due to product differentiation, which means that competition is not intense even if a duopoly exists. As a consequence, the presence of multiple firms within a certain market does not exclude

TABLE 6.1 *An overview of the different orientations of the MAGMA ecosystem*

Undertaking	Ecosystem nature
Google	Informational
Meta	(Consumer) communications
Amazon	Commerce
Microsoft	Productivity
Apple	Luxury

501 See also Van den Boom and Samranchit (n 148) on the topic of Microsoft's acquisitions of LinkedIn in establishing its position in the Sales Intelligence Services and Customer Relationship Management markets.

502 Bostoen and Mandrescu (n 44) 4.

503 Danny Vena, 'Apple Leads the Pack in Survey of Brands Customers Love Most', *Nasdaq* (7 October 2020).

504 Christina Cafarra and others, 'Designing Regulation for Digital Platforms: Why Economists Need to Work on Business Models' 2020 *EUVox* also note that competition between Big Tech ecosystems with different business models may not result in direct competition.

the presence of natural monopoly in these markets: it may be more efficient to have a single system in a market, but differentiation and leveraging the ecosystem has allowed two products in the market to co-exist. This work proposes that the idea that digital ecosystems have reached an equilibrium is supported by the fact that each ecosystem has been able to grow its profits after the multi-product ecosystem became more developed. This is demonstrated through the empirical observations below.

6.3.1 *Empirical Observations on Price Increases in the Maturity Stage*

Profit Maximization in Ad-Centric Ecosystems

According to the Competition and Markets Authority (CMA) in the United Kingdom, both Google and Facebook have been earning profits that are substantially higher than any reasonable estimate of what one would expect in a competitive market.[505] In a study of the UK market, the CMA finds that digital advertising is increasingly displacing traditional media advertising. In the market for digital advertising, they differentiate between search advertising, open-display ad markets, and owned and operated display ad markets. In the market for search advertising, Google earned more than 90 per cent of the £7.3 billion spent on this type of advertising in 2019. Facebook took over 50 per cent of the £5.5 billion spent on display advertising, while Google and Facebook together took around 60 per cent. Around a third was sold through open-display advertising and went to publishers. The CMA estimates that around 80 per cent of all expenditure on digital advertising went to just these two companies.[506]

While this is focussed on the UK market only, there is a clear global trend in the increased revenue extraction by both platforms. After Google became dominant in the market for horizontal search, it had a revenue of USD 0.4 billon, by 2020, Google revenue is USD 18,169 billion.[507] Facebook's revenue increased from 777 million in 2009 to USD 8,596 billion in 2020. These ecosystems do not only see a year-over-year increase in revenue but also a year-over-year increase in profits. These profits have seen both a significant absolute increase as well as a slight percentual increase over the years (Figure 6.1).

This chart aligns well with the idea that digital markets exhibit an outward shifting demand curve combined with economies of scale and scope: the more output these companies deliver, the more profitable they become. The percentual increase in profit over revenue is best visible in Facebook, which still seems to have more room to grow than Google does in search. It can also be argued that the increased

505 Competition & Market Authority (n 69) 42.

506 ibid 58–62.

507 Statista, 'Annual Revenue of Google from 2002 to 2021' (*Statista*) <www.statista.com/statistics/266206/googles-annual-global-revenue/> accessed 15 January 2022.

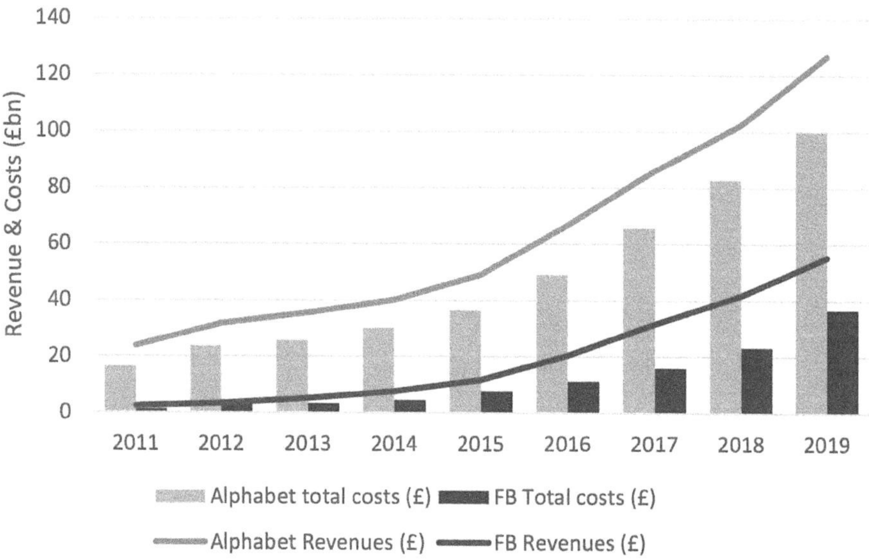

FIGURE 6.1 The CMA analysis of Alphabet Group and Facebook filed 10-K reports Competition & Market Authority (n 69) 66.

profitability is not solely an effect of increased growth but also results from Google's and Facebook's possibility to exercise monopoly power.

For both platforms, it can also be argued that they have gained the ability to extract monopoly profits. Despite observations by Petit on the perceived uncertainty paired with moligopoly competition,[508] this does indicate the presence of classic monopoly harms in digital markets for advertising. While users are not directly charged a higher price, this price increase affects them indirectly as it will be reflected in the prices of goods sold by advertisers. Google, which predominantly works on a cost-per-click basis, has prices that are around 30–40 per cent higher than its closest competitor Bing.[509] Facebook – according to the CMA – has been able to exploit its market power to earn significantly higher revenues per user than its competitors, increasing from an average of £[0–5] per user in 2011 to £[50–60] in 2019.[510]

Google and Facebook's revenue generating platforms are entrenched within their multi-product ecosystem and are sufficiently insulated to extract monopoly rents. These rents are not only extracted in monetary value but also by increased extraction of user data, as exemplified by Google's announcement of increased data combining of publishers in 2016 and Facebook's fine from the Commission over GDPR violations in its WhatsApp service.[511]

[508] Petit (n 13).
[509] Competition & Market Authority (n 69) 235.
[510] Competition & Market Authority (n 69).
[511] *Facebook/WhatsApp* (Case No. M.8228) Commission Decision C(2017) 3192 final [2017] OJ C 134/22.

Profit Maximization in Device-Centric Ecosystems

In device-centric ecosystems, the increases in revenues and profits differ significantly from those in ad-centric ecosystems. Microsoft has seen an increase in revenue from USD 28.37 billion in 2002 to USD 143 billion in 2020.[512] While there is a steady growth in revenue, Microsoft's increase in revenue over the past nineteen years has been around 500%, which pales in comparison to Facebook 8,500% and Google's whopping 45,150% increase in revenues over a similar period of time. Out of Microsoft's USD 143 billion in revenue, USD 39 billion was net income (profit).[513]

Apple increased its revenue from USD 24.5 billion in 2007 – when the iPhone was released – to USD 274.5 billion in 2020.[514] Apple had a net income of 3.5 billion in 2007 and 57 billion in 2020, showing a percentual increase in its revenue to profit ratio (14% in 2007 to 20% in 2020).

Amazon's revenue increase is the most extreme, with a revenue of USD 8.5 billion in 2005 to USD 386 billion in 2020 (an increase of around 4,441%).[515] However, Amazon's strategy of expansion over profits can be seen in its profitability, with fluctuating increases and decreases in profits between 2005 and 2015. In some years Amazon even incurred losses, generating a loss of 241 million as late as 2014. In 2016 however, Amazon's strategy shifts towards profitability and profit increases from USD 596 million to USD 2.3 billion, increasing even more steeply between 2017 and 2018, where profits went from 3 billion to 10 billion in one year. In 2020, Amazon's net profits are 21 billion and still steadily rising.

These numbers provide some intuitions about the different business strategies employed by the device-centric ecosystems. First, Microsoft is focussed on its multi-product software ecosystem. As it already possesses a large market share in its core market and does not aggressively expand into new markets, its increase in revenue is steady but limited. On the other hand, due to Microsoft's focus on maximizing profits in its core markets, it is able to minimize operating costs and maximize net income, resulting in the greatest percentage of net income over profits.

Apple has experienced a greater but similar revenue growth. Apple is able to extract high revenues from the relatively small positions it occupies in the computer and mobile operating system markets. Apple is able to do so as it sells clusters of vertically integrated goods, which means that each sale extracts the maximum potential profits: Microsoft offers products at a low-price point to the majority of customers,

512 Statista, 'Microsoft's Annual Revenue Worldwide from FY 2002 to FY 2022' (*Statista*) <www.statista.com/statistics/267805/microsofts-global-revenue-since-2002/>.

513 Statista, 'Microsoft's Net Income from 2002 to 2022' (*Statista*) <www.statista.com/statistics/267808/net-income-of-microsoft-since-2002/> accessed 16 January 2022.

514 Macrotrends, 'Apple Revenue 2010–2022' (*Macrotrends*).

515 Macrotrends, 'Amazon Revenue 2010–2022' (2022) <www.macrotrends.net/stocks/charts/AMZN/amazon/revenue> accessed 15 June 2022.

while Apple offers a series of highly priced vertically integrated goods to its locked-in user base. The numbers also show that competition is no longer as intense as in the early stages of competition: both undertakings can comfortably extract profits from their market segments by employing an open ecosystem strategy that invites user participation and growth (Microsoft) or closed strategy that relies on vertical integration and central control (Apple).

Finally, Amazon's strategy of aggressive expansion is visible in its profitability. While revenues for Amazon have steadily expanded, its profitability has fluctuated wildly over the past decades, even after it stopped being a consistent loss-leader. However, Amazon has found that its strategy of establishing structural dominance across markets and the achievement of scale and scope came to fruition in the second half of the 2010s, where its profitability exploded.

Once an ecosystem has sufficiently escaped inter-ecosystem competition, it is more likely to set more exploitative terms over time intra-ecosystem. This coincides with the ideas set out in this book: abuses of gatekeeper power – and subsequent monopoly profits – may be linked to diminished inter-ecosystem competition.[516] This book contributes to this discussion through its discussion on the concept of ecosystem power as the other side of the coin to gatekeeper power. This may help to explain – and to assess – when and how decreases in inter-ecosystem competition lead to increased abuses of gatekeeper power. The Section 6.4 sets out a theory as to why inter-ecosystem competition in digital markets is currently weak and does not create sufficient competitive constraints on incumbents.

6.4 STAGE 4: INCUMBENT – INCUMBENCY AND THE SUPPRESSION OF DISRUPTIVE INNOVATION

Stage 4 ecosystem competition happens when a small number of incumbents occupy vast parts of the digital network industry. This book makes the point that the characteristics of digital markets facilitate cross-market expansion due to economies of scale and scope, complementarities, technological linkages, and an inherent expansion drift. This means that if competition is left unchecked, the digital network industry is likely to naturally gravitate towards having a few large firms. Ultimately, a type of oligopoly competition takes hold, except competition between these oligopolies spans across sectors and industries to cover large parts of the digital network. The larger ecosystem operators know that every newcomer will have to depend on one of more of their services to reach end users and business users, giving them access over all the important gateways for entry into competition. The incumbents own infrastructural platforms such as cloud, hardware, and even cables and wires for internet connection, they operate the gateway platforms such as search, operating systems, and marketplaces. Stage 4 ecosystem operators control access

[516] See Cozzolino, Corbo and Aversa (n 99); Rietveld and Schilling (n 47).

points for competition in the digital network industry and have the ability to foreclose competitors by steering away users, preventing funding, entering into killer acquisitions, or poaching talented workers.[517]

The incumbency stage allows large ecosystem operators to continue their reign as the dominant design by preventing the emergence of new and better technologies. The life cycle of the dominant design naturally ends with a decline stage: the once dominant product is displaced by a new product because of technological changes or shifts in user preferences, leading to disruption. While it is possible for the dominant firm to win the new cycle to become the dominant design again, disruption generally happens by outside firms. For the incumbent to leapfrog and enter into the new market themselves, they will have to cannibalize their existing business.[518] As leapfrogging is difficult, monopolists have incentives to try and stop the adoption of new technologies. This can be observed in traditional monopolists as well: the advent of the FM radio was fought by the Radio Company of America, which was a monopolist in AM radio. Similarly, many innovations made in the famous Bell laboratories during Bell/AT&Ts incumbency in telecoms were only released after Bell/AT&T was unbundled.[519] More recently, it was seen by Kodak's failure to move into digital camera technologies which cost it its incumbency in photo cameras.[520] The incumbent monopolist does not want a new technology to cannibalize the profits from its current technology and will generally try to prevent its emergence rather than facilitate it. As potentially disruptive entrants will often have to enter into competition through the multi-actor ecosystem(s) of an incumbent, the incumbent has the ability to identify and foreclose potential disruptors.[521]

By ensuring that no new technologies are developed that favour the entrant over the incumbent the incumbent can prevent discontinuity and protect its current position. Preventing the emergence of new technologies and new entry into the market goes hand in hand: the entrants that are able to create a favourable position for themselves as a consequence of discontinuity were often not active in the market before the discontinuity occurred and may even be the reason that the discontinuity occurred.[522] The idea of stage 4 ecosystem competition introduced here operates on the assumption that incentives for incumbents to cooperate will often outweigh incentives to compete intensely for incumbents. While this work does not create game theoretical models to determine specific incentives to choose cooperation over competition, it does base these insights on literature in law, economics, and

[517] Ezrachi and Stucke (n 1); Lécuyer (n 136); Astrid Krisch and Leonhard Plank, 'Internet Platforms as Infrastructures of the Digital Age' (2019) 45 Der öffentliche Sektor – The Public Sector; Busch (n 2).

[518] Tiwana (n 34) ch 2.

[519] See analyses in Wu (n 344).

[520] Tiwana (n 34).

[521] See chs 5 and 6.2.

[522] See Tiwana (n 34); Cozzolino, Corbo and Aversa (n 99); Ezrachi and Stucke (n 1).

management theory related to oligopoly markets and collusion, as well as empirical observations on competition in digital markets.[523]

Incumbent digital ecosystems can use their combined ecosystem and gatekeeper power, as well as direct or indirect cooperation with other incumbents, to subdue any competitive threats. Specifically, the incumbent may prevent the emergence of new disruptive platforms and technologies which threaten its incumbency by colluding, explicitly, tacitly, or through selective coopetition, rather than competing fiercely with one another.[524] Ezrachi and Stucke describe in depth in which ways incumbents may try to reduce competitive challenges, be it through acquisition, mimicking, denying interoperability, steering users away, or spreading unfavourable information about the possible disruptor.[525] This book builds on those ideas and argues that once the ecosystems have matured, the more intense competition tends to happen on the outer bounds of the ecosystems, which currently include markets for voice assistants, self-driving cars, space exploration, wearables, and virtual reality are not at the core of any of the ecosystems. This is a form of selective coopetition: the stage 4 incumbents prevent disruptive entry by newcomers by competing intensely in these markets and investing heavily. Meanwhile, they collude tacitly or explicitly in other markets to soften competition with one another in their revenue generating markets. By being a first mover in emerging markets – or by foreclosing new emerging platforms before they form their multi-product ecosystems – the incumbent ecosystems can determine the design of the new product and make it complementary to their existing services.[526] While seemingly disruptive at first, the new technology will be transformed into sustained innovation once one of the incumbents has won competition for the emerging market.

The difference between sustained and disruptive innovation is as follows: disruptive innovation entails the introduction of a new technology that replaces the old technology or creates a wholly new market. Sustained innovations are improvements to existing technologies that make them higher quality, more efficient or more cost-efficient to produce. If the disruptive technology is adopted by users, the

[523] cf on collusion Edward J Green, Robert C Marshall and Leslie M Marx, 'Tacit Collusion in Oligopoly' (2014) 2 *The Oxford Handbook of International Antitrust Economics* 464; ibid; Ariel Ezrachi and Maurice E Stucke, 'Sustainable and Unchallenged Algorithmic Tacit Collusion' (2019) 17 Northwestern Journal of Technology and Intellectual Property 217; Marc Ivaldi and others, 'The Economics of Tacit Collusion: Implications for Merger Control' (2007) 282 Contributions to Economic Analysis 217; Rupayan Pal and Marcella Scrimitore, 'Tacit Collusion and Market Concentration under Network Effects' (2016) 145 Economics Letters 266; Lester G Telser, *Competition, Collusion, and Game Theory* (Routledge 2017); Christian Rusche (n 407); Cohen and Zhang (n 387); Heidhues, Köster and Kőszegi (n 329); Petit and Teece, 'Taking Ecosystems Competition Seriously in the Digital Economy' (n 13); Petit (n 13); Cappai and Colangelo (n 14).

[524] ibid.

[525] Ezrachi and Stucke (n 1) ch 3.

[526] Tiwana (n 34).

suppliers of the disruptive technology will generally engage in sustained innovation to further develop their product.[527] Incumbents generally focus on creating sustained innovations to satisfy present and future customers' needs while securing profits and growth. To ensure satisfaction, the sustained innovator will strive to innovate and improve products and services by giving its existing customers something more and better in what they already want, based on their experiences with the incumbent. A disruptive innovator on the other hand is an innovator that delivers a wholly new product, with a very different value proposition than had been available previously. As the disruptor is free form the need to service a large group of existing customers and short-term growth requirements, the disruptor can experiment and offer novel value propositions. Initially, there may be no demand for the disruptors product as it is too novel, but as interest in – and demand for – the product grows, the disruptor becomes able to cannibalize and challenge the incumbent for its market share.[528] Disruption may come in many different forms and market settings, making it hard to determine exactly under what conditions disruption happens.[529] What is however clear is that disruptive innovators must have the ability to unrestrained by anti-competitive behaviour by incumbents and must have access to resources as to enter the market and experiment. Some disruptive technologies are not wholly novel but are a novel application of existing parts. Sometimes these parts can be borrowed from existing incumbents.[530] Disruption may then happen in the form of radical changes in technology, new business models, or other changes that

[527] Joseph L Bower and Clayton M Christensen, 'Disruptive Technologies: Catching the Wave' 12; C Christensen, *The Innovator's Dilemma: When New Technologies Cause Great Firms to Fail* (Harvard Business Review Press 2013); Clayton M Christensen, Michael Raynor and Rory McDonald, 'What Is Disruptive Innovation?' [2015] Harvard Business Review 11.

[528] Christensen (n 528) defines disruptive innovation by the emergence of new products with a very different value proposition from anything available previously. Christensen argues that disruptive innovators will enter into emerging markets with low margins. See also Ezrachi and Stucke (n 1); Carlos Tadao Kawamoto and Renata Giovinazzo Spers, 'A Systematic Review of the Debate and the Researchers of Disruptive Innovation' (2019) 14 Journal of Technology Management & Innovation 73; Rebecca Henderson, 'The Innovator's Dilemma as a Problem of Organisational Competence' (2006) 23 Journal of Product Innovation Management 5 on how this theory has been criticized for being underinclusive of possible disruptive innovations and that it should focus on disruptive business models as well. Alexandre de Streel and Pierre Larouche, 'Disruptive Innovation and Competition Policy Enforcement' (OECD 2015) 4 Define disruptive innovation even more broadly and pose that disruptive innovation offers 'an alternative path to market entry and growth, in addition to the more traditional path of challenging the incumbent firm(s) head on, via sustaining innovation or more statically via cheaper products or superior marketing, for instance. Because it avoids frontal competition, a disruptive innovation strategy can allow the disruptor to grow "under the radar" of incumbent firms and, if successfully executed, can offer more growth potential. Disruptive innovation can thus exist in many ways, whether it be through the development of wholly new products, technologies, processes, business models, superior marketing, new uses of existing technology or entry into an un- or under-utilized product segment. It distinguishes itself mainly as its introduction and adoption disrupt existing business models rather than sustain them.

[529] Ezrachi and Stucke (n 1); Tadao Kawamoto and Giovinazzo Spers (n 529).

[530] Ezrachi and Stucke (n 1).

reduces the modes of supply utilized by today's incumbents to legacy status, including the combining of existing technologies to develop a novel application.[531]

In order to prevent disruption, the incumbent has several tools in its toolbox. First, the incumbent can use exclusionary practices to push a new competitor out of the market or drive it to accept a killer acquisition or potentially foreclosing the competitor. As the incumbent ecosystem enjoys efficiency advantages and the possibility to leverage its network, it can outcompete stand-alone platforms rather easily as long as they do not gain the opportunity to anchor themselves. Faced with the prospect of intense competition, these stand-alone platforms have incentives to allow themselves to be bought out. Refusal to be bought out will result in the mimicking of its services by the incumbent platform and may lead to a market exit.

This type of mimicking has been observed in Facebook's competition with Snapchat,[532] Microsoft's competition with Slack and Zoom, and Amazon's entry into individual product categories, for instance. It is also possible for the ecosystem operator to exclude competitors altogether.[533] For instance, Google's banning of Unlockd from its Play Store may have been because Unlockd competed with Google in the market for advertising. Apple subjects Spotify to disadvantageous treatment by refusing Spotify access to certain technologies, delaying updates through its terms and services and potentially engaging in margin squeeze.[534]

This may help explain why the attractiveness of accepting a killer acquisition grows for a stand-alone company when the ecosystem power held by the incumbent ecosystem is larger. The platforms have the choice to assimilate or die and – depending on the extent of the incumbent ecosystem's power – resistance is often futile. The 2021 market study by the CMA into mobile ecosystems notes similar concerns, arguing that third parties may be discouraged from investing in new and innovative ideas in markets related to mobile ecosystems, as the prospect of competition with Google and Apple makes entry into these markets unattractive.[535]

Second, incumbent ecosystems have the ability and incentives to assimilate the emergence of new potential technologies or icebox them. The CMA study into mobile ecosystems notes these types of innovation harms. Specifically, that weak competition between the Google and Apple mobile ecosystem may lead to certain types of services not becoming available for users, or certain developments and technologies being held up where Apple or Google do not have clear incentives to

531 See Tadao Kawamoto and Giovinazzo Spers (n 647); Rebecca Henderson, 'The Innovator's Dilemma as a Problem of Organisational Competence' (2006) 23 Journal of Product Innovation Management 5.

532 Ezrachi and Stucke (n 3) describe how Facebook first offered purchase Snapchat. After the offer was rejected, Facebook copied Snapchat's main functionalities in order to disincentivize users from adopting Snapchat over Facebook. A similar strategy has been observed in Microsoft's behaviour towards Netscape, see Section 8.2.

533 See the discussion in Section 5.4 and Chapter 6.

534 Bostoen and Mandrescu (n 44) 448 et seq.

535 Competition & Market Authority (n 44) 262–270.

promote these developments.[536] While third-party investments are discouraged if entry into certain markets leads to direct competition with the incumbent ecosystem operator, investments by large digital ecosystems themselves will only be pursued if the new technology or development further entrenches the position of the digital ecosystem as a whole.

Petit noted the continuous investments in R&D by digital ecosystems as an indicator that competitive pressures exist.[537] The presence of continuous R&D investments does however not necessarily indicate that there is direct competitive pressure. Bell/AT&T invested large amounts of money into Research & Development, just like today's incumbent ecosystems do.[538] Yet many important innovations only became available for exploitation and development after AT&T was broken up in the 1980s.[539]

It has been demonstrated empirically that investments in R&D can be made to prevent discontinuity rather than to pursue valuable innovations. As the incumbent ecosystems have the resources to spend large number of resources – likely gained from their dominant position – on innovations that can be patented but never used, R&D to prevent discontinuity can be seen as a harm to innovation rather than an indication that innovation is happening so that ecosystems can escape competition. The possibility that R&D is part of an anti-competitive strategy is discussed in depth in Chapter 9, in light of the Microsoft antitrust case in the US at the turn of the millennium. Here, it is argued that increased investments in R&D may be an indicator of market power if they concur with other anti-competitive strategies that are employed to suppress potential disruption, as happened between Microsoft and Netscape.[540]

The third possibility is to engage in pre-emptive coopetition. As this book focuses on the abuse of market power, it will not dive into issues surrounding potentially illegal agreements made between digital undertakings. Some examples of these agreements have been found in Google's payment to Apple to become the exclusive search engine on iOS or the agreement between Google and Facebook in which they cooperated in the advertising markets.[541]

Bostoen and Mandrescu have also observed beneficial treatment for competing ecosystems that is likely the result of better bargaining power, rather than anti-competitive intent. It has been alleged, for instance, that Amazon is allowed to use

536 ibid 258–265.

537 Petit (n 13).

538 Wu (n 344); Mueller (n 195).

539 Wu (n 344).

540 United States v. Microsoft Corporation, 253 F.3d 34 (D.C. Cir. 2001).

541 California Crane School Inc. v. Google LLC, Alphabet Inc., case 4:21-cv-10001-HSG, 27 December 2021, United States District Court of Northern California; see also Rob Copeland and Tim Higgins, 'Google's Exclusive Search Deals with Apple at Heart of U.S. Lawsuit' *The Wall Street Journal* (20 October 2020); Daisuke Wakabayashi and Tiffany Hsu, 'Behind a Secret Deal between Google and Facebook' *The New York Times* (17 January 2021).

an external payment system for selling its video content, but Netflix as a subscription service is forced to use Apple's in-app payment (IAP) system. Similarly, Apple has exempted Microsoft from billing cloud storage purchases within the app.[542] It is possible that digital ecosystems pre-emptively engage in coopetition as to ensure that no new players emerge that may disrupt the peace found between the ecosystems.

At its core, the incumbents stage is characterized by the ability of the incumbents to take control over access points into competition in the digital network industry, providing them with the power to stop disruptive innovation from taking place, to minimize competition with one another and focus on suppressing competition at the fringes, and the ability to strongly influence users in their decisions towards the adoption of a new product. Ecosystem operators will use their power over resources, positional power, and power over processes to stop threatening entrants from entering into stage 2 or 3 competition, while rewarding entrants that submit to sustaining the innovation of the incumbents. The further inter-ecosystem competition softens, the larger the influence of these ecosystem operators over the entirety of the digital network industry. Rather than acting as gatekeepers over their own segment of the network, they jointly act as gatekeepers for the digital network industry as a whole. It is this measure of power over the network, competition, and competitors that sets apart incumbent ecosystems (stage 4) from mature ecosystems (stage 3). The stages of ecosystem power are not about absolute size, but about size relative to competing ecosystems and the level of control one can exert over parts of the digital network industry.

6.5 CONCLUSION

This chapter has set out the theory of ecosystem competition from which several conclusions can be drawn. First, the emergence of a new platform generally requires the use of launching and growth strategies and potential disruptive innovations as to become the dominant design and aggregate demand on the platform (stage 1 ecosystem competition). Capturing a platform market however, even if this is a monopoly, is not the end of competition in digital markets. Instead, competition continues at the ecosystem level.

Firms that have successfully captured a platform in stage 1 competition will likely attempt to expand into new markets. The creation of a multi-product ecosystem enters the digital firm into stage 2 ecosystem competition, and helps the platform to anchor its position in its captured market by expanding its on-platform cluster and by creating ecosystem linkages between its platforms and products. This allows the platform to create cost-saving efficiencies and value enhancing complementarities. It also provides the platform with staying power, which may help in developing consumer expectations, coordination and compatibility between platforms. At this

[542] See Bostoen and Mandrescu (n 44) 453–454.

stage of competition, the use of leveraging or subsidization to create a multi-product ecosystem that consists of an on-platform cluster or cross-platform offering of goods is likely to create long-run efficiencies, as it allows the platform to challenge the incumbent.

When an ecosystem becomes more mature it enters into stage 3 ecosystem competition. The ecosystem orchestrator can differentiate their strategies and the focus of their ecosystems to soften competition in their core markets. This change of strategy allows the ecosystem to insulate certain markets from competition and to increasingly move competition to the outer bounds of the ecosystem. As inter-ecosystem competition is softened, and the ecosystem operator no longer has to prioritize growth over profitability, it gains the possibility to extract more surplus of the value generated in the ecosystem.

After the ecosystems have matured, they gain incentives to prevent discontinuity. An incumbent (stage 4) ecosystem operator can wield its ecosystem and gatekeeper power to prevent the emergence of new technologies and players in the market. It can do so by abusing its ecosystem power and leveraging its customer base and products as to deny the entrant the possibility to expand, for instance, by denying compatibility between the new service and its existing collection of services (leveraging its position in products) or by mimicking the services offered by the stand-alone competitor and provide the ecosystem's users with incentives to rely on the incumbent's services instead (leveraging its userbase). The incumbent ecosystem can invest heavily in R&D as to enter markets first and appropriate or ice-box certain technologies which may be disruptive, denying entrants to become credible competitors on the emergence of new technologies. If the digital network industry is concentrated under a small number of incumbent ecosystem operators, their incentives can align to engage in pre-emptive (tacit) collusion and selective coopetition, where the incumbent ecosystems collaborate to prevent the emergence of new players which may disrupt their equilibrium.

Recognizing that platform monopolies may be efficient and that competition may persist despite monopoly, as well as the potential long-term efficiencies associated with leveraging and subsidization in creating and establishing multi-product platforms allows for the creation of new types of law and policies that enhance ecosystem competition. The proposed conceptual framework helps to understand where competition is intense (stage 1 and 2 competition), where markets are already insulated from competition (stage 3), and where the use of these tools may lead to the pre-emption of competition (stage 4 competition). Regulation can be used to stimulate intense competition and prevent anti-competitive conduct by incumbents at the ecosystem level, as long as the competitive dynamics of ecosystems of different sizes and orientations are understood.

7

Theories of Harm for Ecosystem Competition

Ecosystem power should be viewed as a distinct form of non-structural economic power. Instead of relating to power *in* a specific market, it relates to the ability to power to expand *across* markets and sectors and *exert control* over key access points for entry into the digital network.[544] Ecosystem power is grounded in the positional power and power over resources held by incumbent ecosystem operators, yet mostly expresses itself through leveraging, and incumbent ecosystem operators are often able to expand rapidly across markets as to capture entire sectors. Ecosystem power is difficult to measure, and harms related to ecosystem powers are hard to capture, as they generally exhibit themselves in the form of long-term strategies where the interdependencies between markets are exploited to entrench the firm's core platform services while occupying emerging markets to pre-empt competition and disruption.

This chapter discusses theories of harm for ecosystem power and sets it apart from theories of harm related to gatekeeper power. Gatekeeper power has found its way into the regulatory vocabulary already with the introduction of the Digital Markets Act (DMA). This type of power is explored in vast literature and lies – implicitly or explicitly – at the heart of a number of EU competition law investigations.[545] Ecosystem power sets itself apart from gatekeeper power by its focus on the technological links between a number of platform and product markets as to determine how the complementarity, modularity, and shared users and resources can be

[544] See Chapter 5.

[545] Abuses of gatekeeper power are central in the enforcement of the DMA; see investigations DMA.100109 Online Intermediation Services – app stores – AppStore – Art. 5(4), Commission Decision of 25 March 2024; DMA.100075, Alphabet – Online Intermediation services – app stores – Google Play – Art. 5(4), Commission Decision of 25 March 2024; DMA.100193, Alphabet – Online Search Engine – Google Search – Art. 6(5), Commission Decision of 25 March 2024; DMA.100055, Meta – Art. 5(2), Commission Decision of 25 March 2024; DMA.100185, Apple – Operating systems – iOS – Art. 6(3), Commission Decision of 25 March 2024; DMA.100206, Apple New Business Terms, Commission Decision of 24 June 2024. In competition law proceedings, Google's role as a gatekeeper is discussed in the *Google Shopping* and *Google Android* cases.

leveraged by incumbent firms to foreclose competition.[546] This results in a complex and forward-looking analysis, which may be hard to operationalize in the existing frameworks for studying the prohibition of cartels and abuse of dominance. It is also observed however that the notion of ecosystems and power that is exerted by ecosystems is already finding its way into merger analyses, albeit in limited forms.[547]

The chapter first explores theories of harm related to gatekeeper power, so that it is clear how this type of power is understood here and to make it easier to highlight the distinctive elements and characteristics of ecosystem power (Section 7.1). The main contributions of this chapter are the provision of clear theories of harm related to ecosystem power and – perhaps equally important – how to distinguish abusive or harmful behaviour related to ecosystem competition from behaviour that has economic rationale (Section 7.2).

7.1 THEORIES OF HARM RELATED TO GATEKEEPER POWER: A PLATFORM-BASED VIEW

The nature of digital platforms operators as gatekeepers in their multi-sided markets has been well studied. A series of expert reports have highlighted theories of harm associated with gatekeeper power to propose possible reforms to competition law or regulatory interventions.[548] Numerous works have highlighted the high degree of influence which the platform operators can exercise over buyers and sellers which are dependent on their platform. Theories of harm related to gatekeeper power often revolve around the ability of the platform operator to exploit the dependency of users on different sides of the market to reach one another, allowing the platform operator to refuse intermediation for some parties (exclusionary behaviour) or extract unfair rents (exploitative behaviour).[549]

546 cf Jacobides, Cennamo and Gawer (n 12); Bourreau (n 28); Jacobides and Lianos (n 12); Jenny (n 14); Hornung (n 65); Manu Batra, Paul de Bijl and Timo Klein, 'Ecosystem Theories of Harm in EU Merger Control: Analysing Competitive Constraints and Entrenchment' (2024) 15 Journal of European Competition Law & Practice 357.

547 See eg Van den Boom and Samranchit (n 148); Batra, de Bijl and Klein (n 546); see also Commission Decision M.10615, Booking/eTraveli.

548 cf Crémer, De Montjoye and Schweitzer (n 4); Zingales and others (n 1); Digital Competition Expert Panel (n 1); OECD, 'Ex Ante Regulation and Competition in Digital Markets' (n 14); Damien Geradin, 'What Is a Digital Gatekeeper? Which Platforms Should Be Captured by the EC Proposal for a Digital Market Act?' [2021] SSRN Electronic Journal <www.ssrn.com/abstract=3788152> accessed 13 December 2022; Geradin, 'What Is a Digital Gatekeeper?' (n 407); Cappai and Colangelo (n 14); Schweitzer, 'The Art to Make Gatekeeper Positions Contestable and the Challenge to Know What Is Fair: A Discussion of the Digital Markets Act Proposal' (n 105); Wagner and others (n 14); Giorgio Monti, 'The Digital Markets Act – Improving Its Institutional Design' (2021) 5 European Competition and Regulatory Law Review 90; Alexandre de Streel and others, 'Recommendations Paper – Making the Digital Markets Act More Resilient and Effective' (CERRE 2021).

549 ibid.

The DMA has operationalized the idea of gatekeeper power in Art. 3(1) DMA. Here, it explains that a platform operator can be considered a gatekeeper of a platform service if it has (i) a significant impact on the internal market; (ii) it provides a (core) platform service which is an *important gateway* for business users to reach end users; and (iii) it is entrenched in this position. The DMA provides a number of quantitative and qualitative criteria to establish whether the platform actually constitutes an important gateway (Art. 3(2) & 3(8) DMA).[550]

The concept of an important gateway is key to the idea of a gatekeeper. The term implies that the platform operator has the ability to decide which business user is able to reach end users through a certain platform, and which business users are not. It is also able to set the terms for access and is able to refuse access to those business users that do not accept these terms.[551] Fulfilling the role of gatekeeper is however a natural part of platform operations: a platform operator has to set rules on the allocation of value between itself and complementors, maintain quality standards, and create reasonable expectations for end users. This is to the benefit of all parties involved: users would likely not engage with business users through a platform if there were no safeguards for fraud, malware, theft, or other serious issues.[552] It becomes a competition problem when the platform operator has gatekeeper power, as well as the ability and incentive to abuse that power.

In many instances, a gatekeeper of a platform does not have significant gatekeeper power. When a platform is intensely competing with other platforms to overcome the chicken-and-egg problem, trying to impose unreasonable terms likely causes business users to leave for another platform that does offer rewards and incentives for joining the network. Issues related to gatekeeper power are therefore mostly present when the gatekeeper is entrenched, and if it has a significant portion of the market.[553] This is not unlike the idea of dominance in a brick-and-mortar market: gatekeeper power exists when the platform has the ability to impose terms on business users and end users unilaterally, as there is a lack of competitive constraints and countervailing buyer power.[554]

Large platforms do have the ability and incentive to abuse their gatekeeper power and have been found to do so. The idea of gatekeeper power is at the heart of a number of important competition law investigations. The *Google Shopping* case has demonstrated how Google can disintermediate comparison shopping service providers and foreclose them. By demoting comparison shopping services in its unpaid search results, while offering its own alternative Google Shopping service in a way that is prominently displayed for users, allows it to push downstream competitors out of the

[550] See Chapter 8.

[551] Geradin, 'What Is a Digital Gatekeeper?' (n 407); Cappai and Colangelo (n 14); Schweitzer, 'The Art to Make Gatekeeper Positions Contestable and the Challenge to Know What Is Fair: A Discussion of the Digital Markets Act Proposal' (n 105).

[552] Tiwana (n 34).

[553] Crémer, De Montjoye and Schweitzer (n 4) 98.

[554] Whish and Bailey (n 404).

market for its own gain.[555] Similarly, the investigation in Amazon Buy Box related to Amazon's preferential treatment of its own retail offerings when compared to competitors.[556] A third example can be found in the mandatory use of its in-app payment (IAP) system for developers that want to proliferate their app through the App store.[557]

The Google Shopping, Amazon Buy Box, and Apple Pay investigations concern cases that relate to gatekeeper power *pur sang*. There is the case of on-platform expansion with direct vertical competition. It is a conflict of interest for Google and Amazon in their roles as the operator of the platform on the one hand and a competitor in a downstream market that is integrated directly into the platform. As the platform operators integrate their own services, the important gateway becomes narrow for complementors: every lead that does not go to third parties because of anticompetitive preferencing by the incumbent goes directly to the gatekeeper. These are abuses of gatekeeper power as it is understood narrowly.

7.2 FROM GATEKEEPER POWER TO ECOSYSTEM POWER: BRIDGING THE GAP

Ecosystem theories of harm are complex, partly because they are often most visible in instances of gatekeeper power but also because we currently do not have equally developed conceptual frameworks to capture them. Jacobides and Lianos have described ecosystem power as powers that relate to a primary market (in this case the platform market) and an undefined number of secondary- or aftermarkets.[558] The platform operator is able to exert its power beyond markets that are directly downstream to the platform market: the firm that manages an Operating System can influence standards, access to the app marketplace, search access points, and so on. Consequently, access to the app marketplace can shape the proliferation of apps, distribution channels, payment systems, and advertising. This type of examination expands harms associated with gatekeeper power beyond the singular platform market and into a broader number of harms that permeate across a number of value chains.[559]

The DMA does well in describing harms that are predominantly related to gatekeeper power through its ex ante obligations. Gatekeeper power allows the ecosystem operator to exert influence over users of its platform or platforms. It entails the ability to block or disintermediate business users, as to make sure that they cannot

555 Case C-48/22 P – Google and Alphabet v Commission (Google Shopping), ECLI:EU:C:2024:14, Judgement of 10 September 2024.

556 CASE AT.40462 – Amazon Marketplace and AT.40703 – Amazon Buy Box, C(2022) 9442 final, Commission Decision of 20 December 2022.

557 Case AT.40437, Apple – App Store Practices (music streaming), C/2024/1307, Commission Decision of 4 March 2024.

558 Jacobides and Lianos (n 12) 1207–2012.

559 cf Jacobides and Lianos (n 12); Lianos and Carballa-Smichowski (n 121); Lianos, Eller and Kleinschmitt (n 121); Batra, de Bijl and Klein (n 546).

reach end users. Disintermediation can take many forms, as described in Art. 5 and 6 DMA: parity clauses, disallowing business users to offer or promote their services through alternative channels; withholding information on performance, competing on the basis of privileged access to data derived from the operation of the platform; and self-preferencing, refusing interoperability (i.e. access to the platform), exclusivity clauses, or any type of behaviour that may lead to disintermediation of the terms of the platform operator are not accepted.

The main limitation of the concept of gatekeeper power, in studying complex interactions across markets and long-term effects, is that the behaviour is studied in the context of *access to a certain platform*. The analysis hereunder shows that ecosystem harms tend to permeate across value chains and often into diagonally or loosely related markets. Firms can use their ecosystem power to foreclose competition in the market quickly after entry, not only after they have become the established monopolist in these markets. Moreover, ecosystem harms are not exhibited as short-term harms towards a certain group of users of a platform, but rather through long-term cross-market leveraging strategies. Harms related to gatekeeper power are often part of the puzzle, but rarely the full picture.

This section first looks at the Microsoft case, where ecosystem power was used to support an abuse of gatekeeper power. Subsequently, it looks at Google Android in light of the long-term strategy employed by Google that began long before the Commission's investigation, to show how ecosystem power can be used to gain control over a market where the firm is not yet dominant.

7.2.1 *Gatekeeper and Ecosystem Power in Conjunction: The Case of Microsoft*

Other cases involve both a dimension of gatekeeper power and ecosystem power. Gatekeeper power relates to abuses that are based on the dual role held by the gatekeeper on a platform and in a vertically related market. Abuses of gatekeeper power happen when the firm uses its rule-setting powers for the platform to prioritize its own products and demote those of others. It can however use its ecosystem power in conjunction with its gatekeeper power to foreclose a downstream competitor. In this case, it does not only set terms that suppress competition on the platform but also leverages its cross-market power into competition with the downstream competitor. Microsoft's foreclosure of Netscape shows how a matter of gatekeeper power can evolve to include abuses of ecosystem power.[560]

Netscape – the supplier of an early web browser in the late 1990s – conquered a large position in the market for web browsers. This sparked concerns for Microsoft that Netscape was capable to develop itself into a form of OS independent middleware, which would diminish the importance of device-based Operating Systems

[560] United States v. Microsoft Corporation, Civil Action No. 98-1232 (TPJ), 14 September 1998, United States District Court.

such as Windows. Netscape provided its web browser software compatible with the Windows OS. After capturing market share in the web browser market, Netscape became increasingly active in developing its own APIs and source code. This allowed software developers to develop OS-independent applications that could be used with Netscape. Microsoft attempted to negotiate with Netscape that Netscape would focus its operations on becoming a pure Windows 95 complementor, rather than a potential competitor to its OS by developing into a middleware platform. After these negotiations failed, Microsoft started to withhold access to crucial APIs in the hope that the threat of incompatibility would dissuade Netscape from developing its middleware platform.[561] Had the Microsoft saga ended with refusal of access, this would have been a classic case of harms related to gatekeeper power.

However, the refusal to deal did not dissuade efforts by Netscape to develop its middleware platform. As a response, Microsoft relied on a combination of tying and predatory innovation. Microsoft pre-installed its Internet Explorer (IE) web browser on its Windows OS free of charge, as to diminish incentives for OEMs or users to pay for the Netscape web browser. At the same time, it significantly increased its efforts in developing IE: it started to invest USD 100 million each year and its team of developers grew from 5 or 6 developers in early 1995 to over one thousand in 1999.[562] By using its privileged access to resources, Microsoft was able to make IE more technologically advanced than the Netscape browser, while offering it for free. It also used exclusivity and revenue sharing agreements with OEMs to exclusively pre-install IE.[563] With this strategy, it starved Netscape in terms of users and revenue until it exited the market.

There is a combination of gatekeeper power on the one hand, refusing access to certain important gateways and preferential treatment of one's own services on the platform. However, there is also a dimension of abuses of ecosystem power: Microsoft was able to leverage its access to resources, its power over processes, and the economies of scope between market A and market B to push Netscape out of the market. This case also provides an insight into the motivation behind abuses of ecosystem power: Microsoft's reason to foreclose Netscape were not based on Microsoft's desire to better monetize its platform service, but to pre-empt disruptive innovation in an adjacent market that may result in a long-term threat to its position across a number of markets.

7.2.2 *The Long-Term Harms of Ecosystem Competition: Google Android in Perspective*

The Google cases show how hard it is to capture ecosystem power, how interlinked harms in different markets are, and the long-term nature of ecosystem-related harms. The EU Google cases look at two distinct parts of the value chain. The

[561] ibid, paras 79–89.
[562] ibid, paras 134–135.
[563] ibid, paras 143–385.

Google Shopping case looked at one specific market that is downstream of horizontal search: the comparison shopping market. Here, it is shown that Google has used its monopoly in search to foreclose downstream competitors as to capture the value that is generated downstream. *Google Android* looked at the part of the value chain that is upstream of the search market. The Commission established how Google has used its position as the operator of Android OS to enter into restrictive Mobile Application and anti-fragmentation agreements (AFAs), as well as revenue sharing agreements, to ensure that Google Search remains the default search engine. Interestingly, Google's payments to Apple to remain the default search engine on Apple devices, which was the focal point of the monopolization case in the US, is completely absent from both the Google Shopping and Android cases, while it was instrumental in Google's monopoly in horizontal search.[564]

It is only by putting these cases together, that one can see that Google's efforts to enter into mobile Operating Systems in 2003, has a direct line to its behaviour in Google Shopping in 2012. When Google acquired Android in 2003, the incumbent in smartphones was Blackberry. There was a risk for Google that if smartphones became the main mode of accessing the internet, it would open up opportunities for new search providers. Google had already secured its position in desktop-based search as it was the main search engine on Windows-based devices and had made an agreement with Apple to be the default search engine on Apple devices in 2002.[565]

In 2007, Apple launched the first iPhone, and by November 2007, Google had entered into agreements with HTC, Samsung, and Motorola to proliferate Google Android OS. Google made Android open source through the Android Open Source Project and started the Open Handheld Alliance. It gave away Android OS for free to Original Equipment Manufacturers (OEMs) to facilitate its proliferation across non-Apple and Blackberry devices. Google invested heavily to develop its offering of applications, including the Play Store, Google Maps, Software Development Kits, testing environments, and APIs. By 2009, it started entering into Mobile Application Agreements. It also offered these applications free of charge to OEMs, if they would use Google Search as the default search engine and Google Play as the default app store. Meanwhile, it continued to pay Apple to remain the default search engine on the iPhone as well as Apple's desktop computers.

By 2011, Blackberry had entered in rapid decline, and by 2012 it had only around 1 per cent market share in smartphone devices. Google's monopoly in search was complete. In the same year, Google made it mandatory for OEMs to enter into an AFA if they wanted to enter into the MADA, limiting competition between diverging versions of Android. It was also in 2012 that Google made the changes to its Panda algorithm that was investigated in Google Shopping, which demoted comparison

[564] See Fiona Scott Morton and Jasper van den Boom, Are Competition Authorities Equipped to Combat Entrenched Digital Monopolies? – Lessons from the US and EU Antitrust Cases against Google, (2025) Illinois Journal of Law, Technology, and Policy.

[565] ibid.

shopping service providers and gave preferential treatment to Google Shopping in its Buy Box. It is only after Google had solidified its position in search through capturing a number of markets, softening competition in a number of adjacent markets to Operating Systems and Search, and foreclosing the last independent competitor that the downstream harms really started to exacerbate.

This is a long-term strategy that should be viewed as an ecosystem-based harm. The harm is not the result of abuses of gatekeeper power in a single platform, but it is the result of a long-term strategy of acquisitions, abundance strategies, agreements, and anti-competitive behaviour that has resulted in the entrenchment of a platform market to ensure that abuses of gatekeeper power are durable. The behaviour by Google described earlier should not only be understood as a way to solidify its position in search but also as a means to pre-empt or delay any type of disruption in the search market. It is also not a matter of gatekeeper power. After all, Google was not even active in mobile handsets when it started its strategy to pre-empt the disruption of its search engine. It entered specifically into this market to prevent a new competitor in search for arising by means of a new technology. Meanwhile, Google also created the contours of competition with another incumbent in desktop markets by agreeing that Apple would not enter into the market for search. A view on ecosystem-based theories of harm explains why this is beneficial for both: if there is no new entrant that has the ability to capture a valuable platform and to build it out into a disruptive innovation, there is less risk to our incumbency in the markets we currently occupy.

A closer look at recent competition between incumbents in new and disruptive markets shows a similar pattern: Google and Apple invested heavily into automotive software and self-driving vehicles. Google, Apple, Microsoft, and Amazon all invested heavily into voice-based assistants. Meta has made an attempt to capture virtual reality. Currently, Google, Apple, and Amazon are all investing heavily into Artificial Intelligence. Studying these patterns shows clearly that as soon as a new disruptive technology arrives, at least one – but usually multiple – of the major incumbents leverages their resources, positional power, power over processes, and gatekeeper power to absorb the new technology in a way that sustains their business models. Automotive entertainment software is dominated by Apple and Google and requires users to link their phones to their cars to access the infotainment system. In this way, Google and Apple ensure that users of their ecosystem remain with their ecosystem, rather than having a third-party offer a smart infotainment system independently. Voice assistants are integrated into the Operating System of the incumbent, with the exception of Amazon, who has used voice-based search to enter into Operating Systems. Meta is now trying to capture its own OS with its Metaverse. Currently, Google and Apple are investing heavily into their proprietary AI services to be tied with their mobile ecosystems, while Microsoft has acquired 51 per cent of ChatGPT and is integrating its co-pilot services into its productivity software. While there is competition on the fringes, it is often one of the existing incumbents that becomes the dominant design for new technologies, either through acquisitions or leveraging.

Harms related to ecosystem power are not about access to a specific platform, or the terms and conditions for access. They are far more complex and pervasive as they relate to cross market and non-structural forms of power. A large incumbent does not need to become dominant in a platform market to exert its power in that market, it can engage in strategies to foreclose and pre-empt competition far earlier. Waiting until the firm has tipped a platform market in its favour means that it is already too late, and preventing one incumbent ecosystem operator from capturing one specific platform market does not restore competition. A look at ecosystem competition, and incumbency, shows that regulators must find ways to structurally open up access points for competition in the digital network industry by protecting entrants and curtailing the power of incumbents.

7.2.3 *A Conceptual Framework for Theories of Harm Related to Ecosystem Power*

While the empirical observations set out above give some indication as to how ecosystem power can be understood, this section attempts to create a conceptual framework that can be operationalized in competition law or regulatory investigations. This section sets out four distinct ecosystem-based theories of harm: entrenchment (or monopolization) strategies; network-wide entry barriers and foreclosure; softening of competition between incumbents; and innovation harms. These types of harm relate to one another but also cause harm independently of one another.

Entrenchment Harms

Entrenchment harms are related to gatekeeper power most directly and are described earlier in the analysis of the Google cases in the EU and the US. The firm can leverage its position across a number of markets to create or maintain a monopoly within a platform market. The idea that expansion of the digital ecosystem through entry into new markets or the integration of new services on the platform leads to entrenchment relates to the complementarity and economies of scope between the primary and secondary market.[566] In assessing the *Google/Fitbit* merger, the Commission raised concerns that Google's increased access to health data could strengthen its dominance in advertising, even though these markets are not part of the same value chain. Similarly, the Commission raised concerns about Amazon strengthening its position as an online retailer if it acquired iRobot. The latter being a producer of an autonomous vacuuming robot.[567] These types of entrenchment harms are not

[566] cf Van den Boom and Samranchit (n 148); AC Hoyng and A Karkaletsi, '22. Competitive Dynamics of Digital Ecosystems and Their Implications for Competition Law Enforcement'; Batra, de Bijl and Klein (n 546).

[567] Hoyng and Karkaletsi (n 566); European Commission, Press release 27 November 2023, 'Commission sends Amazon Statement of Objections over proposed acquisition of iRobot', available at <https://ec.europa.eu/commission/presscorner/detail/en/IP_23_5990>; European Commission, Google/Fitbit (Case M.9660), Commission Decision (2020).

related to gatekeeper power, as they do not relate to the operation of an important gateway for business users to reach end users (or vice versa). Instead, entrenchment is the result of expansion of the ecosystem. The firm is able to leverage the technological linkages, complementarity, or economies of scope to strengthen its position in one market through its activities in a diagonally related market.[568]

The entrenchment effects may not be limited to a singular platform activity. Instead, expansion of the ecosystem and increasing ecosystem power may lead to entrenchment across a number of markets. Take, for instance, the impact of entry into wearables by Apple. Apple has been highly successful in entering the market with the launch of Apple Watch. Apple products are only fully interoperable with the Apple Watch, allowing Apple to leverage its strength from its occupied markets into the market for wearables. Subsequently, Apple's entry into Wearable Operating Systems permeates across a number of downstream secondary markets: Apple integrates its proprietary voice assistant Siri into the Apple Watch as the exclusive digital assistant, impacting competition in the area of voice-based search; it determines which apps become available on the Apple Watch; it integrates its proprietary NFC chip and exclusively allows the use of Apple IAP systems. At the same time, Apple ensures that wearables offered by competitors are not fully compatible with its other services. Competing wearables do not link well with other devices such as the iPhone, and Apple-compatible applications such as the App Store and Apple music are not available.[569] This creates a bidirectional effect: first, Apple steers Apple users to buy an Apple Watch instead of another wearable, solidifying its position in the wearables market by leveraging its existing user base from not only one service, but from its entire ecosystem. Second, it ensures that existing users in the Apple ecosystem that do like the Apple Watch will continue to use Apple's proprietary services. After all, switching costs are increased if the user knows that its Apple Watch will no longer function well if they switch away from the iPhone or other Apple devices. Third, it leverages its existing proprietary services into a new and potentially disruptive market so that it ensures that it remains relevant with the new technology.[570]

These types of cross-market leveraging strategies ensure that the potential for disruptive innovation remains limited. The ecosystem operator leverages its existing

568 ibid; Batra, de Bijl and Klein (n 546) 355–368.

569 These interoperability issues are currently being investigated under the Digital Markets Act, see DMA.100203/4, Apple Interoperability 6(7) DMA, Commission Decision to open proceedings of 9 September 2024.

570 It should be noted that the European Commission is attempting to break open the Apple ecosystem through DMA enforcement, as it is currently in the process of developing a implementing decision related to Apple's interoperability obligations; see European Commission, Commission starts first proceedings to specify Apple's interoperability obligations under the Digital Markets Act, Press Release of 19 September 2024. The DMA, with eye on its objective of promoting contestability, seems most fit to address entrenchment harms, when compared to other ecosystem-based harms. See DMA.100203,204, Apple Interoperability (2024).

position across markets into a new market. Complementarities, economies of scope, and technological linkages create short-term efficiencies: users can use the services that they know and appreciate on a new device, this works relatively well, and it does not require the user to incur any learning costs. In the long-run however, this means that there will be limited or no space for the emergence of new types of voice assistants, wearables-based Operating Systems, marketplaces, or applications.[571] With its success in Apple Watch, Apple successfully appropriated business users, end users, and the distribution channel created with wearables for its own ecosystem.

The effects of these strategies permeate across ecosystems via inter-ecosystem competition: as Apple bolsters its position with its closed strategy, Alphabet moves to capture the rest of the market by maintaining an open strategy. The Apple Watch was launched in 2014, and for a while it competed with Operating Systems offered by Fitbit and Samsung. In 2018, Google acquired Fitbit.[572] In 2021, Samsung switched to Google's Wear OS, abandoning its proprietary Tizen OS.[573] At this point, most if not all non-Apple wearables rely on versions of Google's Wear OS. An emerging market has again been divided between large operators as they leverage their own position, acquire successful smaller platform operators, or enter into agreements with other platform operators to ensure the use of their proprietary Operating Systems. Platform envelopment, or obtaining a dominant position in incipient markets, ensures that large ecosystem operators can absorb innovations to make them sustainable, or simply kill off potentially disruptive innovators.[574] This creates a bidirectional effect: the ecosystem operator simultaneously strengthens their position across its occupied markets and ensures that it becomes the new dominant design in the emerging market. Entrenchment has a significant impact on competition beyond the entrenched market: it is not just a matter of solidifying one's position in market A but also to insulate oneself from competition by enveloping adjacent and potentially competitive markets.[575]

Industry-Wide Foreclosure Strategies

The entrenchment harms have effects that permeate throughout the entire sector, and which are indirectly related to their leveraging activities. These types of harms are even more difficult to capture as they are related to the incentives of third parties, rather than the activities of the incumbent itself. To pre-empt competition, an incumbent may not stop at foreclosing entry to the specific disruptive market. Instead, it may engage in industry-wide foreclosure strategies to occupy or monopolize the potentially disruptive market as well as the surrounding value chain. This

[571] Heidhues, Köster and Kőszegi (n 329) 2–7; Ezrachi and Stucke (n 1).

[572] Case M.9660 – GOOGLE/FITBIT, C(2020) 9105 final, Commission Decision of 17 December 2020.

[573] Romero A, Samsung Has Updated These Galaxy Watch Models to Wear OS 5 (9to5Google, 4 December 2024).

[574] Hoyng and Karkaletsi (n 566).

[575] Australian Competition & Consumer Authority (n 4).

suppresses not only the current threat but also any potential threats of disruption via this sector in the future.

Large ecosystem operators tend to expand across markets rapidly. Stylianou has observed the unprecedented speed and range with which the biggest digital undertakings have expanded, entering into approximately 10 to 15 adjacent markets in a matter of years.[576] The Department of Justice, in its submission to the OECD's roundtable on serial acquisitions, noted that there were 819 non-reported acquisitions by Apple, Amazon, Facebook, Alphabet, and Microsoft between 2010 and 2019.[577] These rapid expansion strategies are part of an effort to identify and absorb new potential distribution channels, innovative activities, or potential competitors. Ultimately, serial acquisitions tend to lead to higher prices and reduced quality for consumers, pre-empt competition and innovation, and lead to highly concentrated sectors.[578] Serial acquisitions have been described as relevant in 'industry roll ups': it is not about dominating a singular market but about enveloping a complete type of industry, activity, and value chain.[579] In digital markets, this process of expansion from sector to sector, allows the digital firm to occupy an increasingly large part of the total digital network. The presence of data-driven information asymmetries allows the digital firm to identify potential threats early and acquire (or foreclose) them before they are on the radar of competition authorities.[580]

The effect of this serial expansion has an impact that permeates across the entire digital network. Start-ups that want to enter the digital network are aware of the risks of competing with Big Tech. It may be a part of their strategy to compete to be acquired, staying in the market long enough to develop a potential disruption so that they are acquired for a premium. While this creates short-term innovations, it does not lead to long-term competition. After all, the new technologies will be absorbed by the incumbent ecosystem operators and either turned into sustained innovation or killed off.[581] For entrants that do want to durably compete, there will be increased barriers to entry. Private investments will be aware of the risks of competing with Big Tech, and incentives to invest will be diminished if there is a risk that Big Tech enters the market.[582] Moreover, large incumbent ecosystem operators will often have expansive networks, or even be active in venture capital themselves. Once the potential disruptive innovation has been identified by large digital players, they will

576 Konstantinos Stylianou, 'Exclusion in Digital Markets', vol 24 (2018) 249.

577 Antonio Capobianco, 'Serial Acquisitions and Industry Roll-Ups – Note by the United States, DAF/COMP/WD(2023)99' 3.

578 ibid; Carl Shapiro, 'Protecting Competition in the American Economy: Merger Control, Tech Titans, Labor Markets' (2019) 33 Journal of Economic Perspectives 69.

579 Capobianco (n 577) 4 et seq.

580 Lécuyer (n 136) online.

581 Ezrachi and Stucke (n 1).

582 See eg Kamepalli, Rajan and Zingales (n 309).

have opportunities to attempt to acquire the start-up outright by offering premiums or, if refused, engage in foreclosure strategies.

In 2024, Google allegedly hired all top talent of Character AI, entering into an exclusive licensing deal, an acquisition in all but name.[583] Similarly, Microsoft has taken a strategic stake in OpenAI, becoming its most important investor and granting it significant power over the company.[584] These types of direct or indirect acquisitions or absorption strategies impact investment incentives: shareholders will not invest in start-ups or small- or medium-sized enterprises beyond a certain point. It may be interesting to gamble on small caps or start-ups with the idea that they may be acquired, but once competition between the entrant and big tech becomes intense there are incentives to withdraw one's investments. This means that the foreclosure effect associated with large digital ecosystems expands across the entire digital network industry, as the deal increasingly becomes assimilate or die. Outside of risk-taking investors, risk-averse long-term investors are more inclined to invest in the large digital ecosystem operators as the value will be directed there over time. At this point, the majority of market cap in America's S&P 500 is concentrated in seven firms (Apple, Amazon, Meta, Alphabet, Microsoft, Tesla, and NVIDIA). These companies are also the main drivers of growth.[585]

This leads to a self-reinforcing harm to innovation, and in the long-term users. As sectors and wealth increasingly concentrates with a small number of firms, these firms increase their ability to identify, acquire, or foreclose potential competitors or disruptors. The firms not only collect data across more sectors, but they also increase their ability to leverage their position and financial resources across a number of markets to acquire any given undertaking at a premium. The ecosystem operators become 'gatekeepers' for entry into any type of digital markets, rather than gatekeepers for their platform. Ultimately, incumbents can come to dominate the means of innovation and production in the digital network industry, as they operate or monitor all key access points and leave no viable markets for entrants to develop their long-term competitive position. This transforms industry wide foreclosure into network-wide foreclosure, as entry into digital markets could only happen sustainably with the approval of the incumbents that control all key access points, and disruptive entry is foreclosed.

Softening of Competition between Incumbents

As the incumbents solidify their control over the digital network industry and concentrate wealth amongst themselves, it becomes easier to divide key markets between one another. Similarly to brick-and-mortar markets, a more transparent

[583] S Goldman, Google's hiring of Character. AI's founders is the latest sign that part of the AI startup world is starting to implode (3 August 2024, *Fortune*).

[584] H Sadiq, 'Microsoft's Strategic Stake in OpenAI Unlocks Unique Investment Avenues' [2024] *Yahoo Finance*.

[585] Just seven companies are carrying the S&P 500 in 2023 (18 May 2023, S&P Global).

and concentrated market increases opportunities for tacit collusion. As the large incumbent firms have found an equilibrium where they are all profitable and able to extract monopoly rents within their ecosystems, their incentives to compete intensely diminish. The longer the market remains stable, and the less the risk of disruptive entry, the greater the ability and incentives for cooperation (tacit or otherwise) become. The competition between incumbents may be reminiscent of oligopoly competition, yet across a wide range of markets captured in their multi-product ecosystem.[586]

Investigations in the United States have unearthed a number of illicit agreements between incumbent ecosystem operators. The recent US v. Google case focuses on the agreement between Apple and Google to make Google the default search engine. There has also been an investigation into Google and Meta, as they were dividing markets in the so-called Jedi Blue agreements.[587] In 2014, the Department of Justice and various big tech firms (Apple, Meta, and Microsoft) made a $435 million settlement after an investigation into their no-poaching agreement.[588] Of course, there is still competition between these firms at the inter-ecosystem level. However, this also creates opportunities for retaliation even if the firms are not competing directly in one another's core markets. The ability to retaliate for intensifying competition relates to the dependency one party has on another at the ecosystem level. One example, although it is not necessarily recognized as a retaliatory action, Apple's decision to introduce its anti-tracking policy significantly impacted Meta's advertising revenue from Apple users.[589] The more these incumbent digital ecosystem operators become intertwined, and the more their interdependence grows, the more attractive it becomes to cooperate.

Digital firms are generally in coopetition, rather than direct horizontal competition. They compete in some areas, while cooperating in others.[590] For instance, if Google, Microsoft, and Apple refused interoperability with Meta's social media services, Meta would not have a platform to reach users. One could consider this an attractive opportunity for the gatekeepers to refuse access, because then they could launch their own social media. However, as Meta's social networks are attractive for users, this could create a risk that users come to rely more on an alternative OS or web-based middleware. This would ultimately threaten the long-term dominance of the first three undertakings. It is in everyone's best interest to cooperate by allowing access and sharing the rents, thus giving preference to cooperation over competition. As the market becomes increasingly concentrated, these firms may only offer these types of grace to one another. Meanwhile, smaller competitors may be refused

586 Ezrachi and Stucke (n 1).

587 S Huijts, EU and UK take on 'Jedi Blue' – Keep Your Friends Close, but Your Enemies Closer?, The Platform Law Blog (2022), online.

588 D Streitfeld, 'Court Rejects Deal on Silicon Valley Hiring' *The New York Times* (4 June 2018).

589 D Newman, 'Apple, Meta, and the $10 Billion Impact of Privacy Changes' *Forbes* (10 February 2022).

590 See eg Cohen and Zhang (n 387).

access to platforms altogether.[591] One can think again of the Apple v. Epic case, where Apple barred Epic access from the App Store, or Google's foreclosure of the Unlockd app after they entered into the market for advertising.[592] The more competition softens between the largest incumbents, the less competition there ultimately is on the fringes of the ecosystems. Incentives to invest in new emerging technologies is diminished, as the incumbents realize that it will not lead to intense long-term competition over time.[593] The incentives to collude for digital incumbents follow a similar rationale as collusion in oligopolies generally: it is easier to divide the profits from the cartel among a smaller number of players, and it is easier to monitor and coordinate a cartel with fewer players. If there are only a few incumbents that control the digital network, it is easier to coordinate where competition is intense and where it is not.[594]

Innovation Harms

The greatest harms associated with abuses of ecosystem power are to innovation, which ultimately results in harms to consumers. As the chokehold of large digital incumbents on the digital network industry tightens, the potential for disruptive innovations to emerge and grow to scale diminish. Large digital ecosystem operators can use exclusion, acquisition, poaching, user-steering, or other forms of economic and financial power to ensure that disruptive innovations never reach the mainstream. Even in situations where the incumbent firms *must* participate in potential disruptive innovation, they engage in sectoral roll-ups to ensure that any disruptive innovation is steered towards a form of innovation that sustains their business models.[595]

Innovation harms are particularly tricky: incumbent ecosystem operators do not take from users by raising prices or lowering quality, they take products from the user that it has never even known. Investments into disruptive innovations by incumbents will only go as far as is necessary to stop the competitive threat. After the incipient markets have been occupied by existing big tech firms, they will reduce investments and streamline the integration into the existing business model. As the market has been occupied by large digital firms, new start-ups will likely avoid entering into these markets and look for other disruptive opportunities, as they realize that their chances of obtaining investments or entering into long-term competition are low. Moreover, their chances of being acquired are lowered if the incumbent ecosystem operator is already present in the market and is able to leverage their position in competition with the entrant by (for instance) emulating their services or simply hiring their talent.[596]

591 Ezrachi and Stucke (n 1).
592 M Han, 'Unlockd Will "Cease to Exist" if Google Blocks the App' *Financial Review* (4 June 2018).
593 Ezrachi and Stucke (n 1).
594 cf Green, Marshall and Marx (n 524); Pal and Scrimitore (n 524); Telser (n 524).
595 Ezrachi and Stucke (n 1).
596 ibid.

This book proposes that ultimately, the predominant harms associated with ecosystems are the following: the presence across markets and key access points for the digital network provides the ecosystem operator with the ability and incentives to pre-empt or absorb potential disruptive innovation. Pre-empting disruptive innovation strengthens their existing entrenchment across markets and grows its power in terms of resources, position, processes and coercive power within its ecosystem and across the entirety of the digital network industry, allowing it to further exploit and exclude its users within the ecosystem. At the same time, entry into incipient markets forecloses any potential disruptors in the incipient market, leading to losses in innovation and investments in new technologies and harming consumers by denying access to potential emerging technologies.

It should be noted that innovation harms are not unique to digital markets. Back in the 1980s, the break-up of AT&T led to the release of a large number of disruptive innovations that were ice-boxed by AT&T as they may have disrupted their existing business model.[597] What distinguishes the modern pre-emption of disruption by Big Tech and the pre-emption of disruption by AT&T is that it happens at an unprecedented scale and across a vast number of markets and sectors, in a highly targeted way due to data-driven information asymmetries, and by firms that individually have market caps and positions that far exceed AT&T even at its prime. The way to combat these harms is by breaking down the stranglehold that incumbent ecosystem operators have over the digital network industry by opening up access points and competitive opportunities for disruptive entrants, while protecting them from anti-competitive activities by stage 4 ecosystem operators so that they can achieve a relatively equal position.

7.3 CONCLUSION

This chapter has briefly set out the links and differences between gatekeeper power and ecosystem power. First, it is discussed how gatekeeper power is exhibited within certain platform markets. The digital firm acts as gatekeeper over an "important gateway" for business users to reach end users. Acting as a gatekeeper is a natural part of offering a platform service, as the platform operator must ensure some level of quality and predictability for consumers. However, once complementors become highly dependent on the platform offered by the gatekeeper, there is a risk of exploitative and exclusionary behaviour by denying access to users or granting access on unreasonable terms. This may include direct or constructive refusals to deal, self-preferencing, discrimination, exploitative prices, terms, or data collection, competing on the basis of privileged access to non-public data, and so on. Harms related to gatekeeper power are well explored in vast literature and have found their way into the DMA.

[597] Wu (n 344).

Harms related to ecosystem power are related to gatekeeper power, yet still underexplored. This book proposes that operators of digital platforms are particularly likely to be capable of abusing their gatekeeper power if they also have strong ecosystem power. Ecosystem power relates to the ability of the digital firm to leverage economies of scope and complementarities, data-related efficiencies, cross-market network externalities, steer users, and intangible forms of power related to access to resources, as well as their positional power and power over processes to entrench their power in existing markets and to capture new markets. This chapter has proposed complex theories of harm for ecosystem power that would require in-depth and forward-looking analyses on their impact across the digital network industry.

The first category of harms is entrenchment in and across markets. This type of harm would be the easiest to observe at the ecosystem level. Here, the incumbent firm uses its ability to leverage its position to strengthen its monopoly in occupied markets or to establish dominance in new markets.

The second category relates to network-wide foreclosure strategies. Here, the digital firm uses its ability to leverage or acquisitions to foreclose players within a certain sector, allowing it to appropriate the sector within its own multi-product ecosystem and to ensure that innovations in this sector support the incumbent's existing business models. By capturing potentially disruptive sectors and occupying key markets and access points there, the incumbent prevents investments in this area as to ensure that there is no potentially disruptive entrant in certain key segments or technologies.

The third category of harms relates to the incumbents ability to soften competition with other incumbents and to coordinate their competitive efforts. As the established stage 4 ecosystem operators grow their reach across the digital network, they become better able to coordinate where they will and will not compete. The core markets of each incumbent are heavily entrenched, and they have found an equilibrium. Competition is then moved to the fringes of the network industry, and focussed on competing in incipient and emerging markets. This means that the incumbents can focus all their resources on pre-empting disruptive innovation. As to make sure that the equilibrium between the incumbents is not upset, they appropriate disruptive innovations and integrate them into their ecosystems in a way that minimizes the competitive pressures on other incumbents, as not to spark retaliation.

Finally, each of these harms to competition result in harms to consumers. For consumers, the greatest loss is in the loss of innovation. Innovation harms are difficult to measure, as they relate to a loss that never came to be realized. This is therefore harder to measure than an increase in price or decrease in quality for existing products. The purpose of digital regulation should be to stimulate disruptive entry and support disruptive innovation. Ultimately, entry in emerging markets by stage one and two ecosystem operators is key to overthrowing the incumbents in their core markets by disrupting the equilibrium and forcing competition between small and large players alike.

PART III

A Regulatory Framework to Govern Ecosystem Competition

This final part of the book looks at existing regulation for digital markets, specifically the DMA, DMCCA, and Section 19a GWB. These three regulatory regimes differ in their nature and underlying principles. The DMA is an ex ante rules-based regime, the DMCCA is a principles-based regime that uses a mix of ex ante and ex post interventions, and Section 19a GWB is a reform of competition law that uses designations to speed up ex post enforcement. These three regimes use different starting points and have different perspectives on the role of ecosystem competition.

The contribution of this part consists of a proposal for progressive ecosystem regulation, which is based on the analyses in Parts I and II and attempts to integrate a rules-based, principles-based, and competition law-based approach into one coherent regulatory framework. The purpose of this regulatory framework is to stimulate dynamic competition by empowering entrants to capture platform markets and innovate disruptively. It is designed as a layered regulation with a heavily regulated, lightly regulated, and protected pool, through which the regulator can take into account the various sizes and degrees of power held by ecosystems.

8

Existing Regulatory Paradigms

EU, UK, and Germany

This chapter discusses three existing regulatory frameworks for digital markets, which each use a distinct approach to govern digital firms and pursue their own objectives. For the purpose of this analysis, the Digital Markets Act (DMA) is considered a rules-based, platform-focussed regulatory approach. This is because the DMA uses clear ex ante rules that apply only to gatekeepers of so-called core platform services. The focus of the DMA and its substantial obligations lie on tackling gatekeeper power in the monopolized platform. It only deals with issues related to ecosystem power, such as denying interoperability and other forms of leveraging, indirectly (Section 8.1).

The DMCCA is viewed as a principles-based sectoral approach. Under the DMCCA, specific activities can be designated with a strategic market status. Designation does not mean that regulatory obligations are imposed directly. Instead, it allows the CMA to impose tailor-made rules to benefit competition in the markets and sector(s) surrounding that activity. To designate an activity, and to impose rules, the CMA must conduct an in-depth study of the relevant activity and sector (Section 8.2).

Section 19a GWB is a competition law-based and ecosystem-focussed approach. Section 19a GWB focuses specifically on digital firms that are dominant in more than one market, which it describes as having paramount significance across markets. In practice, decisions related to the enforcement of Section 19a GWB involve in-depth studies of the functioning of digital ecosystems as to impose rules and restrictions on how they compete (Section 8.3).

The purpose of this section is to explore the existing regulatory approaches and to identify their strengths and weaknesses and is foundational for the development of the system of progressive ecosystem regulation proposed later in this chapter, which integrates these regulatory systems into a singular regulatory approach.

8.1 THE DMA: A RULES-BASED APPROACH TO REGULATING GATEKEEPER POWER

The European Commission has proposed the DMA in 2020. The law was adopted on 14 September 2022 and entered into force on the 2nd of May 2023. The Commission directly announced the first investigations into potential gatekeepers, and designated Alphabet, Apple, Amazon, ByteDance, Meta, and Microsoft on 5th of September 2023. Gatekeepers would have to start complying six months after the date of their designation. On March 7, 2024, the first obligations started to apply on gatekeepers. This means that there has already been quite some early enforcement activity for the DMA at the time of writing, and the impact of DMA compliance is becoming clear. This section provides a bird's eye overview of the DMA, discusses some lessons from early enforcement, and looks at whether the DMA is fit for purpose in terms of regulating digital ecosystems.

8.1.1 *A Bird's Eye Overview of the DMA*

The DMA relies on a system of designations. Firms that are designated with 'gatekeeper power' as understood in the DMA must comply with a number of substantive provisions, aimed at achieving fairness and contestability.

Designations

The regulatory obligations in the DMA only apply to firms designated as gatekeepers. To be designated as a gatekeeper, there are two conditions: (i) operating a core platform service and (ii) meeting the conditions that indicate gatekeeper power. Art. 2(2) DMA provides an exhaustive list of core platform services as recognized under the DMA. This list can be expanded via a market investigation in accordance with Art. 19 DMA. Currently, the list of core platform services includes: online intermediation services, search engines, social networks, video-sharing platforms, number-independent messaging services, operating systems, web browsers, virtual assistants, cloud computing services, and some categories of online advertising services that are connected to one of the other core platform services. The operation of other types of digital services (that are not listed as core platform services in Art. 2 DMA) does not warrant designation, even if the conditions to establish gatekeeper power set out in Art. 3 are met.

A platform operator is considered to have gatekeeper power is they meet three cumulative conditions laid down in Art. 3(1) DMA: it has a significant impact on the internal market; it provides a core platform service which is an important gateway for business users to reach end users; and it enjoys an entrenched and durable position in its operations, or it is foreseeable that it will enjoy such a position in the near future. The DMA takes a pragmatic approach to determining whether these conditions are met. Art. 3(2) DMA provides three quantitative thresholds that correspond to the conditions set out in Art. 3(1) DMA. The operator of a core platform service will be presumed to have gatekeeper power if (i) it has over a turnover of over €7.5 billion in each of the last three financial years, or a fair market capitalization above €75 billion, and provides the core platform service in at least three Member States;

(ii) it has over 45 million end users and 10,000 business users in the EEA; and (iii) both conditions must be met the three preceding financial years.

The presumption created by meeting the quantitative thresholds can be rebutted. Art. 3(5) DMA allows the investigated firm to bring forward any reason by which it can manifestly call into question the applicability of the presumption. The Commission may in turn rebut the relevance of these arguments by bringing forward reasons and evidence of its own. The first designations have proven that gatekeepers are likely to attempt rebuttals of the presumptions. In fact, rebuttals under 3(5) DMA have been raised with respect to most designations of core platform services, and some have succeeded: Samsung's internet browser, Apple iMessage, Microsoft Bing, Edge, and Ads, the X online social network and ByteDance's Ads services have not been designated as a result of this procedure.[598] Most designations however were successful, and over twenty core platform services operated by seven digital gatekeepers are now regulated under the DMA.[599] There has also been a first instance of judicial review with the *ByteDance* case.[600] Here, it became evident that once the Commission decides to proceed with designating a service, it is not easy for the gatekeeper to have such a decision overturned by the Court.[601]

The quantitative criteria are not the only relevant criteria to establish the position of the gatekeeper. Following Art. 3(8) DMA, the Commission can engage in a qualitative assessment. For this, it engages in a market investigation in accordance with Art. 17 DMA. To establish whether the operator of a core platform service should be designated, the Commission can consider (a.o.) the size, number of users, and position of the undertaking, relevant network effects and data-driven advantages, scale and scope effects, the conglomerate structure of the firm, and relevant lock-in effects. The Commission has designated one service where the quantitative thresholds were not met, namely Apple's iPadOS. Here, the Commission found that qualitative considerations warranted designation nonetheless.[602]

Obligations and Prohibitions

The substantive obligations laid down in Art. 5, 6, 7, 13, 14, and 15 apply to all designated gatekeepers. Art. 5 DMA contains the so-called self-executing obligations, and Art. 6 contains obligations that may require further specification (although they are in principle self-executing nonetheless).[603] Art. 7 DMA contains specific obligations

598 Van den Boom and Hornung (n 123).

599 Giorgio Monti and Friso Bostoen, 'The Rhyme and Reason of Gatekeeper Designation under the Digital Markets Act' [2024] SSRN.

600 Case T-1077/23 ByteDance [2024] ECLI:EU:T:2024:478.

601 Jasper Van den Boom and Sarah Hinck, 'ByteDance v. Commission – The EU General Court Has Set First Bars for Gatekeeper Designation Decisions under the Digital Markets Act' (*Verfassungsblog*, 2024).

602 Apple – iPadOS (Case DMA.100047) Commission Decision C(2024) 2500 final [2024].

603 Van den Boom and others (n 8).

related to interoperability for messaging services, which was added to the DMA late. Article 13 is the anti-circumvention obligation, which ensures that gatekeepers do not try to escape the effects associated with the obligations laid down in Art. 5, 6, and 7 through regulatory arbitrage. Art. 14 and 15 DMA are procedural obligations. Following Art. 14, firms must notify mergers even if they do not meet the threshold for review as normally used in EU Merger Control. Art. 15 DMA requires the firm to subject itself to an external audit related to its consumer profiling practices, to submit a report to the Commission, and to publish a non-confidential version of the findings.

Broadly, the obligations laid down in Art. 5, 6, and 7 DMA, which arguably form the core of the DMA, can be categorized as follows[604]:

Types of obligation	Relevant provisions
Data	Art. 5(2), 6(2), (9), (10), (11) DMA.
Anti-steering	Art. 5(3), (4), (5), (7), (8), and 6(3), (5), (6) DMA)
Interoperability	Art. 6(4), (7), (12), 7 DMA.
Transparency	Art. 5(9), (10), 6(8) DMA
Internal management	Art. 5(6)

Data-related obligations concern the collection, use, sharing of, and access to data. Art. 5(2) DMA prohibits gatekeepers from combining data collected on its core platform service and other services without user consent, limiting their ability to leverage their power from one market to another. Similarly, Art. 6(2) DMA prohibits the gatekeeper from using privileged access to non-public data in competition with business users. This limits the advantage that a gatekeeper holds over downstream competitors by preventing the gatekeeper from abusing its dual role as intermediary and competitor. Meanwhile, the gatekeeper must also provide its business users with real-time access to data generated by customer interactions with the services of the business user (Art. 6(10) DMA), reducing information asymmetries. Art. 6(9) DMA contains an enhanced (compared to the GDPR) obligation to provide data portability for users, making switching easier and reducing lock-in. Finally, Art. 6(11) DMA contains a special obligation for gatekeepers that operate search engines to license their data on FRAND basis so that competing gatekeepers can better develop their algorithms. Together, the data-related obligations aim to minimize the advantages held by the gatekeeper while opening up data flows to smaller users and business users, as well as granting data subjects more control over how their personal data is used.

The anti-steering obligations aim to further stimulate user choice and the adoption of new services, both through obligations and prohibitions. Following Art. 5(3)

604 Ibid.

DMA, gatekeepers may not demand exclusivity from business users. Business users should also be free to offer their promotions and subscriptions through any competing channel without restrictions (Art. 5(4) DMA) and to conclude agreements outside of the platform (Art. 5(5) DMA). End users should also not be coerced back into the ecosystems of the gatekeeper. Art. 5(7) DMA prohibits the gatekeeper from making it mandatory for end users to obtain additional services for access to the core platform service, and Art. 5(8) DMA prevents mandatory cross-service log-ins. Art. 6(6) DMA contains a prohibition to impose restrictions on users for switching services more generally. Besides having free choice, users should also be able to uninstall services that are pre-installed by the gatekeeper on its core platform services (Art 6(3) DMA), and the gatekeeper is not allowed to give preferential treatment to its own services under Art. 6(5) DMA. The anti-steering obligations aim to ensure that users do not only have free choice but also that they are not manipulated or coerced by the gatekeeper to stay within the multi-actor ecosystem operated by that gatekeeper. This should not only benefit end users by making it easier to freely choose the preferred service but also benefit contestability by promoting the adoption of services that compete with the gatekeeper.

Interoperability is arranged by mandating technical operability between the platform and third-party applications (Art. 6(4) DMA), specific requirements to provide interoperability for voice assistants and Operating Systems (Art. 6(7) DMA), and to provide FRAND access to App Stores, Search engines, and social networks (Art. 6(12) DMA). Art. 7 DMA imposes interoperability requirements specifically for operators of number-independent communications services.

Transparency is mostly offered to advertisers and publishers by giving them insight into the performance of their strategies and by allowing them to perform an independent verification of their inventories (Art. 5(9), 5(10), and 6(8) DMA). These transparency obligations complement what is already laid down in the Platform-to-Business Regulation, which imposes general transparency duties.[605]

Finally, business users and end users should also not be obstructed from seeking justice in their contact with the gatekeeper. Art. 5(6) prohibits gatekeepers from requiring business users to submit to internal arbitrage before they can raise issues before a competent court.

Together, these obligations should ensure that there is real and lasting change in the competitive conditions of the market. Users should be able to – and actually – adopt competing online platform services and both business- and end users should experience benefits from the DMA. Whether this actually occurs depends on the efficacy of the rules and their implementation by the gatekeeper. Where compliance strategies do not lead to the desired outcomes (i.e. more fairness and contestability), the Commission can enforce the law to ensure *effective* compliance.

[605] Regulation 2019/1150 on promoting fairness and transparency for business users of online intermediation services, OJ L 186 [2019].

Effective Compliance

Art 8 DMA specifies that it is up to the gatekeeper to demonstrate effective compliance with Art. 5, 6, and 7 DMA. Where the gatekeeper does not comply with the self-executing obligations of Art. 5 DMA, the Commission may enforce the law and impose sanctions as to instruct the gatekeeper to revise its compliance solution (Art. 29, 30 DMA). For Art. 6 and 7 DMA, the Commission may either pursue sanctions via a non-compliance procedure, or use the opportunity to specify how the obligation should be implemented. Art. 8(2) DMA gives the Commission the power to impose implementing decisions following a specification procedure, where it explains exactly how the gatekeeper is to comply with an obligations. The Commission is currently using the specification procedure to help Apple develop its interoperability strategy. According to the Commission's preliminary findings, Apple will have to ensure interoperability generally for connections with its hardware devices, and offer interoperability on-demand for a number of software platforms and products.[606]

Tools and Procedures

The Commission has a number of tools to enforce the law and its obligations. Art. 20 DMA specifies that the Commission may open proceedings to pursue the adoption of decision related to Art. 8, 29, or 30 DMA. Art. 29 DMA contains the power to conduct a non-compliance investigation. Where the undertaking has introduced compliance measures that the Commission deems ineffective, it may adopt a non-compliance decision. The Commission endeavours to issue this decision within 12 months of opening the non-compliance investigation (Art. 29(2) DMA). The Commission will first issue its preliminary findings, explaining why the behaviour of the firm is non-compliant and explaining how the gatekeeper should address these problems. After issuing its preliminary findings, the Commission can adopt the non-compliance decision and order a cease and desist of any ongoing non-compliant behaviour by the gatekeeper and order the gatekeeper to provide a timeline and clear explanation of how it will make changes to become compliant (Art. 29(3) & (4) DMA).

Art. 8 DMA contains the possibility for the Commission to implement its implementing decision, where it specifies how the gatekeeper must comply with certain measures. Following Art. 8(2) DMA, the Commission shall adopt the implementing decision within six months of starting the procedure in accordance with Art. 20 DMA. Following Art. 8(3) DMA, the Commission may also enter into a process of negotiations with the gatekeeper, but only if this process is initiated by the investigated entity. If the Commission specifies how the gatekeeper should comply through an Art. 8(2) DMA procedure, and the gatekeeper does not comply with this decision. The Commission may open a non-compliance investigation following Art. 29 DMA.

[606] DMA.100203/4, Apple Interoperability, Commission Decision of 19 September 2024.

Following Art. 18 DMA, the Commission may also start a market investigation into systematic non-compliance. If a gatekeeper has received at least three non-compliance decisions within an eight-year period, the Commission may start such an investigation. If it is found that the gatekeeper is systematically non-compliant, the Commission can impose far-reaching behavioural or structural remedies that are proportionate to achieving effective compliance. The investigation may take up to one year (Art. 18(1) DMA) and preliminary findings must be offered to the gatekeeper after six months (Art. 18(4) DMA). Following Art. 24 DMA, the Commission may use interim measures if there is a serious risk of irreparable damage as the result of the systematic non-compliance of the gatekeeper. The Commission may then adopt a temporary implementing act to ensure compliance while the investigation is pending. The gatekeeper can also try to enter into commitments with the Commission in relation to the behavioural or structural remedies that are to be imposed following the Art. 18 DMA investigation. Commitments are not available for normal non-compliance investigations following Art. 29 DMA.

Article 30 DMA gives the Commission the power to impose fines and sanctions. Where the gatekeeper fails to comply with any of the obligations laid down in Art. 5, 6, or 7, a decision adopted pursuant Art. 8(2) DMA, remedies imposed pursuant Art. 18 DMA, interim measures ordered through Art. 24 DMA or commitments imposed via Art. 25 DMA, a fine of 10 per cent of the total worldwide turnover of the gatekeeper may be imposed for the first infringement. If the gatekeeper is fined for another infringement of the same provision within an eight-year period, this fine may go up to 20 per cent. Following Art. 31 DMA, the Commission may also impose periodic penalty payments of up to 5 per cent of the daily average worldwide turnover until they comply on similar grounds.

The procedural toolbox of the Commission is laid down in chapter V DMA, and includes the power to request information (Art. 21 DMA), the power to carry out interviews and take statements (Art. 22 DMA), the power to conduct inspections (Art. 23 DMA), and collecting information from third parties (Art. 27 DMA). The Commission may issue a 1 per cent fine for failure to comply with any procedural obligation, such as providing information or statements or refusal to submit to an inspection (Art. 30(3) DMA).

Objectives

The enforcement of the DMA and its rules happens to promote two objectives specified in Art. 1 DMA: fairness and contestability. These two objectives are considered intertwined: weak contestability for certain services enables the gatekeeper to engage in unfair practices. In turn, unfair practices by the gatekeeper may reduce the possibility for business users to contest the gatekeeper's position.[607] Contestability, as

[607] Jasper van den Boom, 'What Does the Digital Markets Act Harmonize? – Exploring Interactions between the DMA and National Competition Laws' (2023) 19 European Competition Journal 57.

defined in the DMA, relates to the ability of an undertaking to overcome barriers to entry and expansion and to challenge the gatekeepers on the merits of the products and services of the entrant. Rec. 33 DMA specifies that contestability in core platform services is weakened by the presence of scale economies, network effects, and the effects of data. The DMA should therefore at least stop practices that are liable to worsen entry barriers, by imposing obligations on gatekeepers that lower entry barriers while prohibiting activities that heighten them.[608]

Contestability relates to fairness. Fairness is mentioned throughout the recitals of the DMA in relation to a number of practices and activities, yet at its core seems to mean two things. First, the gatekeeper must avoid acting unfairly. This means that it should not behave in a way that raises entry barriers or departs from competition on the merits. The prohibitions are in place to ensure that there is no unfair behaviour by the gatekeeper. This is similar to the idea of fairness governing EU competition law: the gatekeeper (or in competition law, the dominant company) has the obligation to withhold from activities that harm competition by virtue of their special responsibility (in the case of the DMA, this special responsibility comes with the designation of the gatekeeper). Second, there is the idea that there is an inherent unfairness in digital markets that must be corrected by the DMA. Due to structural characteristics of digital markets, such as scale and scope economies, network externalities, and data-driven advantages, large digital firms are considered able to appropriate larger parts of the generated value, while business users and small competitors are not (always) adequately compensated for their contributions. This type of unfairness is seemingly corrected by the DMA's positive obligations.[609]

Every obligation in the DMA should thus be interpreted in light of fairness *and* contestability, as should effective compliance in accordance with Art. 8 DMA. The obligations themselves are aimed at lowering entry barriers and ensuring that entrants can challenge incumbent gatekeepers by competing with them on the merits. Where there is a structural advantage, the gatekeeper should share with the entrant, for instance, by sharing data. Where there is the possibility of unfair behaviour, the gatekeeper should behave fairly by giving access and not giving its own products preferential treatment. It is up to the gatekeeper how to comply, but its compliance mechanisms should lead to a situation where such contestability is possible. Thus, even if the gatekeeper stops all unfair behaviour, for instance, in relation to refusing access or interoperability or the imposition of unfair trading conditions, it may still not be effectively compliant. The DMA may require of the regulated firm to go further and ensure that its natural structural advantages do not lead to entry barriers as well. As of yet, it is unclear what exactly constitutes effective compliance and how it is measured. As discussed later in this chapter, the Commission has already started non-compliance investigation, yet there is no clarity at the time

608 ibid.
609 ibid.

of writing on whether any of the changes introduced by gatekeepers are considered compliant and able to create fairness and contestability.

8.1.2 *Early Enforcement of the DMA*

The first gatekeepers were designated in September 2023 and included Apple, Amazon, Alphabet, Meta, Microsoft, and ByteDance. These firms were to be compliant with the DMA by 7 March 2024. On the 7th and 8th of March, each of the gatekeepers issued their compliance reports, which significantly varied in length and depth. Outliers were Apple with their 11-page compliance report and Microsoft with its 421-page compliance report, gatekeeper also had to address different issues related to different core platform services. Table 8.1 provides an overview.

The compliance changes highlight how the DMA works in practice. The gatekeeper looks at each of its specific core platform services and makes changes based on the specific obligation in the provision. This creates a situation where the gatekeepers have to invest significant resources and working hours to affect the changes and that the effects the DMA permeate throughout the ecosystem. The DMA does however not seem to require the changes across platforms to be

TABLE 8.1 *Gatekeepers, their core platform services, and relevant provisions*[610]

Designated gatekeeper	Relevant core platform services (CPS)	Provisions that require changes
Apple	App Store, Operating System (iOS), Web browser (Safari)	Article 5(3)(4)(5) Article 6(2)(3)(4)(7)(9)
Amazon	Marketplace (as an 'Online Intermediation Service (OIS)'), Online Advertising Service	Article 5(2)(4)(6)(9)(10) Article 6(2)(5)(8)(9)(10)
Booking	Online intermediation service – vertical search – travel services	Art. 5(2)(3)(4) Art. 6(9)(10)
ByteDance	Online Social Networking Service (OSNS) (= TikTok)	Article 6(9)(10)(12)
Meta	OSNS (Instagram and Facebook), Number-Independent Interpersonal Communications Service (NI-ICS = WhatsApp), Advertising Service, Marketplace (Online Intermediation Service)	Article 5(2)(8)(9)(10) Article 6(2)(5)(8)(9)(10)(12) Article 7(1)(2)
Alphabet	App Store, Online Search Engine, Video-sharing service (YouTube), Web Browser (Chrome), OS (Android), Advertising service, Google Maps (OIS), Google Shopping (OIS)	Article 5(2)(3)(4) Article 6(2)(3)(5)(8)(9)(11)(12)
Microsoft	OS (Windows), Online Social Media (LinkedIn)	Article 5(6) Article 6(2)(3)(7)(9)

610 Taken from: Jasper Van den Boom and Sarah Hinck, 'Compliance Time! Categorizing Risks of Compliance Failures in the DMA' (*SCiDA Blog*, March 2024).

mutually reinforcing or even coherent. Complying with the provisions can require significant efforts of the gatekeeper, but it can also simply require some tweaks to the design and presentation of the core platform service. For instance, compliance with Art. 6(3) DMA has imposed obligations on Apple and Alphabet to offer choice screens for web browsers (Apple) and search engines (as well as browsers, Alphabet), for their Operating Systems. Alphabet already offered a choice screen on its Android devices following the *Google Android* decision but has made tweaks to improve its choice screen. For Apple, the development of the choice screen was a wholly new endeavour.

Similarly, obligations under Art. 5(4), 6(4), and 6(12) DMA required of Google and Apple to make changes to their App Stores as to allow for side-loading and direct promotions, allow for third-party in-app payment systems, and allow for the installation of third-party app stores. This was already available in the Android handheld environment. Alphabet simply had to make it easier for software developers to offer direct links within their apps and set terms for this access. For Apple, linking out, side-loading, and the installation of third-party app stores were previously completely prohibited for software developers in the Apple ecosystem. Apple has reluctantly developed new business terms that allow for activity through side-loading or the installation of third-party app stores, and this reluctance is reflected in its short and negatively phrased compliance report.[611]

There are a number of obligations that affect all gatekeepers, such as the prohibition to combine data laid down in Art. 5(2) DMA. Gatekeepers must ensure that data collected via one core platform service is not used in the provision of other services without user consent. For this, the gatekeepers have to develop systems to label data and make it unavailable for cross-use if users choose not to allow for combination. Again, implementation efforts by gatekeepers were wildly different. Alphabet has explained that it will label data and not collect any data for a given platform if the consent is not given. Meanwhile, Meta has introduced a consent-or-pay mechanism that offers users the choice between allowing for the collection and combination of data, or to pay a monthly subscription fee.

Without discussing each compliance effort in detail, the DMA compliance workshops hosted in March 2024 revealed the practical problems that would arise in enforcing the DMA. First, it became clear that the provisions as laid down in Art. 5 DMA were not exactly clear and unambiguous, and unlikely to be self-executing as intended. Each gatekeeper maintained different ideas on what compliance meant, and most proposed solutions were met with lukewarm or negative responses by business users. Second, it became clear that gatekeepers were reluctant to actually try and achieve effective compliance. Meta's pay-or-consent model, Apple's new business terms, and Google's changes to its horizontal search page were viewed more

[611] J Van den Boom and S Hinck, DMA Compliance Workshop – Apple (SCiDA Blog, March 2024); J Van den Boom and S Hinck, DMA Compliance Workshop – Alphabet (SCiDA Blog, March 2024).

as retaliation by the gatekeeper than compliance efforts by stakeholders.[612] Third, the changes were not as big as expected. Gatekeepers made tweaks to their systems and adhered to the letter of the DMA, but it is not directly evident that there is now increased contestability or more fairness for business users. Furthermore, the effects of the changes are hard to measure as the gatekeepers are unclear about how they have tested these solutions, involved stakeholders and business users, or offered unattractive terms for access.[613] Fourth, the enforcement of the DMA will likely be a serious strain on the resources of the Commission, and changes to the market conditions will be hard fought.

These points are exemplified by the Commission's decision to open five non-compliance investigations only two weeks after compliance became mandatory, and a sixth in the months after. The Commission announced on the 25th of March that it would investigate Meta's compliance with Art. 5(2) DMA, explaining that the pay-or-consent model was likely illegal. It opened an investigation into Apple on the basis of Art. 5(4) DMA, and a separate investigation into Alphabet on the basis of Art. 5(4) DMA, for changes to its app marketplaces. It also started an investigation into Alphabet for the changes to its horizontal search results page on the basis of Art. 6(5) DMA. Finally, the Commission started an investigation into non-compliance by Apple for its changes following Art. 6(3) DMA, which requires Apple to allow uninstallation of its proprietary apps. Three months later, the Commission also announced an investigation into Apple for potential non-compliance in relation to its new business terms, on the basis of Art. 6(4) and a number of other provisions. Again 3 months later, the Commission started its first specification procedure under Art. 8(2) DMA, to explain how Apple can comply with its interoperability obligations under Art. 6(7) DMA.[614]

Each of these investigations must be finished within a period of 12 (non-compliance investigations) to 6 (specification procedures) months. It places significant strain on the Commission's enforcement machine to collect information and develop its theories of non-compliance, which will in turn be litigated. ByteDance, the smallest of the designated gatekeepers, has already had its day in court in relation to its designation. Here, the General Court has ruled in favour of the Commission and maintained the Commission to designate ByteDance's TikTok platform.[615]

612 See Jasper Van den Boom and Sarah Hinck, 'A Week of Compliance Workshops' (*SCiDA Blog*, March 2024).

613 ibid.

614 DMA.100109 Online Intermediation Services – app stores – AppStore – Art. 5(4), Commission Decision of 25 march 2024; DMA.100075, Alphabet – Online Intermediation services – app stores – Google Play – Art.5(4), Commission Decision of 25 March 2024; DMA.100193, Alphabet – Online Search Engine – Google Search – Art. 6(5), Commission Decision of 25 March 2024; DMA.100055, Meta – Article 5(2), Commission Decision of 25 March 2024; DMA.100185, Apple – Operating systems – iOS – Art. 6(3), Commission Decision of 25 March 2024; DMA.100206, Apple New Business Terms, Commission Decision of 24 June 2024.

615 Case T-1077/23, ByteDance v. Commission, ECLI:EU:T:2024:478, Judgement of 17 July 2024.

Other court cases are still to follow for the designations, and will surely follow for the non-compliance investigations.[616]

While this is not the place to enter into the details of each procedure, the Commission has focussed on cases where it considered non-compliance to be *blatant*. This is understandable as the Commission has to prioritize which cases it takes first, and in order to send a signal to unwilling gatekeepers. However, this also means that there are still a number of cases where there is potential ineffective compliance. The more instances of non-compliance there are across a vast range of core platform services offered by a number of gatekeepers, the more risks there are that things will slip through the cracks.[617] Ultimately, the early compliance efforts by gatekeepers may invoke the feeling that the Commission is simply pushing towards the point where it has grounds to investigate systematic non-compliance, so that it can consider more significant remedies and possibly break-up large gatekeeping firms.

8.1.3 *Strengths and Weaknesses: The Ecosystem Perspective*

There are a number of benefits to having the DMA. The DMA should be considered, first and foremost, as a means to resolve the shortcoming of EU competition law. Experiences with the enforcement of competition law in digital markets found that procedures were lengthy and complicated, and that tackling abuses one at a time was too slow to deal with the large number of issues presenting themselves in digital platform markets.[618] The DMA expediates enforcement procedures by introducing ex ante obligations, shifting the burden of proof and intervention, and simplifying procedures.[619] Moreover, as the DMA relies on a system of designations, it makes sure that it does not adversely impact the competitive abilities of small and medium enterprises by raising their costs.

The rules-based approach of the DMA furthermore ensures that problems are tackled across different activities within the multi-product ecosystems and value chains, at least where it relates to the major platforms held by an incumbent. For Alphabet, the DMA designates 7 core platform services, leading to a large number of changes within the Alphabet ecosystem. This should open up new opportunities for business users to promote their offers, gain access, access information or data, etcetera. More importantly, the DMA imposes obligations on all incumbent

[616] M Coulter, 'Apple Files Legal Challenge to EU's Digital Markets Act' *Reuters* (17 November 2023).

[617] Kamil Bazbaz, 'Roadblocks to Competition: Investigate Google's Non-Compliance with the EU Digital Markets Act' (*DuckDuckGo Blog*, 20 November 2024).

[618] Friso Bostoen, 'Understanding the Digital Markets Act' (2023) 68 The Antitrust Bulletin 263; A Fletcher and others, 'The Effective Use of Economics in the Digital Markets Act' (2024) 20 Journal of Competition Law and Economics 1.

[619] Pinar Akman, 'Regulating Competition in Digital Platform Markets: A Critical Assessment of the Framework and Approach of the EU Digital Markets Act'; Podszun (n 233).

ecosystem operators simultaneously. In competition law or antitrust investigations, the decision and imposed remedies only applied to a single undertaking and often a specific market. In the United States, the monopolization case against Google has just been concluded at the time of writing, and a number of remedies are being considered.[620] However, far-reaching remedies against Google would break down the Alphabet ecosystem, while leaving the competing incumbents wholly intact. This may upset the equilibrium found by the incumbent ecosystem operators, but it is not certain that this will restore competition. After all, it may be the case that the other incumbents now occupy the space once held by Google, leading to more concentration in the digital network, rather than less. The DMA ensures that the main issues, as identified through experiences in competition law enforcement, are addressed at once for all gatekeepers simultaneously.

The DMA provides the Commission with a workable, comprehensive, and fast way to address issues in digital markets. It is also targeted, in the sense that it only applies to large digital gatekeepers, thus regulating a small number of large businesses while leaving SME's outside of its scope.[621] It offers business users and end users new opportunities and creates opportunities to escalate for the Commission through findings of systematic non-compliance (Art. 18 DMA).[622] There is certainly added value to the addition of the DMA in the regulatory toolbox.

There are however also shortcomings of the DMA, particularly from the perspective of ecosystem-based competition. The DMA's obligations, while permeating throughout the ecosystem, do not address ecosystem-based harms directly. In fact, the term ecosystem is only mentioned three times in the DMA, all in the recitals. The DMA does not provide a concept of ecosystem nor does it explain how core platform services are related to one another in digital ecosystems and what the relevance of complementarity and economies of scope is in the analyses of the Commission.[623] Despite, the absence of the ecosystem concept in the provisions of the DMA, the ecosystem concept is referred to throughout designation decisions. Gatekeepers are able to raise defences in accordance with Art. 3(5) DMA, and investigated firms including Samsung, ByteDance, Apple, and Meta have all raised the relevance of the size and functioning of their ecosystems.[624] The Commission does attach consequence to the presence or absence of ecosystems in its decisions yet does not provide its own definition or a consistent interpretation. Instead, it is the General Court that has had to provide a definition for the ecosystem concept in the DMA, at least in essence, and explain that in order to raise arguments following Art. 3(5) DMA gatekeepers would have to both explain how their product and actor

620 Department of Justice, 'PLAINTIFFS' INITIAL PROPOSED FINAL JUDGMENT'.

621 Schweitzer, 'The Art to Make Gatekeeper Positions Contestable and the Challenge to Know What Is Fair: A Discussion of the Digital Markets Act Proposal' (n 105).

622 Van den Boom and others (n 8).

623 Hornung (n 65); van den Boom (n 123).

624 Van den Boom and Hornung (n 123).

ecosystems function and what the advantages or disadvantages associated with their ecosystem are.[625]

This raises questions about the role and importance of the size of the total conglomerate and may result in unexpected outcomes. For instance, Microsoft, one of the largest and most valuable companies in the world, has only had to make minor changes to its Windows OS and LinkedIn social media service. For its Windows Operating System, Microsoft now allows the uninstallation of a number of proprietary apps to comply with Art. 6(3) DMA, has made it easier to select defaults in its settings, and will open the Windows Widget Box to users.[626] For LinkedIn, it has introduced additional safeguards for data combinations and expanded its data portability and access tools. Microsoft's productivity software,[627] Office and Teams, its cloud computing service Azure, and its activities in gaming (Xbox) remain completely unregulated under the DMA.[628] There seems to be little to no impact on Microsoft's dominance as an enterprise and productivity ecosystem. Meanwhile, Booking.com has been designated under the DMA in the second round of designations. Booking operates an online intermediation service for travel booking. Booking.com has a market capitalization of ca. €150 billion, as opposed to Microsoft's €3 trillion market cap.[629] Yet the obligation imposed on Booking in terms of prohibiting parity clauses and self-preferencing may be more impactful and costly to implement than Microsoft's changes across its ecosystem.[630]

It can be argued that the DMA's focus on core platform services, while intentionally or unintentionally disregarding ecosystems, leads to a skewed perspective on who is competing with who and what opportunities business users actually have. The theories set out earlier, on the stages of ecosystem competition and ecosystem harms, would actually indicate that the DMA could hinder contestability due to premature designations. ByteDance has tried to raise this line of reasoning before the General Court, launching a 'challenger defence'. ByteDance explained that its small size compared to large incumbent gatekeepers, both on its platform and especially in terms of its digital ecosystem, forces it to compete on the merits. ByteDance argues that it offers users choice, offers lower price points, and invests heavily to bring new services. The Court dismisses these arguments due to a lack of evidence, yet there may be merit in having more analyses of competition at the ecosystem level. As a result of the design of the DMA, a large digital firm with a vast ecosystem is able to escape designation of a core platform service by arguing that the platform is not an important gateway.[631]

625 van den Boom (n 564); *ByteDance*, paras 115–119.

626 Microsoft's Compliance Report for the DMA, Non-confidential summary (2024).

627 Ibid.

628 The European Commission is conducting an investigation into Teams via Art. 102 TFEU, see Cases AT.40721 (Microsoft Teams) and AT.40873 (Microsoft Teams II).

629 Numbers are relevant at the time of writing (December 2024), taken from Yahoo Finance.

630 Booking Compliance Report for the Digital Markets Act, non-confidential summary (2024).

631 van den Boom (n 123).

The focus on platforms specifically may also lead to undesirable situations. For instance, Apple managed to escape designation of *iMessage* by showing that it is not used by business users to reach end users to a great extent. Conversely, opportunities to escape designation are very limited if the firm has a strong position within the platform market. The theory on contestability set out in the chapters above would argue this is counterproductive: it imposes additional burdens on firms that may still be in stage 1 or 2 competition.

In other areas, the focus on platforms may prove to be even more problematic. Cloud computing services, while included under Art. 2(2) DMA as 'core platform services', are often actually not platforms. Infrastructure as a Service (IaaS) such as Azure and AWS is a service where a large digital firm offers online capabilities for storage and virtualization. In principle, customers simply lease storage or computing capacity from the firm itself. These are not platforms, and since they are business-to-business they do not serve as an important gateway for business users to reach end users. This means that these vital infrastructures remain unregulated in the DMA (but they are regulated through the EU Data Act).[632] Similarly, Large Language Models and other Generative AI are offered on the basis of subscription models. This may mean that they too fall outside of the scope of a 'platform' service despite the High Level Group's finding that the DMA is applicable.[633] An ecosystem-based perspective would recognize that protecting competition in digital infrastructure markets (cloud) and potentially disruptive innovations (Artificial Intelligence) is particularly important and should be prioritized. The DMA, as a result of its drafting and personal scope, may be unable to achieve this effectively.

8.2 THE DMCCA: A PRINCIPLES-BASED APPROACH TO REGULATING THE ACTIVITIES OF DIGITAL FIRMS

The United Kingdom has introduced the Digital Markets, Competition, and Consumers Act (DMCCA) as its own response to competition issues in digital markets. The DMCCA relies on a principles-based approach, it sets expectations for digital firms and requires them to develop a code of conduct. Unlike the DMA, the DMCCA does not impose a vast number of ex ante obligations on gatekeepers directly. Instead, the regulator may impose instructions or pro-competitive interventions to stimulate competition, but the DMCCA entails more negotiation and consultation than the DMA.[634]

632 See the market investigations into cloud computing services by the CMA (ongoing <www.gov.uk/cma-cases/cloud-services-market-investigation>) and ACM (ACM, Market Study Cloud Services, Case no. ACM/21/050317 / Document no. ACM/INT/440323 (2023).

633 See European Commission, High-Level Group for the Digital Markets Act Public Statement on Artificial Intelligence, Statement of 22 May 2024.

634 See Van den Boom and others (n 563) for an in-depth overview of the DMCCA's provisions.

8.2.1 A *Bird's Eye View of the DMCCA*

Designations

Under the DMCCA, the Competition & Markets Authority (CMA) can designate a firm if it finds that it is operating an activity with 'strategic market status' (Section 2(1) DMCCA). Unlike the DMA, there is no pre-specified list of services that may be regulated under the DMCCA. Instead, any activity that is provided by the internet, provides one or more pieces of digital content, or is carried out in association with those activities may be considered for strategic market status (Sec. 3 DMA).

The conditions for designation are laid down in Sec. 5–7 DMCCA. Section 6 DMCCA contains the conditions: (i) the undertaking has achieved a position of significant size or scale in respect of the digital activity; (ii) a significant number of other undertakings use the digital activity as carried out by the undertaking in carrying on their business; (iii) the undertaking's position in respect of the digital activity would allow it to extend its market power to a range of other activities; and (iv) the undertaking's position in respect of the digital activity allows it to determine or substantially influence the ways in which other undertakings conduct themselves, in respect of the digital activity or otherwise. Following Section 5, the CMA must conduct a forward looking analysis. This means that the designation does not have to be based on position of the firm as it is now but can also include considerations on where it could be in the near future.[635] Section 7 DMA provides a quantitative thresholds called the turnover condition. According to this section, the total value of the global turnover of an undertaking or, where the undertaking is part of a group, the global turnover of that group in the relevant period exceeds £25 billion, or the total value of the UK turnover of an undertaking or, where the undertaking is part of a group, the UK turnover of that group in the relevant period exceeds £1 billion. If this condition is not met, the CMA cannot designate the activity. This is again different from the DMA, where the Commission can investigate on the basis of qualitative criteria even if the quantitative conditions are not met.

Obligations

If the condition is met, the CMA can enter into an investigation to determine whether designation is necessary. If it decides that it is, it may directly specify what conduct requirements apply to the investigated activity. Conduct requirements are discussed in Chapter 3 DMCCA. According to Section 19, 'conduct requirements' are requirements as to how the designated undertaking must conduct itself in relation to a relevant digital activity. The CMA may choose to impose conduct requirements or a combination thereof for a number of objectives: the fair dealing, open choice, trust and transparency, fair treatment, and ability to interact on reasonable terms

[635] Oles Andriychuk and Eleanor Clayton, 'Experimenting with Regulatory Mechanisms for Shaping Competition in Digital Markets' 9.

objectives. The way in which these conduct requirements are designed or how they are supposed to achieve these objectives is open-ended (Sec. 19 DMCCA).[636]

Conduct requirements can relate to a number of types of measures, these are laid down in Section 20 DMCCA. These include obligations and prohibitions. The types of measures that can be imposed are much more open-ended than those found in the DMA. In terms of obligations, the CMA can impose (for instance) fair trade requirements, create effective processes, or open up defaults or access points. In terms of prohibitions, the CMA may prohibit refusal to interoperate, unfair uses of data, or restricting the ability of users to use the products of other undertakings. While the categories are similar to obligations in the DMA, there is far more room for interpretation as to what exactly these provisions mean and what compliance would entail. Furthermore, the CMA may impose one or more restrictions, they do not apply to all designated undertakings or all simultaneously.[637]

Besides conduct requirements, there is the possibility to impose pro-competition interventions. These interventions may include (i) an order imposing on the designated undertaking requirements as to how the undertaking must conduct itself, in relation to the relevant digital activity or (ii) recommendations made by the CMA to any person exercising functions of a public nature about steps which the CMA considers the person ought to take in respect of the designated undertaking or the digital activity, or otherwise (Sec. 46 DMCCA). The PCI is similar to the specification decision; the CMA clearly specifies what needs to happen to mitigate or remedy the harm caused by the undertaking.[638]

Finally, the DMCCA contains rules on mergers. Sections 57 to 64 contain revised thresholds on 'reporting events'. For regulated firms, a lower thresholds may apply. Moreover, the firms must now notify if they acquire shares that lead to a change in voting rights, this counts when there is a change from under 15% to over 15%, under 25% to over 25%, or under 50% to over 50%.[639]

Procedures

The DMCCA is enforced on the basis of tailor-made remedies and restrictions. The CMA must conduct an investigation before imposing the SMS designation. They give notice to the investigated firm when starting the investigation. This notice will be published (Sec. 10 DMCCA). The CMA must close the investigation within nine

636 Ondrej Kubaric, 'Contours of Contestability: A Comparative Analysis of EU and UK Digital Markets Regulation New EU & UK Rules for Regulating Competition in Digital Markets: A Comparative Perspective' (2024) 10 North East Law Review 11.

637 ibid.

638 Van den Boom and others (n 8).

639 See Spencer Cohen, 'Principles in Transition: What Remains of Competition Law in the Era of Hybrid Competition Enforcement? New EU & UK Rules for Regulating Competition in Digital Markets: A Comparative Perspective' (2024) 10 North East Law Review 87 for more on mergers in the DMCCA.

months of starting it (Sec. 14); it also ends the investigation without issuing a decision (Sec. 12). If an entity is designated, the designation will last for five years.[640]

The CMA can impose its conduct requirements directly upon designating an SMS activity, add conduct requirements or pro-competition interventions later, or remove conduct requirements if they are no longer necessary (Sec. 19–22 DMCCA). If there is reasonable suspicion that a firm has breached a conduct requirement, the CMA may launch an investigation as to impose sanctions and correct the behaviour of the firm (Sec. 26). This investigation must end within six months of being started (Sec. 30). The CMA may find that there is an infringement, may end the procedure without making findings (Sec. 28) or find that there are countervailing benefits (Sec. 29). If the CMA does find an infringement, it may impose enforcement orders to force the firm to adjust its behaviour (Sec. 31). It may also issue interim orders where necessary to prevent irreparable harms (Sec. 32). Enforcement orders will stay active until revoked (Sec. 33–35).

Dialogue and consultations are very important in the DMCCA. Following Section 13 DMCCA, the CMA must launch a public consultation before designating any activity. According to Sec. 27 DMCCA, the CMA must take into account any arguments made by the firm to justify its conduct. Moreover, unlike the CMA, does DMCCA does allow for the agreement of binding commitments (Sec. 36). The CMA may also mediate negotiations between incumbent and third party through the final offer mechanism. Here, the CMA sets terms for a fair transaction between these parties as to resolve an impasse in negotiations (Sec. 38–45).[641]

Pro-competition investigations can only be started after the firm has already been designated.[642] Following Sec. 47 DMCCA, the CMA may open an investigation to determine whether a PCI is necessary and appropriate. The CMA must again notify the investigated entity, and publish a revised version after hearing the firm (Sec. 48 DMCCA). It must also launch a public consultation on the basis of the public notice (Sec. 49). Ultimately, it adopts a PCI decision, where it imposes either a pro-competition order or recommendations. It must do so within 4 months of opening the investigation, with the option to extend the investigation by 2 months (Sec. 50). If the CMA chooses to impose pro-competition orders, it must again open a consultation on the basis of a non-confidential summary of its findings (Sec. 54). Once the orders are imposed, they remain in place until they are revoked (Sec. 53–55). Here, also, binding commitments are available (Sec. 56).

The CMA has a number of investigatory powers available: the power to require information (Sec. 69), to name a senior manager (Sec. 70), to access premises (Sec. 71), to conduct interviews (Sec. 72–76), to issue a warrant (Sec. 77), to collect reports by skilled persons (Sec. 78) and to give orders to preserve information (Sec. 80). It

640 Kubaric (n 635) 18–19.

641 Van den Boom and others (n 8).

642 ibid.

can also impose penalties for breaches of the competition requirements imposed through conduct requirements or competition orders or any procedural infringements. Fines may amount up to 10% of turnover of the group in question depending on the gravity of the infringement, and periodic penalty payments can be up to 5% per day for substantive infringements (Sec. 85–86). For procedural errors, this can be up to 1% fixed payment or a 5% per day periodic penalty payment. The CMA also has the power to fine individuals up to £30.000 of a fixed amount of £15.000 per day periodically.

Objectives

The objectives of the DMCCA can vary. The conduct requirements can be imposed with an eye on the fair dealing, open choice, trust and transparency, fair treatment, and ability to interact on reasonably terms objectives (Sec. 19 DMCCA).[643] Pro-competition requirements are imposed when there is a risk of (or actual) adverse effect to competition. The DMCCA is much more cautious than the DMA in formulating one or two clear objectives that must be pursued through enforcement of the law. Instead, the pursued objectives relate to the tailored remedy. It is clear however that – in line with the application of competition law generally – the DMCCA aims to resolve distortions of competition and ultimately harms to consumers.[644]

8.2.2 *Strengths and Weaknesses in the DMCCA: The Ecosystem Perspective*

The approach taken in the DMCCA differs greatly from that in the DMA. Although there are – at the time of writing – no designations or enforcement actions available, the design of the DMCCA does show how it intends to tackle competition issues.[645]

The DMCCA focuses on designating targeted activities where the CMA believes interventions are required. In the DMA, the Commission can designate platforms or categories of behaviour as well, but then this is applicable to all gatekeepers that have been designated. In the DMCCA, the CMA will impose obligations specifically on Apple, Amazon, Alphabet, or another incumbent player in relation to their operation of a platform or activity in a product market. This affords the DMCCA a great level of flexibility, allowing for the design of bespoke and mutually reinforcing designations and requirements.[646] After all, the SMS-activity does not have to be a platform activity, but merely an important activity that is 'based on the internet'. Moreover, there is a greater opportunity to study the impact of the behaviour of the

[643] CMA, 'Digital Markets Competition Regime Guidance' (2024) Guidance 44.

[644] Van den Boom and others (n 8); Kubaric (n 635).

[645] CMA, 'Digital Markets Competition Regime Guidance' (n 642).

[646] CMA, 'Digital Markets Competition Regime Guidance' [2024] DMCCA Draft Guidance for Consultation; Oles Andriychuk and Eleanor Clayton, 'Experimenting with Regulatory Mechanisms for Shaping Competition in Digital Markets' [2024] NELR.

investigated entity – and the impact of the conduct requirement or competition order – on competition across markets.[647]

The DMCCA grants the CMA the power to add more conduct requirements later or remove them if they are no longer necessary. This allows the CMA to pinpoint and shift regulatory burdens to steer competition in a certain direction. With the DMA, there is the question whether the imposition of the requirements will actually lead to contestability. If not, the requirements will have to be reinterpreted, or compliance standards will have to be changed, to create effective compliance. This means that when the obligations themselves are simply not fit for purpose, it is hard to escape from the framing and design of the obligations themselves. In the DMCCA, the CMA can revoke, update, and add new orders as it sees fit to rebalance competition. This may mean that if an emerging ecosystem operator turns out to be overregulated following the imposition of an order, this can be easily removed. In turn, new orders can be imposed on other incumbents to rebalance competition. This approach seems sensible in regulating digital firms, as it allows the remedy packages to be scaled up or down as market conditions change.[648]

Third, designation with the strategic market status is not limited to platform activities but can include any type of digital activity. This again helps the CMA to target problems where they arise, without having to link them to the operation of a specific (core) platform service. This makes it much easier for the CMA to designate services such as Cloud and Artificial Intelligence, as it is not limited by the need to show that it is a platform-based services.[649] This also means that even in areas where the link between the relevant activity and the rest of the ecosystem are not evident, the CMA can simply designate and intervene on the basis of perceived competition problems. This allows the CMA to escape issues related to market definition or establishing linkages and actually intervene directly where competition is harmed.[650] This is different from the DMA where the regulated activity must relate to the designated platform and is sensible from the ecosystem perspective as harms and anti-competitive effects may permeate throughout the ecosystem and manifest in unexpected ways. By targeting the harm directly, the CMA can start from the idea of resolving the adverse effect and then update or change competition orders as they go build remedies that address the sources of the harm.

Fourth, the CMA is granted investigatory powers that may help to resolve longstanding issues and to acquire information. For instance, the CMA can impose senior managers and dismiss CEO's. If it turns out that far-reaching remedies are necessary, the CMA can appoint trustworthy interim CEO's with reporting obligations that may

[647] Andriychuk and Clayton (n 645); Oles Andriychuk, 'The New EU and UK Regimes for Regulating Competition in Digital Markets: We Finally See What's on the Plate – but Do We Know How to Eat It?' (2024) 12 Journal of Antitrust Enforcement 195; Van den Boom and others (n 8).

[648] CMA, 'Digital Markets Competition Regime Guidance' (n 645).

[649] CMA, 'Potential Remedies' [2024] Market investigation into cloud services.

[650] CMA, 'Digital Markets Competition Regime Guidance' (n 645); CMA, 'Potential Remedies' (n 648).

help to establish why competition failures persist around the digital activity in question. Another power that is promising is the final offer mechanism, which allows the CMA to strike quick deals between regulated firms and third parties, speeding up access on the basis of negotiations between the parties themselves.[651]

While the approach taken in the CMA holds merit, there are some potential shortcomings. First, the enforcement of the DMCCA will likely be resource-intensive and slow to produce results. The CMA must designate activities individually and develop suitable conduct requirements and pro-competitive interventions for each distinct activity.[652] There is space to make sure that these interventions create mutually reinforcing effects between different designated activities, but this requires studies of the relevant markets and their functioning. The DMCCA can build on experiences already gained with the introduction of the DMA and Section 19a GWB, as well as the CMA's own market studies into digital markets,[653] but studying new and evolving markets will be time consuming and resource intensive. Even in areas where the DMA is already active, the CMA will have to justify why the imposition of similar remedies is warranted in relation to different types of activities.

Second, as both a strength and weakness of the DMCCA, it is very much based on negotiations and dialogue. The CMA must launch consultations before it designates or imposes interventions.[654] This again slows down the process and requires the CMA to justify its decision on more grounds and towards more parties. Even after the consultation has been launched and the CMA has motivated its findings, the investigated firm may still try to offer commitments to the CMA, which again requires input from different stakeholders. The negotiations-based focus is straining on resources and opens up opportunities for lobbying and capture.

Third, while the CMA does impose new rules on mergers and acquisitions and goes further than the DMA in this regard, it is questionable if they are sufficient to stop ecosystem operators from engaging in killer acquisitions and rolling up industries. The thresholds for notifications have been revised, but not the thresholds for interventions by the CMA. One may then wonder if this does not lead to the CMA simply having to review and clear *more* transactions, without any material changes in what is permitted. This may again cause an additional strain on the resources of the CMA.

These issues related to resources come together with the enforcement investigations. Investigations into breaches in conduct requirements have to be finished in twelve months, and the imposition of pro-competition orders in six months. With this, the design of the DMCCA raises serious questions about its approach: does

651 CMA, 'Digital Markets Competition Regime Guidance'; Van den Boom and others (n 8).
652 Van den Boom and others (n 8).
653 Competition & Market Authority (n 44); Competition & Markets Authority (n 122); CMA, 'Cloud Services Market Investigation' (2023) Market Investigation.
654 Ibid., CMA, 'Digital Markets Competition Regime Guidance' (n 650).

it foresee in-depth studies of markets and sectors to offer tailor-made and effective remedies, or is the CMA to quickly wrap up its investigations with limited access to resources? This will be shown when the enforcement of the DMCCA starts but will prove vital in the efficacy of the DMA to shape competition.

From the ecosystem perspective, the DMCCA seems to be designed in a much more adaptive and suitable way than the DMA. The question is however whether this approach will remain workable in light of the procedures and resources available to the CMA. This in turn raises the question whether the CMA will be able to sufficiently reign in incumbent stage 4 ecosystems, while simultaneously supporting entrants and small- and medium-sized ecosystem operators.

8.3 SECTION 19A GWB: A COMPETITION LAW-BASED APPROACH TO GOVERNING ECOSYSTEMS

Section 19a GWB is a reform of German competition law. This new competition tool became active in 2021, and precedes the DMA. However, despite being early to arrive, investigations under Section 19a GWB have proven complex and time-consuming. At the time of writing, there are five firms that have been designated with paramount significance in accordance with Section 19a GWB: Microsoft, Meta, Apple, Amazon, and Alphabet.[655] The German Competition Authority (BKA) is actively investigating these firms for potential breaches of Section 19a GWB. Section 19a GWB is unique as it focuses specifically on issues related to the presence of digital ecosystems with cross-market power. The investigations by the BKA not only complement the other regulatory interventions in terms of enforcement but are also valuable in creating new knowledge on – and insights into – competition between digital ecosystems.

8.3.1 *The German Approach to Governing Competition in Digital Markets*

In Germany, Section 19a GWB has been introduced to provide the Bundeskartellamt with tools to identify undertakings with 'paramount significance across markets' and to intervene on the basis of this paramount significance. Unlike the DMA and the SMS regime, Section 19a GWB has been introduced as a reform of competition law rather than a complementary regulatory regime.

Under Section 19a GWB, the BKA can confer a status of paramount significance on those which are particularly capable of extending their position of power across markets or secure their unassailable position due to their financial, technical, or

[655] Alphabet – Case B7-61/21, Bundeskartellamt Decision of 30 December 2021; Meta case B6-27/21, BKA Decision of 02 May 2022; Amazon case B2-55/21, BKA Decision of 05 July 2022; Apple case B 9-67/21, BKA Decision of 03 April 2023; BKA, Microsoft also subject to extended abuse control pursuant to Section 19a GWB – Bundeskartellamt determines paramount significance across markets, Press Release 30 September 2024. The Microsoft decision is not yet published at the time of writing.

data-related resources or due to their [collection of] platforms and their cross-market ecosystems.[656] Article 19a (1) includes a non-exhaustive list of five criteria that may indicate such capabilities; dominance on one or more markets; financial strength and access to resources; vertical integration and activities on otherwise related markets; access to data relevant for competition and; a gatekeeper position.[657]

The introduction of the concept of paramount significance helps to identify risks to competition that are not easily captured under the existing competition law framework. The German legislature identifies three risks to competition that are better captured under Section 19a GWB. First, the existence of network externalities, superior access to data and related feedback loops that trigger strong concentration of markets. Second, the subsequent economies of scale and scope and access to resources that lead to an unassailable market position. Third, the key strategic positions that a firm may hold and that lead to multiple dependencies of market players on their services, which allows the undertaking to distort competition.[658] Moreover, the designation of having paramount significance does not require the finding of dominance in a specific market, allowing the BKA to identify issues related to competition at the ecosystem level.[659]

Designation under Section 19a GWB happens after an investigation into an undertaking. This differs from designation under the DMA as it relies on case-by-case investigations, and from the SMS regime as the designation relates to the undertaking as a whole rather than a certain activity. For undertakings with 'paramount significance', the BKA is able to prohibit certain types of conduct by the firm that it deems anti-competitive. Section 19a GWB contains an exhaustive list of seven practices for which the BKA can impose remedies: (1) self-preferencing; (2) hindering supply or sales activities of other firms (including noncompetitors); (3) hindering competitors in markets where the 19a firm may rapidly expand its position; (4) using collected data to raise market entry barriers or requiring users' permission for such use; (5) hindering competition by denying or impeding interoperability or data portability; (6) withholding information on the 19a firm's performance; and (7) demanding disproportionate (monetary or nonmonetary) compensation from business customers.[660] Similarly to the SMS regime, the BKA can choose which remedies it imposes on a designated undertaking.

[656] Jens-Uwe Franck and Martin Peitz, 'Digital Platforms and the New 19a Tool in the German Competition Act' (2021) 12 16; Deutscher Bundestag, 'Beschlussempfehlung Und Bericht Des Ausschusses Für Wirtschaft Und Energie' (2021) Drucksache 19/25868.

[657] Franck and Peitz (n 655) 7–8.

[658] Franck and Peitz (n 655); Deutscher Bundestag, 'Gesetzentwurf Der Bundesregierung, Entwurf Eines Gesetzes Zur Änderung Des Gesetzes Gegen Wettbewerbsbeschränkungen Für Ein Fokussiertes, Proaktives Und Digitales Wettbewerbsrecht 4.0 Und Anderer Wettbewerbsrechtlicher Bestimmungen' (2020) Drucksache 19/23492.

[659] Franck and Peitz (n 655) 5–7.

[660] ibid 3–4.

For these categories of behaviour, there is a presumption that they may produce anti-competitive effects. An undertaking can however still defend their behaviour by bringing forward efficiency justifications, which is not the case under the DMA.[661] Enforcement is not only sped up by relying on presumptions and the use of ex ante remedies. Section 19a GWB also empowers the BKA to use interim measures as to prevent market tipping or other harms to competition. Moreover, for actions under Section 19a GWB, there is abridged judicial review. Undertakings are able to challenge the decisions of the BKA before the court, but there is no possibility for appeal.[662] The combined effects of these shortcuts greatly speed up enforcement. However, it also increases the risk of false positives. The BKA must therefore be careful in its analysis to ensure that it does not unintentionally harms efficiencies or pro-competitive actions through its interventions.

8.3.2 *Enforcement Experiences in Germany*

Section 19a GWB is already actively enforced in Germany. The Bundeskartellamt has already designated Alphabet,[663] Meta,[664] Amazon,[665] Apple,[666] and Microsoft.[667] Once the entity has been designated, the finding of paramount significance applies to the entity as a whole, and the categories of remedies become available to the BKA in relation to any product or service offered by these undertakings, as long as they can establish competitive harms.

There are already numerous investigations ongoing or concluded on the basis of Section 19a GWB. The Bundeskartellamt has investigated Google in three cases: Google News Showcase, Google Data Processing, and Google Maps & Automotive services.[668] It has issued a decision in the first two cases and accepted commitments in the latter. Amazon has been investigated in relation to its dual role as operator of the market place and logistics provider.[669] Apple is being investigated for its anti-tracking policy as it may favour Apple in its advertising activities.[670] Finally, Meta

[661] ibid 15–16.
[662] ibid 20–22.
[663] Case B7-61/21, Alphabet, Bundeskartellamt Decision of 30 December 2021.
[664] Case B6-27/21, Meta, BKA Decision of 02 May 2022.
[665] Case B2—55/21, Amazon, BKA Decision of 05 July 2022.
[666] Case B 9-67/21, Apple, BKA Decision of 03 April 2023.
[667] Case B 6—26/23, Microsoft, BKA Decision of 27 September 2024.
[668] Case V-43/20, 'Google – Google News Showcase', Decision of 21 December 2022; B7-70/21, 'Google – Data processing', Decision of 6 October 2023; Bundeskartellamt, Google Automotive Services proceeding – Market test regarding commitments proposed by Google, Press Release of 20 December 2023.
[669] Bundeskartellamt, Extension of ongoing proceedings against Amazon to also include an examination pursuant to Section 19a of the German Competition Act (GWB), Press Release of 14 November 2022.
[670] Bundeskartellamt, Bundeskartellamt reviews Apple's tracking rules for third-party apps, Press Release of 14 June 2022.

is being investigated for its activities in virtual reality, as it is combining data and leveraging its activities in social media into these markets.[671]

Some lessons can already be drawn from early enforcement experiences. The investigations into Google have been concluded through commitments. The BKA started these investigations in May and June 2021. Google News Showcase was decided in December 2022, and Google Data Processing in October 2023. In Google News Showcase, the BKA found that the launch of Google's showcase service involved elements that harmed publishers and created risks of self-preferencing through integration in Google's horizontal search page.[672] Google took several measures to address these concerns, including the non-integration of showcase into horizontal search, amending contracts, and ensuring fair treatment.[673] The BKA concluded the case stating that the rights for publishers benefitted from its enforcement actions. In Google Data Processing, the Bundeskartellamt's focus was on Google's approach to cross-service data collection, particularly in relation to user data that could be combined across services such as Google Search, YouTube, and Maps. The Bundeskartellamt found that Google's data practices limited users' control over personal data, giving them insufficient options to prevent their information from being processed across different Google services. Google offered commitments by offering additional user choice on cross-platform data-sharing.[674] The investigation into Meta has been concluded without the adoption of a decision as Meta made voluntary changes to its behaviour and stopped the requirement of logging in with a Facebook account to use the Oculus virtual reality service.[675] Investigations into Apple and Amazon, opened in 2022, are still ongoing.

Early experiences show that the new tool is helpful for the BKA to address novel types of harms that are associated specifically with paramount significance, allowing the BKA to step out of the bounds of abuse of dominance or cartel provisions and to better study the behaviour in the context of platform and ecosystem competition. The designation with paramount significance works a shortcut to establish a special responsibility, so that the investigation itself can focus on the behaviour in question. This should speed up proceedings; nevertheless, the proceedings still take significant amounts of time. In fact, all cases for which the BKA started its investigation have now been – or are potentially – regulated under the DMA. This means that significant resources have been invested in working cases that may only have marginal impact in practice. Nevertheless, the cases are valuable in developing theories of harm and studying the functioning of ecosystems.

[671] Bundeskartellamt, First proceeding based on new rules for digital companies – Bundeskartellamt also assesses new Section 19a GWB in its Facebook/Oculus case, Press Release of 28 January 2021.

[672] Case V-43/20, p. 3 et seq.

[673] ibid 5–9.

[674] Case B7-70/21.

[675] Bundeskartellamt, Meta (Facebook) responds to the Bundeskartellamt's concerns – VR headsets can now be used without a Facebook account, 23 November 2022.

8.3.3 *Strengths and Weaknesses of the German Approach from an Ecosystem Perspective*

There are strengths and weaknesses in the German approach. First, the reform of competition law to recognize competition at the ecosystem level is a valuable addition to competition policy. The German legislature has acted timely to adapt its competition laws as to provide its competition authority with the tools to deal with the novelties of digital markets, identify harms associated to ecosystem competition, and intervene on the basis of new principles and standards.[676] Moreover, introducing the amendment as a reform of competition law – rather than complementary regulation – recognizes the nature of competition policy as a living instrument that is able to evolve alongside the market. The German legislature has made an attempt to ensure that regulation is only introduced when needed, while allowing competition law to govern where possible.

The design of the German tool strikes a balance between speed on the one hand and accuracy on the other hand. Designations with paramount significance, lowered standards of proof, and abridged judicial review help to keep proceedings manageable. Meanwhile, investigations still require the formulation of clear theories of harm and a study of the competitive harms. The depth of the German approach is clear from its designation decisions. The designation of Amazon is motivated through a 215-page decision and studied in depth in judicial review. This decision has really clarified how the German competition authority and court view ecosystems and their operation, engaging with the functioning of Amazon's ecosystem in great detail.[677] Section 19a GWB as a tool is highly suitable to identify new types of harms and further develop theories and experiences with ecosystem-based harms.

This is exemplified well in the BKA's designation decision for Amazon and Microsoft.[678] In its designation of Amazon, the BKA explained what an ecosystem is precisely. Amazon argued in its defence that it did not operate a digital ecosystem per se, but rather that it was active across a number of markets to offer a purchasing and logistics solution. According to Amazon, this conglomeration did not give them power to shape competition in any of these markets specifically. The BKA found, however, with support of the German Federal Court, that Amazon does operate an ecosystem and that it is sufficient 'if strategic and competition possibilities exist, the abstract risk potential which is addressed by the provision. Section 19a (1) GWB is intended to enable the Bundeskartellamt to more effectively control large digital companies whose resources and strategic positioning allow them to have considerable influence on the business activities of third parties, to distort the competitive process to their own advantage and to transfer their existing market power to more

[676] Hornung (n 65).

[677] Case B2-55/21, Amazon, BKA Decision of 05 July 2022; Order of 23 April 2024 – KVB 56/22 – Amazon.

[678] ibid; Case B6-26/23, Microsoft, BKA Decision of September 2024.

and more new markets and sectors.'[679] This case helps to sketch the contours of what constitutes a digital ecosystem: it is not necessary to look at the digital conglomerate from the perspective of its impact on a single market, but rather the extent of its activities across markets as a whole.[680]

In Microsoft, the BKA offers an in-depth explanation of Microsoft's ecosystem power, which it derives from its power over its technological infrastructures (Windows OS, cloud), interfaces (APIs, formats) and its central position in consumer and enterprise computing gives it private rule-setting power. The BKA's analysis, unlike the DMA, does not look at the operation of platform services in isolation, but looks at how Microsoft's activities and behaviour across markets impacts the position of the third parties that depend on them. The BKA finds that Microsoft has the ability and incentives to use this power to influence the behaviour of those that rely on them and gives examples of how it does or has done so. The BKA carefully analyses the sources of Microsoft's paramount significance across markets, and how this power can be used to limit competition. With this, it sets out Microsoft's positional power, its power over processes, resources, and creates an intuition for its degree of ecosystem power.[681]

Section 19a GWB is an important addition to the German competition law toolbox and fulfils a valuable complementary function to the DMA and DMCCA. There are however also shortcomings for the German system. First, while designations have happened rather quickly, investigations into potential anti-competitive behaviour are resource intensive and time-consuming. The investigations into Apple and Meta started in 2022 have still not been concluded, let alone reviewed by courts. While faster than traditional antitrust investigations, the system may still be too slow to address structural competition problems in dynamic digital markets on its own. Second, there is a dissonance between Section 19a GWB as a competition law tool and its system of designation. Designations with paramount significance last up to five years before they are reviewed and are reserved only for very powerful undertakings. Yet, as practice shows, it takes months to years to first designate an entity and then months to years to actually enforce the law (albeit that this is quicker when accepting commitments). The scope of the remedies available to the BKA is also limited and overlaps with the DMA in many instances. This means that while Section 19a GWB is on the one hand very flexible and adaptive, it is less so in terms of remedies and personal scope. The quasi-regulatory nature of this tool may ultimately limit the impact of its enforcement in practice.[682]

Section 19a GWB as a tool has merit, as it allows for the study of ecosystem power and frames ecosystem-related harms in digital markets in a new way, allowing the

679 Order of 23 April 2024 – KVB 56/22 – Amazon (2024).

680 Sarah Hinck and Rupprecht Podszun, 'Beyond DMA: The Amazon Section 19a Case (Germany)' [2024] Journal of European Competition Law & Practice lpae066.

681 Case B6-26/23, Microsoft, BKA Decision of September 2024.

682 van den Boom (n 606).

BKA to consider harms on the basis of economic realities associated with competition in digital markets. At the same time, it can be concluded that this type of competition law reform works best as a complement to sectoral regulation, rather than a substitute. Experiences derived from the enforcement of the provision are best made operational at large scale by translating them into regulatory obligations.

8.4 CONCLUSION

This section has discussed three existing proposals to regulate digital markets. First, the rules-based DMA, which focuses on setting strict and narrowly defined rules to provide a quick solution to problems in digital markets. Second, the SMS regime in the UK, which pursues tailor-made regulations through a dynamic and principles-based regulatory framework that consists of codes of conduct, pro-competition interventions, and revised merger rules. Third, Germany's new competition tool in 19a GWB, which aims to resolve issues in the digital market by introducing the dimension of ecosystem power into competition law analysis.

Each of these regulatory approaches has their own perks and drawbacks and are able to combat competitive issues in digital markets to a certain extent. The different regulatory regimes often complement one another, rather than substitute, even though not all of the regulatory regimes apply in the same jurisdictions, or across the entirety of that jurisdiction.

The rules-based approach as formulated in the DMA is most suitable to regulate the largest and most powerful incumbents. This allows for rapid consequences to the introduction of regulation to resolve the most stringent issues that lead to foreclosure, while preventing undue regulatory burdens on small- and medium sized entities. However, the DMA in itself may prove too static or rigid to be phased out, as it imposes a one-size-fits-all set of obligations and prohibitions on the largest undertakings without a way to gradually reduce regulatory obligations.

The SMS regime proves more flexible in determining which regulatory obligations should govern which players. Developing principles for fair competition provides firms with insights into how they should conduct themselves, while pro-competition interventions ensure that structural problems can be resolved. As interventions are based on principles, evolutions in the market can be taken into account by the relevant authority so that new rules can be formulated and old rules can be removed. The SMS regime allows for deregulation and the introduction of competition yet having to establish clear rules based on principles may afford the largest incumbents with more opportunities to retain their position. At the same time, co-regulation allows the incumbent to capture the regulatory discussion as they still have more access to resources and leverage than their smaller competitors. The DMA and SMS regime therefore complement one another: the DMA creates the initial market opening, while the SMS regime provides flexibility in the process of introducing competition and deregulating afterwards.

Section 19a GWB provides a valuable contribution to competition policy by giving competition authorities tools to identify ecosystem power and harms to ecosystem competition. While it speeds up competition law investigations to some extent, it still requires significant inquiries into the law and facts from the BKA. Consequently, Section 19a GWB may be too slow to act to resolve structural competition issues across a number of markets by itself. However, as Germany is a member state of the EU, the regulatory obligations of the DMA apply in Germany as well. Synergies between the DMA and Section 19a GWB make them highly complementary tools, and the BKA can fulfil an important role as a fact-finder and frontrunner in digital competition cases.

Each of the discussed methods to regulate digital markets has their own perks and drawbacks, and each of them are complementary to one another.

9

A New Regulatory Paradigm

Regulating Ecosystems

This chapter proposes a new type of regulatory framework: progressive ecosystem regulation. This framework integrates a rules-based, principles-based, and competition law-based approach into a single coherent regulatory framework, with the purpose of introducing long-term competition at the ecosystem level and opening up the digital network industry for disruptive entry.

The proposal for progressive ecosystem regulation envisions the creation of three regulatory layers.[683] The largest ecosystem operators (stage 4) are subjected to heavy regulatory burdens that take shape as ex ante rules-based regulation. Ecosystems that are slightly smaller, but still of significant size and with significant ecosystem power (stage 3), are subjected to a regime of lighter regulatory burdens based on principles-based regulation. Here, the relevant authority imposes tailor-made regulatory burdens depending on the observed harms to competition. Emerging platforms and ecosystems (stages 1 and 2) are entered into an 'entrant pool', where they receive protection from – and access to the resources of – the lightly and heavily regulated entities. Progressive ecosystem regulation only regulates interactions between entities in different pools, while competition *within* the three pools happens freely, regulated only through competition law. This means that the larger firms must open up their infrastructures, share resources, and face restrictions in how they compete with smaller firms, but that firms of equal size compete freely with one another. This should strike a balance between maintaining competitive pressure on the one hand while combatting structural competition problems by means of regulation on the other.

The purpose of this regulatory framework is to create an environment conducive to disruptive entry and innovation. The way in which the regulation intends to do so is twofold: first, it attempts to open up the digital network industry for entry by limiting the ability of incumbent ecosystem operators to act as private regulators, so as to reduce their opportunities to raise entry barriers and pre-empt disruption. Second, far-reaching obligations on larger entities to open up their infrastructures, share

[683] How ecosystems are divided into different pools is based on the analyses and categorization of ecosystems from Part II.

data, and support entrants upon request promote the ability of entrants to make use of the resources held by incumbents to experiment and develop new disruptive business models. The underlying idea is that if competition at the ecosystem sufficiently intensifies, it will become harder to devote large amounts of resources to the preemption of entry, as there are more competitive threats from relatively equal market participants and more uncertainty about where disruption might come from.

Section 9.1 explains what progressive ecosystem regulation is at its core and its objectives. Section 9.2 explains the design of the regulatory system. Section 9.3 provides guidance on the regulatory burdens and their justification. Finally, Section 9.4 concludes this chapter.

9.1 A NEW WAY TO THINK ABOUT REGULATION: PROGRESSIVE ECOSYSTEM REGULATION

> Monopoly maintenance in the form of moat building strategies helps protect the erosion of monopoly positions and therefore harms competition…We have to have willingness and the ability to connect related acts and understand how moats protect monopoly power and how competition protects itself in modern markets. More often than not, it is not through an exact replica of the castle, but through insurgents, and allowing those insurgents to thrive in a free durable and uninhibited way, that's competition in a modern market.
>
> —Jonathan Kanter[684]

Progressive ecosystem regulation operates from the idea that the greatest source of competitive pressure in digital markets exists due to risks of disruption.[685] Disruptive entry could wholly displace the existing incumbent in one or more of their

[684] Jonathan Kanter, 'Keynote Remarks at the Stigler Center's 2022 Antitrust and Competition Conference' (21 April 2022) <www.youtube.com/watch?v=FtDZM30OJvA>. 19:22–19:40, Jonathan Kanter acted as assistant attorney general for the US Department of Justice at the time this speech was delivered.

[685] Schumpeter (n 760) included the seminal theory on disruptive competition cycles by referring to this type of innovation as 'creative destruction', where the new technology cannibalizes the legacy technology as a part of economic and societal progress. These types of innovation cycles can also be referred to as 'Schumpeterian competition cycles'; Tiwana (n 20) describes how disruptive innovations may cannibalize the business model of the incumbent. The emergence of a disruptive technology will lead to the decline of the market share of the dominant design of an incumbent technology. Ultimately, the incumbent is faced with the choice to try and 'leapfrog' so that it can capture the next generation of innovation or disappear from the market over time. de Streel and Larouche (n 529) pose that disruptive innovation offers 'an alternative path to market entry and growth, in addition to the more traditional path of challenging the incumbent firm(s) head on, via sustaining innovation or more statically via cheaper products or superior marketing, for instance. Because it avoids frontal competition, a disruptive innovation strategy can allow the disruptor to grow "under the radar" of incumbent firms and, if successfully executed, can offer more growth potential'. Disruptive innovation would also generally lead to positive welfare implications. Ideas on innovation as a part of the goals of competition policy and the system of progressive ecosystem regulation are discussed in depth in Section 9.3.

dominated markets, which may in turn be or become a threat to the competitive power of their ecosystem as a whole.[686] Incumbent ecosystem operators have the ability and incentives to prevent discontinuity, and the larger they grow the better they can do so.[687] Disruptive entry into the digital network industry becomes blockaded when the relative size of a small group of incumbents becomes too large and they can see whatever might be on the horizon early and clearly. As entrants depend on the infrastructures of incumbents, the incumbent can either push them out of the market or coerce them into adopting business models that align with the incumbent's interests.[688] If regulation manages to create a 'fog of war', this allows entrants to build their ecosystems until they can durably compete. In other words, regulation should introduce uncertainty for the incumbent by reducing their view on what is happening in varying parts of the network industry and restore competition by overwhelming them with a mix of regulatory burdens and growing competitive pressures.[689] The layered regulatory approach proposed here intends to do exactly that.

Regulation that is aimed only – or predominantly – at limiting what the largest firm can or cannot do is unlikely to produce sustainable and meaningful competition at the ecosystem level. Only regulation that simultaneously provides access to infrastructures, resources, and access points for entrants (actual and potential) will sufficiently reduce entry barriers to stimulate disruptive entry and long-term competition. The regulatory frameworks discussed in Chapter 10 offer possibilities to provide entrants with resources, in particular the Digital Markets Act (DMA) and DMCCA. However, it is argued here that the needs and interests of entrants should be more central to the design of digital regulation, particularly in terms

[686] Schumpeter (n 684).

[687] Schumpeter (n 760) included the seminal theory on disruptive competition cycles by referring to this type of innovation as 'creative destruction', where the new technology cannibalizes the legacy technology as a part of economic and societal progress. These types of innovation cycles can also be referred to as 'Schumpeterian competition cycles'; Tiwana (n 20) describes how disruptive innovations may cannibalize the business model of the incumbent. The emergence of a disruptive technology will lead to the decline of the market share of the dominant design of an incumbent technology. Ultimately, the incumbent is faced with the choice to try and 'leapfrog' so that it can capture the next generation of innovation, or disappear from the market over time. de Streel and Larouche (n 729) pose that disruptive innovation offers 'an alternative path to market entry and growth, in addition to the more traditional path of challenging the incumbent firm(s) head on, via sustaining innovation or more statically via cheaper products or superior marketing, for instance. Because it avoids frontal competition, a disruptive innovation strategy can allow the disruptor to grow "under the radar" of incumbent firms and, if successfully executed, can offer more growth potential'. Disruptive innovation would also generally lead to positive welfare implications. Ideas on innovation as a part of the goals of competition policy and the system of progressive ecosystem regulation are discussed in depth in Section 9.3.

[688] Ezrachi and Stucke (n 1).

[689] de Streel and Larouche (n 729); Ezrachi and Stucke (n 3) discuss how acquisitions may impact the process of disruptive innovation. Acquisition of a disruptive entrant does not necessarily mean that disruption is pre-empted and may in fact stimulate it, but if the acquisition happens by the incumbent of a legacy technology which is threatened by the disruption, this leads to absorption. These problems have also been discussed in depth in Section 7.4.

of offering them support in developing their multi-actor and multi-product ecosystems, to result in long-term competition. The DMA and DMCCA may also prove to be too incremental in their approach to regulating digital giants: even the DMA, which seemed astounding in the numbers of provisions that it contained and to the number of platforms it applied, has so far mostly resulted in reluctant tweaks to business models and lacklustre implementation of data-sharing obligations.[690] Progressive ecosystem regulation aims to take the regulation a step further, by taking into account ecosystem competition to pry open markets and introduce sustainable competition.

9.1.1 *Key Findings of the Book and the Regulatory Proposal*

The regulatory proposal is based on the key findings presented throughout this book, which are summarized here as to provide a concise answer to the research questions formulated at the start of the book, and to clearly link them to the key characteristics of progressive ecosystem regulation.

The first key finding is that certain platform markets exhibit natural monopoly characteristics. In particular, markets that are highly data-dependent, homogeneous, and fully software based. As a result, digital markets are prone to concentration, and it becomes likely that a single entity intermediates between a relatively homogeneous group of consumers and business users. Product differentiation may lead to duopoly or oligopoly, but the number of players in one specific platform market is likely to remain limited. In other markets, there may not be a natural monopoly, yet competition is still likely to be (strongly) imperfect. Regulation should then aim to promote competition *for* these markets, as opposed to attempt introducing competition *in* the market. In non-digital network industries, the existence of natural monopoly would generally indicate that the regulator should regulate the behaviour of the monopolist in this market while trying to introduce competition in competitive activities up- or downstream in the value chain.[691] In the case of digital self-sustained monopoly however, it may be more effective if regulation focuses on stimulating competition at the ecosystem level. This requires the regulator to take a dynamic view of competitions and cross-market interactions, whereas traditional natural monopoly regulation is often based on static considerations (i.e. the existence of monopoly and the need to redistribute the surplus of generated value). Regulation should then aim to promote efforts to engage in disruptive innovation so as to displace the technology offered by the monopolist with something new and different.

[690] CPI, 'European Sites Criticize Google's Compliance Efforts with DMA' (12 December 2024); N Lomas, 'DuckDuckGo Calls for EU to Widen Its Digital Markets Act Probe of Google' [2024] *TechCrunch*; Bazbaz (n 616); A4E, 'The Implementation of the DMA and Alphabet's Compliance with Its Obligations' (2024). See the non-compliance investigations into the digital incumbents (n 616).

[691] den Hertog (n 15); Decker (n 10).

The second key finding is that the presence of competition at the ecosystem level may provide competitive restraints that prevent harms normally associated with monopoly. This book has argued that the creation of multi-product ecosystems should be viewed as a natural result from the characteristics of digital products and services and the networked nature of digital markets. The modular design of digital goods and their informational nature make the sharing and reuse of components attractive for undertakings, and the networked nature of the digital market makes it important to ensure compatibility between different goods and services, which invites vertical integration or conglomeration. In the digital network, competition between (relatively equal) multi-product ecosystems may create more competitive constraints than competition at the market level. Consequently, monopoly within a market may be less harmful to consumers as long as inter-ecosystem competition is strong, since the existence of competing ecosystems allows users to switch to similar services offered by other ecosystem operators. Thus, an increase in the number of relatively equally positioned ecosystems increases competition throughout the digital network industry.

The third key finding relates to the conditions under which ecosystem competition produces pro- or anti-competitive effects. Ecosystem competition may only provide sufficient competitive restraints to remove harms associated with monopoly if competition between ecosystems is sufficiently intense. The book has identified four stages of ecosystem competition which aim to provide guidance in determining when ecosystem competition is likely to be intense and when anti-competitive behaviour is likely to arise. The book argues that players with emerging ecosystems (stages 1 and 2) are likely limited in their ability to abuse their gatekeeper power in their multi-actor ecosystem as they face intense competition from equal and larger ecosystems in inter-ecosystem competition. Mature ecosystems (stage 3) are likely to change their business models in order to move from a growth to a revenue-generating strategy. Here, the use of gatekeeper power to exclude certain vertical competitors, create lock-in, or extract excessive data becomes increasingly likely. However, entering into a revenue-generating strategy does follow economic rationale as the ecosystem operator will have to develop a durable business model. Competitive problems in ecosystem competition become particularly pronounced when there is a small group of incumbent ecosystems that dominates a large number of markets (stage 4). In this stage, ecosystem operators have the ability and incentives to foreclose entrants by leveraging their ecosystem power and to abuse gatekeeper power in vertical competition to identify and eliminate threats that arise from within their multi-actor ecosystem, as to pre-empt competition by foreclosing or absorbing disruptive innovators. As the incumbents have secured their core revenue-generating markets, and challenging other incumbents for their core markets is costly and difficult, they may look to lead a 'relatively quiet life'. A tacit understanding can come to exist between the existing incumbents that they will prioritize the survival of their existing business models by pre-empting entry across a wide range of markets, deprioritizing competition with one another.[692] This means that for the emergence of new technologies to create competitive pressures, emerging markets should be occupied by small- and medium-sized ecosystems. This warrants supporting stage 1 and 2 ecosystems, while limiting the ability of stage 4 (and to a lesser extent stage 3) ecosystem operators to capture emerging markets.

Based on these findings, the proposed regulatory framework does not attempt to introduce competition within markets but focuses on contestability of these markets. It then goes beyond existing paradigms for regulation by arguing that contestation should not come from undertakings that supply similar services, but rather by allowing differentiated ecosystems to emerge which have the capacity to disrupt the existing business models employed in the core markets of incumbent ecosystem operators. This approach differs from regulation in non-digital network industries, as well as from existing regulatory proposals for digital markets.[693]

9.1.2 *The Objectives of Progressive Ecosystem Regulation*

The purpose of progressive ecosystem regulation is to promote the long-term competitiveness of the digital network industry. It attempts to do so by creating an environment that fosters disruptive innovation by lowering barriers to entry and pry open digital markets despite persistent structural competition issues in two ways: opening up access points for competition for entrants, and protecting and promoting competition at the ecosystem level.

Economic regulation, generally, aims to generate efficiencies that ultimately benefit consumers.[694] In non-digital natural monopoly markets, regulation has often taken shape as price regulation, with a greater or lesser degree of space for productive efficiencies.[695] This has created the perception that regulation and innovation are antithetical.[696] Modern economic regulation is characterized by a shift towards pursuing dynamic efficiencies, in the form of innovation, as a goal in itself. In non-digital networks, it has done so by unbundling vertically integrated monopolists and

[692] See Chapters 7 and 8.

[693] The differences between progressive ecosystem regulation, natural monopoly regulation, and existing regulatory proposals is discussed in depth in Chapter 10.

[694] Posner (n 209); Joskow (n 10).

[695] Decker (n 10).

[696] The tension between regulation and innovation is particularly pronounced in natural monopoly regulation, where access is promoted over competition. However, in many instances the relationship between regulation and innovation is much less clear, competition law has been used to bring forward dynamic efficiencies, and regulation that introduces competition can actually lead to innovation. It is also possible that social regulations related to (for instance) sustainability or security become venues for innovative efforts. For analyses on the relationship between regulation and innovation cf Knut Blind, 'The Impact of Regulation on Innovation' (2012) 12 NESTA working paper series; Philippe Aghion, Antonin Bergeaud and John Van Reenen, 'The Impact of Regulation on Innovation' (2023) 113 American Economic Review 2894.

introducing competition where possible.[697] Competition is then the vessel by which innovation arrives, and regulation serves to guide it.[698]

There are several popular theories on what drives innovation. Arrow's theory presupposes a monopolist that faces no competitive pressures. Such a monopolist – without any risks of displacement and no alternatives for its customers – will not have any incentives to innovate. Thus, a monopolist will only invest in innovation to pre-empt the emergence of a potential competitor: competitive pressure is then a prerequisite for innovation to happen.[699] Aghion's theory on innovation has refined Arrow's theory and argues that innovation and competition have an inverted U relationship. While monopoly is not conducive to innovation, if a market is extremely competitive, innovation may slow down because the small firms do not have the resources to invest and cannot always appropriate the benefits associated with their R&D investments. A monopolist has relative certainty that if it invests to pre-empt the entry of a competitor, it can reap the benefits of operating the new technology. In a situation of (extremely) intense competition however, prioritizing investments into R&D may lead to market exit if the investments do not pay out. This has led to Aghion's curve, where most innovation takes place when there is some level of competition, but that competition is not too intense.[700]

Arrow's theory may have missed some real market constraints. First, Arrow's model assumes a monopoly in both production and innovation. This is however not necessarily the case, an incumbent will be skilful in generating innovations that fit within their existing business model (sustained innovation), but will be hesitant to engage in innovation that cannibalizes their business model (disruptive innovation).[701] Entrants that are able to produce disruptive innovations may have the opportunity to displace the monopolist. While the rewards of sustained innovation are incremental, the reward of successful entry can be enormous. Thus, entrants may choose to invest heavily even if chances are low if they see an opportunity for 'disruptive' innovation.[702]

Christensen coined the theory of disruptive innovation: a small firm will invest – likely with the support of private capital – in efforts to displace the monopolist by

[697] Posner (n 10); Joskow (n 10); Decker (n 10); den Hertog (n 15); Marneffe and Vereeck (n 15); Ibáñez Colomo (n 15).

[698] Cave (n 15); Marc Bourreau, Pınar Doğan and Matthieu Manant, 'A Critical Review of the "Ladder of Investment" Approach' (2010) 34 Telecommunications Policy 683; Blind (n 695); Phillippe Aghion and others, 'Competition and Innovation: An Inverted-U Relationship' (May 2005) 120 The Quarterly Journal of Economics 701–728.

[699] KJ Arrow, 'Economic Welfare and the Allocation of Resources for Invention' in Charles K Rowley (ed), *Readings in Industrial Economics: Volume Two: Private Enterprise and State Intervention* (Macmillan Education UK 1972) <https://doi.org/10.1007/978-1-349-15486-9_13>.

[700] Aghion and others (n 697).

[701] Richard J Gilbert, *Innovation Matters: Competition Policy for the High-Technology Economy* (The MIT Press 2020) <https://doi.org/10.7551/mitpress/12686.001.0001> accessed 22 January 2025.

[702] ibid; Bower and Christensen (n 528).

producing new technologies. Christensen's seminal work *Disruptive Technologies: catching the wave* opened with the quote 'one of the most consistent patterns in business is the failure of leading companies to stay at the top of their industries when technologies or markets change... The pattern of failure has been striking in the computer industry'.[703] In 1995, when the digital network industry was in its infancy, the competitive conditions for disruptive entry and cycles of destructive innovation were present. This meant that the giants of yesteryear, be it IBM, Altavista, MySpace, or Blackberry failed to pre-empt disruptive entry by means of sustained innovation. In Chapter 6, it is set out how today's digital incumbents competed and occasionally narrowly avoided bankruptcy. The risk of displacement is what drove the wave of rapid innovation seen 2000s and 2010s. These early examples help to show that while the digital network industry is prone to concentration, competition is possible. It is the case that *some* markets heavily favour a monopoly as a result of natural market forces, but it is not the case that competition and competitive pressures are completely absent.[704] The diminished competitiveness of smaller firms now should be attributed to the presence of large ecosystems that span across a vast range of markets, rather than the structural competition issues within a particular market. Much like non-digital markets, regulation can serve the purpose of identifying whether there are core network activities, where there is actually a natural monopoly and where competition cannot be durably introduced. Here, it can focus on introducing competition in adjacent markets with the purpose of allowing challengers to duplicate the necessary infrastructure so as to ultimately contest this monopoly.

Regulation should thus aim to intensify the existing competitive pressures, rather than achieving a better allocation of welfare for existing monopolies. This is also the rationale underlying the DMA, which promotes fairness and contestability, as well as the DMCCA, which focuses on protecting competition by regulating certain strategic activities. While both aim to allow for contestation of a monopoly by lowering barriers to entry, the mechanism behind contestability remains unclear. There is no focus on ecosystem competition, but rather a focus on opening up certain platforms to competition. It remains questionable whether these interventions will suffice to create long-term and intense competition between firms if ecosystem power is not taken into account. Early implementation strategies following the introduction of the DMA show that large gatekeepers are able to modify their strategies and shift their resources to maintain a moat surrounding their platform monopolies.

It is proposed here that there are two persistent risks that threaten the position of the incumbent. The first is disruption: if regulation manages to lower entry barriers, an entrant can come in to contest the monopoly and potentially displace it. The idea of competition *for* markets, rather than in markets, relies on the idea that a

703 Bower and Christensen (n 528).

704 Ducci (n 11); Petit and Teece, 'Innovating Big Tech Firms and Competition Policy: Favoring Dynamic over Static Competition' (n 13); Petit (n 13).

disruptive innovator is able to displace the monopolist.[705] The second risk is not as well recognized in existing regulatory frameworks, the presence of inter-ecosystem competition: if there is an ecosystem operator of equal size, they are better positioned to challenge the monopolist for their core markets than small entrants.[706] Rather than contestability, this implies a dimension of sustained competition at the ecosystem level. Progressive ecosystem focuses on stimulating the latter: opening up resources across not only platforms but entire ecosystems creates novel opportunities for entry, which may be harder to detect than entry that comes from competition on the platforms offered by incumbents.

Today's incumbents have reached the size and the level of control over the digital network industry that allows them to pre-empt or absorb competition successfully. The dynamism of digital markets of the time where Facebook challenged MySpace or Google challenged Altavista is no longer present: incumbents simply have too much insight into where competitive threats are coming from and how to pre-empt them. Progressive ecosystem regulation attempts to recreate the conditions for sustainable competition and real competitive constraints by again introducing the element of uncertainty and risk of disruption. By fostering an environment where disruptive innovation thrives, progressive ecosystem regulation attempts to shape the incentives of incumbents, challengers (medium-sized ecosystems), and entrants to compete.[707]

Progressive ecosystem regulation relies on three key objectives: (i) incumbent firms must be limited in their ability to pre-empt disruptive innovation; (ii) ecosystems of equal size must be incentivized to prioritize competition with one another; (iii) entrants must be incentivized to enter into long-term, meaningful, and disruptive competition. Progressive ecosystem regulation incorporates these three components by introducing a layered regulatory structure, where obligations on firms vary on the basis of the size of their ecosystem, and where these obligations only apply with respect to smaller ecosystems than the firm that is regulated. This results in the creation of three distinct pools:

- Heavily regulated – incumbent ecosystems with significant ecosystem power and control over access points for competition (stage 4 ecosystems)
- Lightly regulated – mature ecosystems with significant ecosystem power (stage 3 ecosystems)
- Protected: Entrants with small ecosystems that are trying to capture a platform market and enter into meaningful competition at the ecosystem level (stage 1 and 2 ecosystems).

The first objective is served by introducing far-reaching prohibitions and negative obligations on the stage 4 ecosystem competitors, the incumbents, which are entered into the heavily regulated pool. By taking away their ability to steer users away from

[705] Petit (n 13).
[706] Jacobides, Cennamo and Gawer (n 12); Jacobides and Lianos (n 12); van den Boom (n 123).
[707] van den Boom (n 123).

potential disruptors or abuse their power over resources, processes, and their positional power, the regulatory framework intends to 'pry open' markets to allow for meaningful competition. This intervention aims to restore competition that has been lost by the pervasive and systematic suppression of competition by incumbents.

The second objective is promoted by distinguishing between heavily and lightly regulated entities and the creation of a protected entrant pool. Regulatory obligations do not govern competition within these pools, but only how players in one pool compete with another: the burdens on heavily regulated entities govern their behaviour towards the lightly regulated and entrant pool, obligations in the lightly regulated pool only create obligations towards entrants, and entrants are free to compete while enjoying access to the resources and facilities of larger ecosystem operators. Ecosystems of a relatively equal size are not hindered in how they compete with one another, while the regulation ensures that access points for competition remain open. This carefully constructed operationalization of the regulatory burdens creates incentives to comply where necessary and compete where possible. The burdens on heavily regulated entities should be designed to be too heavy to bear (at least in the long term). This is a means of restoring competition to its pre-disrupted state: the incumbents have enjoyed the rewards of their monopolization efforts, and must now carry the costs of re-introducing competition. This should make incumbent firms want to escape the heavily regulated pool. They may be able to do so by means of significant interventions in their business models, for instance, divestments of parts of their ecosystem. If they manage to prove that they no longer have power over access points for competition, they can be entered into the lightly regulated pool. This is greatly beneficial to them as it both removes their obligations towards lightly regulated entities and relieves them of part of their duties towards entrants. Rather than just being regulated, large firms are encouraged to end their monopoly.

Firms that are in the lightly regulated pool can compete with one another freely, creating incentives to compete intensely. These pools are still governed by competition laws, so larger lightly regulated firms may still find to have abused their monopoly. For larger firms, the risk associated with disrupting competition too much is re-entry into the heavily regulated pool. As lightly regulated firms are relatively equal, they should be able to exercise competitive pressures on one another. After all, firms of a relatively equal size are best positioned to invest in efforts to overthrow the incumbent in a specific market.

Meanwhile, the third objective is promoted as entrants will have better opportunities to enter the market in a meaningful way as competition in the rest of the digital network intensifies. As ecosystems of an equal size compete more heavily with one another, they will be able to dedicate less resources to identifying and pre-empting threats from competitive entry. Meanwhile, entrants are invited to experiment and innovate by granting access to the infrastructures and resources of the larger ecosystem operators. This means that existing ecosystems may be challenged from within (on the basis of their own infrastructures) or from outside of the ecosystem (through innovations by entrants on the infrastructure of another regulated ecosystem operator). This makes disruptive entry hard to predict, as entrants can emerge rather quickly and the challenged firm does not necessarily have privileged access to data or insights on the competitive movements of the entrant.

Uncertainty as a driver of competition seems to be the foundation of competition in the digital network industry.[708] Currently, the unregulated network industry has become too transparent for large incumbents. Progressive ecosystem regulation, through its complex structure and mix of obligations and prohibitions, reintroduces the uncertainty that drove intense competition when the digital network industry was forming.

9.2 THE REGULATORY LAYERS AND POOLS OF PROGRESSIVE ECOSYSTEM REGULATION

This section sets out the idea behind the heavily regulated, lightly regulated, and entrant pool in detail. It explains in depth how it is decided which entities are entered into which pools, and what the effects of such a designation are. Progressive ecosystem regulation imposes different positive and negative obligations on regulated entities depending on which pool they are designated to.

Heavily regulated entities are subjected to a rules-based regime which includes a number of positive and negative obligations. In terms of positive obligations, the heavily regulated entity must provide access to technologies, licenses, and data, generally free of charge. It is also subjected to prohibitions on certain leveraging behaviour, abuses of gatekeeper power or otherwise exclusionary behaviour, and limitations to their ability to acquire entrants.

In the lightly regulated layer and pool, the starting point of the regulation is to develop certain principles for fair competition in the digital network industry. Lightly regulated entities may be subjected to tailor-made regulatory burdens to ensure the effectiveness of these principles or to resolve certain recurring problems which entrants face when engaging in competition with a lightly regulated entity. Here, regulatory burdens may include for instance the provision of FRAND (yet under certain circumstances free) access to technologies, licenses, or data, prohibitions to exclude, or limitations in one's ability to abuse their gatekeeper power. Players in the lightly regulated pool will also enjoy access to the resources held by incumbents for free or under FRAND conditions, where it is facilitated through the regulation.

Entrants will not face additional regulatory burdens but will instead gain access to resources and infrastructures held by the regulated entities. They will also enjoy increased protection from anti-competitive behaviour by heavily- and lightly regulated entities through the regulation. The entrant pool should create a safe haven for entrants and provide them with access to the resources required to overcome

[708] Petit (n 13); Dattée, Alexy and Autio (n 104); Petit and Teece, 'Taking Ecosystems Competition Seriously in the Digital Economy' (n 13).

the chicken-and-egg problem and to enter into competition. Heavily regulated entities will have to make available more resources than lightly regulated entities. This ensures access for entrants to the resources of ecosystems that control the most and reflects the asymmetric competitive position of heavily and lightly regulated entities. Lightly regulated entities can also still acquire entrants without additional limitations, ensuring that entrants who wish to be absorbed have options to be acquired.

An important distinctive feature of progressive ecosystem regulation is that it only regulates the interactions *between* the different pools, not competition *within* these pools. This means that players of an equal size can compete freely with one another, while safeguards are imposed to deal with asymmetries in size and power. Competition within the heavily regulated, lightly regulated, or entrant pool remains intense, while the safeguards prevent incumbents from pushing potential disruptors out of their markets. This allows entrants to experiment and find ways to differentiate themselves from both larger firms (without the risk of being coerced into behaviour that supports the incumbent's business models) and one another (by not imposing needless restrictions on firms in their ability to compete with those of an equal size). Meanwhile, incumbents are incentivized to compete intensely with one another as they cannot focus their resources on foreclosing entrants, and to instead use these resources to maintain their position through competition on the merits.[709]

Figure 9.1 shows how this governance of the interactions would look, before moving on to the details of how players are entered into pools and how the regulation impacts them.

9.2.1 *The Heavily Regulated Pool: A Rules-Based Regime for Digital Giants*

The introduction of the heavily regulated pool is intended to resolve the most pressing issues related to ecosystem competition and competition in digital markets generally. For this, the heavily regulated pool uses a DMA-style approach: an ex ante regime consisting of self-executing rules.[710] Once competition intensifies, entities

[709] See also Pablo Ibáñez Colomo and Andriani Kalintiri, 'The Evolution of EU Antitrust Policy: 1966–2017' (2020) 83 The Modern Law Review 321 describe how 'market shaping' interventions under competition policy generally can harm incentives to invest. Here, the authors rely on the example of how a duty to supply may negatively impact incentives to invest and innovate in the relevant market and that this may harm long-term competition in light of stimulating short-term rivalry. This book has argued – more specifically for digital markets and ecosystem competition – that undermining the ecosystem operator's ability to differentiate oneself from competing ecosystems undermines its ability to engage in inter-ecosystem competition and leads to a similar outcome where long-term competition is harmed as a result of stimulating short-term rivalry. One example may be the obligation on Apple and Google to allow one another's app stores on their mobile OS: by diminishing the ability of Apple to differentiate itself from Google and maintain its high-quality standards, such an obligation is a threat to the viability of Apple's business model. Apple's ability to differentiate its products from those in other ecosystems lies in its exertion of greater quality control and unique complementarities.

[710] van den Boom and others (n 8).

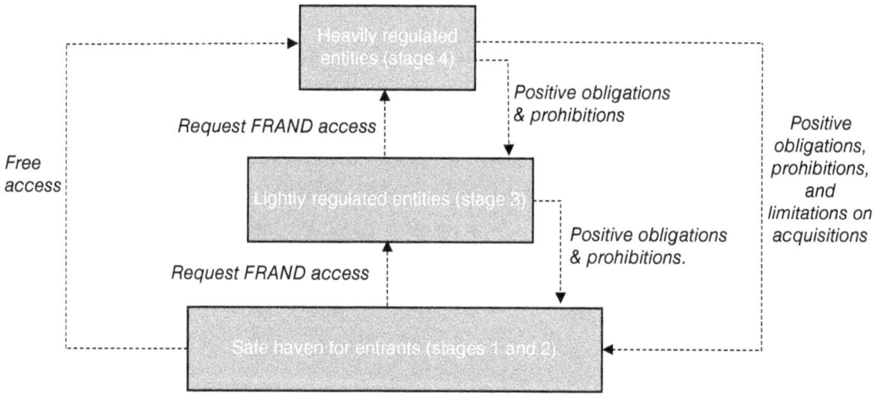

FIGURE 9.1 An exemplary overview of the regulatory pools and burdens in progressive ecosystem regulation

should gradually be moved from the heavily regulated pool to the lightly regulated pool until there are no heavily regulated entities left. Light regulation should be the primary modus operandi, and introduction in the heavily regulated pool should be reserved for exceptional circumstances (as currently faced in the digital network industry under the GAFAM incumbency). The lightly regulated pool will allow for varying degrees of regulatory burdens imposed on entities within that pool to facilitate this transition.[711]

The heavily regulated layer should be reserved for the most entrenched and powerful incumbents in digital markets, categorized in this book as entities in stage 4 ecosystem competition. Determining whether – and how – an assessment takes place will ultimately be up to the regulator, but some guidance is provided here. For this assessment, it would likely be suitable to on a qualitative assessment with some minimum thresholds.

In terms of thresholds, undertakings should only be entered into the heavily regulated pool if they are durably dominant (or have a similar significant presence) in at least two digital markets, of which at least one is a platform market. The second dominated market can be a platform market but does not necessarily have to be. A qualitative assessment should however demonstrate that a second non-platform market has strategic significance. This could be the case, for instance, if the platform operator provides cloud-based infrastructure (Infrastructure as a Service; IaaS) services. IaaS services, such as Microsoft's Azure or Amazon AWS, are not platform services. However, from the perspective of ecosystem competition, such markets have significant value as they provide the ecosystem operator with a key access point for competition in digital markets. This threshold serves the purpose of establishing

[711] This is discussed in Section 9.2.2.

that the incumbent ecosystem operator holds *entrenched* dominance in at least one platform market, as well as a strong position (or dominance) in a market that is an important potential entry point for competition. This indicates that the firm is at least in stage 3 ecosystem competition (i.e. operating a mature ecosystem) and is likely to be in stage 4 ecosystem competition.

The finding that the firm is in stage 4 ecosystem competition should be further substantiated by looking at its activities in vertically integrated or adjacent markets. If the ecosystem operator is active in a large number of horizontally or diagonally related markets or has a significant ability to manipulate their multi-actor ecosystem due to vertical integration, designation is likely warranted. The additional activities help the regulator to assess whether this is a case of stage 3 and 4 ecosystem competition. If there are indicators that the ecosystem operator does not have strong cross-market significance, or if they are not dominant in at least one platform market and one additional digital market, it may be more suitable to enter the ecosystem operator into the lightly regulated pool.

For the qualitative assessment, the regulator can look into similar characteristics of the platforms and ecosystem as a whole as used in the DMA, DMCCA, and Section 19a GWB: the number of end users, business users, the value of the firm, conglomeration, access to data, or other indicators may help to determine which regulatory pool is most suitable.[712] These indicators should be looked at as part of a qualitative assessment, not to establish presumptions on the basis of certain quantitative thresholds. This better reflects the dynamic nature of digital competition and the idea that relative power between ecosystems is leading in the assessment. Via a comprehensive assessment, regulators can not only determine the importance of the ecosystem as a whole but also use numbers of active users and revenues per platform to determine whether the ecosystem operator has a strong position in certain platform markets.

This assessment for designation into the heavily regulated pool combines two elements. First, it looks at whether there is an expansive multi-product ecosystem by looking at the number of markets in which the entity operates. This excludes players with small ecosystems, despite their potentially strong position within one certain market. Subsequently, the assessment looks at whether the ecosystem operator actually has relative power within at least one core market within this ecosystem that provides the ecosystem operator with the ability and incentive to foreclose entry and pre-empt disruptive innovation. This element excludes undertakings that operate across a number of markets but do not have the ability or incentive to foreclose competition or pre-empt entry in any of these markets. The designation is then only limited to incumbent ecosystem operators: those with an expansive multi-product ecosystem, in which they are entrenched in their activities in core revenue-generating markets and which have the ability to foreclose entry or

[712] See art 3 (2) Digital Markets Act.

pre-empt disruption as a result of their incumbency. The other types of players: those with a strong position or monopoly in one platform market and no multi-product ecosystem, or those with a multi-product ecosystem but no strong position in any market, should be designated to the lightly regulated pool.

The assessment is likely to capture the usual suspects such as Google, Apple, Amazon, Meta and Microsoft. Not only do they operate expansive ecosystems, but their historical behaviour demonstrates their ability to pre-empt competition or absorb innovation. Each of these ecosystem operators has entered into a great number of acquisitions – as well as high profile acquisitions – and most of these firms are, or have been, subject to antitrust proceedings due to their anti-competitive behaviour.[713] With undertakings of this magnitude, entry into the heavily regulated pool could help to quickly intervene as to resolve the most pressing issues related to the most important players. It should be noted that this pool should remain of limited size and only include a handful of firms. However, the obligations that are imposed on these firms should be significant, (far) exceeding those imposed under the DMA. The regulatory framework should allow for quick adjustments in its prohibitions and obligations, likely faster than the DMA. The rules-based framework must prioritize effectively prying open markets for competition and minimizing entry barriers. It cannot be left up to the firm to comply in the way that it prefers if this does not produce quick and observable results, and the idea of how proportionality is balanced may have to be reassessed: it should not only be about finding the least intrusive measures but also about whether a less intrusive – and potentially ineffective – measure disproportionally affects the entry and the competitive process.[714] Similarly to the DMA, effectiveness means clear rules, no case-by-case analysis of harmful effects, limited exceptions, and quick enforcement.[715] The difference is then mainly the gravity of the rules and the idea that new rules will keep piling on as long as there is no observable change in competitive pressures and market dynamics. The main concern should be preventing under-enforcement, while over-enforcement may even be viewed as a feature of the regulatory system since firms can be moved to the lightly regulated pool if the position and structure of their ecosystem changes.[716]

Such an approach is suitable for the heavily regulated layer for four reasons. First, similarly to the DMA, the undertakings that face the heaviest regulatory burdens are also the ones that have developed the greatest competitive advantage by virtue of the absence of regulation and lack of experience in enforcing competition

[713] Geoffrey Parker, Georgios Petropoulos and Marshall Van Alstyne, 'Platform Mergers and Antitrust' (2021) 30 Industrial and Corporate Change 1307 note that together, the so-called GAFAM companies have concluded a total of 855 acquisitions since their inception. The largest number of acquisitions is by Google, followed by Microsoft and Facebook.

[714] Jasper van den Boom and Fiona Scott Morton, Recalibrating Regulation 1/2003: How to Restore Proportionality in EU Remedy Design (March 22, 2025). Available at SSRN: https://ssrn.com/abstract=5189659 or http://dx.doi.org/10.2139/ssrn.5189659.

[715] The substantive obligations are laid down in articles 5–7 of Digital Markets Act.

[716] Cappai and Colangelo (n 14) 24 et seq.

law in digital markets.[717] Second, a rules-based approach which uses ex ante self-executing obligations ensures that results are produced quickly in terms of changing the behaviour of a number of firms. The DMA produces behavioural changes (and venues for enforcement against non-compliance) from the date that compliance becomes mandatory. Other regulatory systems, such as the DMCCA and Section 19a GWB, still require (lengthy) investigations or negotiations after the initial designation.[718] The point of the heavily regulated pool is to break down barriers to entry and open up access to resources quickly, despite potential justifications that the regulated firm may want to bring forward. Third, unlike the DMA, the heavy burdens imposed on these undertakings would only apply towards entrants and – to a lesser extent – lightly regulated entities. Progressive ecosystem regulation would mainly ensure that these undertakings pass on the benefits they have obtained from a lack of regulation when capturing their markets to the undertakings that are entering into competition now. Fourth, the possibility that heavily regulated entities are moved to the lightly regulated pool allows ecosystem operators to escape their heavy regulatory burdens if the regulation works as intended.

While the first two reasons align with the rationale and effects of the DMA, the latter two reasons diverge from the DMA. With respect to passing on benefits, the DMA does not scale which benefits are passed on depending on the size and position of those that obtain those benefits. Instead, it seems to maintain a 'top-down' approach where powerful undertakings are simply restrained in what behaviour is allowed or disallowed for them. While it is clear that the DMA provides more rights to third parties and competitors to use core platform services in a meaningful way, it is unclear how the DMA actually empowers entrants to enter into durable competition. If there is one, the DMA at least does not clearly express what this type of competition would look like. It therefore remains unclear what contestability means beyond breaking down barriers to entry. With respect to deregulation and the introduction of competition, there seems to be no mechanism in the DMA to gradually relieve the gatekeepers from regulatory burdens when market conditions change. It seems to be an 'all or nothing' regulatory regime. As noted by Colomo, there is no clear presumption that free competition is ultimately a desirable outcome within the DMA.[719] The intermediate regulatory layer created in progressive ecosystem

717 The DMA describes how contemporary gatekeepers have obtained a disproportionate advantage over business users due to their privileged access to resources such as data, their intermediary position, and other structural characteristics of platform markets. Recital 33 states that 'unfairness should relate to an imbalance between the rights and obligations of business users where the gatekeeper obtains a disproportionate advantage', the DMA aims to ensure fair economic outcomes by allowing third parties to adequately capture the benefits from their innovative efforts. The DMA is based on the idea that digital gatekeepers – due to the characteristics of digital markets, anti-competitive behaviour, and/or the absence of a regulatory framework – have unfairly gained, used, or entrenched their position. See to this extent recitals 1–4, 7, 13–34 Digital Markets Act.

718 See the comparison in van den Boom and others (n 8).

719 Ibáñez Colomo (n 15) 4–5.

regulation would provide for a mechanism to gradually deregulate by allowing to impose varying degrees of regulatory burdens on undertakings within this pool. This possibility for deregulation should push heavily regulated entities to comply, as it makes being an incumbent restricting and punishing, and shrinking and refocussing the ecosystem may again allow them to compete more freely.

9.2.2 *The Lightly Regulated Pool: Tailor-Made Regulatory Obligations*

The lightly regulated pool consists of players who are in stage 3 ecosystem competition. These are entities that have developed mature ecosystems and have shifted – or have shown the ability to shift – from growth to profitability. However, they do not have control over multiple important access points for entry into competition in the digital network. This regulatory pool should be larger than the heavily regulated pool, but the burdens on lightly regulated entities will not be as heavy. Lightly regulated entities will generally be subjected to fewer obligations, and the obligations that are imposed on them only work towards players in the entrant pool.

The lightly regulated pool relies on a principles-based approach to regulating, like the DMCCA. Tailor-made burdens are imposed to ensure that competition in the digital network is not distorted by ecosystem operators that are dominant (or have a similar significant presence) in strategic activities, mainly infrastructures or facilities that serve as access points to competition. Players in the lightly regulated pool have no obligations towards those in the heavily regulated pool and may compete freely with incumbents and other lightly regulated entities, at least within the bounds of competition law and other applicable regulation.[720] The purpose of the lightly regulated pool is threefold: first, it offers a venue for the regulator to quickly impose conduct requirements or regulatory burdens if it finds that a mature ecosystem operator is hindering or blocking entry, or has other detrimental impacts on competition.[721] Second, it ensures that ecosystem operators that have been able to grow into mature ecosystem by the benefits they obtain from the regulation will also pass those benefits on to entrants. This should contribute to creating an innovative environment where entrants can thrive and enter into durable competition. Third, it provides a way to gradually relieve heavily regulated entities from their regulatory burdens as to reflect changes in the competitive realities of the digital

[720] Where the regulator wants to create horizontally applicable regulation that also governs competition between players in the same pool, they can do so through complementary regulatory regimes. The recently proposed European Commission, Proposal for a Regulation of the European Parliament and of the Council on Harmonised Rules on Fair Access to and Use of Data, COM(2022) 68 final of 23 February 2022 (Data Act); Regulation (EU) 2022/2065 of the European Parliament and of the Council of 19 October 2022 on a Single Market For Digital Services and amending Directive 2000/31/EC, OJ L277/1 (Digital Services Act) is another example of regulation that can complement progressive ecosystem regulation without these regulatory systems encroaching on one another.

[721] This follows a similar rationale as the imposition of the DMCCA itself.

network. The latter creates opportunities for gradual deregulation that are missing in the DMA.

The lightly regulated pool, with its principles-based and tailored approach,[722] can be more extensive in terms of the number of entities that are designated without creating adverse effects on competition. The regulator sets out baseline principles for acceptable conduct in the market and may impose substantive regulatory obligations where necessary.[723] Examples of principles underlying the lightly regulated pool may include fair, reasonable, and non-discriminatory access for entrants to facilities or infrastructures operated by lightly regulated entities, withholding from anti-competitive conduct (also in the absence of market dominance), facilitating switching between services as to reduce user lock-in, and developing effective infrastructures for sharing and porting data. While lightly regulated entities are expected to act in accordance with such principles, the approach includes a 'no harm, no foul' principle: as long as there is no observed harm related to the behaviour of firms, there is no consequence to their designation.

The assessment on whether undertakings should be assigned to the lightly regulated pool can occur in three different settings: currently unregulated firms become regulated; firms are moved from the heavily regulated pool to the lightly regulated pool; or firms are moved from the entrant pool to the lightly regulated pool.

Regulating Currently Unregulated Firms

First, an example of determining whether a currently unregulated entity should be designated. There are a number of large digital firms that are not regulated under the DMA, DMCCA, or Section 19a GWB at the time of writing. For the DMCCA and Section 19a GWB, there are still opportunities to do so, but for the DMA it is the case that they either do not operate a core platform service (e.g. Netflix), or it was found that they do not exhibit sufficient gatekeeper power to be designated (e.g. X Holding Corporation). Assessing whether these undertakings should be entered into the lightly regulated pool again depends on market circumstances. The Commission can look at their position within a single platform or digital market, their cross-market position, their ability to steer users or extract profits from their user-base, and other indicators such as market cap and users' numbers.

[722] Tania Van der Brande, 'Rules-Based versus Principles-Based Regulation – Is There a Clear Front-Runner?' (*Ofcom News Centre*, 3 August 2021) <www.ofcom.org.uk/news-centre/2021/rules-versus-principles-based-regulation>.

[723] Secretary of State for Digital, Culture, Media and Sport and Secretary of State for Business, Energy and Industrial Strategy, *A New Pro-Competition Regime for Digital Markets* (Great Britain 2021) discusses the proposed regulatory regime that relies on the finding of a strategic-market status. This is principles-based regulation but allows for the regulator to impose additional rules specifically aimed at undertakings that operate a certain bottleneck market. The imposition of additional rules under progressive ecosystem regulation would be similar to these 'pro-competitive interventions' under the SMS regime. A comparison between progressive ecosystem regulation and the UK regulatory regime is provided in Chapter 9.

Netflix – while not operating a core platform service under Art. 2(2) DMA – does arguably operate a stage 3 ecosystem. The Netflix video-streaming platform is the leading global streaming platform, there is a significant level of vertical integration due to Netflix' in-house studios, and its sequential price increases in recent years show that it has the ability to pursue profitability over growth. The latter is also demonstrated by Netflix's ongoing efforts to stop user-sharing, which does not seem to stifle its growth despite unpopularity among users. This indicates that users are unlikely to switch, possibly due to a lack of viable alternatives. This, combined with Netflix's market cap, creates a reasonable case for entry into the lightly regulated pool.[724] As a result of such a designation, Netflix may be required by the regulator to – for instance – license titles in their portfolio to specialized streaming services. This would allow entrants to offer a curated selection for users at a lower price, thus stimulating competitive pressures on the incumbent. This could open up new venues for competition and innovation in on-demand streaming.[725]

Another unregulated entity is the X Holding Corp. The Commission has investigated whether the X social media platform should be designated under the DMA but has found this to be unwarranted in light of the platform's diminishing position in terms of business and end users. At the same time, the X Holding Corp, which includes Tesla, a highly impactful social media platform, space exploration, and other business ventures may be a target for some regulatory restraints. The system of progressive ecosystem regulation would not look at the X social media platform in isolation, but rather at the impact of the activities across markets as a whole. While the analysis here leaves in the middle whether and how this should lead to the imposition of regulatory burdens related to one or more of their business ventures, it does show the flexibility of the system of progressive ecosystem regulation when compared to the DMA.

Moving Firms from Heavily Regulated to Lightly Regulated

When competitive conditions change, scenarios arise where it is no longer suitable to impose heavy regulatory burdens on a firm. Periodical assessments of

[724] Netflix could qualify as having a strong position in the market for video-streaming services with 39 per cent market share, 209 million subscribers in 2022, and many more. It is also vertically integrated into content production and mobile video games, see Mansoor Iqbal, 'Netflix Revenue and Usage Statistics (2022)' (*Business of Apps*, 27 October 2022); Stephanie Chan, 'Netflix's Rivals Grow Share of U.S. Streaming App Usage to 61% in Q1 2022' (*SensorTower*, 21 April 2022); it does operate a large conglomerate of integrated services which qualifies them as an operator of a multi-product ecosystem, Affan Shaik, 'The Walt Disney Company – A Conglomerate beyond Mickey Mouse And Marvel Studios' [2020] *Brand Hopper* provides an overview of the Disney congelation which includes several animation and other content production studios, news networks, sports networks, and alternative streaming platform Hulu. Disney's lack of a strong position in a platform market means that it does not qualify to be entered into the heavily regulated pool, but does allow designation into the lightly regulated pool.

[725] See eg Eli M Noam, 'Overcoming Market Power in Online Video Platforms', *Regulating Big Tech* (Oxford University Press 2021).

competition in the digital network should point out whether an incumbent is no longer in control of important access points, or if their position across markets is waning.

The question about what level of regulation is suitable is also relevant in the DMA, but this system does not provide for a gradual change in the applicable regulation. Booking.com and ByteDance are two firms that are currently subjected to ex ante rules as they are designated with gatekeeper power. While regulating their gatekeeper power may benefit consumers, these firms do not hold significant ecosystem power in comparison to firms such as Microsoft, Apple, Google, or Amazon. Their control over the digital network industry is also significantly lower, and they are often dependent on the infrastructures of other incumbent ecosystem operators to offer their services to end users. It raises questions about whether it is proportional to designate these firms in the same way as the GAFAM companies, and subject them to the same set of rules.[726] By entering them into a lightly regulated pool, the regulator can impose some restrictions (i.e. parity clauses, prohibitions to disintermediate, or restrictions on advertising), without unduly hindering their ability to compete with incumbent ecosystems.

The example of DMA designations helps to explain how incumbent players can transition both from the heavily regulated and entrant pool into the lightly regulated pool. For heavily regulated entities, the majority of the substantive obligations it faced under the rules-based approach may stay in place, while only the ones that are no longer deemed necessary are removed. The previously heavily regulated entity will be subjected to the same or similar obligations to entrants but can now compete freely with lightly regulated entities. Regulatory burdens can be adjusted or removed over time depending on market realities. To remain within the example of TikTok, if ByteDance would overtake Meta as the incumbent in social media platforms, Meta can be designated to the lightly regulated pool and its regulatory obligations towards TikTok gradually removed. Meanwhile, TikTok can be subjected to additional rules or – if circumstances demonstrate that it is necessary – it can even be considered for heavy regulation.

Moving Firms from the Entrant Pool to the Lightly Regulated Pool

Players that transition from the entrant pool to the lightly regulated pool after capturing a platform market and growing their ecosystem would become subject to the principles associated with lightly regulated entities but would not necessarily face additional regulatory burdens immediately. This ensures that regulatory burdens on the newly emerging ecosystem are minimized while it further develops its business model. The transition will however mean that the ecosystem operator loses the privileges in terms of access and protection offered by the entrant pool. These

[726] van den Boom (n 123).

mechanisms should enable a smooth transition both for entities which move from the heavily regulated pool or entrant pool into the lightly regulated pool.[727]

The choice for a rules-based approach in the heavily regulated pool – as opposed to the principles-based regulation in the lightly regulated pool – is justified by the differences in speed of implementation and enforcement.[728] The imposition of tailor-made substantive obligations is costly in time and efforts. As competition in the digital network industry is harmed by the presence of large incumbent ecosystems, resolving the most pressing issues rapidly may outweigh ensuring the precision of regulation to only target what is necessary. Temporarily introducing the heavily regulated pool buys the regulator time to find fitting solutions without delaying necessary interventions.[729]

9.2.3 *The Entrant Pool: A Safe Haven for Entry and Experimentation*

The entrant pool is not as much a pool as it is a layer, as any undertaking that does not meet the criteria to be entered into the lightly or heavily regulated pool potentially ends up here. Any firm that is – actively or potentially – entering into stage 1 ecosystem competition receives the protection and rights granted to those in the entrant pool under progressive ecosystem regulation. There should, however, be some limiting requirements, as including any undertaking in the entrant pool would allow any undertaking to invoke rights following the obligations imposed on entities in the lightly or heavily regulated pool. This may not be desirable as this would allow undertakings in the unregulated pool to request access to data or other resources without any vested interest, creating unnecessary costs for regulated entities.

In order to ensure that there is such a vested interest, there should be some mechanism to verify whether the firms are actual or potential entrants which: operate in a digital platform market (actual competitors); are dependent on the platforms operated by regulated entities (i.e. business users); or trying to enter into a digital product- or services market (i.e. potential competitors). Undertakings that want to invoke rights granted to players in the entrant pool should be able to demonstrate that they are – or have serious intentions – of developing digital products, or that they contribute to the value generated in a multi-actor ecosystem. In other words, they must reasonably show that they are entering into stage 1 ecosystem competition. While this limits the scope of who can rely on the regulatory framework to obtain benefits generated in the digital network industry, the entrant pool should remain

[727] Section 9.3.2 describes how designation as a gatekeeper under the DMA would mean that a newly emerged gatekeeper would be subjected to *all* regulatory burdens after a transition period of three years in which is subjected to none of the regulatory burdens.

[728] Geradin, 'What Is a Digital Gatekeeper?' (n 407) 2; Wagner and others (n 14) 1002–1003.

[729] The discussion on choices related to quick enforcement and tailor-made solutions underpinning progressive ecosystem regulation is continued in Section 10.2, where it is compared to regulatory proposals in the EU, UK, and Germany.

relatively broad and easy to enter. To exemplify, one could think of the resources granted to Fintech start-ups under the Payment-Services Directive. Here, third-party providers of financial services are granted access to resources and information held by banks so that they can innovate, as long as they pass an authorization scheme.[730] This creates minimum requirements to determine who is eligible to enjoy the benefits associated with the regulation, without raising regulatory hurdles.[731]

It is possible to limit this scope further, for instance by setting maximum thresholds concerning revenue, the undertakings positioned in non-digital markets, or other qualitative criteria. This would prevent players with a strong position in non-digital markets from extracting the benefits from the regulation. However, it is not evident that this is necessary or desirable. After all, larger undertakings with access to resources could contribute meaningfully to competition in digital markets and facilitating this access may be justified.[732] Moreover, undertakings that are successful in capturing a platform market and expanding into an ecosystem quickly will also rapidly be moved to the pool of lightly regulated entities. It may therefore be more attractive to include large entities in the entrant pool, as they may be able to rapidly develop new innovations and then pass these benefits on to entrants upon entry into the lightly regulated pool. There could however still be reasons to limit access to players of a certain size, for instance to prevent small- and medium-sized enterprises (SMEs) from being pushed out of competition by entrants that operate large undertakings in non-digital markets. If SMEs cannot enter into competition effectively, this may diminish the likelihood of new disruptive ideas and defeat the purpose of the entrant pool of creating a safe haven for experimentation and the development of new business models. The upper and lower bounds of entry into the protected pool should be determined by the regulator and may prove fertile ground for research if such a scheme is implemented.

Entrants that successfully expand into a multi-product ecosystem will eventually be assigned to the lightly regulated pool. Notwithstanding the potential regulatory burdens that are paired with being assigned to the lightly regulated pool, the biggest transition for entrants who transition into the lightly regulated pool is the loss of their protected status and privileged access to resources. As entrants may have built their products and services (partly) on the basis of access to resources offered by regulated entities, they may have to rethink parts of their business models once they transition into the lightly regulated pool. To ensure that the entrant has time

[730] Directive (EU) 2015/2366 of the European Parliament and of the Council of 25 November 2015 on payment services in the internal market, amending Directives 2002/65/EC, 2009/110/EC and 2013/36/EU and Regulation (EU) No 1093/2010, and repealing Directive 2007/64/EC.

[731] By David Parker, 'PSD2 Open Banking: The Challenges of Third-Party Provider Identity and Regulatory Checking', *The PayTech Book* (2019) <https://doi.org/10.1002/9781119551973.ch19> accessed 22 January 2025.

[732] For instance, Disney's entry into video-streaming has led to (some level of) competition with leading streaming provider Netflix.

to adjust its business model to cope with the transition, there should be some delay between the notification by the regulator that they will be assigned to the lightly regulated pool and the loss of these rights. However, as entrants are aware that they will leave the entrant pool once they grow their ecosystem, they should already prepare for this eventuality on their own initiative. The transition period then does not have to be long, but can be as short as 6 months to a year. This reflects the dynamic nature of digital markets, where innovation cycles are often short and pushes firms to think actively about how they will expand once they lose their privileged status.[733] This system of temporary access to resources helps to mitigate issues related to free-riding and promotes disruptive innovation as entrants cannot simply offer duplicate services to the incumbent indefinitely.

9.2.4 *The Role of Competition Law: Protecting Competition, Discovery, and Future-Proofing*

While the regulatory burdens address the most prominent harms related to ecosystem competition, competition law still plays three important roles: protecting competition, discovery, and future-proofing.

In the proposed regulatory system, the regulatory obligations will only relate to interactions between players in different pools. Competition law investigations may then help first and foremost to regulate competition within these pools. In the heavily regulated pool, competition law may ensure that the incumbents have to choose competition over cooperation, even if cooperation seems attractive to retain their incumbent position. In the lightly regulated pool, it prevents the emergence of new cartels or forms of collective dominance that may create long-term harms to competition or short-term harms to consumers. Competition in the entrant pool may also be regulated via competition law to a certain extent, but one can also consider block exemptions for firms under a certain size to maximize their space to compete creatively.[734]

Competition laws such as those laid down in Section 19a GWB facilitate the study of competition within and between ecosystems, bring to light competitive dynamics and the effects of certain types of behaviour, and lead to the formulation of new theories of harm, thus creating a process of discovery. The complementarity between

[733] Under the DMA, regulatory obligations on gatekeepers which have been designated under article 3 DMA only start to apply after three years, as this would lead them to meet the condition of being entrenched set out in article 3 (2) DMA. A period of three years may be justifiable under the DMA as designation means that all regulatory burdens set in out articles 5, 6, and/or 7 DMA would apply, but that a shorter period is suitable for a transition from the entrant pool to the lightly regulated pool as the burdens imposed on the newly regulated entity are much more limited.

[734] Block exemptions for vertical restraints and opportunities for horizontal cooperation between smaller firms are commonplaces in EU competition rules, see the Vertical Block Exemption Regulation, Commission Guidelines on Horizontal Cooperation Agreements.

regulation and competition law helps to create a mutually reinforcing system: competition law creates generalizable lessons for the regulatory regime, indicating which rules must be added or removed. At the same time, the regulatory regime helps to establish benchmarks for competition law, so that investigations can be sped up when theories of harms for certain types of behaviour become established.

Giving an active role to competition law, integrated into the regulatory system in turn helps to future-proof the regulatory framework itself. The system of progressive ecosystem regulation should, if working as designed, lead to intensified competition at the ecosystem level. This should in turn diminish the need for a heavily regulated layer as there is more competition in the digital network. As the heavily regulated pool shrinks, and the lightly regulated pool grows, competition will increasingly happen between players of an equal size that do not have regulatory restrictions on how they compete with one another. The regulatory system can then be phased out by removing or readjusting regulatory obligations to create safeguards for entrants, while competition law is used to prevent heavy concentration of the digital network industry under incumbent ecosystem operators.

Competition law investigations can also reveal gaps in the regulatory framework. Some of these gaps are likely best addressed by adjustments to the regulatory obligations, while others require a more flexible marker harnessing toolkit. It may be the case that behaviour is captured by neither the regulatory framework nor existing competition law provisions, this would warrant the development of new competition tools such as Section 19a GWB, a European Market Investigation Tool, or others. By giving competition law a highly specific and clearly demarcated role in the regulatory framework, it is easier to understand how they can be enforced symbiotically. This still raises questions in the enforcement of the DMA, where there may be parallel investigations into similar behaviour or services depending on their classification (or lack thereof) as gatekeeper. In the system of progressive ecosystem regulation, competition law is leading in governing intra-pool competition and combatting cartels. In inter-pool competition, it works symbiotically with the regulatory framework as it discovers and tests whether new regulatory burdens should be introduced, or as a safety net for behaviour that slips through the cracks of the regulation.

9.3 PRACTICAL IMPLEMENTATION OF THE REGULATORY FRAMEWORK: DISTINGUISH PROGRESSIVE ECOSYSTEM REGULATION FROM EXISTING LEGAL FRAMEWORKS

This section provides some ideas as to what regulatory obligations could look like for different pools, and how their application differs from the DMA or DMCCA. These suggestions are not exhaustive. After all, the system in the lightly regulated pool is flexible and consists of tailor-made obligations. The rules laid down in the heavily regulated system should be carefully considered, yet rules should be added or revised depending on enforcement experiences. The purpose of this section is to give insights as to what types of rules can be considered, how they would apply, and how this system differs from existing regulatory regimes.

9.3.1 *Data Sharing*

Access to data – in particular creating access to data held by operators of large ecosystems with operators of smaller ecosystems or entrants – is vital to stimulating competition in digital markets. Access to large quantities of data creates increasing returns to scale, while having access to various datasets – potentially from various sources – creates economies of scope. While not all digital services are equally data-dependent, access to data can be used to generate a variety of cost-saving innovations by training algorithms, identifying user preferences, personalizing, or targeting services.[735] Aside from the competitive advantages enjoyed by the dominant undertaking with superior data access, which are derived from economies of scale and scope, market failures as a result of data may arise due to externalities, information asymmetries, and missing markets because of high transaction costs and risk.[736]

In the context of progressive ecosystem regulation, data-sharing obligations are an important tool to stimulate competition and disruptive innovation. First, these obligations reduce the competitive advantage held by the largest undertakings and thereby increase opportunities for entrants. As entrants gain access to more information to compete with, the threat of competition by specialists towards the incumbent intensifies, creating more competitive constraints on the incumbent.[737] Second, access to data with low transaction costs provides entrants with opportunities to experiment and enter ventures that are left unoccupied by the incumbent. As access to data is viewed as a key input for innovation, sufficient access to it for entrants should stimulate the potential for disruptive entry.[738]

While there are clear benefits to data-sharing obligations, there are also risks that these obligations have a negative impact on welfare. Mandated data-sharing may adversely impact the incentives of the monopolist to innovate and collect this data, risks related to hold-up and increased risks of data-leaks.[739] Sharing data could lead to short-term innovation but may lead to harms in the long run if the regulatory obligations are too strict.[740]

735 cf University of Antwerp and others (n 250); Junqué de Fortuny, Martens and Provost (n 244); Duch-Brown, Martens and Mueller-Langer (n 250); Prüfer and Schottmüller (n 249); Bertin Martens and others, 'Business-to-Business Data Sharing: An Economic and Legal Analysis' 56; Fast, Schnurr and Wohlfarth (n 70).

736 Martens and others (n 734) 29–32.

737 Bourreau (n 28) 6–9.

738 Krämer and Schnurr (n 274) 11; Martens and others (n 734) 19 et seq.

739 Martens and others (n 734) 26.

740 See eg Graef and Prüfer (n 266) 4.

One way to mitigate these risks could be to limit data-sharing obligations to a relatively small number of markets that are highly data-dependent. For instance markets for search, advertising, and markets that rely heavily on recommendation systems such as e-commerce.[741] Another way is to limit the type of data that is shared. Graef and Prüfer argue that it is optimal to only share raw user data and exclude processed data or algorithms for which the sharing party has already invested resources and effort. This minimizes disincentives while providing competitors and entrants with the data that is most vital to creating innovative services.[742] If only raw user data is shared however, Prüfer and Schottmüller propose that in theory, mandating *all* firms active in data-driven markets to share their user information in order to maximize the total amount of data available in the industry.[743]

Progressive ecosystem regulation tries to strike a balance between the incentives of undertakings that are mandated to share their data and the efficiencies generated for competitors. These findings inspire the obligations imposed on heavily and lightly regulated entities by introducing differing gradations of mandatory data sharing on each group.

Heavily regulated entities can be subjected to strict data-sharing measures. Larger undertakings are better able to afford costs of compliance, have a higher marginal benefit from collecting data due to economies of scale and scope, and have the ability to compete with privileged access to data.[744] Imposing strict data-sharing measures should help mitigate information asymmetry between the incumbent ecosystem operators and operators of emerging ecosystems, allow entrants to enjoy some benefits from economies of scale generated through access to their datasets and allow for novel innovations. As such, larger undertakings may be subjected to obligations to share raw – and even processed – data with both lightly regulated entities and entrants. Heavily regulated entities may also be required to allow entrants to access their algo-

741 cf Argenton and Prufer (n 280); Prüfer and Schottmüller, 'Competing with Big Data' (n 20); Argenton and Prüfer (2012) and Prüfer and Schottmüller (2017) have advocated for data-sharing in highly data-dependent markets for search engines, relying on models that demonstrate that the benefits of data sharing outweigh any disincentives. Argenton and Prüfer showed that – at least in markets for search – incumbents will continue to invest in data collection even when faced with strict data-sharing obligations.

742 Jens Prüfer and Inge Graef, 'Governance of Data Sharing: A Law & Economics Proposal' (2021) 2021-004 CentER, Center for Economic Research Working Paper 24.

743 Prüfer and Schottmüller (n 266) 968 et seq; Prüfer and Graef (n 741) 4.

744 The proposed data sharing in Prüfer and Graef (n 22) would not be limited to markets and sectors which are already dominated but can also be used to prevent tipping (p 12). The authors recommend the imposition of data-sharing obligations on undertakings with more than 30 per cent market share (p 3). This would differ greatly in practice from the limited data-sharing obligations under the DMA. Here, gatekeepers only have to share data upon the request of business users or competitors under art. 6 (1)(i) DMA or where it concerns search engine data on a FRAND basis under art. 6 (1)(j) DMA. In practice, this means that only a very small number of entities will actively share data with a limited number of third parties.

rithms for in-situ data access.[745] This would place a heavy burden on a small set of large ecosystem operators, yet it is justified in light of the generated efficiencies. Providing entrants with access to data at low or zero costs and in-situ data rights should help them overcome existing barriers to using data as a resource. Ensuring that entrants can utilize these resources should promote technological advancements which ultimately benefit the consumer. Lightly regulated entities would gain access to data in order to develop their own algorithms, while entrants can learn through insights derived from in-situ data rights. Alstyne and others describe potential applications of in-situ data rights, allowing entrants to develop services related to price comparisons, fact-checking fake news, or other specialized services which may improve on the technologies offered by contemporary incumbents.[746] While these far-reaching data-sharing obligations may generally pose risks to long-term innovation, this is likely less problematic in the system of progressive ecosystem regulation. After all, it operates on the idea that innovation is stifled exactly due to the presence of large monopolists. Sharing their data and limiting their incentives to innovate should then presumably only bring marginal negative effects while allowing access to data for smaller competing ecosystems could lead to disruption.

Lightly regulated entities could be required to make available, by matter of principle, raw user data upon the request of entrants under FRAND conditions. This would ensure that entrants continue to have access to data with which they can innovate and compete, even when the heavily regulated pool shrinks. Moreover, by tailoring regulatory obligations imposed on lightly regulated entities to their business models, the regulator is able to introduce additional data-sharing obligations with respect to heavily data-dependent activities. By sharing as much raw data as possible, entrants can catch up to the data-driven advantage of lightly regulated entities more rapidly. Meanwhile, adverse impacts to collect data are minimized by significantly limiting the sharing of processed data and ensuring that raw data is only made available on request.[747]

As a result of the imposed obligations, entrants would enjoy – potentially free – access to significant quantities and types of data from heavily regulated entities. Entrants would also have the right to request access to raw user data from lightly regulated entities under FRAND conditions. Together, these obligations provide entrants with access to different types of data and databases that allow for experimentation, continued research on the basis of existing technologies, and entry into competition with fewer obstacles related to the data-driven advantages of existing ecosystem operators. The mechanism by which data is shared from large undertakings to smaller undertakings ensures that data sharing does not strengthen the position of dominant incumbents.

[745] Marshall Van Alstyne and others, '"In Situ" Data Rights' (OpenBU 2021) Communications to the Autoriteit Consument en Markt.

[746] ibid.

[747] See eg Graef and Prüfer (n 266) 4; Martens and others (n 734) 26–32.

9.3.2 *Data Portability*

Data portability is – similarly to data sharing – a tool to regulate the allocation of data across entities in an industry.[748] However, data portability obligations complement data-sharing obligations in multiple ways. First, the right to data portability complements data-sharing obligations by virtue of its objectives. Data-sharing obligations provide competitors in the market with access to a relevant input with beneficial effects on their ability to compete. Data portability is a user-centric right, where the user can demand that their data is ported from one undertaking to another specifically. Data-sharing rights then have a more horizontal nature (all undertakings that are subjected to sharing obligations should share the data with all beneficiary undertakings with the right and desire to receive it) while data portability only focuses on one-to-one transactions (the undertaking that receives the request by the data subject to port the data must port this data to another undertaking).[749]

Second, data portability complements data sharing as it provides tools to give the data-subject consent to share their personal data. While the sharing of personal data with a large number of undertakings under data-sharing obligations is likely undesirable, sharing personal data at the request of the data subject may in fact empower the user. Allowing users to port their data reduces switching costs and lock-in for users of a platform, as they become able to 'take their data and leave'. It is due to this user-centric element of data portability that it found inclusion in the GDPR under article 20, as it supports the rights of the data subject to take control over their personal data.[750]

The importance of data portability as a tool to stimulate competition in digital markets has been affirmed in policy reports and the inclusion of an obligation to ensure effective data portability in art. 6(1)(h) DMA.[751] Data portability can enhance the free flow of data and competition in a market by complementing data sharing: data sharing can be viewed as a top-down obligation aimed at the proliferation of data across the market generally, while data portability provides a bottom-up route to proliferating specific data at the request of the data subject.

With these complementary functions, data-portability rights are important in contributing to the achievement of the goals of progressive ecosystem regulation. While data-sharing obligations provide entrants with access to resources, data portability

[748] Inge Graef, Martin Husovec and Nadezhda Purtova, 'Data Portability and Data Control: Lessons for an Emerging Concept in EU Law' (2018) 19 German Law Journal 1359.

[749] cf ibid; Jan Krämer, Pierre Senellart and Alexandre de Streel, 'Making Data-Portability More Effective for the Digital Economy – Economic Implications and Regulatory Challenges' (CERRE 2020) CERRE Project Report; OECD, 'Data Portability, Interoperability and Digital Platform Competition' (2021).

[750] Graef, Husovec and Purtova (n 747) 1361 et seq.

[751] cf Crémer, De Montjoye and Schweitzer (n 4); Digital Competition Expert Panel (n 1); Zingales and others (n 1); Australian Competition & Consumer Authority (n 4); Subcommittee on Antitrust (n 1).

obligations may help entrants in gaining access to a customer base. The right to data portability can reduce switching costs for end users and business users.[752]

For instance, in platforms that provide social networks, the ability for customers to transfer their photos, videos, and comments to another platform eliminates the need for end users to 'start over' on another platform. As noted in *Microsoft/LinkedIn*, switching costs for end users can become quite high if the creation of a profile costs significant efforts in its creation and curation.[753] The US House Subcommittee has noted that effective data portability is required to enhance switching from networks such as those offered by Facebook. Here, the Subcommittee argued that the data portability by Facebook was insufficient to create such effects, inspiring calls for the imposition of more effective data portability tools.[754] Similar wording is used in art. 6(1)(h) DMA, where gatekeepers are required to provide 'effective' data portability upon request of the business- or end user of the platform. Whether imposed in heavily or lightly regulated pools of entities, the regulator can review the data portability offered by entities to ensure its effectiveness.

Data portability also facilitates switching for business users: the ability to transfer one's reviews from one platform to another, to transfer transaction histories or other matrixes used for trade can significantly reduce the opportunity cost associated with switching providers and multi-homing. Multi-homing is facilitated by data portability as it does not require the transferring platform to delete their databases, but merely to make the data available to the receiving party as well. Increased abilities to multi-home do not only stimulate competition on the ecosystem level but also diminish the ability of the dominant ecosystem operators to abuse their gatekeeper power, at least as long as alternative platforms emerge. Multi-homing also allows new platforms to generate data through increased interactions by users with the platform, again diminishing the competitive advantage of the incumbent in terms of superior access to data.[755]

In the EU, the right to data portability has been regulated in the General Data Protection Regulation. Under the GDPR, undertakings must port data provided by the data subject on request of the data subject in a one-off modality. Article 6 (1)(h) DMA confers further-reaching responsibilities on gatekeepers of core platform services by noting that these undertakings must provide 'effective data portability'. This book argues that this heavier burden is not formulated clearly, and that it is not clear how effective data portability differs from data portability rights under the GDPR. Heavier burdens in terms of providing effective data portability may include enlarging the scope of the data shared. For instance, not only sharing data provided by the data subject but also inferred data that is related to the individual. Alternatively, it

[752] Krämer, Senellart and de Streel (n 748) 56–60.
[753] See Microsoft/LinkedIn (Case M.8124) Commission Decision C(2016) 8404 [2016], OJ C 388/4.
[754] Subcommittee on Antitrust (n 1) 121–122.
[755] Krämer, Senellart and de Streel (n 748) 55–60.

may mean that the undertaking has to share data over a longer period of time, for instance by periodically or continually porting data on the individual rather than in a one-off modality.[756] Whichever categories of heavy burdens are chosen, this book argues that these heavier burdens should be reserved only for undertakings in the heavily regulated pool. Moreover, the additional rights obtained by the receiving undertakings should be limited to the lightly regulated entities and entrants. Data sharing between heavily regulated undertakings should be governed by article 20 GDPR or any other regulation which exists besides progressive ecosystem regulation. This ensures that progressive ecosystem regulation does not introduce rules of competition between players in the same pool.

Data portability obligations on lightly regulated entities and entrants can be limited to those introduced under article 20 GDPR or other complementary regulation. Developing data portability infrastructures can be costly for undertakings, and these investments may be wasted if users do not end up using the right to data portability. In order to minimize costs imposed on entrants and developing ecosystems, it is most efficient to impose uniform obligations on data portability infrastructures on smaller undertakings and emerging ecosystems.[757] Emerging ecosystem operators in the lightly regulated pool of entities are unlikely to have similar capabilities to lock users in as those in the heavily regulated pool of entities. It should be viewed on a case-by-case basis whether imposing heavier burdens related to data-portability rights is efficient or desirable. It is also not desirable to give entrants exemptions to the provision of data portability rights. Data-portability rights under article 20 GDPR exist predominantly to empower data subjects by granting them more control over their data. Denying users such a right to protect entrants may clash with the objectives pursued under data protection legislation. Data subjects should have the right to port their personal data such as their photos or written texts from one undertaking to another, irrespective of their competitive position.

In short, data portability does not only have the effect of increasing access to data for competitors and entrants (like data sharing) but also lowers switching costs and facilitates multi-homing. This creates increased opportunities for entrants to gain access to an installed base, which is a requirement for the emergence of successful ecosystem competition.[758] At the same time, data portability under the GDPR exists to empower data subjects to take control of their data. This aspect of data portability should not be lost by providing exemptions to it.

While data-portability complements data-sharing rights, they may not be sufficient to ensure entrants' access to a customer base. While data portability may help consumers to overcome initial obstacles to switching, there are still other technical

756 See discussions on types of data and continuous data porting in Krämer, Senellart and de Streel (n 748); OECD, 'Data Portability, Interoperability and Digital Platform Competition' (n 748).

757 OECD, 'Data Portability, Interoperability and Digital Platform Competition' (n 748) 39.

758 Krämer, Senellart and de Streel (n 748) 8.

barriers or defaults that prevent users from switching. In order to eliminate these barriers, technical interoperability obligations may be necessary to facilitate actual switching. For instance, allowing users of a messaging service to send messages cross-platform may reduce switching costs associated with network externalities. Data portability alone may not be enough here, as allowing the user of a messaging service to port their messages and shared media from one service to another but does not allow them to port their network. As messaging services have strong network effects, allowing data alone to be ported is insufficient to induce actual switching. Similarly, data portability alone is not enough to stimulate competition absent data-sharing obligations. Practice has proven that users are reluctant in exercising their data portability rights. Moreover, the limited scope of data-portability rights (both in terms of data shared and receiving entities) would limit the access to data enjoyed by entrants (and to a lesser extent lightly regulated entities).[759]

9.3.3 *Interoperability*

Mandatory interoperability has been used in network industries as well as remedies in competition law cases.[760] It is therefore not surprising that interoperability, standard-setting, and access unbundling have been identified as a core issue in the EU's Digital Agenda.[761] Since then, a variety of scholars have called for mandatory interoperability to strengthen competition in digital markets.[762] Compelled interoperability can address many competition issues without interfering with the structures that make networked digital platforms attractive and contribute to economic growth in a multitude of ways. Interoperability can expand network effects, create commons where assets become shared between the incumbent and third parties and introduce competition on the basis of those assets or facilities.[763]

The literature distinguishes between a number of types of interoperability which produce different effects. First there is data interoperability,[764] Hovenkamp distinguishes between dynamic interoperability which facilitates real-time data sharing and access and static interoperability which requires portability but not necessarily real-time actions.[765] Issues related to data interoperability have been discussed in

[759] ibid 75 et seq.
[760] Bourreau, Krämer and Buiten (n 231) 36 et seq.
[761] ibid 36.
[762] cf Oscar Borgogno and Giuseppe Colangelo, 'Data Sharing and Interoperability: Fostering Innovation and Competition through APIs' (2019) 35 Computer Law & Security Review 1; Chris Riley, 'Unpacking Interoperability in Competition' (2020) 5 Journal of Cyber Policy 94; Scott Morton and others (n 230); Noam (n 724).
[763] Herbert Hovenkamp, 'Antitrust Interoperability Remedies' (2022) 2814 Faculty Scholarship at Penn Carey Law.
[764] Bourreau, Krämer and Buiten (n 231) 13.
[765] Hovenkamp (n 762) 27–28.

Sections 9.3.1 and 9.3.2. This section will focus on technical interoperability, for which Bourreau and others distinguish between protocol interoperability, which allows third parties to offer complementary services on a platform, and full protocol interoperability, which refers to the implementation of technical standards that allow substituting services to interoperate.[766] Both data interoperability and technical interoperability can be horizontal, between activities at the same level of the value chain, or vertical, between activities at different levels of the value chain. Within vertical interoperability, Bourreau and others distinguish between within-platform interoperability and cross-platform interoperability. Within-platform interoperability allows third parties to integrate their products into a platform (for instance their like buttons or extensions into a social media platform). Cross-platform interoperability goes further as it requires not only within-platform interoperability but also the standardization of interfaces so that third parties can integrate their complementary services across all similar platforms.[767] Technical and data interoperability are viewed here as complementary: where users have a technical means to switch but cannot do so because of the data they have aggregated on a platform, data interoperability may allow them to port their data and switch. When data is not the obstacle for users to switch, but lock-in is the result of technical integrations, bundling, or the maintenance of exclusive rights of certain infrastructures, technical interoperability facilitates switching.

When interoperability is mandated by regulators, they should account for the different effects produced by each type of interoperability. Horizontal interoperability – while beneficial in allowing users to multi-home between providers within a single network – may also entrench the current network as the standard. When entrants are guaranteed access to the existing network, there are few incentives to create an incompatible network as to compete.[768] There is likely a trade-off between short-run benefits for consumers and long-run incentives to be disruptive. However, in situations where users are locked in due to the network externalities, horizontal interoperability may be necessary to create meaningful competition.[769]

Imposing cross-platform interoperability also warrants caution. As described throughout the book, the ability of platform and ecosystem operators to differentiate themselves from one another is an important source of competition at the ecosystem level. Introducing cross-platform interoperability between equal players may harm their ability to differentiate themselves and eventually lead to a loss of

[766] Bourreau, Krämer and Buiten (n 231) 13–14, 21 et seq provide examples of protocol interoperability and full protocol interoperability. The first may require the operator of an Operating System to allow apps by third-party app developers, and the latter may require the operators of messaging systems to allow users to send their messages directly across platforms.

[767] ibid 17–19.

[768] This has also been observed in providing unlimited access for third parties to infrastructures of the incumbent in non-digital network industries, see Cave (n 15); Bourreau, Doğan and Manant (n 697).

[769] See eg Scott Morton and others (n 230) 1028–1035, 1050.

consumer choice and diminished incentives to ensure quality. Under the DMA, Apple may be required to open up its walled garden to Google's Play Store and allow side-loading.[770] Here, two distinct but interrelated problems arise. As a result of the obligation to allow side-loading, Apple may not be able to guarantee the quality of applications available on the iPhone as it had in the past.[771] As quality assurance is a cornerstone of Apple's competitive strategy, the interoperability requirements from the DMA may have unintended side effects as users may perceive the iOS as less safe, possibly reducing their willingness to pay. While such a defence has been lodged by Apple on multiple occasions in relation to the DMA, this idea is controversial and is viewed as a means for Apple to escape its obligations.[772] However, mandating Apple to allow the installation of Google Play on iOS may strengthen the position of Google as an operator of App Stores and diminish Apple's capacity to distinguish its mobile iOS from Google's Android, strengthening Google's position in these markets. Under progressive ecosystem regulation, Apple would have to allow the installation of third-party App stores operated by entrants, intensifying competition with smaller players, while retaining the right to refuse the installation of Google Play. Also in situations where cross-platform interoperability is limited to providing access to players from other pools, there should be a balance between access for newcomers and ensuring that the ecosystem operator can engage in quality assurance to allow ecosystem operators to differentiate their products in terms of quality.

The latter point may also apply to vertical interoperability. While it is *prima facie* desirable that complementors are better protected when offering their goods to a platform, the platform operator should still be able to govern its multi-actor ecosystem.[773] Ensuring access for all may result in the proliferation of low-quality and potentially harmful goods and services. While the assessment of the suitability of a complementary product should be based on objective, fair, and non-discriminatory criteria, there are efficiencies associated to gatekeeping by the platform operator. This would limit the ability of the incumbent to retaliate by denying vertical interoperability in a discriminatory manner while allowing it to govern its ecosystem at the same time.[774]

The optimal level of 'openness' mandated from platforms is recognized as one of the potential inefficiencies associated with vertical interoperability, along with the risk of double marginalization and reductions in economies of scale and scope.[775]

[770] Art. 6 (4) Digital Markets Act.

[771] See the discussions in Sections 4.1.3 and 6.3.

[772] Apple has argued this in their DMA compliance report of 6 March 2024.

[773] See again Section 4.1.3.

[774] An example of retaliation through denying interoperability can be found in United States v. Microsoft Corporation, 253 F.3d 34 (D.C. Cir. 2001). Here, Microsoft attempted to dissuade Netscape from developing middleware by refusing access to information failed, and Microsoft switched to a mimicking strategy to foreclose Netflix.

[775] Bourreau, Krämer and Buiten (n 231) 25–29.

However, the benefit of ensuring access for complementors to a platform – and limiting the ability of the ecosystem operator to exclude potential competitive threats – can outweigh these inefficiencies. The double marginalization problem is of lesser concern in markets where competition between complementors is intense. The emergence of new opportunities and access to new distribution channels, as well as access to resources for entrants that may offer such complements, is likely to intensify competition. Initial 'growing pains' of the regulation should be diminished once competition across ecosystems intensifies.[776] Moreover, platforms have proven to accept leading losses in order to foreclose competition. Price-based exploitative harms are rare in digital markets when compared to exclusionary harms.[777]

Similar considerations apply surrounding diminished economies of scale and scope. In traditional network industries, economies of scale and scope were required to offer the service cost-efficiently. In digital markets however, increasing returns to scale and scope tend to result in high barriers to entry and insulated markets.[778] This book again proposes that the emergence of competition outweighs the benefits associated with a greater cost advantage of the incumbent. As noted in Section 9.3.3, regulation that aims to maintain the position of the monopolist to safeguard economies of scale and scope will generally lead to second-best outcomes compared to competition.[779]

The imposition of technical interoperability requirements should be approached cautiously. This book proposes that in the heavily regulated pool, undertakings should mostly be subjected to vertical interoperability obligations as well as a limited number of cross-platform interoperability requirements. Vertical interoperability enhances participation by complementors and places limits on the ability of the incumbent to pre-empt competition by excluding potentially threatening players in its ecosystem, which is a cornerstone of progressive ecosystem regulation. Cross-platform interoperability may be suitable where multi-homing is important for complementors and the costs to port a complementary service from one provider to another are high. Ensuring that there is a single standard for third parties to offer their complementary services across platforms may help to reduce their entry costs in such cases.[780] However, the imposition of cross-platform interoperability should be limited to ensure that ecosystem operators in the heavily- and lightly regulated pool can still differentiate themselves from one another.

The imposition of horizontal interoperability should be limited to business models where this is absolutely necessary to induce switching. One activity which may require horizontal interoperability could be number-independent messaging

776 ibid.
777 Khan (n 267).
778 See Chapter 5.
779 Marneffe and Vereeck (n 15).
780 Bourreau, Krämer and Buiten (n 231) 13 et seq.

services which are characterized by strong direct network effects. In the final version of the DMA, the EU legislature has made the choice to impose horizontal interoperability obligations on providers of these services (Art. 7 DMA).[781] Horizontal interoperability in this type of messaging services is not new, as it also exists in telecommunications (where network operators must allow users to call and text one another) and email. For progressive ecosystem regulation, horizontal interoperability would be limited to creating interoperability between the services provided by heavily regulated entities and players from the lightly regulated or entrant pool, or players from the lightly regulated pool and entrants. Due to this asymmetry in the workings of the obligations, progressive ecosystem regulation may not be the most suitable regime to include horizontal interoperability obligations. In order to ensure that the system of interoperability is understandable for market participants, this may be more suitably arranged through complementary regulation. This is one potential weak point of progressive ecosystem regulation. The effects of this weakness on the efficacy of progressive ecosystem regulation should however be limited as it does not focus on creating horizontal interoperability but rather on vertical interoperability which facilitates the development of competing infrastructures.

In the lightly regulated pool, vertical interoperability should be reflected in the principles underlying the regulation. The idea behind progressive ecosystem regulation is that entrants into digital markets can build on the infrastructures of those that came before them. Ensuring technical interoperability between a platform and its complementors reflects this idea underlying the regulatory system. The imposition of vertical interoperability requirements should be relatively common when ecosystem operators in the lightly regulated pool become more powerful. This ensures that they do not focus on pre-empting disruption themselves after they have captured their position in the market. Cross-platform interoperability should again only be imposed to the extent that this is necessary to foster entry and competition. It is particularly important for emerging ecosystem operators to have the ability to differentiate themselves from others so as to raise their value proposition.

The conditions for access for entrants may differ per pool. The requirements to facilitate access should be stricter for entities in the heavily regulated pool than the lightly regulated pool. First, following the findings of the book, the incumbents have

[781] Article 7 DMA introduces horizontal interoperability obligations on the providers of number-independent messaging services. Here, the EU legislature has decided that the need for increased competition and consumer choice in markets for messaging services warrants the creation of a single system. See also recital 64 DMA:

> The lack of interoperability allows gatekeepers that provide number-independent interpersonal communications services to benefit from strong network effects, which contributes to the weakening of contestability. Furthermore, regardless of whether end users 'multi-home', gatekeepers often provide number-independent interpersonal communications services as part of their platform ecosystem, and this further exacerbates entry barriers for alternative providers of such services and increases costs for end users to switch.

the strongest incentives and ability to pre-empt disruption or absorb innovation. This should be reflected in the regulatory burdens. Second, emerging ecosystems are more likely to aim their operations at growth and will have incentives to include third-party complementors to expand their multi-actor ecosystems. For the lightly regulated pool, vertical interoperability obligations are more likely to become necessary when the ecosystem operators in the lightly regulated pool become more mature and change their business models from growth to profits. It is here that mandated access should become widespread. This also relates to the third point, heavily regulated entities and larger ecosystem operators in the lightly regulated pool will have more access to resources to facilitate interoperability. Imposing unnecessary regulatory burdens on growing ecosystems may harm their ability to compete with new larger ecosystems that emerge, hindering the achievement of the objectives set out in the regulatory framework.

9.3.4 *Prohibitions*

The prohibition to engage in exclusionary behaviour such as self-preferencing, tying and bundling, or mimicking aims to give effect to the positive obligations set out above by preventing incumbents from engaging in circumventive measures that diminish possibilities for entry. Incumbents that are obligated to provide access – whether it be to data, infrastructure, or other resources – may attempt to engage in behaviour that results in the same anti-competitive outcomes *de facto*. Instances of such anti-competitive behaviour have been observed in telecommunications in *Deutsche Telekom*, *TeliaSonera*, *Telefónica*, and *Slovak Telekom* in both regulated and deregulated parts of the network industry. Here, incumbents attempted to restrict competition on the service level through margin squeeze or the imposition of unfair terms.[782] As such, a prohibition to exclude is necessary to ensure the effectiveness of progressive ecosystem regulation. The added benefit of prohibitions to exclude is that it provides public authorities with a shortcut to intervene against anti-competitive behaviour. Prohibiting certain behaviour ex ante diminishes the need for an in-depth case-by-case assessment. The DMA also relies heavily on ex ante

[782] Case T-167/08, Microsoft Corp. v European Commission [2012] ECLI:EU:T:2012:323; Case T-30/89, Hilti v Commission of the European Communities [1991] EU:T:1991:70; Case 53/92, Hilti AG v Commission of the European Communities [1994] ECLI:EU:C:1994:77; Case T-612/17, Google LLC v European Commission [2021] ECLI:EU:T:2021:763; Case T-271/03 Deutsche Telekom v. Commission of the European Communities [2008] ECLI:EU:T:2008:101; Case C-280/08 P Deutsche Telekom v European Commission [2010] ECLI:EU:C:2010:603; Case T-336/07, Telefónica, SA and Telefónica de España, SA v European Commission [2012] ECLI:EU:T:2012:172; Case C-295/12 P, Telefónica SA and Telefónica de España SAU v European Commission [2014] ECLI:EU:C:2014:2062; Case C-52/09, Konkurrensverket v TeliaSonera Sverige AB [2011] ECLI:EU:C:2011:83; C-165/19 P, Slovak Telekom v. Commission [2021] ECLI:EU:C:2021:239; see also Fernando Díez, 'Jurisprudence of the EUJC on Margin Squeeze: From Deutsche Telekom to TeliaSonera and Beyond … to Telefonica!' [2011] SSRN Electronic Journal 21.

prohibitions to speed up enforcement and even includes its own anti-circumvention clause in article 13 DMA, which aims to ensure that the prohibitions and obligations laid down in articles 5, 6, and 7 DMA are effective and that gatekeepers do not create artificial constructions which amount to circumventions of these obligations.[783]

The DMA has based its obligations on lessons from applying competition law. The anti-competitive effects of self-preferencing and tying and bundling have been discussed in the *Microsoft*, *Google Shopping*, and *Google Android* cases.[784] Moreover, concerns related to tying and bundling appealing to user defaults or inertia or product proliferation have been discussed across merger cases involving big digital platforms.[785] Prohibitions of exclusionary acts that may lead to foreclosure in regulation should be aimed at ensuring the effectiveness of access rights held by entrants and emerging ecosystems, rather than serving as a regulatory short-cut. Negative obligations in the DMA have been critiqued to serve as a regulatory short-cut, as having ex ante prohibitions removes the need for case-by-case analyses, proving anti-competitive effects.[786] While such ex ante obligations to speed up enforcement are attractive to regulators or competition authorities, interventions in digital markets should still be based on the perceived harmful effects of the behaviour. In progressive ecosystem regulation, interpreting negative obligations in light of the positive obligations imposed on regulated entities so as to ensure their effectiveness provides a justification for intervention and limits the scope of the ex ante prohibitions. In this sense, the prohibition to exclude could itself be formulated as an anti-circumvention clause with respect to the positive obligations imposed on heavily and lightly regulated entities.

There is however an important difference between prohibitions that aim to address issues related to competition at the ecosystem level and as it is used in the DMA. In the DMA, the prohibitions apply specifically towards leveraging from and to the regulated core platform service. In a system of ecosystem competition, access should be available – at least to those in the lightly regulated or entrant pool – to *all* infrastructures and interfaces held by the stage 4 incumbent firm. For instance, the obligations laid down in the DMA ensure access to the offer of one's service on the Windows Operating System. In order to fully address concerns related to ecosystem competition however, the entrant should also be guaranteed easy and

[783] Pierre Larouche and Alexandre de Streel, 'The European Digital Markets Act: A Revolution Grounded on Traditions' (2021) 12 Journal of European Competition Law & Practice 542; Cappai and Colangelo (n 14) 5 et seq.

[784] Commission Decision in Google Shopping, Commission Decision in Google Android.

[785] Google/DoubleClick (Case M.4731) Commission Decision C(2008) 927 final [2008] OJ C 184/10; Microsoft/Skype (Case M.6281) Commission Decision C(2011) 7279 [2011], OJ C 268/12; Facebook/WhatsApp (Case M.7217), Commission Decision C(2014) 7239 [2014] OJ C; Microsoft/LinkedIn (Case M.8124) Commission Decision C(2016) 8404 [2016], OJ C 388/4; Apple/Shazam (Case M.8788) Commission Decision C(2018) 5748 [2018] OJ C 106/16; Google/Fitbit (Case M.9660) Commission Decision C(2020) 9105 [2020] OJ C 210/32.

[786] Cappai and Colangelo (n 14) 14; Ibáñez Colomo (n 15).

favourable integration into functionalities such as the search and taskbar, Microsoft productivity software such as Word, Teams, and Outlook, and other proprietary apps. In order to ensure equal treatment, Microsoft would have to ensure that if you can send a Teams link easily through Word or Outlook, it is equally easy or easier to send communication links offered by a third party. For this, one may consider prohibitions to pre-install only one's proprietary service, but require the integration of all approved third-party suppliers and offering the ability to send a link through a drop-down menu. This will leave stage 4 ecosystem operators with two choices: either provide a link with multiple choices that are presented equally or do not integrate any choice at all. If the incumbent chooses the first, this stimulates competition in the downstream markets. If it chooses the latter, it opens itself up to competition from another ecosystem provider that is willing to provide an integrated or holistic experience.

Here, there may also be a role for private litigation and interpretation by EU and Member State courts. By relying on private litigation, injured parties are not dependent on the public authority to intervene. Monti has noted the advantages and disadvantages of introducing private enforcement as part of a regulatory system in a review of the DMA. Here, Monti argues that the regulated entities (in this case gatekeepers) are best placed to internalize compliance and that their clients are in the best position to see if there is non-compliance. Private litigation would provide claimants with direct access to judicial review, allow them to seek redress in terms of damages, and facilitate compliance through the imposition of injunctive relief. The risk of having to pay damages should also have a deterrent effect on non-compliance for the regulated entities. There are also potential risks to private enforcement, as private litigation before national courts may lead to diverging interpretations on when the regulated entity effectively complies with the obligations imposed on it. Moreover, it may prove complex for the claimant to gather and analyse evidence that there is an infringement of the obligations resting on the regulated entity.[787]

In the system of progressive ecosystem regulation, reserving private litigations for cases of *de facto* non-compliance with positive obligations imposed on the regulated entity may limit these concerns. The role of courts will be limited to assessing whether the entity has engaged in behaviour that limits the effectiveness of the regulatory burdens imposed on them. Thus, the court does not have to determine whether the compliance with the positive obligation is effective, but simply whether the regulated entity has engaged in behaviour that may have diminished the effectiveness of the positive obligation. Referral of prejudicial questions to European courts may also limit divergence in the interpretations of national courts while allowing EU courts to develop case law on non-compliance and anti-competitive

[787] See Monti (n 548).

behaviour which ultimately translates into lessons and principles for the application of general competition law. As such, progressive ecosystem regulation may facilitate the use of private enforcement in furthering its objectives.

The application of such prohibitions, or anti-circumvention measures, should be similar towards undertakings in the lightly regulated pool. It is however possible to introduce additional standards of assessment for behaviour by lightly regulated entities. For instance, one could argue in favour of allowing efficiency justifications for lightly regulated entities and not for heavily regulated entities. The latter are incumbents – at least in part – due to the efficiency advantages associated with scale. As such, one can wonder whether an increase in efficiency outweighs anti-competitive effects of the incumbent vis-à-vis a smaller undertaking. Lightly regulated entities will have varying positions of relative strength with their ecosystems and may be in different stages of ecosystem competition. As such, certain behaviour with potential anti-competitive effects may be warranted if it allows lightly regulated entities to mature their business models and develop sustainable competitive strategies. Maintaining such an approach would reflect that progressive ecosystem regulation is based on the different stages of ecosystem competition and takes into account the asymmetric position of ecosystem operators in the digital networks. Relying on ex ante prohibitions that forego or abridge the case-by-case analysis, while allowing the defendant to raise efficiency justifications, strikes a balance between the rights of the defendant and the desire to facilitate dynamic competition.

9.3.5 *Line of Business Restrictions and Limitations to Acquisitions*

The imposition of line of business restrictions or limitations on acquisitions may be considered to further reduce the ability of ecosystem operators to leverage their power into new markets and to stimulate the emergence of new ecosystems.

Line of business restrictions may help to ensure that incipient markets are not occupied mostly or only by large digital firms. We have seen in recent years that large digital firms will either acquire suppliers of prominent emerging technologies such as AI and voice-based assistants or leverage their ecosystem power into competition to dominate these markets. While there has been some evolution in how mergers are notified and assessed with the DMA and DMCCA, it is unlikely that these changes are sufficient to address this type of pre-emptive competition.

Stage 4 ecosystem operators should be prevented from, or at least limited in their ability, to engage in serial acquisitions and industry roll-ups. There are multiple ways in which this can be achieved. In a ranking from most restrictive to least restrictive, one could first think of a complete prohibition of acquiring firms in the entrant pool, under a certain market cap, or within a certain period of time for heavily regulated entities. Such an outright prohibition would grant stage 1 and 2 ecosystem operators the time to grow their ecosystems to a certain size before they have to face the decision of being acquired or entering into intense competition with the incumbent. This would also require the imposition of some line of business restrictions or other protections, so that the incumbent cannot simply foreclose the entrant by abusing its positional power through other means (such as refusing interoperability or discrimination). While heavily regulated entities are restricted in their ability to acquire the firms, this does not mean that entrants cannot enter the market for the purpose of being acquired. Lightly regulated entities should face no restrictions in acquiring an undertaking of any size unless specified in the tailor-made rules. This also means that lightly regulated entities can issue their bids before stage 4 ecosystem incumbents can even make an offer. This gives the entrant a third choice: be acquired by a stage 2 or 3 ecosystem operator before entering into competition with the stage 4 incumbents, waiting until stage 4 ecosystem incumbents are able to bid to see if it can extract a premium, or preparing for long-term competition. While the entrant is in the protected pool, it will enjoy the benefits of access and protection granted by their regulatory framework, giving them a strong position. Once the shift from the protected entrant pool to the lightly regulated pool comes into view, the entrant can consider whether it wishes to continue or be acquired.

A less intrusive and more creative option could be the next best offer mechanism. If a stage 4 ecosystem incumbent makes a bid to acquire an undertaking, an opportunity is granted to players in the lightly regulated pool to issue their bids. The competition authority may then determine that the entrant may only consider the second-best offer if this is lower than the offer issued by the incumbent ecosystem operator. It has been seen in the past that operators of large ecosystems offer significant premiums to acquire start-ups that seem beyond the bounds of reason for undertakings without extreme power over resources. Meta bought WhatsApp for €19 billion, even though it generated no revenues. A second-best offer system would, without disclosing the bid, open up an auction to the lightly regulated pool. Firms in the lightly regulated pool are attended to the fact that the firm may be of potential interest since it is a target of acquisition for one of ecosystem incumbents, sparking bids. As the acquired firm may only consider the second-best offer and below, it can only consider the offer by stage 4 ecosystem incumbent if this is not the highest bid. If there is a lightly regulated entity that would offer more money for the same service, one can consider that the acquisition happens at a reasonable price. If the bid of the stage 4 ecosystem incumbent is significantly higher, the regulatory authority could consider this as an indication that the stage 4 incumbent is abusing its access to resources, and impose line of business restrictions on suspicion of anti-competitive intent. Lightly regulated entities are incentivized to make competitive bids: if they bid too high they may outbid the ecosystem incumbent, risking intensified competition in the related sector, if they bid too low they may lose the bid to another entity of the same size, or the potential acquiree may reject the bid.

A third option would be to make adaption to the notification thresholds and the assessment of serial acquisitions. The regulator can prevent industry roll-ups by treating subsequent small transactions as a singular transaction, and to assess the effects of the joint transactions on the specific sector. If it is found that the firm has acquired too much of the sector over a number of years, the regulatory authority could roll back the previous acquisitions and enforce divestments.[788] While proportional, this would likely require significant study and efforts from the regulator.

Aside from stronger merger rules for heavily regulated entities, there could be some general line of business restrictions. These types of restrictions are hard to implement and justify, as they would exclude a potential innovator from entering into a new technology or industry. The auctioning mechanism proposed above could lead to a justification of a temporary line of business restriction. Similarly, line of business restrictions could be imposed on incumbent ecosystem operators in relation to markets where the regulator has issued structural separations, so as to ensure that they do not pick apart the divested entity and integrate it into their own ecosystems.[789] Overall however, restrictions on how and where to enter business should be governed mostly by prohibitions related to leveraging and abusive behaviour as described previously.

9.3.6 *Direct Subsidies*

The proposal for progressive ecosystem regulation is focused on creating the market conditions where competition may thrive by facilitating disruptive innovation. However, there are still significant entry barriers that may delay or prevent entry. Direct public subsidies (i.e. industrial policy) may help entrants to overcome these barriers to entry by providing funding for initiatives. These subsidy schemes are complements to progressive ecosystem regulation and do not fall within the framework itself. The proposal for progressive ecosystem regulation aims to create conditions that facilitate innovativeness but is not aimed at stimulating certain types of innovation or to determine desirable outcomes of competition. This section aims to highlight that if there is a desire to 'pick winners and losers', this would be a matter for other instruments such as industrial policy. This section highlights that it is possible to use such an instrument to create desired outcomes in a direct or indirect way. The question whether this is desirable, and which principles should govern the use of such a tool, is outside of the scope of this research.

Ezrachi and Stucke have suggested the creation of innovation support policies as a possible solution to the pre-emption of disruptive innovation. Here, the authors argue that among other things, financial grants, tax breaks, loans, guarantees, and capital investments may speed up entry and disruption of the business models of

[788] Capobianco (n 577) 2–9.
[789] See eg Cooper, van den Boom and Arnao (n 473).

existing incumbents. Aside from these direct subsidy measures, policies can also help with technology transfers, commercializing innovations, or providing the needed inputs. They note that a challenge is to ensure that public funds and incentives are channelled effectively to those who create value and enhance innovation diversity. As identifying promising undertakings and technologies can be challenging, the authors recommend for instance to subsidize research which can then be incorporated by entrants for disruptive innovation.[790]

While there is no guarantee that investments in specific entrants may pay off, let alone certainty that all investments pay off equally, this book proposes that it may be worth investing significantly in disruptors that meet certain criteria. Article 10 of the proposed European Chips Act identifies several conditions that undertakings must meet to qualify so as to receive subsidization: they must establish a first-of-a-kind facility, their operations must have a clear positive impact on the Union's semiconductor value chain with regards to the security of supply and an increasingly qualified workforce, there must be an absence of certain extraterritorial application of public service for third countries and the undertaking must commit to invest in the next generation of chips.[791] While these conditions relate to a manufacturing industry, similar conditions can be developed to strengthen the competitive position of SMEs in digital competition.

The focus of these conditions is to be determined by the relevant authority. However, in the European context, one can think of several principles that may be leading. First, it has been noted that Europe lags behind the United States and China in the competitiveness of their platform economy.[792] Consequently, there is significant dependence of the EU on foreign digital platforms. One concern that has been raised in the past is digital sovereignty, referring to Europe's (or any nation's) ability to act independently in the digital world.[793] The promotion of digital sovereignty could be one of the conditions on the basis of which funding is granted, for instance by promoting regional differentiation through language, geographical markets, or adherence to European values and principles developed as a part of the funding framework.

Second, industrial policy may try to steer the outcomes of innovation. Some forms of innovation are considered to be 'toxic innovation'. Coad and others have written on the possible downsides of bad innovation, denoting the risks such as harms to human health or environmental damage.[794] Ezrachi and Stucke have writ-

[790] Ezrachi and Stucke (n 1) 205–208.

[791] European Commission, Proposal for a Regulation of the European Parliament and of the Council establishing a framework of measures for strengthening Europe's semiconductor ecosystem (Chips Act), COM(2022) 46 final, 8 February 2022.

[792] Stolton S, EU 'punching well below its weight' in digital technologies, von der Leyen warns' (Euractiv, 5 February 2021).

[793] Madiega T, Towards a more resilient EU, European Parliament – EPRS Ideas Paper, July 2020.

[794] Alex Coad and others, 'Editorial: The Dark Side of Innovation' (2021) 28 Industry and Innovation 102.

ten extensively on toxic or bad innovations, arguing that harms resulting from bad innovation in the digital realm may expand far beyond economic harms and privacy but even constitute a threat by undermining democracy.[795] Issues related to platform's role of informing the public have also been noted in government and expert reports.[796] Funding through innovation support policies could set conditions on which types of innovation are granted support. One can think of platforms that set high standards for privacy and data protection, which engage in voluntary fact-checking, which aim to develop benevolent algorithms that steer away from harmful content or fake news or platforms which develop non-advertising-based business models. While it is not possible to micro-manage undertakings, the framework could include transparency and reporting measures and sanctions for non-adherence to the funding agreement. This should provide the relevant authority with influence on the development of new technologies.

9.3.7 *An Overview of the Regulatory Burdens*

The obligations and prohibitions proposed in this section are intended as examples. The exact wording and content of the provisions would have to be determined through a legislative process. Here, legislators can draw from experiences from competition law enforcement and the enforcement of the DMA, DMCCA, Section 19a GWB, and other digital regulations imposed globally. There is a vast spectrum of possible interventions, and the listed burdens above are just a sample platter of possibilities that can be considered. Table 9.1 summarizes the regulatory burdens that have been proposed throughout Section 9.3.

TABLE 9.1 *Obligations for the different regulatory layers under progressive ecosystem regulation*

Obligations	Specific obligations for different regulatory pools
Data sharing	**Heavily regulated**: make large amounts and different categories of data available (potentially raw user data, non-personal data); free of charge for entrants, free or FRAND access for lightly regulated entities depending on the circumstances. **Lightly regulated**: make available smaller amounts and fewer categories of data to entrants under FRAND conditions, or free if warranted due to circumstances.

[795] Ariel Ezrachi and Maurice E Stucke, 'Is Your Digital Assistant Devious?' [2016] SSRN Electronic Journal 1; Maurice E Stucke and Ariel Ezrachi, 'How Digital Assistants Can Harm Our Economy, Privacy, and Democracy' (2017) 32 Berkeley Technology Law Journal 1239; Ezrachi and Stucke (n 1).

[796] Australian Competition & Consumer Authority (n 4); Zingales and others (n 1); Digital Competition Expert Panel (n 1); Subcommittee on Antitrust (n 1).

Obligations	Specific obligations for different regulatory pools
Data portability	**Heavily regulated**: provide effective data portability for users; includes more categories of data than user-provided data; regulator may set sharing architecture and mandate functionalities that make porting data easier (a data portability button for instance). **Lightly regulated and Entrants:** provide data portability in line with other regulatory frameworks (GDPR, Data Act).
Interoperability	**Heavily regulated**: requirements for vertical and cross-platform interoperability towards entrants and lightly regulated entities. Horizontal interoperability if warranted due to the nature of certain markets. **Lightly regulated:** requirements for vertical and cross-platform interoperability to guarantee access to entrants.
Prohibitions to exclude	**Heavily regulated:** ex ante prohibitions on behaviour that is presumed harmful to competition with a 'quick look' analysis and without efficiency justifications. **Lightly regulated**: ex ante prohibitions with a 'quick look' analysis but allow for efficiency justifications.
Limits on acquisitions	**Heavily regulated:** additional limitations on the acquisition of entrants or lightly regulated entities; option to introduce second-best offer mechanism; focus on serial acquisitions. **Lightly regulated:** no additional limitations on acquisitions.
Direct subsidies	**Entrant pool:** direct investments by public authorities into entrants, line of business restrictions for heavily regulated entries in relation to entrant firms.

9.4 CONCLUSION

This chapter has set out a comprehensive regulatory framework based on the findings of this book in combination with insights from regulation theory. The regulatory framework – dubbed progressive ecosystem regulation – pursues the creation of dynamic efficiencies by facilitating competition that may lead to disruptive innovation. It does so by opening up access points, limiting the ability of incumbents to pre-empt competition, and creating uncertainty for incumbents. It is proposed to divide ecosystems into three regulatory pools depending on their size: the heavily regulated, lightly regulated, and entrant pool. Obligations laid down in the system of progressive ecosystem regulation only govern the interactions and competitive efforts between players that operate in different pools, while competition within the pools remains governed by competition policy.

Heavily regulated entities are subjected to positive and negative obligations towards the lightly regulated entities and entrants. Lightly regulated entities have additional obligations towards entrants only. Entrants enjoy rights to access data, infrastructure, and other resources and protection from potentially exclusionary behaviour. The proposed regulatory framework also recommends limitations on the ability of heavily regulated entities to engage in mergers.

Through this system of regulation, a balance is struck between the freedom of entities to compete with players that are equal, while protecting competitors that are potentially as efficient but which have not yet had the chance to grow. By protecting entrants and emerging ecosystems from incumbents – and affording them access to valuable inputs – they have increased opportunities to experiment and develop new business models or act as a complementor to growing ecosystems. As entrants are protected from exclusionary behaviour, the incumbents' ability to pre-empt disruption is diminished. As the heavily regulated – and to a certain extent lightly regulated – entities are limited in their ability to pre-empt competition or absorb innovation, they are forced to compete on the merits to maintain their advantage over entrants.

The prospect of deregulation strengthens the incentives to compete as incumbents will try to conquer a durable position when regulatory limitations governing it are removed. These ideas are based on insights derived from theories on regulating natural monopoly markets in non-digital networks, as well as the process of deregulation in these markets.

The chapter has also set out guidance on the implementation of substantive obligations, specifically data sharing, data portability, interoperability, prohibitions to exclude, and limitations on certain categories of mergers. Here, it has been set out how these obligations may apply differently in the heavily and lightly regulated pool and the intended effects of imposing such obligations.

10

Conclusions

This book has explored how theories on the regulation of network industries can inspire the regulation of digital markets. This exploration provides novel perspectives on the regulation of digital market and develops new methods to regulate digital markets. Specifically, it proposes a regulatory framework that is based on idea surrounding competition in and between digital ecosystems, aimed at stimulating sustainable long-term competition by creating conditions conducive to disruptive entry. The book contributes to the literature in multiple ways: it develops a framework for the assessment of digital natural monopoly, as well as theories on the competitive dynamics of ecosystems. It also attempts to define ecosystem power as a complement to gatekeeper power, theorizes on stages of ecosystem competition, and proposes a regulatory framework based on the findings of these analyses.

This section summarizes the main findings and discusses how the book has contributed to the discussion on the regulation of digital markets. Section 10.1 discusses the findings from Part I, setting out the parallels and differences between competition in digital and non-digital network industries. This part has developed an anatomy of the competitors in the digital network industries and developed the theory of digital natural monopoly.

Section 10.2 discusses the findings of Part II, answering questions on the dynamics of competition between digital ecosystems within the digital network. This part of the book has developed a concept of ecosystem power as well as stages of ecosystem competition, providing novel perspectives on the competitive pressures experienced by digital undertakings.

Section 10.3 discusses the findings of Part III, answering questions on how regulation should take shape in light of the findings throughout the book. This part answers questions on what a desirable regulatory framework for the digital network industry could look like. Through the proposed regulatory framework, the part has highlighted which principles and mechanisms for regulation can be derived from the book.

Finally, Section 10.4 answers the question at the core of this research, highlighting in what ways focussing on the nature of digital markets as a network industry can shape regulation. This section concludes the book by highlighting the contributions of this book in the discussion on how digital markets cand and should be regulated.

10.1 PART I: THE COMPETITORS IN THE DIGITAL NETWORK INDUSTRY

Part I has explored questions on the nature of digital markets and the parallels and differences between digital and non-digital network industries. First, it is highlighted that there are some shared characteristics between non-digital and digital network industries, as both are characterized by network effects, economies of scale and scope, the need for complementarity, compatibility and standards, and the presence of switching costs and lock-in. As a result, the digital network industry – much like traditional network industries – is prone to the existence of bottleneck markets, especially when there are markets that exhibit natural monopoly characteristics. After setting out the parallels, the book looks into the differences between digital and non-digital markets, looking into a series of characteristics that make digital goods and services unique.

The uniqueness of digital markets is related to the nature of digital goods as modular information goods, as well as the presence of data-driven efficiencies. As digital goods have an informational nature, they are non-exhaustible and reusable. This inspires abundance strategies where undertakings give away free goods, or free versions of the good, as to attract a large network of users. Unlike with non-digital goods, these abundance strategies can be maintained for a long time due to the (near-)zero marginal cost of duplicating and distributing digital goods.

The modular design of the goods generates economies of scope, which promote the sharing of components, involving third parties as to co-generate value and expanding across markets. Undertakings which proliferate digital goods are therefore likely to attract both a large network of consumers, as well as a network of business users. Consumers are attracted through abundance strategy and the digital undertaking can attract business users by providing them with a technology to offer their goods and services and compete with one another. This technology is generally the digital platform. The platform operator and the third parties that depend on its platform create a multi-actor ecosystem where the actors co-generate value, cooperate and compete with one another.

Reliance on the digital platform strategy is attractive for digital undertakings as it eliminates the need to produce everything in-house. Instead, the value proposition of the digital platform undertaking exists in its ability to match producers of goods and services to end users who consume them. The efficiency of this model is further amplified by the presence of data-driven efficiencies, as this allows the platform operator to improve their matching capabilities and increase their value as an intermediary. Thus, while the principles underlying traditional networks and digital networks are similar, the employed business models and competitive strategies differ substantially as the digital operator chooses to use multi-sided market strategies.

The nature of digital goods also explains the prevalence of multi-product ecosystems in the digital network industry. For the purpose of this book, multi-product ecosystems have been defined as a collection of goods and services built around a digital platform or a group of digital platforms for which one undertaking is able to exercise control on terms for activities such as determining compatibility, coordination and the setting of standards. Reliance on the digital platform model requires the digital undertaking to attract as many users as possible as to improve its intermediation services. By expanding into new markets, the digital undertaking is able to enrich the offering on its platform by integrating new functionalities, access new groups of users, and create new multi-actor ecosystems. The modular and informational nature of digital goods and data-driven efficiencies also facilitate the expansion across markets, as the digital undertaking can reuse its resources to enter into new markets more easily. The platform may choose to engage in cross-platform expansion to capture new platforms, on-platform expansion to enrich the offering on its platform or vertically integrate as to enhance its control in determining the value proposition of the platform and the allocation of value in its multi-actor ecosystem.

The digital platform business model is associated with strong indirect network externalities, economies of scale and scope, and other data-driven efficiencies. As a consequence, it has been argued that digital platform markets are prone to market failures. This book has therefore explored whether these characteristics lead to natural monopoly in digital markets. In traditional networks, natural monopoly often exists in markets where there are high sunk and fixed costs with subsequent economies of scale. This mostly occurs in infrastructure markets, where the incumbent must invest vast amounts of resources to develop an infrastructure and then spread out the costs over a large number of customers. The book has concluded that digital markets may also exhibit natural monopoly but under different circumstances.

The book develops both single-product and multi-product perspectives on digital monopoly. It finds that digital platforms exhibit feedback loops that result in concentration, how imperfect competition depends on the level of economies of scale and the fixed costs, and whether the platform is purely software-based or (partly) physical, the homogeneity or heterogeneity of the goods and related possibilities to diversify, and the level of data-driven incumbency advantages. From a single-output perspective, monopoly is only likely to occur in pure software platforms with highly homogeneous demands and strong data-driven advantages, such as horizontal search engines. This may be different when taking a multi-output perspective, if differentiated goods and services can be integrated onto a single platform, the market may concentrate towards monopoly even if there is some level of heterogeneity. Unlike non-digital natural monopoly, digital monopolies are dynamic, and the cost of entry and economies of scale depend on whether there are already mature platform and ecosystem operators in the market. The more mature a market is, the higher the sunk and fixed costs associated with entry are likely to be.

Through the analyses, three self-reinforcing feedback loops that contribute to this monopolization are identified. First, the nature of the platform operator as an intermediary means that the installed base on either side of the platform serves as an input for supplying the intermediation service: any consumption of output on one side of the market is also an input to provide intermediation on the other side of the market. Second, each interaction with the platform generates data, which is an input itself. As this data is automatically generated with these interactions, the platform enjoys increasing returns to scale. There are thus increasing returns to scale in adoption of the service: increases in users lead to supply-side efficiencies in intermediation, which attracts more interactions from these users, which generates more data, which helps to further improve the service and attract more users. This leads to the third feedback loop: as the efficiency advantage of the incumbent grows with scale, the fixed costs that must be incurred to offer an equal service grow with the maturity of the platform. As monopolization is related to these feedback loops, the digital natural monopoly distinguishes itself from non-digital natural monopolies. For the latter, there was generally subadditivity of the single firm as the infrastructure was so costly that it was not economically viable to build duplicate (competing) infrastructures. Consequently, all demand had to be aggregated on that infrastructure as to make its operation cost-efficient. Non-digital infrastructures are therefore often natural monopoly *until* a certain range of demand. Conversely, the digital natural monopoly is demand induced: the more users aggregate on the platform, the more the efficiency advantage of the incumbent operator grows. This indicates that in digital platform markets, natural monopoly comes to exist *after* a certain level of demand is aggregated in the platform.

The dynamism of digital markets leads to complex effects. On the one hand, the analyses shows that the existence digital ecosystems and associated economies of scope and complementarity helps the monopolist to not only sustain their monopoly but also enter in adjacent markets. Thus, self-sustaining dominance in one market is likely to lead to expansion across markets. The resulting ecosystem serves as a moat, allowing the firm to protect their core platform markets from competition. On the other hand, the existence of multi-product ecosystems within the digital network industry create a distinct form of competition: ecosystem competition. Rather than competing in a market, digital firms are able to challenge the monopolist by leveraging their position across markets in competition *for* a market. This means that even if a market is monopolized, the presence of strong competing ecosystems may create competitive constraints, limiting opportunities for the monopolist to extract rents.

This finding means that digital monopoly should not be regulated in the same way as non-digital natural monopoly. As there are opportunities for competition, regulation should aim to foster the dynamic competition that exists within the digital network industry. The book has explored the competitive dynamics of ecosystem competition in its second part.

10.2 PART II: THE DYNAMICS OF COMPETITION BETWEEN DIGITAL ECOSYSTEMS

Part II starts by distinguishing between inter-ecosystem, intra-ecosystem, and vertical competition. Here, the book distinguishes between ecosystem power, that is, the ability of the ecosystem operator to act anti-competitively in competition with other product ecosystems, and gatekeeper power, the ability to act anti-competitively towards users that are dependent on a certain platform in the ecosystem. This book argues that gatekeeper power is akin to market power, as it allows the ecosystem operator to distort competition in the platform market, in vertically related markets or by exploiting the consumer in that market. Abuses of ecosystem power on the other hand are novel and relate to the ability of the ecosystem operator to pre-empt competition in a wide variety of markets that are loosely connected to the markets that are occupied by the ecosystem operator.

The book then moves on to explore the competitive dynamics of competition between ecosystems as to understand how ecosystem power arises and exhibits itself. Here, the book combines theoretical and empirical insights to develop four stages of ecosystem competition:

Stage 1 ecosystem competition occurs as competition *for* a platform market, a new platform market emerges and players compete to tip this market in their favour. As markets are prone to tipping – and some exhibit natural monopoly characteristics – there is likely one winner that takes most or all of that market.

Stage 2 ecosystem competition is characterized by the emergence of multi-product ecosystems. Winners in their respective 'core' platform markets leverage their resources and installed bases into vertically related or adjacent markets, they use this expansion to develop their on-platform cluster or cross-platform ecosystem. This allows the emerging ecosystem operator to both insulate their core markets from challenges by competitors and differentiate their ecosystem as to challenge markets occupied by existing ecosystems or to explore new opportunities. Both of these stages of ecosystem competition are marked by intense competition where today's winner in a market can still turn into tomorrow's loser.

Stage 3 ecosystem competition happens when the existing ecosystems find an equilibrium. The ecosystems are sufficiently differentiated from one another that each ecosystem in the market can independently find their path to revenue generation and profitability. As inter-ecosystem challenges diminish, the ecosystem operator can shift strategies to extract additional profits from its users. As this period is marked by diminished uncertainty, the ecosystem operator gains the ability to enjoy the profits of their competitive success. This stage of ecosystem competition also provides increased risks for the abuse of gatekeeper power, as users are more likely to be locked in with their ecosystem and alternatives are becoming increasingly scarce.

Stage 4 ecosystem competition happens when the largest ecosystem operators set their sights on the pre-emption of new entrants into digital markets. As the ecosystem operators have acquired vast resources, have locked in their users, and face diminished competitive threats, they can set their sights on ensuring that no new disruptive competitor arises. In this scenario, ecosystem operators have the resources to engage in killer acquisitions, offer discounts to exclude entrant ecosystems, and to force entrants to engage in sustained innovations that complement the existing ecosystems under threat of exclusion. As a result, innovation in digital markets slows down, especially disruptive innovation. Ecosystem operators also have no incentives to compete intensely with one another, as the potential benefits from intense competition with equals is lower than preventing disruption of the current revenue sources. Stage 4 ecosystem competition is where the competitive situation in the market becomes dire and entry barriers and market failures become systematic.

This book argues that the digital network is currently characterized by the prevalence of stage 4 ecosystem competition: a select group of ecosystems has the ability to pre-empt challenges to their incumbency. These ecosystem operators have enjoyed first mover advantages and market or legal conditions that have allowed them to expand across a wide variety of markets without the competitive threats of other incumbents.

It is proposed that the presence of incumbents leads to long-term harms as a result of a number of distinct yet interrelated types of harms: entrenchment harms make it harder to contest the monopoly for competing ecosystems and easier for the incumbent to leverage their power from that monopoly into new markets. To preserve its power in and across markets, the ecosystem operator may engage in industry-wide roll-ups, taking over not only core markets but also entire value chains that may constitute access points for competitive entry. Once a small number of incumbents takes over large parts of the digital network industry, they have incentives to soften competition for one another's core markets while competing intensely in emerging and incipient markets, which pushes out potential entrants and smaller ecosystem competitors. For those that do succeed to enter the market, the incumbents can use acquisitions or anti-competitive behaviour to absorb entrants, coerce them to innovate in a way that serves the incumbent's business model, or push them out of the market entirely. These exclusionary harms result in harms to end-consumers in the form of innovation harms: not only do consumer not get access to new and disruptive technologies, but they also miss out on the period of intense competition between emerging ecosystems. This minimizes the allocation of the generated value towards consumers, while incumbents can appropriate these gains to further solidify their position in the network.

10.3 PART III: A REGULATORY FRAMEWORK TO GOVERN ECOSYSTEM COMPETITION

Part III sets out a regulatory framework that combines the insights derived from economics literature and management theory with regulation theory. This book proposes a regulatory system it calls progressive ecosystem regulation, where entities in digital markets are divided across three pools: the entrant pool, the lightly regulated pool, and the heavily regulated pool. Actors within each pool can compete freely with one another, while the regulation governs interactions and competition between entities in different pools.

The purpose of progressive ecosystem regulation is to create long-term and sustainable competition by fostering an environment that stimulates disruptive entry and protecting ecosystem competition. The framework relies on three key components to achieve these objectives: (i) incumbent firms must be limited in their ability to pre-empt disruptive innovation; (ii) ecosystems of equal size must be incentivized to prioritize competition with one another; and (iii) entrants must be incentivized to enter into long-term, meaningful, and disruptive competition.

Progressive ecosystem regulation imposes heavy regulatory burdens on stage 4 ecosystem operators. These firms have to adhere to a strict set of ex ante, horizontally applicable rules that entail prohibitions and obligations to provide smaller firms with access to data, infrastructures, and other resources. The burdens are supposed to be sufficiently heavy that the costs of continued monopolization of their part of the network industry outweighs the cost of losing that position. In effect, firms are not only regulated in what they can or cannot do but pushed to work towards a redistribution of markets and market shares and to shrink their multi-product ecosystem. Firms that do so are entered into the lightly regulated pool. Once they enter into the lightly regulated pool, they can compete freely with other lightly regulated entities and are relieved of a part of their burdens vis-à-vis entrants. Thus, by working towards ending their incumbency, they regain their freedom to compete.

Over time, this should result in a larger number of relatively equal ecosystems (stage 3) competing with one another. As these firms compete intensely, they have less resources available to identify potentially disruptive markets and pre-empt competition. Meanwhile, the ecosystems in the lightly regulated pool still have the means to invest in innovation and to outcompete their contemporaries.

Persistent competitive entry is promoted as entrants are protected through the regulatory framework and granted access to the infrastructures and resources of lightly regulated entities. This should create an environment where entrants can experiment to find opportunities to disrupt the status quo, while preventing lightly regulated entities from closing the door behind them.

Progressive ecosystem regulation attempts to (re)introduce an element of uncertainty into digital competition by removing the control of large incumbent ecosystem operators over the digital network industry. Progressive ecosystem regulation opens up access points for entry into competition in the digital network, grants entrants access to infrastructures and resources, and promotes a stable competitive equilibrium in the network. This harnesses the dynamism inherent to digital competition, without unduly limiting opportunities for firms to differentiate themselves or obtain rewards from their competitive efforts.

10.4 THE DIGITAL NETWORK INDUSTRY: LESSONS FOR REGULATION

The contribution of this book lies with its novel approach to regulation and regulatory tools, which create a bridge between different streams of literature. The book has combined insights from economics and management literature to explain why competition in the digital network industry has taken shape as it does, how the interests of different parties can be accounted for, and what competitive pressures arise. These insights have been brought together with theories on the regulation of network industries to create new principles and perspectives on regulation specifically for digital markets.

By looking at the nature of digital markets as a network industry, it became possible to focus on competition in the network as a whole, rather than looking at competition in or for markets or the role of the platform operator as a gatekeeper towards its users. Maintaining this focus on the network resulted in an in-depth exploration of the dynamics of inter-ecosystem competition in the digital network as to explain why ecosystem operators tend to focus on a long-term strategy of cross-market expansion. This perspective on competition in the digital network also helps to explain how the presence of digital natural monopoly may create bottleneck markets, but that the impact of monopoly in a market on competition differs between digital and non-digital networks. In the latter, the existence of natural monopoly would warrant the regulation of the monopolist in their market due to a lack of competitive constraints. In the first, competitive pressures at the ecosystem level may be sufficient to prevent harms associated with monopoly. The book concludes that by looking at digital markets as a network industry, it becomes clear that regulators must adopt new perspectives on competition and new paradigms for regulation: the regulatory framework must reflect the dynamic and unpredictable nature of digital markets and competition between ecosystems. The regulatory framework proposed in this book has explained how regulation can be used to pursue these objectives.

The book acknowledges the importance of the structure and characteristics of individual markets, recognizing that the existence of natural monopoly – or strongly imperfect competition – may lead to foreclosure of competition in certain digital markets. At the same time, the book recognizes the importance of competition at the level of the ecosystem and the competitive pressures that this type of competition provides. By relying on economics literature and management theory, the regulatory framework attempts to internalize and maximize the efficiencies associated with the achievement of economies of scale and scope in natural monopoly markets *and* the efficiencies associated with competition. As digital markets are dynamic and characterized by short innovation cycles, regulation which focuses on stimulating disruptive innovations as to create durable competition is more suitable than imposing long-lasting and burdensome regulatory obligations.

The regulatory framework balances the interests of the regulated entities, entrants, and public authorities. It ensures that regulated entities can compete freely with players that are at an equal level, preventing undue restrictions in their ability to determine their business models and strategies. At the same time, they are limited in engaging certain behaviour if this negatively affects players that are potentially as efficient but have not yet had the chance to develop. The interests of public authorities are safeguarded by relying on obligations that do not require high direct regulatory costs, and by creating a system that allows for the participation of national competition authorities. As the regulation is aimed at being phased out, risks of regulatory capture are also diminished.

The flexibility of the proposed regulatory regime is also reflected when comparing it to the current proposals for regulation or the reform of competition law. Progressive ecosystem regulation was compared to existing regulatory proposals in the EU, UK, and Germany to demonstrate that each of these proposals can be incorporated into a system of progressive ecosystem regulation. The pool of heavily regulated entities can be subjected to rules-based regulation, lightly regulated entities can be subjected to principles-based regulation, and competition within pools can be governed by an amended version of competition policy. By incorporating these different approaches into a coherent system, the strengths of each approach can be safeguarded while addressing some of the weaknesses of the current proposals.

The proposal for progressive ecosystem regulation provides fruitful ground for discussion on the regulation of digital markets in the future. The purpose of the proposal has not been to develop a fully functional operational framework. Instead, it invites regulators and academics to think differently about competition in digital markets by highlighting competition within the digital network industry as a whole, the role that ecosystem competition and dynamic competition should play in shaping regulation and the regulatory objectives that should be pursued. The book has answered the question on how the nature of digital markets as a network industry should shape regulation by emphasizing the need to empower entrants so that they can become competitors in the network, facilitate disruptive innovation so that entrants can displace incumbents, and use regulation to intensify competition throughout the network industry so that users do not have to become dependent on just one platform or ecosystem.

Bibliography

A4E, 'The Implementation of the DMA and Alphabet's Compliance with Its Obligations' (2024)

Accenture, 'Tackling the Costs of a 5G Build' (3 August 2018)

Adner R, 'Ecosystem as Structure: An Actionable Construct for Strategy' (2017) 43 *Journal of Management* 39

Adomavicius G and others, 'Do Recommender Systems Manipulate Consumer Preferences? A Study of Anchoring Effects' (2013) 24 *Information Systems Research* 956

Aghion P, Bergeaud A and Van Reenen J, 'The Impact of Regulation on Innovation' (2023) 113 *American Economic Review* 2894

Aghion P and others, 'Competition and Innovation: An Inverted-U Relationship' (May 2005) 120 *The Quarterly Journal of Economics* 701–728.

Akman P, 'A Preliminary Assessment of the European Commission's Google Android Decision' (2018) *Competition Policy International* (December Issue) 8

Akman P, 'A Web of Paradoxes: Empirical Evidence on Online Platform Users and Implications for Competition and Regulation in Digital Markets' (2022) 217 *Virginia Law and Business Review* 1

Akman P, 'Regulating Competition in Digital Platform Markets: A Critical Assessment of the Framework and Approach of the EU Digital Markets Act' (2024) 30 *European Law Journal* 112

Almunawara MN and Ansharib M, 'Multi-sided Networks of Digital Platform Ecosystem: The Case of Ride-Hailing in Indonesia' (2020) 30 *Asia Pacific Journal of Information Systems* 808

Anderson C, *The Long Tail – Why the Future of Business Is Selling Less of More* (Hyperion e-book 2016)

Andriychuk O, 'The New EU and UK Regimes for Regulating Competition in Digital Markets: We Finally See What's on the Plate – but Do We Know How to Eat It?' (2024) 12 *Journal of Antitrust Enforcement* 195

Andriychuk O, 'Shaping the New Modality of the Digital Markets: The Impact of the DSA/DMA Proposals on Inter-Platform Competition' (2021) 44 *World Competition* 261

Andriychuk O and Clayton E, 'Experimenting with Regulatory Mechanisms for Shaping Competition in Digital Markets'

Andriychuk O and Clayton E, 'Experimenting with Regulatory Mechanisms for Shaping Competition in Digital Markets' [2024] NELR

Areeda P and Hovenkamp H, *Antitrust Law: An Analysis of Antitrust Principles and Their Application* (Aspen 1978)

Argenton C and others, 'Can Abuse of a Dominant Position Be Tackled More Effectively?' [2023] *Report for the Dutch Ministry of Economic Affairs & Climate*

Argenton C and Prufer J, 'Search Engine Competition with Network Externalities' (2012) 8 *Journal of Competition Law and Economics* 73

Armstrong M, 'Network Interconnection in Telecommunications' (1998) 108 *Economic Journal* 545

Armstrong M, 'Competition in Two-Sided Markets' (2006) 37 *The RAND Journal of Economics* 668

Arnold R and others, 'Is Data the New Oil? Diminishing Returns to Scale' [2018] 29th European Regional ITS Conference, Trento 2018 17

Arrow KJ, 'Economic Welfare and the Allocation of Resources for Invention' in Charles K. Rowley (ed), *Readings in Industrial Economics: Volume Two: Private Enterprise and State Intervention* (Macmillan Education UK 1972) https://doi.org/10.1007/978-1-349-15486-9_13

Arthur C, 'Microsoft Threatened as Smartphones and Tablets Rise, Gartner Warns', *The Guardian* (4 April 2013)

Arthur C, 'iTunes Is 10 Years Old Today, Was It the Best Idea That Apple Has Ever Had', *The Guardian* (24 May 2017)

Australian Competition & Consumer Authority, 'Digital Platform Inquiry' (2019)

Autio E, 'Orchestrating Ecosystems: A Multi-layered Framework' [2021] Innovation 1

Autio E and Thomas L, 'Innovation Ecosystems: Implications for Innovation Management' (2014)

Baer D, 'The Real Reason Facebook Bought Oculus: "Virtual Reality Will Be the On-Ramp to Optical Computing"', *Business Insider* (21 November 2014)

Barabasi A-L and Albert R, 'Emergence of Scaling in Random Networks' (1999) 286 *Science* 4

Baronian L, 'Digital Platforms and the Nature of the Firm' (2020) 54 *Journal of Economic Issues* 214

Batra M, de Bijl P and Klein T, 'Ecosystem Theories of Harm in EU Merger Control: Analysing Competitive Constraints and Entrenchment' (2024) 15 *Journal of European Competition Law & Practice* 357

Bauer JM, 'Platforms, Systems Competition, and Innovation: Reassessing the Foundations of Communications Policy' (2014) 38 *Special Issue on Moving Forward with Future Technologies: Opening a Platform for All* 662

Bazbaz K, 'Roadblocks to Competition: Investigate Google's Non-Compliance with the EU Digital Markets Act' (*DuckDuckGo Blog*, 20 November 2024)

Berg SV and Tschirhart J, *Natural Monopoly Regulation: Principles and Practice* (Cambridge University Press 1988)

Blind K, 'The Impact of Regulation on Innovation' (2012) 12 NESTA Working Paper Series

Borgogno O and Colangelo G, 'Data Sharing and Interoperability: Fostering Innovation and Competition through APIs' (2019) 35 *Computer Law & Security Review* 1

Bostoen F, 'Online Platforms and Pricing: Adapting Abuse of Dominance Assessments to the Economic Reality of Free Products' (2019) 35 *Computer Law & Security Review* 263

Bostoen F, 'Understanding the Digital Markets Act' (2023) 68 *The Antitrust Bulletin* 263

Bostoen F and Mandrescu D, 'Assessing Abuse of Dominance in the Platform Economy: A Case Study of App Stores' (2020) 16 *European Competition Journal* 431

Bostoen F and Petit N, 'Platforms' Treacherous Turn' [2023] *SSRN Electronic Journal* <www.ssrn.com/abstract=4664056> accessed 22 August 2024

Bostoen F and Petit N, 'Platforms' Treacherous Turn' [2023] *Network Law Review*

Bourreau M, 'Some Economics of Digital Ecosystems' (OECD 2020) Note for the OECD DAF/COMP/WD(2020)89

Bourreau M, de Streel A and Graef I, 'Big Data and Competition Policy: Market Power, Personalised Pricing and Advertising' (2017) CERRE Project Report

Bourreau M, Dogan P and Manant M, 'Modularity and Product Innovation in Digital Markets' (2009) 6 *Review of Network Economics* 1

Bourreau M, Doğan P and Manant M, 'A Critical Review of the "Ladder of Investment" Approach' (2010) 34 *Telecommunications Policy* 683

Bourreau M, Krämer J and Buiten M, 'Interoperability in Digital Markets' (CERRE 2022) Final Report

Bower JL and Christensen CM, 'Disruptive Technologies: Catching the Wave' 12

Bowers S, 'Google Hits on Profit Formula' *The Guardian* (8 August 2001)

Bresnahan T, Greenstein S and Henderson RM, 'Schumpeterian Competition and Diseconomies of Scope: Illustrations from the Histories of Microsoft and IBM', *The Rate and Direction of Inventive Activity Revisited* (National Bureau of Economic Research, Inc 2011)

BRICS Competition Law and Policy Center, 'Digital Era Competition: A BRICS View' (BRICS 2021)

Brin S and Page L, 'The Anatomy of a Large-Scale Hypertextual Web Search Engine' (1998) 30 *Computer Networks and ISDN Systems* 107

Brown I, 'Interoperability as a Tool for Competition Regulation' (LawArXiv 2020) preprint <https://osf.io/fbvxd> accessed 7 February 2022

Brynjolfsson E, Hu Y (Jeffrey) and Smith MD, 'Long Tails vs. Superstars: The Effect of Information Technology on Product Variety and Sales Concentration Patterns' (2010) 21 *Information Systems Research* 736

Brynjolfsson E, Hu YJ and Smith MD, 'From Niches to Riches: The Anatomy of the Long Tail' [2006] *MIT Sloan Management Review* 13

Busch C, 'Regulation of Digital Platforms as Infrastructures for Services of General Interest' (2021) 09 WISO Diskurs

Cabral and others, *The EU Digital Markets Act: A Report from a Panel of Economic Experts.* (Publications Office 2021) <https://data.europa.eu/doi/10.2760/139337> accessed 14 December 2022

Cafarra C and others, 'Designing Regulation for Digital Platforms: Why Economists Need to Work on Business Models' 2020 *EUVox*

Caillaud B and Jullien B, 'Chicken & Egg: Competition among Intermediation Service Providers' (2003) 34 *The RAND Journal of Economics* 309

Capobianco A, 'Serial Acquisitions and Industry Roll-Ups – Note by the United States, DAF/COMP/WD(2023)99'

Cappai M and Colangelo G, 'Taming Digital Gatekeepers: The "More Regulatory Approach" to Antitrust Law' (2021) 41 *Computer Law and Security Review* 1

Cave M, 'Encouraging Infrastructure Competition via the Ladder of Investment' (2006) 30 *Telecommunications Policy* 223

Chan S, 'Netflix's Rivals Grow Share of U.S. Streaming App Usage to 61% in Q1 2022' (*SensorTower*, 21 April 2022)

Chandler A, *The Visible Hand: The Managerial Revolution in American Business* (Belknap Press 1993)

Christensen C, *The Innovator's Dilemma: When New Technologies Cause Great Firms to Fail* (Harvard Business Review Press 2013)

Christensen CM, Raynor M and McDonald R, 'What Is Disruptive Innovation?' [2015] *Harvard Business Review* 11

Christian R, 'On Gatekeepers and Structural Competition Problems' (2021) 56 *Intereconomics* 205

Church J and Gandal N, 'Systems Competition, Vertical Merger, and Foreclosure' (2000) 9 *Journal of Economics & Management Strategy* 25

Claici A and others, 'The Economic Rationale for Vertical Integration in the Tech Sector: Hardware Devices to Software to Services: Strategic Risk-Taking, Innovation and Investments in the Pursuit of Efficiency and Consumer Value' (Copenhagen Economics 2020)

Clemons EK and Madhani N, 'Regulation of Digital Businesses with Natural Monopolies or Third-Party Payment Business Models: Antitrust Lessons from the Analysis of Google' (2010) 27 *Journal of Management Information Systems* 43

CMA, 'Cloud Services Market Investigation' (2023) Market Investigation

CMA, 'Digital Markets Competition Regime Guidance' (2024) Guidance

CMA, 'Digital Markets Competition Regime Guidance' [2024] DMCCA Draft Guidance for Consultation

CMA, 'Digital Markets Competition Regime Guidance'

CMA, 'Potential Remedies' [2024] Market Investigation into Cloud Services

Coad A and others, 'Editorial: The Dark Side of Innovation' (2021) 28 *Industry and Innovation* 102

Coase RH, 'The Nature of the Firm' (1937) 4 *Economica* 386

Cohen JE, 'Law for the Platform Economy' (2017) 51 *Davis Law Review* 72

Cohen MC and Zhang R, 'Competition and Coopetition for Two-Sided Platforms' (2022) 31 *Production and Operations Management* 1997

Cohen S, 'Principles in Transition: What Remains of Competition Law in the Era of Hybrid Competition Enforcement? New EU & UK Rules for Regulating Competition in Digital Markets: A Comparative Perspective' (2024) 10 *North East Law Review* 87

Colangelo G, 'Evaluating the Case for Regulation of Digital Platforms' (2020) 26 *The Global Antitrust Institute Report on the Digital Economy* 1

Competition & Market Authority, 'Online Platforms and Digital Advertising' (2020) Online Platforms and Digital Advertising Market Study – GOV.UK

Competition & Market Authority, 'Mobile Ecosystems Market Study – Interim Report' (2021) Market Study Interim Report

Competition & Markets Authority, 'Online Platforms and Digital Advertising Market' (2019) Online Platforms and Digital Advertising Market Study – GOV.UK

Constantiou ID and Kallinikos J, 'New Games, New Rules: Big Data and the Changing Context of Strategy' (2015) 30 *Journal of Information Technology* 44

Cooper A, Van den Boom J and Arnao Z, 'Considerations for Effective Search Competition Remedies' (2024) Knight Georgetown Institute Report

Cooper G, 'Bluesky Boasts More than 30 Million Users, Thanks to "Twitter Quitters"' *CNET* (31 January 2025)

Copeland R and Higgins T, 'Google's Exclusive Search Deals with Apple at Heart of U.S. Lawsuit' *The Wall Street Journal* (20 October 2020)

Coulter M, 'Apple Files Legal Challenge to EU's Digital Markets Act' *Reuters* (17 November 2023)

Cowling J, 'A Brief History of Microsoft – The Worlds Biggest Software Company' (*DSP Explorer*, 8 February 2016) <https://content.dsp.co.uk/a-brief-history-of-microsoft-the-worlds-biggest-software-company>

Cozzolino A, Corbo L and Aversa P, 'Digital Platform-Based Ecosystems: The Evolution of Collaboration and Competition between Incumbent Producers and Entrant Platforms' (2021) 126 *Journal of Business Research* 385

CPI, 'European Sites Criticize Google's Compliance Efforts with DMA' (12 December 2024)

Crampes C, 'Network Industries and Network Goods' 39

Crane DA, 'Ecosystem Competition and Antitrust Laws' (2019) 98 *Nebraska Law Review* 412

Cranz A, 'There Are over 3 Billion Active Android Devices' *The Verge* (18 May 2021)

Crémer J, De Montjoye Y-A and Schweitzer H, 'Competition Policy for the Digital Era' (2019)

Crunchbase, 'List of Google's 4 Funding Rounds Totaling $26.1M' (online, 2000) <www.crunchbase.com/search/funding_rounds/field/organizations/funding_total/google> accessed 16 December 2022

Curran K, Graham S and Temple C, 'Advertising on Facebook' (2011) 1 *International Journal of E-Business Development* 26

Cusumano MA, Gawer A and Yoffie DB, *The Business of Platforms: Strategy in the Age of Digital Competition, Innovation, and Power* (Harper Business 2019)

Datacenter Knowledge, 'Google Data Center FAQ, Part 2' (26 August 2008)

Dattée B, Alexy O and Autio E, 'Maneuvering in Poor Visibility: How Firms Play the Ecosystem Game When Uncertainty Is High' (2018) 61 *Academy of Management Journal* 466

Davies T and Georgieva Z, 'Zero Price, Zero Competition: How Marketization Fixes Anticompetitive Tying in Monetized Markets'

de O. Melo C and others, 'Interpretative Case Studies on Agile Team Productivity and Management' (2013) 55 *Special Section: Component-Based Software Engineering (CBSE), 2011* 412

de Streel A and others, 'Recommendations Paper – Making the Digital Markets Act More Resilient and Effective' (CERRE 2021)

de Streel A, Bourreau M and Giet L, 'Digital Conglomerates and EU Competition Policy' (CERRE 2019)

de Streel A and Larouche P, 'Disruptive Innovation and Competition Policy Enforcement' (OECD 2015)

Decker C, *Modern Economic Regulation: An Introduction to Theory and Practice* (Cambridge University Press 2015)

den Hertog JA, 'Review of Economic Theories of Regulation' (Utrecht School of Economics 2010)

Department of Justice, 'Plaintiffs' Initial Proposed Final Judgment'

Deutscher Bundestag, 'Gesetzentwurf Der Bundesregierung, Entwurf Eines Gesetzes Zur Änderung Des Gesetzes Gegen Wettbewerbsbeschränkungen Für Ein Fokussiertes, Proaktives Und Digitales Wettbewerbsrecht 4.0 Und Anderer Wettbewerbsrechtlicher Bestimmungen' (2020) Drucksache 19/23492

Deutscher Bundestag, 'Beschlussempfehlung Und Bericht Des Ausschusses Für Wirtschaft Und Energie' (2021) Drucksache 19/25868

Díez F, 'Jurisprudence of the EUJC on Margin Squeeze: From Deutsche Telekom to TeliaSonera and Beyond … to Telefonica!' [2011] *SSRN Electronic Journal* 21

Digital Competition Expert Panel, 'Unlocking Digital Competition' (2019)

Dokko G, Kane AA and Tortoriello M, 'One of Us or One of My Friends: How Social Identity and Tie Strength Shape the Creative Generativity of Boundary-Spanning Ties' (2014) 35 *Organization Studies* 703

Ducci F, *Natural Monopolies in Digital Platform Markets* (Cambridge University Press 2020)

Duch-Brown N, 'The Competitive Landscape of Online Platforms' (2017) 4 *JRC Digital Economy Working Paper* 1

Duch-Brown N, Martens B and Mueller-Langer F, 'The Economics of Ownership, Access and Trade in Digital Data' (2017) 1 JRC Digital Economy Working Paper

Economides N, 'The Economics of Networks' (1996) 14 *International Journal of Industrial Organization* 673

Economides N, 'Public Policy in Network Industries' (2006) 06-17 Working Paper Series New York University 469

Economides N and White LJ, 'Networks and Compatibility: Implications for Antitrust' (1994) 38 *European Economic Review* 651

Evans M, 'Google Strikes Deal with Hospital Chain to Develop Healthcare Algorithms' *The Wall Street Journal* (26 May 2021)

Evans PC and Gawer A, 'The Rise of the Platform Enterprise – A Global Survey' (2019) <www.thecge.net/app/uploads/2016/01/PDF-WEB-Platform-Survey_01_12.pdf>

Ezrachi A and Stucke ME, 'Is Your Digital Assistant Devious?' [2016] *SSRN Electronic Journal* 1

Ezrachi A and Stucke ME, *How Big-Tech Barons Smash Innovation – and How to Strike Back* (HarperCollins 2022)

Farrell J and Klemperer P, 'Coordination and Lock-In: Competition with Switching Costs and Network Effects' (2007) 3 *Handbook of Industrial Organization* 1967

Fast V, Schnurr D and Wohlfarth M, 'Regulation of Data-Driven Market Power in the Digital Economy: Business Value Creation and Competitive Advantages from Big Data' (2022) 0 *Journal of Information Technology* 202

Federal Trade Commission, 'The "Sharing" Economy – Issues Facing Platforms, Participants & Regulators' (2016)

Filistrucchi L and others, 'Market Definition in Two-Sided Markets: Theory and Practice' (2014) 10 *Journal of Competition Law and Economics* 293

Filistrucchi L, Geradin D and van Damme EEC, 'Identifying Two-Sided Markets' [2012] *SSRN Electronic Journal* <www.ssrn.com/abstract=2008661> accessed 14 September 2021

Fletcher A and others, 'The Effective Use of Economics in the Digital Markets Act' (2024) 20 *Journal of Competition Law and Economics* 1

Franck J-U and Peitz M, 'Market Definition and Market Power in the Platform Economy' (2019) CERRE Tech, Media, Telecom Report

Franck J-U and Peitz M, 'Digital Platforms and the New 19a Tool in the German Competition Act' (2021) 12 *Journal of European Competition Law & Practice* 16

Fraz S, 'A Journey through Time: The Progression of Search Engines from Altavista to Google' *Medium* (9 August 2023)

Freeman C and Louçã F, *As Time Goes By: From the Industrial Revolutions to the Information Revolution* (Oxford University Press 2001)

Funding Universe, 'Amazon.Com, Inc. History' (Funding Universe) <www.fundinguniverse.com/company-histories/amazon-com-inc-history/>

Fzrachi A and Stucke ME, 'Sustainable and Unchallenged Algorithmic Tacit Collusion' (2019) 17 *Northwestern Journal of Technology and Intellectual Property* 217

Gal MS and Rubinfeld DL, 'The Hidden Costs of Free Goods: Implications for Antitrust Enforcement' (2015) 80 *Antitrust Law Journal* 521

Gambhava H, 'How Much Does Hardware Product Development Cost?' *eFour* (online, 16 September 2022) <www.efour.co/blog/hardware-product-development-cost/>

Gawer A, 'Digital Platforms' Boundaries: The Interplay of Firm Scope, Platform Sides, and Digital Interfaces' (2021) 54 *Long Range Planning* 1

Gawer A and Cusumano M, 'Industry Platforms and Ecosystem Innovation' (2014) 31 *Journal of Product Innovation Management* 418

Gawer A and Cusumano MA, 'How Companies Become Platform Leaders' (2008) 49 *MIT Sloan Management Review* 28

Gawer A and Henderson R, 'Platform Owner Entry and Innovation in Complementary Markets: Evidence from Intel' (2007) 16 *Journal of Economics & Management Strategy* 1

Geradin D, 'What Should EU Competition Policy Do to Address the Concerns Raised by the Digital Platforms' Market Power?' (2018) DP 2018-041 TILEC Discussion Paper

Geradin D, 'What Is a Digital Gatekeeper? Which Platforms Should Be Captured by the EC Proposal for a Digital Market Act?' [2021] *SSRN Electronic Journal* <www.ssrn.com/abstract=3788152> accessed 13 December 2022

Geradin D, 'What Is a Digital Gatekeeper?' (*Platform Law Blog*, 24 February 2021)

Geradin D and Katsifis D, 'Strengthening Effective Antitrust Enforcement in Digital Platform Markets' [2021] *European Competition Journal* 1

Gerbrandy A and Phoa P, 'The Power of Big Tech Corporations as Modern Bigness and a Vocabulary for Shaping Competition Law as Counter-Power' in Huub Brouwer, Michael Bennett and Rutger Claassen (eds), *Wealth and Power* (1st edn, Routledge 2022) <www.taylorfrancis.com/books/9781003173632/chapters/10.4324/9781003173632-11> accessed 16 August 2024

Gilbert B, 'Facebook Blames Apple after a Historically Bad Quarter, Saying iPhone Privacy Changes Will Cost It $10 Billion' *Business Insider* (3 February 2022)

Gilbert RJ, *Innovation Matters: Competition Policy for the High-Technology Economy* (The MIT Press 2020) <https://doi.org/10.7551/mitpress/12686.001.0001> accessed 22 January 2025

Giorgio Monti, 'The Digital Markets Act' (2021) 5 *European Competition and Regulatory Law Review* 90

Graef I, 'Data as Essential Facility Competition and Innovation on Online Platforms' (Katholieke Universiteit Leuven 2016) <http://lib.ugent.be/catalog/rug01:002276080>

Graef I, Husovec M and Purtova N, 'Data Portability and Data Control: Lessons for an Emerging Concept in EU Law' (2018) 19 *German Law Journal* 1359

Graef I and Prüfer J, 'Mandated Data Sharing Is a Necessity in Specific Sectors' 103 *Economisch Statistische Berichten* 298

Graham M and Elias J, 'How Google's $150 Billion Advertising Business Works' *CNBC* (13 October 2021)

Green EJ, Marshall RC and Marx LM, 'Tacit Collusion in Oligopoly' (2014) 2 *The Oxford Handbook of International Antitrust Economics* 464

Greenfield R, 'What the Web Looked Like before Google' *The Atlantic* (27 September 2013)

Greer M, *Electricity Cost Modeling Calculations* (Academic Press/Elsevier 2011)

Griggs B and Leopold T, 'How iTunes Changed Music, and the World' *CNN* (26 April 2013)

Grossman PZ and Cole DH, *The End of a Natural Monopoly: Deregulation and Competition in the Electric Power Industry* (Elsevier 2003)

Gundlach G and Moss DL, 'Systems Competition and Challenges to Antitrust Thinking: An Introduction' (2011) 56 *The Antitrust Bulletin* 1

Hagiu A and Wright J, 'Multi-sided Platforms' (2015) 43 *International Journal of Industrial Organization* 162

Hamilton NW and Caulfield AM, 'The Defense of Natural Monopoly in Sherman Act Monopolization Cases' 33 *De Paul Law Review* 31

Han M, 'Unlockd Will "Cease to Exist" if Google Blocks the App' *Financial Review* (4 June 2018)

Hartung A, 'How Facebook Beat MySpace' *Forbes* (14 January 2011)

Hartung A, 'How Facebook Beat MySpace' *Forbes* (14 February 2011)

Haselton T, 'Departing Windows Chief Terry Myerson Explains Why Microsoft Failed in Smartphones' *CNBC* (29 March 2018)

Hawker NW, 'Automotive Aftermarkets: A Case Study in Systems Competition' (2011) 56 *The Antitrust Bulletin* 57

Heidhues P, Köster M and Kőszegi B, 'A Theory of Digital Ecosystems' [2024] *SSRN Electronic Journal* <www.ssrn.com/abstract=4991830> accessed 13 December 2024

Hein A and others, 'Digital Platform Ecosystems' (2020) 30 *Electronic Markets* 87

Henderson R, 'The Innovator's Dilemma as a Problem of Organizational Competence' (2006) 23 *Journal of Product Innovation Management* 5

Hinck S and Podszun R, 'Beyond DMA: The Amazon Section 19a Case (Germany)' [2024] *Journal of European Competition Law & Practice* lpae066

Ho SY and Lim KH, 'Nudging Moods to Induce Unplanned Purchases in Imperfect Mobile Personalization Contexts' (2018) 42 *MIS Quarterly: Management Information Systems* 757

Holcombe RG, 'Economic Power' in Randall G Holcombe (ed), *Coordination, Cooperation, and Control: The Evolution of Economic and Political Power* (Springer International Publishing 2020) <https://doi.org/10.1007/978-3-030-48667-9_3>

Hornung P, 'The Ecosystem Concept, the DMA, and Section 19a GWB' [2023] *Journal of Antitrust Enforcement* jnad049

Hovenkamp H, 'Antitrust and Platform Monopoly' (2021) 130 *Yale Law Journal* 1952

Hovenkamp H, 'Antitrust Interoperability Remedies' (2022) 2814 *Faculty Scholarship at Penn Carey Law* 1

Hoyng AC and Karkaletsi A, '22. Competitive Dynamics of Digital Ecosystems and Their Implications for Competition Law Enforcement'

Hutter M, 'Information Goods' in Ruth Towse (ed), *A Handbook of Cultural Economics* (Edward Elgar Publishing 2003)

Ibáñez Colomo P, 'The Draft Digital Markets Act: A Legal and Institutional Analysis' (2021) 12 *Journal of European Competition Law & Practice* 561

Ibáñez Colomo P and Kalintiri A, 'The Evolution of EU Antitrust Policy: 1966–2017' (2020) 83 *The Modern Law Review* 321

IBM Cloud Education, 'Application Programming Interface (API)' (2020) <www.ibm.com/cloud/learn/api>

Iqbal M, 'Netflix Revenue and Usage Statistics (2022)' (*Business of Apps*, 27 October 2022)

Ivaldi M and others, 'The Economics of Tacit Collusion: Implications for Merger Control' (2007) 282 *Contributions to Economic Analysis* 217

Jacobides MG, Cennamo C and Gawer A, 'Towards a Theory of Ecosystems' (2018) 39 *Strategic Management Journal* 2255

Jacobides MG and Lianos I, 'Ecosystems and Competition Law in Theory and Practice' (2021) 30 *Industrial and Corporate Change* 1199 <https://doi.org/10.1093/icc/dtab061>

Jenny F, 'Competition Law Enforcement and Regulation for Digital Ecosystems: Understanding the Issues, Facing the Challenges and Moving Forward' (2021) 3 *Concurrences* 38

Joskow P, 'Regulation of Natural Monopoly' in A Mitchell Polinsky and Steven Shavell (eds), *Handbook of Law and Economics*, vol 2 (Elsevier 2007) <https://EconPapers.repec.org/RePEc:eee:lawchp:2-16>

Jullien B, 'Competition in Multi-sided Markets: Divide and Conquer' (2011) 3 *American Economic Journal: Microeconomics* 186

Junqué de Fortuny E, Martens D and Provost F, 'Predictive Modeling with Big Data: Is Bigger Really Better?' (2013) 1 *Big Data* 215

Kamepalli SK, Rajan R and Zingales L, 'Kill Zone' (2020) No. 27146 National Bureau of Economic Research Working Paper Series <www.nber.org/papers/w27146>

Kanter J, 'Keynote Remarks at the Stigler Center's 2022 Antitrust and Competition Conference' (21 April 2022) <www.youtube.com/watch?v=FtDZM30OJvA>

Kaplan KA, 'Facemash Creator Survives Ad Board' *The Harvard Crimson* (19 November 2003)

Kaplow L, 'Market Definition: Impossible and Counterproductive' (2013) 79 *Antitrust Law Journal* 361

Kapoor R, 'Ecosystems: Broadening the Locus of Value Creation' (2018) 7 *Journal of Organization Design* 12

Katz ML and Shapiro C, 'Network Externalities, Competition, and Compatibility' (1985) 75 *The American Economic Review* 424

Katz ML and Shapiro C, 'Systems Competition and Network Effects' (1994) 8 *Journal of Economic Perspectives* 93

Kenney M and Zysman J, 'The Rise of the Platform Economy' (2016) 32 *Issues in Science and Technology* 61

Kesler R, 'The Impact of Apple's App Tracking Transparency on App Monetization' [2022] *SSRN Electronic Journal* <www.ssrn.com/abstract=4090786> accessed 30 August 2024

Khan LM, 'Amazon's Antitrust Paradox' (2017) 126 *The Yale Law Journal* 710

Khan LM, 'The Separation of Platforms and Commerce' (2019) 119 *Columbia Law Review* 126

Krämer J and Schnurr D, 'Big Data and Digital Markets Contestability: Theory of Harm and Data Access Remedies' [2021] *SSRN Electronic Journal* <www.degruyter.com/document/doi/10.1515/9781400879762-024/html> accessed 26 October 2021

Krämer J, Senellart P and de Streel A, 'Making Data-Portability More Effective for the Digital Economy – Economic Implications and Regulatory Challenges' (CERRE 2020) CERRE Project Report

Krisch A and Plank L, 'Internet Platforms as Infrastructures of the Digital Age' (2019) 45 *Der öffentliche Sektor – The Public Sector*

Kubaric O, 'Contours of Contestability: A Comparative Analysis of EU and UK Digital Markets Regulation New EU & UK Rules for Regulating Competition in Digital Markets: A Comparative Perspective' (2024) 10 *North East Law Review* 11

Lancieri F and Sakowski PM, 'Competition in Digital Markets: A Review of Expert Reports' [2020] Working Papers 303, The University of Chicago Booth School of Business, George J. Stigler Center for the Study of the Economy and the State

Laney D, '3D Data Management: Controlling Data Volume, Velocity and Variety' [2001] Meta Group Research Note

Larouche P and de Streel A, 'The European Digital Markets Act: A Revolution Grounded on Traditions' (2021) 12 *Journal of European Competition Law & Practice* 542

Lécuyer T, 'Digital Conglomerates and Killer Acquisitions – A Discussion of the Competitive Effects of Start-Up Acquisitions by Digital Platforms' [2020] Concurrences

Lemley M and Wansley M, 'Coopting Disruption' [2024] 105 *Boston University Law Review* 457

Leong C and others, 'Platform Leadership: Managing Boundaries for the Network Growth of Digital Platforms' (2019) 20 *Journal of the Association for Information Systems* 1531

Leswig K, 'Apple's Ad Privacy Change Impact Shows the Power It Wields over Other Industries' *CNBC* (13 November 2021)

Lianos I and Carballa-Smichowski B, 'A Coat of Many Colours – New Concepts and Metrics of Economic Power in Competition Law and Economics' (2022) 18 *Journal of Competition Law & Economics* 795

Lianos I, Eller KH and Kleinschmitt T, 'Towards a Legal Theory of Digital Ecosystems' (2024) <www.ssrn.com/abstract=4849340> accessed 22 August 2024

Lomas N, 'DuckDuckGo Calls for EU to Widen Its Digital Markets Act Probe of Google' [2024] *TechCrunch*

Macrotrends, 'Amazon Revenue 2010–2022' (2022) <www.macrotrends.net/stocks/charts/AMZN/amazon/revenue> accessed 15 June 2022

Macrotrends, 'Apple Revenue 2010–2022' (*Macrotrends*)

Mandrescu D, 'Tying and Bundling by Online Platforms – Distinguishing between Lawful Expansion Strategies and Anti-competitive Practices' (2021) 40 *Computer Law and Security Review* 1

Marneffe W and Vereeck L, 'The Meaning of Regulatory Costs' (2011) 32 *European Journal of Law and Economics* 341
Marsden P and Podszun R, 'Restoring Balance to Digital Competition – Sensible' (Konrad Adenaufer Stiftung 2020)
Martens B and others, 'Business-to-Business Data Sharing: An Economic and Legal Analysis' 56
Martínez-López FJ and others, 'Behind Influencer Marketing: Key Marketing Decisions and Their Effects on Followers' Responses' (2020) 36 *Journal of Marketing Management* 579
Mazzucato M, Entsminger J and Kattel R, 'Reshaping Platform-Driven Digital Markets' in Martin Moore and Damian Tambini (eds), *Regulating Big Tech* (Oxford University Press 2021)
McGirt E, 'Facebook's Mark Zuckerberg: Hacker. Dropout. CEO' *Fast Company* (1 May 2007)
McIntyre DP and Srinivasan A, 'Networks, Platforms, and Strategy: Emerging Views and Next Steps' (2017) 38 *Strategic Management Journal* 141
Mies YA, Wagner H-T and Vodosek M, 'Understanding the Antecedents of Lock-In, Switching Costs and Network Externalities in the Context of Digital Innovation' in Tomás Bayón and others (eds), *Dynamic Capabilities and Relationships: Discourses, Concepts, and Reflections* (Springer International Publishing 2021)
Montero J and Finger M, *The Rise of the New Network Industries* (Routledge 2021)
Montero JJ and others, 'Digital Platforms – The New Network Industries? How to Regulate Them?' (2019) 21 *Network Industries Quarterly* <http://mir.epfl.ch/>
Monti G, 'The Digital Markets Act – Improving Its Institutional Design' (2021) 5 *European Competition and Regulatory Law Review* 90
Monti G and Bostoen F, 'The Rhyme and Reason of Gatekeeper Designation under the Digital Markets Act' [2024] SSRN
Moore J, 'Predators and Prey: A New Ecology of Competition' (1999) 71 *Harvard Business Review* 75
Moore K, 'Google Advertising Statistics for 2021' *Digital Third Coast* (2022)
Moore M and Tambini D (eds), *Regulating Big Tech: Policy Responses to Digital Dominance* (Oxford University Press 2021)
Mueller CE, 'Computer Software Is a Natural Monopoly – Predatory Pricing and Efficient Scale' (1998) 29 *Antitrust Law & Economics Review* 99
Mueller M, *Universal Service: Competition, Interconnection and Monopoly in the Making of the American Telephone System* (Syracuse University Books 2013)
Murphy H, 'Facebook Confronts Growth Problems as Number of Young Users in US Declines' *Financial Times* (22 October 2021)
Nalebuff B and Brandeburger A, *Co-Opetition* (Profile Publishers 1997)
Newman D, 'Apple, Meta, and the $10 Billion Impact of Privacy Changes' *Forbes* (10 February 2022)
Newman JM and others, 'Antitrust in Digital Markets' (2019) 72 *Vanderbilt Law Review* 1497
Newton C, 'How YouTube Perfected the Feed' *The Verge* (30 August 2017)
Noam EM, 'Overcoming Market Power in Online Video Platforms' in Martin Moore and Damian Tambini (eds), *Regulating Big Tech* (Oxford University Press 2021)
Nooren P and others, 'Should We Regulate Digital Platforms? A New Framework for Evaluating Policy Options: Evaluating Policy Options for Digital Platforms' (2018) 10 *Policy & Internet* 264
Nowag J, 'The UBER-Cartel? UBER between Labour and Competition Law' [2016] *SSRN Electronic Journal* 1
Nowviskie B, 'Eternal September of the Digital Humanities' in Matthew K Gold (ed), *Debates in the Digital Humanities* (University of Minnesota Press 2012) <https://doi.org/10.5749/minnesota/9780816677948.003.0025> accessed 22 August 2024

OECD, 'Big Data: Bringing Competition Policy to the Digital Era' (OECD 2016) Background Note by the Secretariat

OECD, 'Quality Considerations in Digital Zero-Price Markets' (2018) DAF/COMP(2018)14

OECD, 'Data Portability, Interoperability and Digital Platform Competition' (2021)

OECD, 'Ex Ante Regulation and Competition in Digital Markets' (OECD 2021)

OECD, 'Glossary of Industrial Organisation Economics and Competition Law'

Oestreicher-Singer G and Sundararajan A, 'The Visible Hand? Demand Effects of Recommendation Networks in Electronic Markets' (2012) 58 *Management Science* 1963

Pacces AM and Visscher L, 'Methodology of Law and Economics' in Bart van Klink and Sanne Taekema (eds), *Interdisciplinary Research into Law* (Mohr Siebeck 2011)

Pal R and Scrimitore M, 'Tacit Collusion and Market Concentration under Network Effects' (2016) 145 *Economics Letters* 266

Parker BD, 'PSD2 Open Banking: The Challenges of Third-Party Provider Identity and Regulatory Checking', *The PayTech Book* (2019) <https://doi.org/10.1002/9781119551973.ch19> accessed 22 January 2025

Parker G, Petropoulos G and Van Alstyne M, 'Platform Mergers and Antitrust' (2021) 30 *Industrial and Corporate Change* 1307

Parker G, Van Alstyne M and Jiang X, 'Platform Ecosystems: How Developers Invert the Firm' (2017) 41 *MIS Quarterly* 255

Pereira MP and others, 'Standards Wars: Google vs. Altavista' (Aalborg University – Course: Standardization 2015) <www.researchgate.net/publication/277311538>

Perry MK, 'Vertical Integration: Determinants and Effects' (1989) 1 *Handbook of Industrial Organization* 183

Petit N, 'The Proposed Digital Markets Act (DMA): A Legal and Policy Review' (2021) 12 *Journal of European Competition Law & Practice* 529

Petit N and Teece DJ, 'Taking Ecosystems Competition Seriously in the Digital Economy' (OECD 2020)

Petit N and Teece DJ, 'Innovating Big Tech Firms and Competition Policy: Favoring Dynamic over Static Competition' 41

Pizio AD, 'People Think Amazon Is an E-Commerce Company, but 74% of Its Profit Comes from This Instead' [2024] *Motley Fool*

Podszun R, *Digital Markets Act – Article-by-Article Commentary* (Hart-Beck-Nomos 2024)

Podszun R, Bongartz P and Langenstein S, 'Proposals on How to Improve the Digital Markets Act' [2021] Social Science Research Network

Pollitt MG and Steer SJ, 'Economies of Scale and Scope in Network Industries: Lessons for the UK Water and Sewerage Sectors' (2012) 21 *Utilities Policy* 17

Porter J, 'The Rise and Fall of iTunes: Apple's Most Hated App' [2019] *The Verge*

Portuese A, 'The Digital Markets Act: A Triumph of Regulation over Innovation' [2022] *Information Technology* 24

Posner RA, 'Natural Monopoly and Its Regulation' (1969) 21 *Stanford Law Review* 548

Prat A and Valletti TM, 'Attention Oligopoly' (2022) 14 (3) *American Economic Journal: Microeconomics* 530–557.

Pruden R, 'How Facebook Used White Space to Crush Myspace' *TechDirt* (19 January 2011)

Prüfer J and Graef I, 'Governance of Data Sharing: A Law & Economics Proposal' (2021) 2021-004 CentER, Center for Economic Research Working Paper 24

Prüfer J and Schottmüller C, 'Competing with Big Data' (Tilburg University, Tilburg Law and Economic Center 2017)

Prüfer J and Schottmüller C, 'Competing with Big Data' (2021) 69 *The Journal of Industrial Economics* 967

Rahman-Jones I and Gerken T, 'Threads: Meta's Rival to Elon Musk's X Launches in EU' [2023] *BBC*

Rietveld J and Schilling MA, 'Platform Competition: A Systematic and Interdisciplinary Review of the Literature' (2021) 47 *Journal of Management* 1528

Rietveld J, Schilling MA and Bellavitis C, 'Platform Strategy: Managing Ecosystem Value through Selective Promotion of Complements' (2019) 30 *Organization Science* 1232

Riley C, 'Unpacking Interoperability in Competition' (2020) 5 *Journal of Cyber Policy* 94

Rochet J-C and Tirole J, 'Platform Competition in Two-Sided Markets' (2003) 1 *Journal of the European Economic Association* 990

Rochet J-C and Tirole J, 'Two-Sided Markets: A Progress Report' (2006) 37 *The RAND Journal of Economics* 645

Rubinfeld D and Gal M, 'Access Barriers to Big Data' (2016) 59 *Arizona Law Review* 339

Sadiq H, 'Microsoft's Strategic Stake in OpenAI Unlocks Unique Investment Avenues' [2024] *Yahoo Finance*

Schmoll N, 'What Is the Difference between a Regular Phone Line & a DSL Line?' *It Still Works* (29 August 2017)

Schumpeter JA, *Capitalism, Socialism, and Democracy*, vol 37 (Harper and Brothers 1942)

Schweitzer H, 'Digitale Plattformen als private Gesetzgeber: Ein Perspektivwechsel für die europäische "Plattform-Regulierung"' [2019] *ZEuP*

Schweitzer H, 'The Art to Make Gatekeeper Positions Contestable and the Challenge to Know What Is Fair: A Discussion of the Digital Markets Act Proposal' (2021) 3 *ZEuP* 35

Scott Morton FM and others, 'Designing Regulation for Digital Platforms: Why Economists Need to Work on Business Models' *VoxEU* (4 June 2020)

Scott Morton FM. and van den Boom J, Are Competition Authorities Equipped to Combat Entrenched Digital Monopolies? – Lessons from the US and EU Antitrust Cases against Google, (2025) *Illinois Journal of Law, Technology, and Policy*

Scott Morton FM and others, 'Equitable Interoperability: The "Super Tool" of Digital Platform Governance' (2021) 4 Digital Regulation Project, Policy Discussion Paper 1

Secretary of State for Digital, Culture, Media and Sport and Secretary of State for Business, Energy and Industrial Strategy, *A New Pro-Competition Regime for Digital Markets* (Great Britain 2021)

Shaik A, 'The Walt Disney Company – A Conglomerate beyond Mickey Mouse And Marvel Studios' [2020] *Brand Hopper*

Shao S, 'Antitrust in the Consumer Platform Economy: How Apple Has Abused Its Mobile Platform Dominance' (2021) 36 *Berkeley Technology Law Journal* 355

Shapiro C, 'Protecting Competition in the American Economy: Merger Control, Tech Titans, Labor Markets' (2019) 33 *Journal of Economic Perspectives* 69

Shapiro C and Teece DJ, 'Systems Competition and Aftermarkets: An Economic Analysis of Kodak' (1994) 39 *The Antitrust Bulletin* 135

Sharkey WW, *The Theory of Natural Monopoly* (Cambridge University Press 1982)

Sharpe N and Olufunmilayo A, 'Is Apple Playing Fair? Navigating the iPod FairPlay DRM Controversy' (2007) 5 *Northwestern Journal of Technology and Intellectual Property* 332

Shipilov A and Gawer A, 'Integrating Research on Interorganizational Networks and Ecosystems' (2020) 14 *Academy of Management Annals* 92

Shy O, *The Economics of Network Industries* (Cambridge University Press 2004)

Sidak JG and Teece DJ, 'Dynamic Competition in Antitrust Law' (2009) 5 *Journal of Competition Law & Economics* 581

Silver S, 'August 6, 1997 – The Day Apple and Microsoft Made Peace' (*Apple Insider*, 6 August 2018)

Sinn H-W, 'The Subsidiarity Principle and Market Failures in Systems Competition' (1996) 5411 NBER Working Paper Series

Sinn H-W, 'The Selection Principle and Market Failure in Systems Competition' (1997) 66 *Journal of Public Economics* 247

Statista, 'Annual Revenue of Google from 2002 to 2021' (*Statista*) <www.statista.com/statistics/266206/googles-annual-global-revenue/> accessed 15 January 2022

Statista, 'Microsoft's Annual Revenue Worldwide from FY 2002 to FY 2022' (*Statista*) <www.statista.com/statistics/267805/microsofts-global-revenue-since-2002/>

Statista, 'Microsoft's Net Income from 2002 to 2022' (*Statista*) <www.statista.com/statistics/267808/net-income-of-microsoft-since-2002/> accessed 16 January 2022

Streitfeld D, 'Court Rejects Deal on Silicon Valley Hiring' *The New York Times* (4 June 2018)

Streitfeld D, 'Google's Profits Soar as Revenue Rises 62 Percent' *New York Times* (29 July 2021)

Stucke ME and Ezrachi A, 'How Digital Assistants Can Harm Our Economy, Privacy, and Democracy' (2017) 32 *Berkeley Technology Law Journal* 1239

Stylianou K, 'Exclusion in Digital Markets' (2018) 24 *Michigan Technology Law Review* 181

Subcommittee on Antitrust C and AL of the C on the J, 'House Investigation of Competition in Digital Markets' (2020)

Sverdlik Y, 'Google: From 112 Servers to a $5B-Plus Quarterly Data Center Bill' *Datacenter Knowledge* (23 July 2014)

Tadao Kawamoto C and Giovinazzo Spers R, 'A Systematic Review of the Debate and the Researchers of Disruptive Innovation' (2019) 14 *Journal of technology management & innovation* 73

Teel J, '9 Costs That Factor into Mass Manufacturing a Hardware Product' (2017) <https://makezine.com/article/digital-fabrication/3d-printing-workshop/cost-manufacture-new-electronic-hardware-product/>

Telser LG, *Competition, Collusion, and Game Theory* (Routledge 2017)

'Testimony before the Subcommittee on Antitrust, Commercial, and Administrative Law' (28 July 2020) Statement by Jeff Bezos to the U.S. House Committee on the Judiciary

Thompson B, 'Apple's Middle Age' (*Stratechery*, 5 February 2018) <https://stratechery.com/2018/apples-middle-age/>

Tiwana A, *Platform Ecosystems: Aligning Architecture, Governance, and Strategy* (Morgan Kaufmann 2013)

Tiwana A, 'Evolutionary Competition in Platform Ecosystems' (2015) 26 *Information Systems Research* 150424094525000

Trusov M, Ma L and Jamal Z, 'Crumbs of the Cookie: User Profiling in Customer-Base Analysis and Behavioral Targeting' (2016) 35 *Marketing Science* 405

Tucker C, 'Network Effects and Market Power: What Have We Learned in the Last Decade?' [2018] Antitrust 72

UNCTAD, 'Value Creation and Capture: Implications for Developing Countries' (United Nations Conference on Trade and Development 2019)

University of Antwerp and others, 'Mining Massive Fine-Grained Behavior Data to Improve Predictive Analytics' (2016) 40 *MIS Quarterly* 869

Van Alstyne M and others, '"In Situ" Data Rights' (OpenBU 2021) Communications to the Autoriteit Consument en Markt

van den Boom J, 'What Does the Digital Markets Act Harmonize? – Exploring Interactions between the DMA and National Competition Laws' (2023) 19 *European Competition Journal* 57

van den Boom J, 'Incumbent or Challenger? – Assessing Ecosystem Competition in the DMA' (2024) 20 *Journal of Competition Law & Economics* 409

Van den Boom J and others, 'Digital Regulation Synthesis: Comparative Analysis of the DMA, Sec. 19a and the DMCCA' (2024) (1) SCiDA Discussion Paper, SSRN

Van den Boom J and Hinck S, 'ByteDance v. Commission – The EU General Court Has Set First Bars for Gatekeeper Designation Decisions under the Digital Markets Act' (*Verfassungsblog*, 2024)

Van den Boom J and Hinck S, 'A Week of Compliance Workshops' (*SCiDA Blog*, March 2024)

Van den Boom J and Hinck S, 'Compliance Time! Categorizing Risks of Compliance Failures in the DMA' (*SCiDA Blog*, March 2024)

Van den Boom J and Hornung P, 'Ecosystems in the DMA – Bridging the Gap between Legal Text and Economic Reality' [2025] *Journal of European Competition Law & Practice*

Van den Boom J and Samranchit P, 'Digital Ecosystem Mergers in Big Tech – A Theory of Long-Run Harm with Applications' [2021] *Journal of European Competition Law & Practice* 1

Van den Boom, J and Scott Morton, FM, Recalibrating Regulation 1/2003: How to Restore Proportionality in EU Remedy Design (March 22, 2025). Available at SSRN: https://ssrn.com/abstract=5189659 or http://dx.doi.org/10.2139/ssrn.5189659

Van der Brande T, 'Rules-Based versus Principles-Based Regulation – Is There a Clear Front-Runner?' (*Ofcom News Centre*, 3 August 2021) <www.ofcom.org.uk/news-centre/2021/rules-versus-principles-based-regulation>

van Dijck J, Nieborg D and Poell T, 'Reframing Platform Power' (2019) 8 *Internet Policy Review* 1

Van Eijk N and others, 'Digital Platforms: An Analytical Framework for Identifying and Evaluating Policy Options' (TNO 2015) <www.tno.nl>

Varian H, *Microeconomic Analysis* (3rd ed., Norton 1992)

Varian HR, 'Markets for Information Goods' 19

Vena D, 'Apple Leads the Pack in Survey of Brands Customers Love Most' *Nasdaq* (7 October 2020)

Wagner G and others, 'Taming the Giants: The DMA/DSA Package' (2021) 58 *Common Market Law Review* 987

Wakabayashi D and Hsu T, 'Behind a Secret Deal between Google and Facebook' *The New York Times* (17 January 2021)

Wang G and Unger J, 'A Strategy to Move Taiwan's IT Industry from Commodity Hardware Manufacturing to Competitive Cloud Solutions' (2013) 1 *IEEE Access* 159

Wen W and Zhu F, 'Threat of Platform-Owner Entry and Complementor Responses: Evidence from the Mobile App Market' (2019) 40 *Strategic Management Journal* 1336

Whish R and Bailey D, *Competition Law* (11th edn, Oxford University Press 2024)

Wilson J, 'How Amazon Video's ECommerce Approach Is Giving Them An Edge in the Streaming Industry' *Forbes* (29 August 2022)

Wright J, 'One-Sided Logic in Two-Sided Markets' (2004) 3 *Review of Network Economics* 42

Wu T, *The Master Switch: The Rise and Fall of Information Empires* (Alfred A Knopf 2011)

Zhang X-Z, Liu J-J and Xu Z-W, 'Tencent and Facebook Data Validate Metcalfe's Law' (2015) 30 *Journal of Computer Science and Technology* 246

Zhu F and Liu Q, 'Competing with Complementors: An Empirical Look at Amazon.Com' (2018) 39 *Strategic Management Journal* 2618

Zingales L and others, 'Stigler Committee on Digital Platforms – Final Report' (Stigler Center 2019)

Zubanoff S, *Surveillance Capitalism* (Profile Books 2019)

Index

19a GWB, 4, 24, 183, 185, 205–213, 227, 229, 231, 236–237, 256

abundance, 27
access rules, 33
access to the resources, 214, 223–224
acquisitions, 109, 124, 129, 131, 146, 150, 154, 159, 173, 177–178, 182, 205, 216, 228, 252, 254, 257, 264
ad-centric, 23, 98–99
advertisements, 22–23, 46, 73, 75, 122
advertisers, 22–23, 27, 40, 42, 44–45, 57, 60, 99, 116, 118, 126, 132, 156, 189
aftermarkets, 35, 51, 61, 66, 127, 169
aggregation, 27
algorithm, 70–71, 73, 77, 93, 103, 118, 139, 172
Alphabet, 21, 27, 34–36, 40, 42, 52, 64, 65, 108, 117, 122, 156, 163, 166, 169, 176–178, 186, 193–196, 203, 206, 208, 217
Amazon, 21, 27, 36, 40, 46, 52, 71, 73, 79, 97–98, 117–118, 121–123, 138, 140, 143–145, 149–154, 157–158, 162–163, 169, 173–174, 177–178, 186, 193, 203, 206, 208–211, 226, 228, 233
Android, 27, 34, 37, 46, 91, 107, 116–118, 122, 127, 128, 145, 148–149, 152, 154, 166, 170–172, 193–194, 246, 250
anti-circumvention, 188, 250, 252
anti-steering, 188
API, 19
app stores, 62, 64, 132, 166, 194–195, 225
Apple, 21, 26, 34–38, 46, 49, 52, 61, 64–66, 98, 107, 116–118, 122, 127, 132–134, 137–138, 141–143, 145–150, 152–154, 157, 162–164, 166, 169, 172–173, 175–179, 186–187, 190, 193–197, 199, 203, 206, 208–209, 211, 225, 228, 233, 246, 250
applications. *See* apps
apps, 19, 27, 31–32, 44, 61, 71, 97, 101, 118, 122, 147–148, 153–154, 169, 175, 194–195, 198, 208, 245, 251
architecture, 30–32, 35, 257
artificial intelligence, 21, 116, 173, 199, 204
auctions, 34

barriers to entry, 3, 92, 94, 128, 177, 192, 219, 221, 229, 247, 254
Big Data, 25, 29, 57, 68–70, 72, 74, 76–77, 81, 239
BKA, 206–213
Bundeskartellamt, 206, 208–210
business users, xiii, 2, 27, 34, 82, 92, 96, 109, 116, 119, 125, 151–152, 158, 168–169, 175–176, 181, 186, 188–189, 191–192, 194, 196–199, 217, 227, 229, 234, 239, 242, 260
buyers, 22–23, 60, 99, 125, 167
ByteDance, 37, 128, 186, 195, 197–198

case-by-case investigations, 207
chicken-and-egg problem, 3, 23, 28, 34, 42, 58, 93, 101, 120, 125, 136, 168, 225
CMA, 75, 155–156, 162, 185, 199–206
command-and-control, 32–33
commerce ecosystem, 153
Commission, 2–4, 27, 36–37, 65–66, 68, 75, 91, 93, 98, 100, 107, 118, 123, 127–128, 132, 142, 148–149, 156, 166–167, 169–170, 172, 174–176, 185, 187–192, 195–200, 203, 230–232, 236, 242, 249–250, 255
communications ecosystem, 153
community, 17–19, 67, 140, 144
competition between systems, 48, 50–51, 81, 115
competition law, 2–5, 8, 10, 83, 107, 124–125, 127, 166–168, 174, 183, 185, 192, 196–197, 203, 206–207, 210–214, 219, 229–230, 236–237, 244, 250, 252, 256, 267
competition law-based, 185, 206, 214
competition policy, 66, 210, 213, 215–216, 225, 257, 267
competition rules, 34, 236
competitive threat, xiv, 180
complementarity, 60, 62, 102

complementors, 19, 24–25, 33–34, 36, 39, 49–50, 72, 75, 115–121, 125–126, 129–134, 136–137, 141, 144–145, 148, 151, 168–169, 181, 246–249
compliance, 186, 189–197, 201, 204, 217, 229, 239, 246, 251
compliance workshops, 194
component sharing, 18–19
conduct requirements, 200–205, 230
congestion, 20, 56, 97
constant returns to scale. *See* economies of scale
content, 2, 18, 20, 23, 27, 29–30, 33–34, 41–42, 44–45, 51, 68, 73, 75–77, 95, 99–101, 121, 126, 141–142, 150, 164, 200, 232, 256
contestability, 74, 91, 108–109, 175, 186, 189, 191–192, 195, 198–199, 201, 204, 219, 221–222, 229, 248
coopetition, 24, 39, 117, 160, 163, 165, 179
coordination, 26, 28–31, 39, 48–49, 51, 56, 61, 66, 69, 71, 80–81, 97–98, 164, 261
coordination costs, 28–29, 31, 61, 67, 98
co-products, 60, 76, 89, 102
cost-saving efficiencies, 69, 73, 78–79, 96, 102, 164
countervailing benefits, 202
cross-platform expansion, 40–42, 47, 105–106, 144, 261

data, xiii–xiv, 2–4, 10–11, 15, 19, 21–22, 25, 28, 37–39, 41, 46–48, 50, 53, 58, 67–73, 75–80, 82, 84, 93–94, 96–104, 106–107, 109–111, 115–116, 119, 122, 129, 132–134, 137–141, 146, 148–149, 152, 154, 156, 170, 174, 177–178, 181–182, 187–188, 192, 194, 196, 198, 201, 207, 209, 215, 217–218, 224, 227, 229, 231, 234, 238–244, 249, 256–258, 260–262, 265
data dependency, 98, 100, 146
data portability, 188, 198, 207, 241–243
data-driven efficiencies, 67, 69, 71, 73, 80, 84, 101, 110, 260–261
data-driven network externalities, 58, 69, 80, 95–96, 100, 107, 110
datasets, 42, 68–71, 74, 77–79, 238–239
data-sharing, 73, 209, 217, 238–241, 243–244, 258
de facto regulator, xiii, 5, 25, 33, 51, 108, 134
decentralized, 28–30, 69
decreasing returns to scale. *See* economies of scale
Department of Justice, 107, 177, 179, 197, 215
developers, 19, 26, 27, 31–32, 34, 46, 118, 122, 126, 145, 148, 152, 169, 171, 194, 245
differentiation, 100, 115, 121–124, 146, 152, 154, 217, 255
digital business models, 3, 11, 19, 53, 68
Digital Markets, Competition, and Consumers Act, 2, 4, 199
digital network industry, xiii–xiv, 5, 7, 9–11, 13, 51, 53–54, 62, 65, 81–82, 108, 111, 115, 130, 134–137, 143, 158, 164–165, 174, 178, 180–182, 214–216, 218–219, 221–222, 224, 226, 233–234, 237, 259–262, 264–267
digital platforms, 2–4, 7–8, 13, 15, 22, 24–31, 34–35, 39–40, 43, 46, 49–51, 70–71, 75, 80, 83, 85, 91–97, 99, 102, 106–111, 123, 128, 136, 167, 182, 196, 234, 244, 250, 255, 260–262
direct competition, 116
direct network externalities, 56–57
direct subsidies, 254, 257
discovery, 34, 236
display advertising, 45, 70, 75, 104, 116, 141, 150, 153, 155
disruptive, 5, 7, 41, 113, 130–131, 137, 139, 141–142, 158–161, 164–165, 171, 173, 175–182, 199, 214–220, 222, 224, 227, 235–236, 238, 245, 254, 257, 259, 264–265, 267
disruptive innovation, 139, 160–161, 177, 180–182, 215–216, 220, 236, 254, 264
disruptors, 159, 161, 178, 181, 223, 225, 255
Digital Markets Act (DMA), 2, 4, 8, 24, 36, 64–66, 91, 127–128, 166, 168–169, 175, 183, 185–201, 203–208, 211–213, 216–217, 221, 225, 227–229, 231–234, 236–237, 239, 241–242, 246, 248–250, 252, 256
DMCCA, 4, 183, 185, 199–206, 211, 216, 221, 227, 229–231, 237, 252, 256
dynamic competition, 8, 81, 148, 183, 252, 262, 267

economies of scale, 58
economies of scope, 46, 60–61, 76, 90–91
ecosystem, xiii–xiv, 5, 7, 9, 11, 24–25, 27, 29, 31–32, 35–42, 47, 49–52, 54, 61, 64–66, 81–85, 91, 94, 99, 104–105, 108–109, 111, 113, 115–125, 127–136, 139–142, 144–154, 156–160, 162, 164–167, 169–171, 173–183, 185, 193–194, 196–199, 203–207, 209–219, 221–257, 259, 261–267
ecosystem linkages, 39, 47–48, 50, 105, 111, 116–117, 130, 132, 151, 154, 164
ecosystem power, xiv, 7, 113, 115, 124, 127, 129–132, 134, 158, 162, 164–167, 169–171, 174–175, 180–182, 185, 211–214, 218, 221–222, 233, 252, 259, 263
ecosystems, xiii–xiv, 3, 5, 7–9, 11, 13, 15, 27, 35–40, 42, 44–45, 47–54, 62–65, 81–84, 91, 98–99, 105–111, 113, 115–116, 118, 120, 122–126, 128–137, 144–146, 150–155, 157, 160, 162–165, 167, 173, 176, 178–183, 185–186, 189, 196–198, 206–207, 209–210, 214, 216–219, 221–223, 225, 227–228, 230, 233–234, 236, 238–239, 243, 247, 249–250, 252–254, 257–259, 261–266
end users, 34

entrant pool, 214, 223–225, 230–231, 233–236, 248, 250, 252, 257, 265
entrants, 3, 7, 83–84, 108–111, 118, 130, 137, 146, 150, 159, 164–165, 174, 177–178, 181, 183, 192, 206, 215–216, 218–220, 222–225, 229–235, 237–241, 243, 245–248, 250, 253–258, 264–267
entrenched, 37, 82, 107, 124, 126, 144, 156, 168, 176, 182, 186, 226–227, 229, 236
entrenchment harms, 174
ex-ante rules, 185
exhaustive, 4, 16, 20, 50, 72, 77, 186, 207, 237

Facebook, 23, 26–27, 36, 41, 48, 52, 67, 75, 78, 80, 92, 96, 100, 116, 118, 133, 136–138, 140–141, 145, 148–150, 152–153, 155–157, 162, 163, 177, 193, 209, 222, 228, 242, 250. *See also* Meta
fair dealing, 200, 203
fair treatment, 200, 203, 209
fairness, 2, 186, 189, 191–192, 195, 221
feedback loop, 79–80, 95–102, 106, 121, 262
final offer mechanism, 202, 205
fines, 191
fixed costs, 59, 73, 86–89, 92–94, 96, 102, 107, 110, 261–262
foreclosure, 109, 128, 130, 170, 174, 176, 178, 180, 182, 212, 250, 266
forward looking analysis, 200
FRAND, 188–189, 224, 239–240, 256
Freemium, 17, 24
full protocol interoperability, 245
future-proofing, 236

gatekeeper power, 133, 166, 169–170
gatekeepers, 4, 7–8, 33, 115, 120, 124–125, 129, 131–132, 134, 151, 158, 160, 164–171, 173–174, 178–179, 181–182, 185–199, 203, 207, 218, 221, 224, 229, 231, 233–234, 236–237, 239, 242, 248, 250–251, 259, 263–264, 266
gatekeeping, 31, 196, 246. *See also* gatekeepers
gateway, 22–23, 84, 92, 105, 158, 168–169, 175, 181, 186, 198–199
General Court, 91, 128, 187, 195, 197–198
General Data Protection Regulation, 2, 242
Generative AI, 199
German Federal Court, 210
giveaways, 17, 20–21, 27
Google, 3, 23, 26–27, 30, 34, 36–37, 45–47, 65, 75, 77, 79, 85, 91–93, 102, 104–105, 107–108, 116, 118, 121–122, 127–128, 132, 134, 137–141, 145, 148–150, 152–157, 162–163, 166, 168–174, 176, 178–180, 193–197, 208–209, 217, 222, 225, 228, 233, 246, 249–250
Google Android, 128, 145, 148, 194
Google/Fitbit, 127, 174, 250
hardware, 20–21, 48–50, 52–53, 59, 66, 72, 93, 98, 141, 143, 148, 158, 190
heavily regulated, 26, 183, 214, 222–234, 236–237, 240, 243, 247–248, 252, 254, 257–258, 265, 267
heterogeneous, 39, 42, 68, 97, 100–101, 149
High Level Group's, 199
homogeneous, 76, 97, 100–101, 110, 217, 261
horizontal interoperability, 245, 248, 257
horizontal search, 38, 45, 93, 101–105, 117, 132, 137–139, 141, 149, 155, 172, 194–195, 209, 261

incipient markets, 176, 180–181, 252, 264
increasing returns to scale. *See* economies of scale
incumbent, xiv, 5, 24, 41, 66, 75, 84, 92, 94–95, 101, 105, 108–110, 113, 130, 132–134, 137, 139–140, 144–146, 151, 158–167, 169, 172–174, 176–177, 179–182, 192, 196, 198, 202–203, 206, 212, 215–216, 218–223, 225, 227, 230, 232–233, 234, 236–239, 242, 244–247, 250, 252–254, 261–262, 264–265
indirect competition, 81, 108, 116–117, 142, 147–148
indirect network externalities, 56–57, 79, 95, 110, 261
industry-wide foreclosure, 176
information goods, 15–17, 20, 30, 53, 72, 260
infrastructures, xiii–xiv, 20, 23, 25, 27, 29, 42, 46, 51–53, 55, 59, 61–62, 69, 72–73, 79, 81, 83–84, 86–91, 94, 102, 107–110, 118, 120, 131, 137, 151, 199, 214–216, 221, 223–224, 226, 230–231, 233, 243, 245, 248–250, 257, 261–262, 265–266
innovation, xiv, 1, 4, 6–8, 19, 39, 47, 48, 107, 109, 113, 122, 124, 131, 134–135, 139, 141, 158, 160–164, 171, 173–175, 177–178, 180–183, 215–217, 219–220, 222, 227–228, 232, 236, 238, 240, 249, 254–255, 257–258, 264–265, 267
innovation harms, 180, 182
inter-ecosystem competition, 116, 118, 120–121, 129, 131–132, 134–136, 141, 151, 158, 164–165, 176, 218, 222, 225, 266
interim orders, 202
intermediary, xiii, 22–23, 25–26, 29, 51, 57, 95–96, 100, 119, 125, 188, 229, 260, 262
intermediate, 24, 43, 95, 99, 229
interoperability, 63, 65–66, 175, 188–190, 241, 243–244, 257
intra-ecosystem competition, 118
investigatory powers, 202, 204
iOS, 26–27, 34, 38, 46, 107, 117–118, 122, 148, 152, 163, 166, 193, 195, 246
iRobot, 174

Large Language Models, 199
leverage, xiii–xiv, 3, 7, 39, 49, 51, 58, 64, 84, 117, 124, 127, 129–134, 137–138, 144, 147, 162, 171, 174–176, 178, 180, 182, 188, 212, 252, 263–264

lightly regulated, 183, 223–232, 233–237, 239–240, 242–244, 247–248, 250, 252–253, 256–258, 265, 267
line of business restrictions, 252
Linux, 26, 33
living instrument, 210
lock-in, 66
long tail, 30, 60, 71, 74

marginal costs, 6, 17, 27, 50, 59, 72–73, 77, 86–88, 90, 92, 94, 97–98, 107
market, xiii–xiv, 1, 3, 5–8, 10–11, 17, 21–23, 25–27, 29, 32, 34, 36–37, 41–51, 57–58, 60–61, 64–65, 70, 75, 77–78, 80, 82–95, 98–99, 101–104, 106–107, 109–111, 115–116, 118–120, 122, 124–125, 127–134, 136–150, 153–182, 185–189, 191, 195, 197–200, 203–208, 210, 212, 215–218, 220–223, 225–229, 231–235, 238–239, 241, 248, 252, 254, 259–266
mergers, 100, 127, 188, 201, 205, 252, 257–258
Meta, 21, 26–27, 35, 41, 48, 52, 68, 80, 116–118, 122–123, 154, 166, 173, 178–179, 186, 193–195, 197, 206, 208–209, 211, 228, 233, 253
Microsoft, 21, 26, 36, 49, 64, 92–93, 98, 100, 116–117, 122–123, 137–138, 141–142, 145–150, 152–154, 157, 162–164, 170–171, 173, 177–179, 186–187, 193, 198, 206, 208, 210–211, 226, 228, 233, 242, 246, 249–251
middleware, 142, 170–171, 179, 246
mimicking, 160, 162, 165, 246, 249
mobile ecosystems, 133, 162
modular, 18, 20, 40, 50, 78, 104–105, 111, 121, 218, 260–261
modularity, 3, 18–19, 30, 61, 104, 111, 118, 166
monopoly, 3, 5–8, 10, 13, 45–46, 63–64, 80, 83, 85–92, 94, 96, 100–101, 106–107, 109–111, 124–125, 131–132, 136, 138, 140, 144, 147–149, 155–156, 158, 164–165, 172, 174, 179, 182, 215, 217–221, 223, 228, 258–264, 266
multi-actor ecosystem, 24–25, 29, 31, 36–37, 39, 42, 46, 51, 94, 115, 119–121, 125, 133–134, 147–148, 159, 189, 218, 227, 234, 246, 260–261
multi-home, 67, 131–132, 242, 245, 248
multi-output perspective, 7, 89, 91, 102, 261
multi-product ecosystem, 36–39, 48, 105, 111, 116, 120, 128–129, 142–143, 145, 150–151, 155, 165, 227, 265
multi-sided, 22, 24–25, 32, 44, 56, 99, 102, 167, 260
'must have', 125–126

nascent competition, 81
natural monopoly, 6, 10, 13, 83, 85–90, 92, 97, 101, 106–107, 131–132, 140, 217, 221, 261–262, 266–267
networks, xiii–xiv, 2–3, 5–11, 13, 16–17, 19, 22–23, 26–28, 30, 37, 39–40, 44, 49, 51–67, 69, 73–74, 79–88, 90–101, 107–111, 113, 115–116, 121, 124, 126–128, 130, 134–137, 139, 141–143, 149, 151, 158, 162, 164–166, 168, 174, 177–182, 186–187, 189, 192, 197, 207, 214–219, 221–224, 226, 230, 232–234, 237, 242, 244–245, 247–249, 252, 258–262, 264–267
network effects. *See* network externalities
network externalities, 55
non-digital goods, 15, 20, 50, 260
non-structural market power. *See* ecosystem power

OEMs, 27, 145, 148, 152, 171–172
online intermediation service, 193
on-platform expansion, 105
open choice, 200, 203
Operating Systems, 19, 21, 26, 37, 44, 46, 48, 52, 54, 58, 64–65, 107, 116–118, 141, 145, 147–149, 169–170, 172–173, 175–176, 189, 193–194, 198, 245, 250
orchestration, 30–32, 35

paramount significance, 185, 206–211
pay-or-consent, 194–195
peak loads, 56
personalization, 3, 68, 73
platform operator, 3, 19, 24–25, 28–29, 31, 33–36, 39–42, 51, 57–58, 95–96, 108–109, 115, 118–121, 125–126, 133–134, 136–137, 144–145, 167–170, 181, 186, 226, 246, 260, 262, 266
platforms, xiii, 2, 8, 15, 19, 22–26, 28–32, 34–35, 37–44, 46–48, 51–53, 61, 72, 75, 80–84, 91, 94–97, 99–101, 106–111, 115, 117, 120, 122, 124–126, 128–129, 134–137, 143–146, 152–153, 155–156, 158, 160, 162, 164–165, 168–169, 180, 186, 190, 193, 196, 199, 203, 207, 214, 217, 221–222, 227, 233–234, 242, 245–247, 256, 261
positive obligations, 192, 224, 249–251
pre-empting, 181
principles-based, 183, 185, 199, 212, 214, 230–231, 234, 267
private litigation, 251
procedural obligation, 191
pro-competition interventions, 201–202, 212
profiling, 74, 188
progressive ecosystem regulation, xiv, 11, 183, 185, 214–217, 219, 222, 224–226, 230–232, 234, 237–238, 240–241, 243, 246–252, 254, 256–257, 265, 267
public goods, 16

quality improvements, 3, 71, 73–74, 80, 98, 107

reasonable terms, 200
recommendations, 11, 41, 71, 73–75, 78, 100, 104, 143, 201–202
regulatory short-cut, 250
remedies, 4, 9, 61, 191, 196–197, 201, 204–208, 211, 244
rivalrous, 16, 20, 50, 72, 77
rules-based, 183, 185, 196, 212, 214, 224–225, 228–229, 233–234, 267

safe haven, 224, 234–235
sanctions, 190–191, 202, 256
scale, 26–30, 37, 50–52, 54, 56, 58–59, 67–69, 71–73, 79–80, 83–84, 86–92, 94, 96, 98, 101–102, 107–108, 110–111, 137–139, 142–144, 155, 158, 180–181, 187, 192, 200, 207, 212, 229, 238–239, 246–247, 252, 260–262, 267
scarcity, 15–16, 125
SDKs, 31
self-executing, 187, 190, 194, 225, 229
self-preferencing, 4, 170, 181, 198, 207, 209, 228, 249–250
sellers, 22–23, 27, 31, 60, 143–144, 167
serial acquisitions, 177, 252, 254, 257
services, xiii–xiv, 3–5, 11, 15–16, 19, 21–24, 26–33, 35–36, 38–47, 49, 51–55, 57–59, 61–62, 64–65, 67–69, 71, 73, 75–79, 81, 83–85, 89–111, 116–123, 125–126, 128–131, 134, 136–139, 144, 146, 149–154, 158, 160–162, 165–166, 168–171, 173–176, 179–180, 185–189, 191, 193–200, 204, 207–209, 211, 218–219, 226, 229, 231–235, 237–240, 242, 244–248, 260–261
shared inputs, 38, 60, 102
SMS designation, 201
softening of competition, 178
software, 15–16, 19–21, 24, 26–27, 31, 33–34, 46, 49–50, 53, 59, 61, 64, 66, 68, 73, 82, 92, 98, 101, 105, 122–123, 126, 138–139, 142–143, 146, 149, 153, 157, 171, 173, 190, 194, 198, 217, 251, 261
stable core, 19, 42, 46, 50, 61, 83, 105, 120
stage 1, 136–137, 144, 146, 164–165, 199, 214, 218, 222, 234, 252
stage 2, 146, 164, 214, 253
stage 3, 146, 151–152, 164–165, 214, 218, 222, 227, 230, 232, 265
stage 4, 113, 152, 159–160, 164–165, 206, 214, 218, 222, 226–227, 250, 253, 264–265
standard, 63, 67, 81, 84–85, 97, 116, 135, 244, 245, 247
start-up, 178
static interoperability, 244
strategic market status', 200
sunk costs, 3, 16, 59, 72, 77, 88–89, 92, 94, 107–108, 130, 137
super intermediary, 25
sustained innovation, 161, 220–221
switching costs, 66

tailor-made, 185, 201, 206, 212, 214, 224, 230, 234, 237, 253
targeted advertising, 71, 73, 75–77, 80, 102, 104, 137, 139–140
technical interoperability, 244–245, 247–248
theories of harm, 109, 166–167
third-party, 19, 24, 29, 31–32, 42, 51, 75, 143–144, 148–149, 163, 173, 189, 194, 208, 245–246, 249, 251
TikTok, 40, 117, 193, 195, 233
transaction platform, 23, 44
transactions, 16
transparency, 122, 188–189
trust and transparency, 200, 203
turnover condition, 200
tying and bundling, 130, 249–250

Uber, 30, 71, 74, 98, 118, 121, 126, 140
undertaking, 3, 7, 17, 19, 22, 27, 29, 36, 39, 48–49, 53, 58, 63–64, 66, 69, 73–74, 77–79, 89, 91–92, 94, 96, 98, 100, 127, 130, 140–141, 178, 187, 190, 192, 197, 200–201, 207–208, 234, 238, 241, 243, 252–253, 255, 260–261
user-generated content, 30, 95

vertical ecosystem competition, 115, 119
vertical integration, 29–30, 36, 51, 61, 72, 115, 119, 121, 134, 138, 145, 151, 158, 207, 218, 227, 232
vertical interoperability, 245–249
viewers, 22

web browser, 193
WhatsApp, 26, 95, 100, 116, 126, 149, 156, 193, 250, 253
Windows, 21, 26–27, 34, 52, 66, 92, 123, 138, 141, 147, 149, 171–172, 193, 198, 211, 250

YouTube, 30, 40, 42, 98, 101, 105, 121–122, 193, 209

zero cost, 16, 27, 122

www.ingramcontent.com/pod-product-compliance
Lightning Source LLC
LaVergne TN
LVHW011808200926
848484LV00005B/1102
* 9 7 8 1 0 0 9 6 7 1 6 9 9 *